Here Today, Gone Tomorrow

To Miloska,
my wife,
and my four grandchildren,
William and Thomas Nott and Saffron and Siena Swire

HERE TODAY, GONE TOMORROW

RECOLLECTIONS OF AN ERRANT POLITICIAN

John Nott

First published in Great Britain 2002
by Politico's Publishing
8 Artillery Row, London, SW1P 1RZ, England

Tel. 020 7931 0090
Email publishing@politicos.co.uk
Website http://www.politicos.co.uk/publishing

A catalogue record for this book is available from the British Library.

ISBN 1 84275 030 5

Printed and bound in Great Britain by Creative Design and Print.
Typeset in Bembo by Duncan Brack.
Cover design by John Berry.

CONTENTS

ILLUSTRATIONS

Between pages 82 and 83:
Lieutenant, 2nd Gurkha Rifles, 1955
Miloska, 1968
Major General Sir William Nott, GCB
'Encampment of the Kandahar Army under General Nott outside the walls of Kabul on the evacuation of Afghanistan by the British' (Published by Hering and Remington, 137 Regent Street, 1848)

Between pages 178 and 179:
My parents' marriage, 1930
My mother and me aged 10 months
Grandfather and great-grandfather Francis outside Bridestowe Rectory on Dartmoor, 1910: 'A hunting parson and his son'
Signals Officer, 1/2 Gurkha Rifles, Malaya, 1954
Defence Secretary, presenting sword of honour, Sandhurst passing-out parade, 1982
Captain Narbir Tharpa, 2nd Gurkha Rifles, the first Queen's Orderly Officer
2nd Lieutenant, 1st Battalion the Royal Scots; escort for battalion train to Berlin, 1951
My scout car with signalman, Malaya, 1953
Rifleman Bhimbahadur Gurung with kukri and patchet gun
Family photo for election address, 1970: with Julian, William and Saša
Miloska, daffodil fields
William and Thomas Nott, mackerel fishing off St Michael's Mount
Another grandchild: Saffron Swire with Lillie
Admiral Fieldhouse, Commander of the Falklands Task Force, and myself during the campaign
Caspar Weinberger, US Secretary of Defense, and myself in a Tornado just before the Falklands crisis
Trewinnard, 1835 – our home in Cornwall. It is still like this today
Woodcocks – our small sporting estate in Cornwall

Between pages 338 and 339:
Private Eye, 9 April 1982
'We are doing everything to seek a negotiated solution' (Garland, *Daily Telegraph,* 27 April 1982)
'Nott's Navy Cuts' (Garland, *Daily Telegraph,* 26 June 1981)
'Ah, John! The good news is we've got a job for you in the city – the bad news is it's in Palermo!' (Jak, *Evening Standard,* 7 October 1982)

INTRODUCTION

Most politicians have five minutes of fame before they disappear for ever. My descent into obscurity was, however, suspended for several years as a result of walking out of a rather silly interview with Robin Day. It seemed then, and still seems now, to have been an incident of utter triviality. But the BBC, as an entertainment medium, thrives on triviality, and it therefore thought fit over a period of almost twenty years to replay the conclusion of the interview repeatedly.

With Robin Day's sad death two years ago, television viewers may now be spared the regular sight of my unprepossessing features on the screen. But as I shall be remembered, if at all, for this minor episode, I have decided to open these recollections by recalling it for the final time.

The interview occurred at the Conservative Party conference at Brighton in October 1982, shortly after the victory in the Falklands. I had made my valedictory address as Defence Secretary, which was followed by a rather extended standing ovation. As the cheers and clapping echoed around the hall, I wished rather fervently that the delegates would resume their seats so that I could escape from the platform back to my farm in Cornwall – the conference being the annual low point of my political year.

As I left the platform under the beaming features of Margaret Thatcher, some minion thrust a list of requested interviews into my hand. Foolishly I decided to delay my departure by responding to one request, and I therefore found myself in the studios of the BBC. I was fed up with politics and was longing to get out, having recently announced my retirement. Robin Day and I were already good friends and I sat down in the proffered chair, not caring overmuch to be there at all, let alone awaiting a list of fatuous questions. Whether I was to put up a good performance on the television would have been a concern to me in earlier years – a politician, like an actor, is only as good as his last performance. Indeed, in the cockpit of the House of Commons, performance is everything, content not quite nothing but nearly so.

Chapter Eight of this book is about my disagreements with the top brass of the Royal Navy. And because my Defence Review in 1981 had created substantial controversy, the motions on the order paper put down for debate by the naval lobby, before the Falklands had actually occurred, were full of criticism of what I had done. But in the euphoria following the Falklands victory, no word of criticism of the Defence Secretary arose at all. For the first and last time in my entire political career, I was something of a hero in the Conservative Party. Robin Day, poor fellow, whose own reputation was based on asking awkward questions, was in a jam. How was he to stir it up when the delegates had wilfully failed to play his game? So he decided to create his own agenda.

As his questions were monotonously repeated, the major part of my brain was dwelling on my farm, the autumn colours, the conclusion of the harvest, the green fields of England – and here was this famous controversialist desperately trying to generate a row out of something which, for my part, was already part of history. My brain reacted: 'What the hell? I don't need to sit here re-fighting the Defence Review with a journalist, however famous.' So I walked out.

What caused this reaction? Here is a shortened version of what eventually appeared in Robin Day's book of interviews with the famous. Beside the Pope, Gorbachev, Thatcher and the Almighty, I was very small fry; so Robin left me out of the first edition. This provoked a massive reaction that his most famous interview of all, the one with me, had been omitted; the publisher insisted that it should be included in all subsequent printings.

> Sir Robin Day: Mr Nott, is it not remarkable that whereas in the conference agenda there is resolution after resolution calling on you to re-think, re-assess, re-examine, reverse, re-appraise your defence policies in the light of the Falklands conflict, none of this came out? Do not many of the resolutions reflect the criticism publicly made by Admiral Sir Henry Leach, the First Sea Lord, saying that we've got to retain the three Invincible class anti-submarine carriers, we've got to improve the effectiveness of weapons and destroyers and frigates, and retain, you know, more of them?
>
> Rt Hon. John Nott MP: You'd hardly expect the First Sea Lord to say anything else, would you?
>
> RD: Another of the criticisms (again reflected in the conference resolutions)

by Sir Henry Leach is that the Navy is saddled with the whole of the Trident missile costs.

JN: But as you say, it didn't come up in the debate.

RD: No, well it ought to have done, oughtn't it?

JN: No, I don't think so. It's for the speakers themselves to decide what they wish to say, not what the media want them to say.

RD: On the merits of the point, for the benefit of many Conservatives and others who are worried that the Navy may be saddled with too much of the Trident missile costs and will, therefore, be run down more than it should, what's the answer to that?

JN: Well, the Navy – the real sum of money we're spending on the Navy to-day is very much greater than when we came into power. On the conventional Navy, without nuclear weapons, it's about half a billion pounds more than when we came to office, and the Navy's share of the total defence budget will remain at round about a quarter of the total defence budget, in our forward plans.

RD: But Sir Henry Leach said – and I apologise for quoting him again, but he'd been forty-five years in the Navy and I suppose he knows something about it – 'The cuts in the Royal Navy's budget plans are twice the Army cuts and seven times the RAF cuts.'

JN: The forward plans had to be trimmed because they were greater than the sum of money available. You would hear a different story, if you wished to quote it, from people in the other services. My task is to maintain a balance between all three services, and most expert opinion is of the view that we've probably got the balance about right.

RD: But why should the public, on this issue, as regards the future of the Royal Navy, believe you, a transient, here-today and, if I may say so, gone-to-morrow politician, rather than a senior officer of many years ...

JN: I'm sorry, I'm fed up with this interview. Really it's ridiculous.

(EXIT the Secretary of State for Defence)

RD: Thank you, Mr Nott.

As I wandered back among the mingling delegates, Michael Jopling, the Chief Whip, came up to me and said, 'John, I hear you've caused a frightful commotion on the BBC.' To which I replied, 'Michael, I'm not sure why you say that. What am I meant to have done?' 'Oh,' he said, 'You have walked out of an interview with Robin Day – I don't know that will go down at all well, John.' So I said, 'Well, Michael, you are just the Chief Whip and I do not think anyone is going to take much notice of your view of the matter!'

Michael Jopling and I knew each other well, and he laughed and we parted. But soon the story was filtering out among the delegates; I do not think either the assembled media or the delegates felt that it was an incident of any particular consequence, but they were all greatly entertained when the walk-out was played back to them on the evening news.

I went back to the conference hotel to collect my bags and saw that the assembled hacks were drinking, as normal, around the bar. So I walked into the bar, where Robin Day was being given the most appalling ribbing by his media peers. I went up to him and said: 'Robin, I quite enjoyed the incident. What about you?' It was perfectly clear to me that he was completely miserable about the whole affair. He felt in some way that he had let his profession down. I don't know why.

According to my private secretary, the excellent David Omand, I received about 850 letters after the walk-out, with only about twenty or thirty saying I had behaved petulantly and should have had the professional skill to sit it out. The overwhelming view was that it was high time that Robin Day and all those other interviewers were given their comeuppance, and they congratulated me whole-heartedly on what I'd done.

I conclude this introduction by reflecting on the irony of the fact that I shall be remembered only for a media event – when I was always uninterested, almost uniquely unskilled for a senior politician, and rather contemptible of the whole media charade.

I would be happy to have as my political epitaph what John O'Sullivan of the *Daily Telegraph* wrote about me in 1978:

There are people in gossip columns who are famous for being famous. But Mr John Nott, the Shadow Minister for Trade in Mrs Thatcher's team, is at some risk of being famous for being obscure.

What bliss; unless vast numbers buy this tome, I have arrived, belatedly and subject to the whim of the BBC, at the happy resting place of all former politicians. I hope only that my grandchildren will enjoy these recollections, because this book is dedicated to them.

John Nott
January 2002

Chapter One

ECHOES OF EMPIRE

Mark my words, there will be a signal catastrophe in Afghanistan.

(General Keane on his departure for England, 1839)

I start my story in Afghanistan.

My ancestor (my great-great-great-grandfather, to be precise), Major General Sir William Nott GCB, was a 'Sepoy General' of the East India Company. He fought in the First Afghan War (1838–42), which saw one of the greatest disasters in British military history. Seventeen thousand British and Indian soldiers, and their camp followers, were slaughtered by the Afghans in the mountain passes – one man survived to tell the tale. My grandfather was fortunate; he was elsewhere commanding an army in Kandahar and following the disaster, together with General Pollock, he recovered Afghanistan for the British. As a result, to this day the medal commemorating the battles of Kandahar, Ghuznee and Kabul adorn my family coat of arms – so the events of the recent past are known territory in my family history.

I also believe that the story of a 'life' is somehow diminished without the inclusion of the family characteristics and experiences of the author's forebears; those not interested should skip to Chapter Two! As a part-time farmer I am conscious too of what breeders call the 'pre-potent sire', the bull that stamps his characteristics on his progeny. I think my ancestor, for better or worse, stamped his mark on me!

Moreover, his experiences, now more than 150 years ago, in several ways are mirrored in my own. Both of us became involved in a colonial war – his role was to maintain the integrity of the British Empire in India, my small part was to resist aggression in almost the last outpost of the Empire: the Falkland Islands. The First Afghan War was provoked by the expansionist ambitions of Russia in Asia; my two years in the Ministry of Defence were overwhelmingly concerned with resisting the expansionist ambitions of Russia in Europe – the

Cold War. When my grandfather, as the commander of the Kandahar Army, recovered Afghanistan for the British in 1842, he did so in opposition to the Afghan tribes; in 1982, at the height of the Cold War, I co-operated with the CIA to arm these same Afghan tribes against the Russians. Some of these same arms are still in use today.

Now the sun has set on the British Empire and the Russian Empire has collapsed, not least because of the Soviet ten-year bloodletting in Afghanistan.

The substance of the interview with Robin Day was about my differences with the Board of Admiralty and, in particular, with Sir Henry Leach, its chief. At the heart of this dispute was the relationship and tension between a 'politician' and a 'sailor'. Great Britain's military history is, in part, the story of the relationships between the senior officers of the three services and their political masters. It is demonstrated to perfection in the experience of my grandfather.

When we launched the Falklands Task Force, I remembered the lessons taught by him in 1840:

> The Envoys and Ministers … will state to you from time to time the services which they may wish the troops to accomplish; when the manner of performing and carrying them into full effect, must depend entirely on your judgement, and for which you alone will be responsible to government.
> (Order from General Nott to Lt. Col Wymer, commanding a detachment –
> Kandahar 1840)

Not so easy to accomplish in later days when instant communications enable presidents and ministers to interfere with military operations in the field.

My hesitation at the outset of the Falklands War in 1982 was whether the logistics of the operation could stand the strain. In 1839 the unopposed 'Army of the Indus' in which my grandfather commanded the 1st Division, struggled with 50,000 men and women and 30,000 camels for a thousand miles across the plains and deserts of India and into the mountains of Afghanistan. There it suffered one of the great military and logistic disasters in British military history.

I remembered this story in my family history, and also the shambles of Suez in 1956, when on a Wednesday evening at the start of April 1982, alone with Margaret Thatcher, I expressed my doubts about the logistic viability of recapturing the Falkland Islands some 8,000 miles away. We did – and sadly, but incredibly, we lost no more than 255 killed out of the 31,000 afloat in over a hundred ships. Fortune smiled on us.

In the last resort, one can only judge oneself as people see you; just as one can only judge other people as you see them. Margaret Thatcher, after I resigned and retired to business (one of the few senior ministers to do so voluntarily), ever since has behaved towards me as if she was a deserted wife – in her memoirs she called me a mixture of 'gold, dross and mercury'. Some compliment.

Robin Oakley – a lobby journalist and sometime Political Editor of the BBC – interviewed my colleagues in 1978 when I was in the Shadow Cabinet. 'John Nott's independence', he reported, 'can take the form of an irritating impatience, a tendency not to suffer fools gladly, a refusal to be burdened with commitments that others have to accept.' And he quoted one colleague: 'You never know where you are with him. He has such a contrary streak, you can't predict which way he will jump – whether he will take the high-minded approach or seize on the practical politics of an issue.' Another put it succinctly: 'He hates to be caged in, and he is very quickly bored.'

I suppose of all the kind or critical things that have been said about me, I like best the comment made about me by Admiral of The Fleet Lord Lewin (as he was to become), the Chief of the Defence Staff, who worked with me intimately for two difficult years in the Ministry of Defence. In lecture notes made at the end of 1981 he summed me up as follows:

> Individual style – makes own decisions; doesn't like long papers, big meetings, monolithic bureaucracy; gets on with the job, tends to concentrate on one issue at a time to exclusion of all else; very very able politician; Nott [a pun] a military genius or defence expert, nor does he have to be.

My own judgement is that I was always regarded as a maverick, too independent to be relied on, not a joiner. Amusing, good fun (depending on mood), competent and clever – but a poor team player. 'I cannot alter my nature,' General Nott said. 'I cannot change and divest myself of the independent disposition that God has given me.'

The *Dictionary of National Biography* says of Sir William Nott that he 'was a self-reliant man who when the opportunity offered showed a genius for war … he was impatient of control and freely criticised the conduct of his superiors'. 'Reserved in manner, he was intimate with few; but to those few he was a true friend.' When you read in this chapter about my forebears, and in particular my grandfather, you must judge for yourself whether their genes flow in my veins.

~

Let me begin with William's father. Charles Nott was born in 1753 on the family farm at Shobdon in Herefordshire. He was the second son and left home to seek his fortune. As a young boy, he travelled to London where a richer branch of the family lived. The *Dictionary of National Biography* again, says of Roger, the father of Sir Thomas Nott, a Royalist, that he 'was a wealthy citizen of London who suffered much for his loyalty in the Civil War'. Charles Nott met a young lady from Norfolk, Miss Bailey, and married her in the church of St Andrew's, Holborn. He stayed in London for a time, but he was a farmer's son and enjoyed a reputation as an agriculturist. So he left London, probably in the 1780s, and farmed in several places in Wales, including Neath and Cowbridge, where his sons went to the local grammar school. He finally arrived in Carmarthen and rented a series of farms from Lord Cawdor, then the greatest landowner in South Wales.

He was something of an entrepreneur and towards the end of the eighteenth century he bought the Ivy Bush Inn. As the first coaching inn on the road to London from the Irish ferry at Fishguard, the Ivy Bush was an astute purchase. (It is now the leading hotel in Carmarthen.) Moreover, not only was Charles a prosperous farmer and innkeeper, but he was also a mail contractor – one of the most profitable occupations before the coming of the Penny Post. To post a letter from Carmarthen to London in those days cost 12d, equivalent to about £10 in today's money, and the charge for a pair of horses to travel from five to twenty miles was between 20d and 30d. A traveller, 'Mr. M.', recorded in his diary a visit to Carmarthen with his wife and son. It was at the time of the French Wars:

Monday, 7 September 1801
    We drove to the Ivy-bush Inn, a very ancient built house, with oak stairs and floors to the rooms rubbed brown, but good accommodations and civil people; indeed Mr. Nott, the master, appears to be far above the common rank of Inn-holders in Wales. He possesses a very large farm about a mile from the town, and undoubtedly has the best Chaises and Horses in the country.

    While dinner was preparing we surveyed the town, which is considered as the principal one of South Wales. It is well supplied with everything, the shops are good and well furnished, and plenty seems to abound.

    The streets were full of soldiers, the Cardigan Militia were quartered here and the Carmarthen Fencibles. The 'Bush' alone had 35 privates and 5 Officers quartered there.

After agreeing with Mr. Nott for a chaise for a few days to be ready in the morning, we retired to rest. Our berths were not of the first-rate, but we slept well, having long since got the better of being over nice ...

Monday, 14 September

A fine grey morning, we were ready to set off at 7 o'clock. Mr. Nott was already risen, and had prepared tea with us, which he refused to charge for, indeed the attention and polite behaviour of this gentleman and his family, the superiority of his horses and carriages, the skilfulness and civility of his drivers entitle him to that preference which he so eminently receives.

In a stout, well-built chaise, and four fine horses, we set off for Aberystwyth, a journey of 50 miles, to be performed in one day, and with the same poor animals – we dreaded the very idea, but Mr. Nott assured us the horses would go through it with ease ...

Nott itself is a Scandinavian name which changed slightly over the centuries. In the *Dictionary of English Surnames*, Knott, Cnut, Knut, Canut are all prominent. In Iceland, the only reasonably pure Viking race left in Europe – the Icelanders can still read the Viking sagas in their original form – the telephone book in Reykjavik is full of Knutrs and also has a few Notts. Probably my forebears came as part of the Danish invasions in the tenth century, because the surviving people of our name seem to be concentrated on the Herefordshire/Worcestershire border, the Devon/Cornwall border and in Yorkshire. All of these places are on the borders of the restless and invading Britons. There my forebears farmed through the centuries and my distant cousins are still doing so today, substantial yeoman farmers on the rich Herefordshire soil.

The first John Nott that I can trace was Sheriff of London several times and, as an early predecessor of Ken Livingstone, was Mayor of London in 1363–64. He was a pepperer. The pepperers, who preceded the grocers, superintended the weighing of goods in *'averia ponderis'*. I hope that his ghost haunts the metric system and the officials who now police it. Whilst he was Mayor, a writ was issued by Edward III to him and the Sheriffs insisting that greater diligence was shown in suppressing usury. The Jews had been expelled from the City of London in 1290, and this writ was an attempt to strengthen ecclesiastical law, with the usurers to be tried by the Mayor and other named personages. Given that I was to become a merchant banker – the most usurious of all occupations – the King's writ makes interesting reading:

> Whereas heretofore the City of London has sustained great mischiefs, scandals, and damages, and in time to come might sustain the same, by reason of certain persons who, neither for fear of God nor for shame of the world, do daily exert themselves, to maintain the false and abominable contract of usury, under cover and colour of good and lawful trading; which kind of contract, the more subtly to deceive the people, they call 'exchange'; whereas it might more truly be called 'wickedness', seeing that it ruins the honour and the soul of the agent, and sweeps away the goods and property of him who appears to be accommodated, and destroys all manner of right and lawful traffic …

Am I a descendant of John Nott? I do not know, but the coat of arms of John Nott, Mayor, and the Hereford and Worcestershire Notts are very similar.

~

Charles Nott of Carmarthen had several sons. His youngest son William, my great-great-great-grandfather, was born in January 1783. 'I frequently fancy that if it had been my fortune to have received a proper education', he would write many years later of his childhood, 'I should have been exalted and conspicuous among the John Bulls. I never received any schooling, but what my own fist knocked into my own dull head after I left our fatherland.'

William helped his father in his farming operations and inherited the paternal attachment to agriculture, which he retained to the day of his death. I share it today. He used to boast, when he had reached high military rank, that he had often guided the plough. By the time that William approached his fourteenth birthday, the French were planning an invasion of England. His devoted Victorian biographer, J.H. Stocqueler, memorably describes the atmosphere:

> The whole country was inspired with military fervour; every boy girded on a sword, and longed to confront the enemy; even mercantile London forgot the vulgar selfishness of commerce in the chivalry of the moment, and not only gave her money but formed her citizens into urban soldiery to oppose the French regicides. But it was in Wales that the fire of patriotism burnt with the most intense brilliancy. The hardy Cambrians could not forget, in the ruins of castles scattered over the principality, how the land had once groaned under

Norman tyranny and feudalism, and they dreaded a repetition of scenes which had prostrated their daring ancestors.

Well over a thousand Frenchmen landed at Fishguard on 22 February 1797 and for several days held possession of the town, while the remaining invasion force stayed offshore waiting to land. The Pembroke Fencibles, the Cardiganshire Militia, the Fishguard and Newport Principals, and the Cawdor Yeomanry headed for Fishguard. 'Lord Cawdor, commander of the Pembroke Yeomanry, was summoned from dinner to be told that the French had landed,' was how one later account put it:

He hastened across the county with a makeshift militia armed largely with scythes and pitchforks to meet some 1500 equally makeshift Frenchmen, half of them released from Paris jails for the occasion and almost all of them to-tally drunk on brandy looted from a wreck. The heroic yeomanry had no trouble rounding up the sozzled invaders, who according to legend had been reduced to a state of abject terror by Welsh women in scarlet cloaks dodging among the rocks to look like redcoats. To this day the yeomanry bear on their cap badges the proud legend 'Fishguard' – the only domestic battle honour earned by any British regiment.

Foremost of the counties in arming to resist invasion was Carmarthenshire, where a volunteer corps was formed. William Nott, 'sharing to a great degree in the general enthusiasm', enrolled as a member in 1798, 'tho he was but a boy of 15'. And often in later years he 'laughably told the tale of this his first and bloodless campaign; what heroes he and several of his companions thought themselves as they marched back from the scene of their first military essay into their head-quarters in Carmarthen'. Indeed, these brief days of military glory determined his destiny. 'Having once imbibed a military atmosphere, nothing could or would content his soul but a commission in the army.'

Happily, commissions at this time were much more easily obtained than in the nineteenth century, and William's elder brothers were granted commissions in the Royal Army; William by contrast secured a Bengal cadetship of the East India Company. Subsequently, throughout his military service, he would display much fury at the patronage granted to the officers of the Royal Army over the more experienced officers of the East India Company. His attitude might have been different if he had taken a commission in the Royal Army himself.

After an appalling voyage lasting five months and involving shipwreck in South America and severe injury at the hands of French privateers in the Indian Ocean, William Nott landed at Calcutta 'in utter destitution, sick and suffering'. Fortunately, he had reached a town 'where hospitality was proverbial, and he immediately received all the care and attention kindness could devise'.

Ensign Nott was promoted lieutenant in February 1801, and three years later he was selected to command a detachment under Captain Hayes of the Bombay Marine, later called the Royal Indian Navy (my uncle, Rear Admiral Martin Nott, subsequently became its last British Chief of Staff). This was an expedition against the tribes on the west coast of Sumatra, a Dutch settlement which had joined with the French in their privateering upon the commerce of the Eastern seas. Off the coast of Sumatra, retribution was taken by this expedition against pirates who had inhumanely butchered so many English men and women on the high seas.

What is of interest is how a companion of William Nott remembered him at this time:

I was a great deal with Nott in 1803, 1804 and 1805. He was rather tall, but not lusty; neither was his figure such as indicated agility; still he moved about without awkwardness. He had a fine oval head, dark hair, sallow complexion and not a joyous countenance; on the contrary, without being morose, it was expressive of a calm observation of what was passing, for he was rather a looker-on, than a delighted participator of the gaieties of his associates. His temper was impetuous, yet he could curb it so as not to be disagreeable to his companions; there was enough in it, however, to scare away indiscreet familiarity.

I was his junior officer when on shore at Muckee, and passed the nights with him shut up in one of the stockades; he was then, if I may so express myself, in his glory: no precaution was omitted to prevent a surprise, his unwearied vigilance rendered it impossible, and his preparations to resist any attack which might be made, proved what might be expected from him when he might become the commander of an army. Those nights welded us together for ever.

I cannot say whether he was studious or idle: at that period the world was in arms; life was passed in action rather than study; books seldom fell in our way; our minds were solely engaged with the General Orders of the day.

I suspect that something similar might have been said of me whilst I was serving with the Gurkhas in Malaya. Although I was a keen and conscientious officer, I do not think that I have ever had a 'joyous countenance' and my temperament has always scared away 'indiscreet familiarity'. I regret it. I was never 'a delighted participator' in the 'gaieties' of my associates and I hated mess nights.

In 1811 Nott was made 'Superintendent of Native Pensions and Paymaster of Family Pensions' at Barrackpore. The pension in old age and infirmity, and the provision for the family, constituted the chief inducement to take service with the East India Company – and still do today for our Gurkhas. For these soldiers, the wages and the honour of fighting for their European masters are as nothing compared to the certain provision that the army provides for their future. Thrift and the hope of long years of retirement, when the physique has become enfeebled, are the understandable ambitions of the recruit.

William Nott fulfilled his important duties as the pensions paymaster; and as the father of the family which now began to cluster around him. He had married Letitia, the daughter of a solicitor practising in Calcutta, and had fourteen children, but only five survived him. In India at this time, there were few means of educating European youth, and most parents therefore, even at the risk of an expenditure beyond their immediate means, despatched their children back to England.

Charles, the eldest, and William, the second son, were sent to school with a Mr Williams of Carmarthen. A wonderful Victorian-style letter received from their father read as follows:

I hope I shall find that you have made great progress in learning. I should be sadly disappointed indeed were I to find it otherwise, as my best and fondest hopes of happiness depend upon the knowledge of my boys.

I have requested your uncle to send you immediately to some public school, which will probably be Eton, where I fully trust your conduct will be such as I could wish and that you will be conspicuous for your attention to the precepts of your learned teachers, and for your honourable and gentlemanly behaviour.

I am depriving myself of many comforts to enable me to see you well educated; but I shall feel myself amply, nobly repaid, if your conduct equals my fond expectation.

I trust you will be particularly careful in forming acquaintances while at Eton. Always bear in mind that virtuous poverty is far preferable to titled vice and indolence. Not but you may meet with those among the rich and great, who are possessed of every good and desirable quality; however, never lose sight of the old proverb – *noscitur a sociis* [the people you associate with]. It is not easy to get rid of evil companions where an intimacy has once subsisted with gay and dissolute young men. I would therefore have you be cautious in forming friendships. Never allow the supercilious smile of the idle and super-ficial, or the loud laugh of the ignorant, to lead you, even for a moment, from the path of learning, honour, truth, and virtue; the pride of the supercilious is even beneath contempt, and the loud laugh of the presumptuously ignorant will meet with self-punishment. But though you will meet with many such characters, you will also find every good principle and disposition combined in others, whose acquaintance will confer honour, and whose friendship I would have you cultivate …

You must be great tall fellows by this time; your mother and myself anx-iously look forward to the period of meeting. Farewell my much loved boys. Your mother joins in love to all. Write to me frequently, and tell of all you see and think.

Yours, affectionately,
William Nott
Barrackpore, Feb. 9, 1819

I sent a copy of this letter to my younger son, William, whilst he was at Eton, but it provoked no response! But I am glad to say that both my sons, Julian and William, followed their forebears to Eton – Julian went to Oxford and William subsequently followed me and his forebears to Trinity College, Cambridge.

~

William Nott was still in India when in 1836 the new Governor General, Lord Auckland, arrived to take up his post. One of Auckland's earliest moves was to seek to establish commercial relations with Afghanistan. The background was briefly this: the time had arrived when it was clear that the East India Company must sooner or later establish closer commercial and political relations with Afghanistan and the surrounding states in Central Asia and, to this end, create an understanding with these neighbouring powers. These considerations led to the employment of Captain Burnes upon a long-contemplated commercial mission to Afghanistan in 1836. Burnes had not been long at Kabul before he discovered that the Russians were at work to persuade Dost Mohammed, the Emir, to form an alliance with Persia.

Subsequently, from November 1837 to September 1838, a powerful Persian army laid siege to Herat – traditionally regarded as the key to India, because it stands on the high road between Afghanistan and Persia. Moreover, the Shah of Persia made it clear that it was not his intention to let his Eastern conquests stop short at the possession of the city of Herat. He claimed also the principalities of Kabul and Kandahar.

These developments aroused great alarm in both India and England, with Russia being seen as the instigator and as likely to reap the benefit of any gains made by the Persians. Palmerston, then Foreign Secretary, took the robust view that urgent measures were needed to nip in the bud such dangerous schemes. The British press likewise advocated prompt intervention, as innumerable pamphlets revealed Russia's planned encroachment and declared that the invasion of India was the eventual objective. Finally, after long and anxious discussions at Simla in the Himalayas, Auckland decided to send a force across the River Indus, which formed the border between India and Afghanistan.

'It is difficult to convey a notion of the enthusiasm which pervaded the Indian Army when it became known [in August 1838] that a force was to be assembled in the northwest', Nott's biographer would write. The Army had been long inactive – indeed, the officers had almost degenerated into 'mere pleasure seekers, or carping critics at the measures of the government'. However, he went on:

> The faintest sound of the war-trumpet produced a magical change in their feelings. To fight with any power which had braved the British flag was agreeable, but to contend at the head of sepoys against the European cohorts of the Czar in regions beyond the Indus, was an honour so rare and unexpected, and was fraught with so much promise of distinction and advancement, that not a soldier in the whole length and breadth of India could for a moment tolerate the idea of being left behind.

It was decided that a considerable force should ascend the Indus from Bombay under the command of Lieutenant General Sir John Keane; and that this force would form a junction with the Bengal detachment on the River Indus. Until then, the command of the Bengal Army devolved upon Major General Sir Willoughby Cotton, and that of the First Division of the Army of Indus upon Major General Nott.

The movement of the Bengal column began on 12 December. The total strength in fighting men was reckoned at nearly 10,000 and, as each man in an Indian force required four people to wait upon him in some form or another, there were, including the camel drivers, not less than 40,000 camp followers and 30,000 camels. Nott would not have disagreed with the views of his biographer:

> The movements and establishments of the Persians under Xerxes and Darius were here repeated upon at least the same scale. The officers regarded the expedition as little else than an extensive pleasure promenade – an enormous picnic.

One officer even boasted that his mess had 'two camel loads of the best manillas', and in general scant attention was paid to the instruction to commanding officers to 'move disencumbered of every article of baggage which could, without compromising the efficiency of the corps, be dispensed with'. In Stocqueler's scornful words again:

> Jams, pickles, cheroots, potted fish, hermetically-sealed meats, plate, glass, crockery, wax-candles, table-linen, &c., were all deemed indispensable to the 'efficiency of a corps'. Many young officers would as soon have thought of leaving behind them their swords and double-barrelled pistols as march without their dressing-cases, their perfumes, Windsor soap, and eau-de-cologne.

It reminds me of visiting the officers' mess of Guards battalions on exercises in the British Army of the Rhine!

Notwithstanding all this superfluous baggage, few problems were experienced in the early stages of the march across India. By the end of February 1839, however, the original enthusiasm had waned: provisions were beginning to get scarce in camp, camels had dropped on the road, and their loads were necessarily left prey to marauders and followers who hung about the line of march.

As time wore on, things got worse and worse. Nott's biographer gave the situation the full treatment:

> The annals of the British campaigns in India, or indeed in any other part of the world, do not furnish a parallel to the miseries and losses experienced by

the unopposed 'Army of the Indus'. The marches lay through extensive sandy deserts and dry jungles; the water was everywhere extremely scarce, and such as was obtained was muddy, brackish, stagnant, poisonous; forage was obtained with great difficulty; the camels died by fifties and hundreds; the Baluchi mountaineers plundered at every opportunity, assassinating stragglers and bearing off their burthens; the sun was powerful, the glare distressing; communication with the rear was seriously interrupted, for the marauding propensities of the Scinde robbers extended to the dawks (the letter carriers), and not one letter in a dozen ever reached its destination.

Nott himself reported at one stage that 'the 4th Brigade alone has lost during the last four days 244 camels by death – namely starved', and that 'my horses have not had a blade of grass or any forage for four days'. Finally, on 6 April, General Sir John Keane with the Bombay column joined up at Quetta with the Bengal column, and new arrangements were made for command.

At this point, it is worth recording a passage in a book, *The Choice of a Profession*, published in 1857. The author had this to say of the Army of the East India Company:

> This splendid army, great in emoluments, and eminent in services, though looked down upon by the Queen's officers, can afford to hold its own, both on the ground of the magnificent empire it has won and keeps for Britain, and the high character and military talents of its officers … The supercilious Queen's officer, whilst affecting to despise the servant of the Company, is forgetting his early training in London drawing rooms, and has few opportunities of showing his superiority to his fighting brother of the Company, except in blackballing him at his club. At the same time the Company's officer is winning empires in the East, and enjoying a hearty grumble that an ancient professional jealousy excludes him from general command.

Now, in spring 1839, General Nott saw once again the Queen's officers being placed above those of the Company Army, and he resolved to seek an interview with Sir John Keane, the Commander of the Army and well known for his rough tongue. 'Your Excellency is aware,' began Nott, 'that the column about to advance is composed almost entirely of Bengal troops; that in this column there will be no less than four of Her Majesty's General Officers, but not one Company's, unless I am to go.' There ensued a fierce argument on this score, prompting

Keane to say to Nott: 'Your conduct, for an officer of your rank, is very extraordinary – the most extraordinary I have ever heard of.' The encounter (described by Nott to his son Charles) ended without any meeting of minds:

'General Nott, I see clearly that nothing that I can say will convince you.' 'No, your Excellency, nothing that you have said on this subject can convince me.' 'You insult my authority.' 'I am not aware that I have; what I have said is my deliberate judgment, which nothing can change.' After much more debate, warm on his part, cool on mine, I said, rising to retire: 'Well, your Excellency, I trust that I have left no ill impression upon your mind. I see the whole affair; I am to be sacrificed because I happen to be senior to the Queen's officers.' 'Ill impression, Sir! I will never forget your conduct as long as I live!' 'Oh! your Excellency, since that is the case, I have only to wish you a very good evening.'

With all these black marks against his name, it was hardly surprising that General Nott's protests were of no avail. He was left behind in Quetta in charge of a brigade, and General Keane marched towards Kandahar and onwards to Kabul with the bulk of the army. It arrived outside the walls of Kabul on 6 August 1839. There, Shah Soojah – the British choice – was put on the throne by force in the place of Dost Mohammed. It was to prove, as it does today, that outsiders cannot impose their choice of government upon the Afghan people.

There were no signs of welcome for the invading army and the inhabitants of Kabul looked on with 'the most complete indifference'. As Shah Soojah rode in, Macnaghten (the appointed Envoy to Kabul) and Burnes (the appointed Resident) rode alongside him in the full fig of the diplomatic service. Their resplendent uniform comprised 'a cocked hat fringed with ostrich feathers, a blue frock coat with raised buttons, richly embroidered on the collar and cuffs, epaulettes not yielding in splendour to those of a field marshal, and trowsers edged with very broad gold lace'. Such are still the pretensions of our envoys living in fine palaces around the world, in spite of the reduced circumstances of our country. On this occasion the British in their finery quite outshone the Shah, and only a prophet could have known that it would not be long before both Macnaghten and Burnes would be hacked to death and hung in pieces around the walls of Kabul.

General Keane's arrival in Kabul was greeted as a triumph back in England. Keane was made a baron and, with a neat sense of timing, retired to England. He handed over command to General Cotton, who was subsequently succeeded by General Elphinstone. As Keane departed for India and England, he famously said: 'Mark my words, there will be a signal catastrophe in Afghanistan.'

~

The appointment of General Elphinstone proved to be a disaster – and led to one of the most shameful episodes in the annals of the British Empire, namely the slaughter by the Afghans of the entire retreating, 17,000-strong British Army. Elphinstone's qualifications for the post were slender; he was a sick man and did not want the job. But according to a contemporary, he was of 'good repute, gentlemanly manners and aristocratic connexions', and certainly he was loved by his men. He had last seen service on the field of Waterloo, a quarter of a century before. Emily Eden (the sister of Lord Auckland, the Governor General) said of 'Elphy Bey', as she called him, that he was 'in a shocking state of gout, poor man. One arm in a sling and very lame. He cannot, of course, speak a word of Hindoostanee.' General Nott, always prone to cause the greatest offence, simply said of him that he was 'the most incompetent soldier that was to be found among the officers of the requisite rank'.

The British Army of 'Occupation' in Kabul, having placed the hated Shah Soojah on the throne, settled down to turn Kabul into yet another little England. The wives arrived, always a fatal turn of events in India, and 'gave themselves great airs', with 'snobbery and catty behaviour much in evidence'. It was, after all, the earlier arrival of the British memsahib in India that had divided the conquering British men from their Indian wives and mistresses, setting up the racial distinctions and barriers which survived right through until the departure of the British at Indian independence in 1947.

Slowly the English began to find the place endurable. The fine climate braced and exhilarated them. They rode races, they played cricket, they got up dramatic entertainments, they went out fishing, they went out shooting. When the winter fell upon them, to the infinite astonishment of the Afghans, they skimmed over the smooth surfaces on their skates. But all was not well. 'There are truths which must be spoken,' one account soon afterwards frankly conceded. 'The temptations which are most difficult to withstand, were not withstood by our English officers. The attractions of the women of Kabul they did not know how to resist – and the Afghans were very jealous of the honour of their women.'

The fire of rebellion rose amongst the Afghans and the flames spread with amazing rapidity: 'The sword of numerous tribes was unsheathed, and every European and all who served with them – every spot they occupied – was threatened.' At that time General Nott intercepted a document sent around the Afghans. It read as follows:

> To the high and exalted Nobles, leaders and Moslem followers of the Chief of All Prophets (on whom be peace) among the Belooch and Brahoe tribes.
>
> … the followers of Islam believing His Majesty Shah Soojah in full possession of uncontrolled power [i.e. the backing of the Army of the Indus] joined him with all their strength. But few understood the real truth; so the English threw aside the veil and day by day employed themselves in uprooting the religion and causing separation among the followers of Islam.
>
> Hence the warriors and champions of Islam from among the Dooranees, Ghilzies, Persians, Kohistanees and Lohuzurees, with men of other districts, girded up the loins of valour for the restoration and strengthening of the Moslem religion, and spared neither their lives, their honour, nor their wealth in their holy cause, but according to the Sacred Book, placing not regard on the smallness of their worldly means, have drawn forth the sword of honour …

An interesting commentary on recent events.

By November 1841 Kabul was in turmoil. Burnes, eagerly waiting to inherit the post of Envoy from Macnaghten, was murdered. The British retreated to the military cantonments outside the walls, where Elphinstone's physical condition was rapidly deteriorating. He dithered, and under the urging of the appeasing diplomat, Macnaghten, refused to take firm action against the insurgent rebels.

At the same time, the tribes in lower Afghanistan were about to rise up. General Nott, by now promoted to command all the troops in lower Afghanistan and Scind, spent two years, from 1840–42, in Quetta and Kandahar quelling various rebels, reducing rebel forts and dispersing concentrations of Afghan troops, who were intent on expelling the British invaders. On 13 January 1842 a force of 15,000 to 20,000 Afghans laid siege to Kandahar, but after a fierce battle they were defeated by Nott with 9,000 British and sepoy troops and driven from the field.

On the very same day as the battle at Kandahar, he heard of the murder of Macnaghten in Kabul, and he received an order from General Elphinstone that he was to withdraw all his troops to India. Nott refused to obey, believing – quite correctly – that Elphinstone had issued the order under coercion.

Writing to his daughter at the start of November 1841, he had already given his opinion of the cause of the incipient disaster at Kabul:

> This country is in a sad state. Sir William Macnaghten's mistakes and weak system begin to tell most woefully; it must be changed, or we must walk out of this world. Lord Auckland should long ago have placed all power here, civil and military, in the hands of a General Officer, who would have used it humanely, honourably, but when needed, roughly, and even sternly. Half measures will not do here, among an indignant, half-civilized race, who have had a hated King forced upon them ... Macnaghten and General Elphinstone have made a pretty mess of it; and what is worse, the moral influence of their doings is fast extending over the whole country from Persia to the Attoch.

The disaster that duly befell Elphinstone in Kabul was recorded with due solemnity by Nott's biographer:

> Capitulating to the Afghans, the troops commanded by General Elphinstone evacuated Kabul under a pledge of *sauf conduit* ... The snow covered the ground, the officers and soldiers were depressed, half-starved, ill-clothed and badly supplied with ammunition; the Afghans, the Ghazees, the Morrunds, the Ghilzies, accompanied them into the passes; here the treachery of the tribes disclosed itself in fearful colours. From the heights, where thousands of Afghans were assembled, a deadly fusillade was poured upon the columns, and bodies of furious horsemen charged them in the defiles, and blocked up their passage. Bravely and desperately they fought in spite of bad leadership; but numbers, the snow, and their disorganized condition, were against them ... The savage hordes were unremitting in their attacks, nothing could slake their thirst for the blood of the infidels. For three or four days the contest continued, and only terminated with the massacre of some 17,000 officers, soldiers and followers; 150 were made prisoners, including several ladies and children, and only one man, a Dr Bryden, escaped during the conflict to tell the piteous tale ...

This account almost understates the horrors of the retreat from Kabul in the days after 6 January 1842, and the treachery of the Afghan chief, Akbar Khan (the son of Dost Mohammed), who had promised them safe conduct.

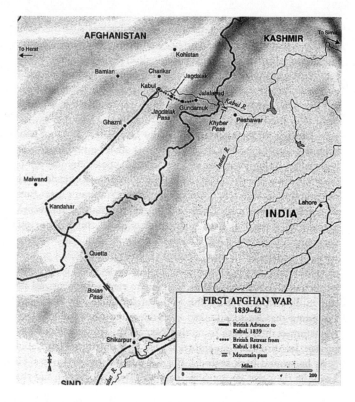

When the news from Afghanistan reached India, each instalment was more calamitous than the last. Auckland was appalled. As his period of office drew to a close and he prepared to hand over to Lord Ellenborough, his successor, his whole policy of resisting the incursion of the Persians and Russians into India, through Afghanistan, lay in tatters. Back in London, the dismay and panic was even worse. The 'I told you so' brigade, led by the most famous Englishman of all, the Duke of Wellington, was in full flow. Queen Victoria was horrified – and Parliament, as so often in a crisis helping to make the worst of it, was in turmoil. I tell the tale in Chapter Nine of the hysterical behaviour of the House of Commons after the invasion of the Falkland Islands.

A reluctant Ellenborough was persuaded that, in order to uphold the honour of the Empire, a relief force would have to be sent. He was also induced to put in command General George Pollock, a 'Company officer'. Pollock was a veteran of the Company's army, and it was clear that neither snobbery nor nepotism had played any part in his choice. Indeed, he and Nott were from the same mould. They respected and liked one another.

Pollock was still in Jalalabad and Nott in Kandahar – some 300 miles apart – when the surprising order reached both of them to withdraw speedily back to India from Afghanistan. Pollock and Nott were aghast, and the two generals adopted delaying tactics, explaining why military retirement was at that moment out of the question. The argument between the generals and the high command in India continued throughout May, June and July, until at last Ellenborough, the new Governor General, solved the problem by throwing the whole burden of decision on the generals. If Nott chose, he might 'withdraw by way of Kabul', which was in the opposite direction to India, while Pollock 'might advance to the capital and co-operate with that General'. Ellenborough, in a despatch to Nott, stated:

> It [i.e. retreat via Kabul] is an object of just ambition, which no one more than myself would rejoice to see effected: but I see that failure in the attempt is certain and irretrievable ruin, and I would endeavour to inspire you with the necessary caution, and make you feel that, great as are the objects to be obtained by success, the risk is great also.

Nott could hardly complain about having the whole responsibility placed on the generals. After all, throughout his service he had tried to insist on 'a becoming jealousy of the independence of a commanding officer'.

Slowly the First Afghan War drew to its conclusion. Nott advanced on Kabul from one direction, fighting as he went; and Pollock from the other. They met victorious in Kabul, not knowing that each of them had taken the decision to 'withdraw' via there. Pollock arrived two days before Nott, and eventually somewhat indiscriminate retribution was meted out to the Afghan population.

Nott and Pollock became Victorian heroes and returned to India laden with honours – Nott being given 'the new title of "Envoy to the King of Oude", in substitution of the lesser title of Resident at the Court of Lucknow', then the most profitable of all appointments in British India. But by now he was a sick man, and he did not last long in Lucknow – to the distress of Ellenborough, with whom he had developed a strong mutual affection, in contrast to his contempt for Auckland. Late in 1843 or early in 1844 he set sail for England.

Great were the celebrations there at the recovery of British honour. The prime minister, Sir Robert Peel, moved a motion of grateful thanks to General Nott in the House of Commons; he was given the Freedom of the City of London; and he was invited to Apsley House by the Duke of Wellington. The young Queen Victoria even asked him to stay at Windsor. But it was all too much. He wanted nothing more than to return home to Carmarthen and to take up residence at his estate, Job's Well. How right he was – 'And what have kings that privates have not too, save ceremony …?' His entry into Carmarthen on 9 September 1844 touched him more than all the honours and feting in the capital. All activity in the town ceased for the day, and the whole population came out to welcome him.

He lived for only a few more months and died on 1 January 1845. His statue stands to this day in Nott Square, Carmarthen, where there has been no Ken Livingstone to remove it, although he is today a forgotten general of the Empire from a forgotten war. So many episodes in his story encapsulate what command is all about in time of war. So much depends on the twists and turns of fortune. 'Is he lucky?' asked Napoleon about one of his generals.

Emphatically Elphinstone was not a lucky general; he died whilst in captivity with the Afghans.

~

Unlike his several military brothers and cousins, General Nott's son William became a fashionable parson and was given a Crown living in Sutterton, Lincolnshire. He married into a rather grander family than his own – Miss Farrer, of another Eton family, was the daughter of Major General James Farrer of the Coldstream Guards. The Revd William Nott's son, my great-grandfather, also William, became a regular soldier in the Hampshire Regiment, serving in the Sudan and India. His marriage to Rosalie Woolf caused great disapproval. She came from prosperous commercial stock (her family owned a large ceramics factory near Pontefract) and her brother Lewis was a Liberal MP in the 1880s – altogether a somewhat degrading combination to stomach for a fashionable Tory parson and a proud regiment, not helped by the fact that the Woolf family was Jewish and of pacifist inclinations. As a result he left the regiment under a cloud and served in several staff assignments, retiring as a colonel.

My grandfather Lewis was born in India in 1869, whilst his father was serving there. From early in his life his abiding interest and indeed his motive force was his religious conviction – everything was subordinated to his evangelical beliefs. I remember as a young boy during the Second World War visiting my grandparents. We had family prayers twice a day; playing cards were banned and dice were the instruments of the devil. To my surprise, my grandparents played backgammon every night – very strange! My grandmother regarded the Pope and all bishops of the Church of England as being part of the army of Satan.

After leaving Woolwich – 'the Shop', the Victorian alternative to Sandhurst – my grandfather was commissioned as a regular officer in 1890 into the York & Lancaster Regiment; but after a number of years he resigned his commission. The boisterous nature of mess life, the gambling, drinking and womanising of the young officer class offended him.

He joined an evangelical group which was known as 'The Group of Seven', and he and Bishop Tugwell went out as missionaries to the Hausa country in northern Nigeria; there they created a calligraphy for the Hausa dialect and translated the New Testament into that language. He also learned Arabic in this Muslim country. My grandfather wrote a volume of children's stories in Hausa which is still used in some of the schools in northern Nigeria today. (It was proudly shown to me when I visited northern Nigeria as Secretary of State for Trade in 1981.)

After a few years he caught blackwater fever and was forced to return to England. He became the land agent to an immensely rich lady, a Miss Bell, who owned 360 acres in Tooting – and reputedly half Cannon Street. She was also a great evangelical and together they ran a Christian mission in the East End of London. When she died, she left my grandparents an annuity which supplemented their modest family income.

At the outset of the 1914–18 war, he rejoined his regiment – the York & Lancaster – and, in due course, joined the staff of General Allenby in Cairo. After Allenby conquered Palestine, my grandfather became part of the military government there. He spent four years as military governor of Gaza and was then posted as governor in Tulkarm & Nablus, one of the four main administrative centres in Palestine. He thus became involved for several years in some of the earliest tensions between the Arab population and the early Jewish settlers. I remember him telling me of his sympathies for the Palestinian Arabs – and he was one of the few local governors who spoke fluent Arabic – but he became disenchanted by Arab disorganisation and hopelessness beside the much smaller but more determined and ambitious Jewish population.

The Balfour Declaration in 1917 committed Britain to the establishment of a 'National Home' for the Jews in Palestine. Although there was an underlying moral sentiment for the Jews in Lloyd George's government in London, it was just as much an imperialist move to counteract the Middle Eastern influence and ambitions of the French. The Mandate over Palestine was formally assigned by the Allied Power to Britain in 1920.

For two years the Commonwealth armies had fought the Turks, the Ottoman rulers of Palestine for 400 years. Thirteen thousand British and Commonwealth soldiers lost their lives. The Revd Spence told them: 'In the Middle Ages you remember how the armies of Christendom came to this land to fight against the infidels for the possession of the Holy Places. And we too are Crusaders, soldiers of the Christian faith, fighting so that the spirit and teaching of Jesus Christ may prevail throughout the world.' (The cap badge of chaplains to the Forces contains even today the vision of Constantine: 'In this sign conquer'.)

My grandfather's work for the early Jewish settlers (who were, after all, responding to the Balfour Declaration's commitment to the creation of a homeland for Jews) in no way conflicted with his Arab friendships. My grandfather was a considerable Arab scholar, based on his time in the Hausa country; he spoke fluent Arabic and was steeped in Islamic literature. He entertained King Abdullah of Transjordan, who visited Nablus with his caravan in 1925, and the two of them struck up a lifelong friendship; they conversed only in Arabic. When King Abdullah made a state visit to England in about 1936, he expressed the wish to see my grandfather; my uncle recalls that my grandfather (never a rich man) gave the king a dinner in Brown's Hotel which cost a small fortune, as Abdullah brought with him a substantial retinue. The two of them conversed about Arab literature long into the night.

~

Overall, looking back over the story of my Nott forebears, I realise that I was very much born a child of the Empire. By contrast, Europe was unknown to me. This was to change.

Chapter Two

THE LITTLE BOY WHO COULDN'T SAY SORRY

Brilliant work and speedy progress must not be expected of this boy, but he will be facing and overcoming difficulties undismayed, when his more alert competitors have sunk into despondency.

(School Report – aged 12)

I was born on the outskirts of London on 1 February 1932. At that time my parents were living in a delightful late-Georgian house called Stoberry Cottage. It still stands today – it has become the vicarage of Bromley Parish Church – but the large garden has been partly replaced by a rather ugly post-war housing estate and a multi-storey car park. In those days, the house was in an excellent position near to the church – private, quiet and with a wonderful untrammelled outlook over the open land of St Martins Hill.

Stoberry Cottage was not a large house, but it accommodated my parents, my elder sister and me, and some three or four servants. There was always a cook, a parlour maid, a housemaid, a gardener and our nanny; but they were an ever-revolving team because my mother was always quarrelling with one or another of them. When I left politics, one journalist wrote of me that 'he was a good cook as cooks go, and as all cooks go, he went'. That would certainly have applied to the domestic regime at Stoberry Cottage.

From as early as I can remember I had wanted to be a soldier. The engine driver phase passed me by. One of my earliest recollections is of standing outside the gate of our house, dressed in the uniform of the Blues – the Horse Guards. My mother had given me a silver breastplate, with a helmet and plume; and dressed up in all my glory, I stood waiting for the passers-by to put money in a box that I held in my hand. The money that I collected, ostensibly for charity (and no doubt this will be reported to the Charities Commission) was usually spent on buying soldiers or a new fort.

The projects that I devised to collect money were incredibly complex and, looking back on some of my earliest exploits in the field of finance, I am even now impressed by the childish genius of them. I do not think that I have ever been particularly interested in money as such, but I have quite enjoyed making it – and, at one stage in my life, it became a question of necessity, not pleasure.

One day, I arranged an elaborate fire alarm system whereby the dining room bell was connected to a piece of string which hung down outside the main gate, backing on to St Martins Hill. A large notice was posted beside the bell informing everyone that, should fire break out, they should put some pennies in the box and pull on the string. No-one ever pulled on the string, but I always recovered a good crop of pennies from the box. Clearly I was destined to spend some time in my life as a merchant banker.

Having inherited a rather belligerent nature from my mother, a constant war raged between myself and my nannies. I can remember that it was unusual for any nanny to last for more than a few months, and with the exception of Nanny Collins, I hated the lot of them. When I behaved badly, which was frequently, my mother always took my side and consequently the nanny left in a huff. My father, on the other hand, said that they were not strict enough.

One of the main sources of conflict was my refusal ever to say 'sorry'; somehow I just could not bring myself to say it. My mother used to show dogged determination in trying to make me apologise, but the shame of ever doing so far outweighed any punishment that could be bestowed on me. The outcome of this clash of wills was always the same – a sort of compromise. I used to shut myself inside the dark hotcupboard and eventually whisper the one word 'sorry' to my mother, who put her ear to the keyhole on the other side of the hotcupboard door. Even then my embarrassment was so intense that I used to remain inside the hotcupboard for some time before coming out.

Nonetheless I remember the first seven years of my life at Stoberry Cottage as happy ones. My pedal car brought me special pleasure, and I had a circular route around the garden – and sometimes on to the common. This did not seem to bother anyone very much, because in those days it seemed natural for boys to wander and explore – the idea that it was necessary to keep a continual watch on young children to protect them from child abuse and other dangers never seemed to enter anyone's mind.

I saw my parents rather formally at tea time when I was delivered by my nanny into their presence. My father, who commuted daily to his business in the City, seemed a remote figure, rather uninterested in his children. I never quite got over this impression. His passion was his garden. The care and state of the lawns were far more important than having somewhere for his children to play. If anyone ever complained, he invariably replied that he was 'only working hard on it, so that it would look nice for you'. After a shower, the lawn was always barricaded to prevent heel marks ruining the grass.

I must have seen my mother very frequently during the day, but I have no real recollection of having done so. I know that she read a story to me every night at bedtime. My world indoors was entirely circumscribed by the nursery, which had a green linoleum floor that I remember vividly. There was a table by the window which I also recall as the scene of fierce battles with my nanny, who was for ever ordered to stuff cod-liver oil and other ridiculous medicines down my throat – violent contests that were good training for Cabinet government under Mrs Thatcher.

Recently, after a lapse of sixty years, I returned to Stoberry Cottage. The house was awaiting the arrival of the new vicar but a delightful lady, one of the churchwardens, showed my wife and me around. The hotcupboard was just as I had remembered it, so was the nursery. But it had lost its green linoleum floor. Looking out of the nursery window, there were new housing estates in the far distance.

In the 1930s I think we lived in an atmosphere of what could be described as bourgeois gentility. But today the fence around the house is covered with graffiti and the vicar has barred exit on to the Common, itself strewn with uncleared rubbish – not a great advertisement for the local council.

Bromley's main street is now a pedestrian precinct and is just like every other shopping metropolis catering to our supermarket society. I speak with authority from my distinguished service as Chairman of Etam, the well-known women's lingerie chain! Marks & Spencer, Next and Ann Summers jostle for the custom of the passer-by, while Starbucks and Costa Coffee provide temporary relief from the weariness of modern shopping. No-one, neither the workers nor the customers, had ever seen or exchanged a word with the proprietors of these establishments. There is a box for complaints.

My visit to Bromley High Street made me wonder about my politics. I was passionately concerned in my early days in that profession to switch power from the producer to the consumer. What seems to have happened is that now that the consumer is triumphant there is over-production of everything, which has driven down prices but at great cost to our society. Political parties no longer represent differing interests; instead, they invite us to cringe to a single interest, the consumer's great god, money. It is why political leadership has debased itself to the focus group. No government dares to challenge the supermarkets, which many feel are ripping off consumers with their gross profit margins, often double those on the Continent. This is because the supermarkets seem to politicians to be powerful representatives of the consumer interest – and that means votes. So much for my visit back to Stoberry Cottage!

~

The onset of the Second World War changed all our lives. In 1939, as war seemed inevitable, my father decided to evacuate us to Devonshire, to the home of my maternal grandparents. I was seven years old, and these next six years were the most impressionable of my life.

My mother's family was called Francis. They could not have been more different from the Notts, who were travelled, fairly sophisticated, well-read and no longer based in one place. The Francis family, on the other hand, was bog Devon; they hardly ever left the county, even to visit London which they rather despised, although most of the boys were sent to Oxford, after Blundell's.

My father tried to join the Royal Navy in 1939, but was rejected due to his age. He therefore volunteered for the nearest that he could get to the sea, namely the Air-Sea Rescue service of the RAF at Devonport, which he joined as an ordinary aircraftsman. After a year on the air-sea rescue launches, he was persuaded to take a commission in the RAF and I hardly saw him for the next five or six years, apart from a sojourn in Belfast where he was stationed during the Belfast Blitz. Possibly the Belfast Blitz was the nearest that I ever came to real war. Sitting under the kitchen table with my mother and sister, it was frightening as the bombs and parachute mines fell all around us. A phosphorous flare, on a parachute, attached itself to the house and we had to be evacuated immediately. I have always wondered ever since, particularly when I sent men to war, how I would behave in a nasty, bloody battle. Certainly I would have been frightened – but duty, tradition, and a determination not to let the side down would probably have seen me through. Nevertheless, how can one know? We were eventually taken up the hill to Belfast Castle, where we lived in the cellars whilst Belfast docks were effectively being destroyed in the harbour below us.

Meanwhile, my Francis grandfather became my surrogate father. He was a lovely man. He was the local GP in Northam, Appledore and Westward Ho! But in those days, as a qualified surgeon, he also performed a number of operations in Bideford Hospital, which then had four doctors; its successor, the North Devon District Hospital in Barnstaple, has over sixty. He operated his own private health service, charging his richer patients but never sending in a bill to the poor families of the area, in particular to Appledore, a struggling fishing village.

My grandmother, who loved me dearly, came from a Cornish family – the Symons of Falmouth. They were a prosperous boat-building family, but left for Brazil in the early nineteenth century when Cornwall was going through one of its many depressions (as a result of the collapse of the tin mining industry). In Brazil they entered the cotton trade, married into the Portuguese community – consequently I have a Portuguese great-great-grandmother – and then, after two or three generations, returned to Lancashire to set up cotton mills. They were well-known cotton spinners in the late nineteenth century, playing a part in local Conservative politics. It was a large Victorian family, and I spent much time in later years visiting my grandmother's unmarried sisters – the rather impoverished Symons maiden aunts.

But it was to the Francis family, and in particular to my grandfather, that I owe my greatest debt. They were true country people, and it was from them that I learned my love of the countryside – and country sports – now the most important thing in my life. Maybe my love of the land and farming comes from my Nott yeoman ancestors, but it was the Francises that taught me about birds and butterflies and fish – and the quiet wonder that one can get from standing beside a river with a rod in the hand. I spent a lot of time with my grandfather. He had a beautiful collection of butterflies and birds' eggs; he had a particular passion for dormice, and was happiest when upside-down in a hedge looking for them. Before he got a car, he used to bicycle forty miles or more to fish in the River Torridge, for we lived in the two valleys of the Taw and the Torridge – the world of Tarka the Otter and Salar the Salmon. During the war, he and I made frequent trips to fish in the reservoirs of the area, in his car that he was allowed to keep as a doctor. He kept his guns and fishing rods in pristine order.

Unlike the Notts, the Francis family was Norman, and had been one of

Devon's landowners. The first Francis that we know about is William Francis of Bolham in 1347. The Francis family members – or Franceis as they were then known – were landowners in Combe Florey, East Chevithorne, Bolham and Talaton on the borders of Devon and Somerset. Over the generations they married into nearly all of the leading families of the West Country. There are some remarkable fourteenth- and fifteenth-century Francis tombs in the nave floor of the church at Combe Florey, where they lived for 400 years.

Great-grandfather Francis was the Rector of Bridestowe, on the edge of Dartmoor, for thirty-eight years. He had a large Victorian family, four boys and six girls, and they lived in an enormous rectory which still stands today, but has been converted into an old people's home. It still has pictures of the Francis family hanging on the walls. The rectory was run by Auntie May, great-grandfather's sister; she sat at one end of the large table and Auntie Madge sat at the other. It was quite normal to have thirty members of the family and relations staying there at the same time. According to my mother, meals were chaotic with a lot of shouting, not least because the maiden aunts were very deaf – Auntie Madge had an ear trumpet. My grandfather took charge of the bread, which had to be thrown from one end of the table to the other. 'Auntie May had the best pudding at one end, and Auntie Madge had the rice pudding at the other; you had to finish the rice pudding first. Auntie Madge was responsible for the bread and butter and Auntie May looked after the cake.'

The life of the family was wholly integrated with the village. Aunties May and Madge were the godparents of practically every child in the village, many of them illegitimate. Between them they took responsibility for the rectory and its many servants; my mother says that the children were never allowed into the domestic quarters or the kitchens. My great-grandfather took all this in a paternalistic way. Life was taken up with shooting, fishing, riding and picnics. His great preoccupation was bowls. He had a few friends in the district, including the Baring-Goulds at Lew Trenchard. The Revd Baring-Gould, the famous writer of 'Onward Christian Soldiers', was remembered by my aunt as 'a horrible man' who 'married a mill girl from the North and treated her terribly'.

One topic never mentioned in the Francis family was money. The Notts were always short of money and one was conscious of it. The Francises had it from somewhere, no-one quite knew from where exactly. In fact, it came mainly from farms in Somerset and Devon, many of which were sold at rock-bottom prices in the agricultural depression of the 1930s; my grandfather owned the Queen's Hotel at Portsmouth and other properties around and about, but no-one knew how or why. It was never discussed.

I find the whole subject of my forebears interesting, because in their very different ways they sum up an England that has passed. The Notts came from Scandinavia and survived through the centuries in Hereford & Worcester as small landowners and yeoman farmers. Then one of them achieved some fame and the family consequently drifted away from the land, in the process becoming rather rootless, like the vast majority of people today. The Francises, being Normans, no doubt expropriated land owned by people like the Notts, the original Danish and Anglo-Saxon settlers. The Francises were landowners in the West Country, but slowly through the generations their wealth diminished and they entered the professions, the Church and medicine. I feel very English, though of my sixteen great-great-grandparents I number one Jewish, one Portuguese and one French great-great-grandmother (Emilie de Sievrac, from Toulouse); altogether, not much of a dilution.

~

I was sent to a number of preparatory schools as a boarder, and I was deeply unhappy at some of them – not without just cause. There was a particularly nasty one in Honiton called The Grange, where the headmaster was remote except when he enjoyed himself by beating boys on their bare bottoms. The food was based on disgusting war-time rations, and I learned nothing. I still have a rather forlorn letter home to my parents:

> Thank you very much for my parcel with the sweets. We had a run up to Dumpdown Hill. It is very very steep and about 3 miles from here. We picked sides. I was the team leader of one side. Joker Mr Booker's dog was on my side. This is how the points went. 1st person 12 points, 2nd person 11 points and so on. I got up there first ... I am glad you are coming here on Wednesday as it is a half holiday ... Do any aeroplanes go from W. [a coded reference to where my parents were living] to bomb Germany? I WANT A LETTER FROM DADDY ...

Then, by some twist of good fortune, my life was changed. My mother discovered a preparatory school called King's Mead which had been evacuated to Bideford from Seaford. It was located in a large manor house called Moreton, owned by the Stucley family. The headmaster, Douglas Shilcock, was, I think, a great man – one of a very small contingent that has influenced my life for the better. Douglas loved his boys and devoted every waking hour to building up their confidence, caring for them physically – and intellectually. He had the headmaster's dormitory, which adjoined his bedroom. Each morning the elite who occupied this dormitory used to pile into his bed for conversation, ragging, and the odd pillow fight. I was a favourite and, although I spent very many mornings in his bed, he never touched me, nor any other boy, I believe.

I have exchanged these reminiscences about Douglas' dormitory with several of my distinguished contemporaries, and I know of none who would take a different view. Today, of course, if it was known that we had played games in his bedroom, he would be locked up in Pentonville as a sex abuser, and a great influence for good would have been lost to the world. Douglas Shilcock, who was a rich man, dressed immaculately in wonderful clothes and shaved in the bath every morning. He had hoarded huge quantities of tinned food when the war began, and these provisions, supplemented by the large walled garden at Moreton and the local black market, ensured that we lived a life of considerable luxury.

I remember many schoolboy anecdotes about which we used to joke with Douglas. One of the richer boys was a scion of Colman's Mustard. His mother used to be adorned with hugely expensive jewellery – the war notwithstanding – when she visited her son. The headmaster had a sort of game with senior boys as to how we could steal her pearls, which she wore in the bath. How we knew she wore her pearls in the bath, I never knew, but it enhanced our imagination and competitive spirit.

It was at Moreton that, aged twelve, I fell in love for the first time. She was called Mimi, a famous music-hall star later known as the Countess of Suffolk & Berkshire. By the time I came to meet her she was a very beautiful widow in her thirties. She was kind and solicitous of me, by then one of the young prefects in the school. Her husband, the Earl, received a posthumous George Cross for dismantling unexploded bombs and landmines – the most dangerous of which he kept for himself. I never knew what sort of relationship she had with Douglas Shilcock, but we often wondered whether she managed to divert his feelings away from his boys. Her two sons, Michael and Maurice, were at King's Mead, and she used to come and stay with the Stucleys in order to visit them – or was it Douglas Shilcock …? Once I confiscated Micky Suffolk's penknife for carving his name on the wooden desks and evidently failed to give it back.

I received a charming letter bearing a coronet on the writing paper of the Savoy asking if I could return the penknife. I was most impressed, particularly with the Savoy writing paper.

When the school returned to Seaford, I was made head boy. I would never attain such a grand position again. No Prime Minister can ever be as important as the head boy of a prep school. I was captain of cricket, captain of football and *victor ludorum* – alas, none of these sporting triumphs was to survive into my public school. I used to play God with the dormitories, shifting these poor young boys from one dormitory to another trying to create a coherent team, and driving matron mad until Douglas Shilcock stepped in.

What sort of schoolboy was I? My report for the summer term of 1944 perhaps gives some idea:

Classics. Self assurance is gradually coming. He is a very keen worker and always gives of his best. Grammar he learns easily and he has a retentive memory. His composition always shows evidence of care and application but his translation is a weakness.

Mathematics. He is not a natural mathematician and finds this subject rather difficult. However, by dint of dogged work, he gradually masters his disabilities and in the end light is shed on dark ways. Brilliant work and speedy progress must not be expected of this boy, but he will be facing and overcoming difficulties undismayed, when his more alert competitors have sunk into despondency.

French. His learning is still too mechanical and, while in grammar he is well above the average, he frequently misses the point in translations by lack of common sense and imagination.

English. As keen as ever and, as ever, a pleasure to teach. In a subject like this, without the comfortably hard & fast rules of the classics, he is not so much at home. Most of his difficulties are, I am sure, figments of his own too conscientious imagination.

Headmaster's report. One of the soundest and best boys in my school.

My parents wanted me to go on to Marlborough but Douglas Shilcock was very keen on Bradfield. He thought that a small school in the country, without too many athletic and intellectual pressures, would suit me best. So to

Bradfield I went in 1945. I was happy there. It had a wonderful location, beautiful countryside, a regime of muscular Christianity, terrible food, cold baths every morning, limited homosexual activity, but nothing too offensive. I only climbed into bed with another boy on one occasion and I enjoyed it. I have never had any homosexual inclinations, but I have often wondered what I have missed.

For some extraordinary reason, I only excelled in two activities – boxing and chess. Being tall and stringy, I used to hold out my straight left, and those tough little buggers from Wellington, Marlborough, Radley and the rest used to walk straight into it. I have a strange memory that it was only the boys from Catholic public schools that were short, nasty and vicious; it must have been that their regime was tougher and more masochistic, conducted as it was by monks.

There was a school chess competition and, in my second year, I reached the final. This caused a real scandal: an unknown twerp beating all the older boys. It was my chess expertise that taught me never to play a straight bat in White-hall. There the whole system of inter-departmental committees, organised by the civil service, is designed to ensure that nothing radical ever happens. You have to beat the system and manoeuvre around it, and chess prepares you for the tricks of the trade.

I left Bradfield in 1950 relatively well-equipped to face the Army. This was not least because of the discomforts, the atrocious food, the fagging, and the unbelievably cold dormitories – in short, communal living in Spartan post-war austerity conditions, but made bearable, even congenial, by the comradeship of the House and its admirable housemaster, Murray Argyle, now dead. What did I miss at Bradfield? Girls; there were none. It was a highly artificial atmosphere for a teenage boy. Bradfield today has been transformed for the better by the presence of girls. I would love to see my grandsons attend that admirable school, but I fear they are destined to follow their father and their earlier fore-bears at Eton.

~

Around 150,000 eighteen-year-olds were conscripted every year into the armed forces right up until 1960. No-one who went through this experience will ever forget it. British male society today is divided into those who have experienced military service and those who have not. It remains a cultural divide of some significance.

National Service, as it was called, probably did more good than harm to the youth of Britain, but some succumbed to temptation. Everything in military life is a mixture of intense activity, occasional excitement and prolonged periods of boredom. Inevitably, periods of inactivity and leisure led to what today would be the 'laddish' pursuits of booze and women. In those days most young men were virgins on enlistment, but service in the Far East, the Middle East and Germany did not extend their innocence for very long. Every young soldier was encouraged to equip himself with a prophylactic kit of condoms, cotton wool, antiseptic cream, and instructions; and these provided limited safeguards, but also some encouragement to visit the brothels of Singapore, Berlin, Aden and all points of the compass.

National Service began with a medical examination and an interview. With a mixture of extreme apprehension and some enthusiasm, I reported early – only to founder at my first military hurdle by an inability to provide the urine sample. I could not fill the bottle. I was put to the end of the queue and, late in the afternoon, an impatient medical officer assisted me by turning on all the taps in his examination room. Humiliation No. 1!

Within six weeks of the interview, the buff envelope arrived containing an enlistment notice, a rail warrant and a postal order for four shillings, being an advance of pay. On Thursday, all over England, decrepit steam trains pulled out of stations delivering their quota of raw recruits to Inverness, Darlington, Preston, Worcester, Brookwood and Aldershot. Knowing my family history, I had requested at the initial interview a preference either for the cavalry or the infantry – preferably, for family reasons, the Royal Hampshire or the York & Lancaster Regiments. With typical military precision, I was consigned to the Royal Army Service Corps (RASC). Later I came to realise that my education, slim build and limited muscular development qualified me to drive a lorry, but not for arm-to-arm combat in the infantry. My interviewing officer was absolutely right, and no doubt he eventually retired as a millionaire head-hunter, or a poverty-stricken NHS psychiatric consultant.

The first six weeks in the Army were traumatic for most young men, but not for the public schoolboys, who were already inured to a life of humiliation, grilling, discipline and extreme discomfort. For the majority who had never left home and had been indulged by a loving mother, it was a dreadful change. Suddenly all these young men were thrown together, in rowdy dormitories, with Brummies, Mancunians, Cockneys, Jocks, Geordies, borstal boys, graduates, illiterates and public schoolboys. The coarseness, vulgarity and language of the barrack room must have come as a real shock. Sex was the only unifying force – and was virtually the only topic of conversation; banter and the boasting of personal sexual achievement marked out the men from the boys. We had one recruit from Blackpool who boasted that he had 'f★★★★d' hundreds of girls standing up against walls outside dance halls, and he was believed. He was the hero of our barrack room.

The horrors and absurdities of the first six weeks of Army basic training will live in the memory of everyone who did National Service – and, indeed, everyone who has subsequently joined the Army, because I do not think the shock tactics have changed very much.

My recollection of events is that on arrival at Oudenarde Barracks, Aldershot, we were issued with our 'bibles', namely an AB64 Part One (Soldiers Service book) and Part Two (Pay book). We were then doubled away for an Army haircut, a savage sheep-shearing with clippers, which was followed by a medical and a batch of inoculations. It was wise to be at the front of the queue, because the needle became very blunt after it had been plunged into thirty arms. Kitting out was interesting and followed the Army maxim, 'If it fits, you must be deformed.' No item of kit had a simple name. 'Drawers, cellular green, other ranks, two pairs; blouses, battledress, khaki, other ranks, one', etc.

There were two theatres of war: the drill ground, on which we spent a third of our time, and the barrack room. The latter was dominated by blancoing webbing, pressing trousers (achieved with an iron on damp brown paper after shaving the rough wool along the crease), scouring all brasses and badges with a wire brush until they could take Brasso, and preparing the 'best boots'. This latter exercise was performed by scalding off the leather pimples with a hot spoon, or burning off the surface with meths, before applying heated polish and spit over prolonged periods long into the night. This made the boots useless for everything except the parade ground.

Just as a child remembers only the sunny days on an English beach, rather than the frozen Atlantic sea and the biting wind; just as a young Gurkha subaltern remembers the wonderful early evenings in the jungle camp rather than the six-hour trek through swamps with a 60lb pack; so an ex-National Serviceman remembers the good things about Army training rather than the horrors of it all.

It is hardly to be believed, fifty years on, but after I received my National Service commission in the RASC – following a stint at Mons Officer Cadet

School under the legendary RSM Brittain – I was posted back to Oudenarde Barracks, Aldershot as a platoon commander, in charge of these very same recruits that I have just described. At the time I was appalled, because I wanted to travel and see the world, and I wondered what the defect was in my character and military prospects that had led to such a posting. In fact, it was a great education for future life because I was actually responsible every six weeks for a fresh batch of my newly conscripted countrymen, and I still think that they were amazing. The so-called football hooligans of today would if necessary save this country in the future, as they have so often in the past.

By the end of a fortnight, the conscripts were transformed from a disparate and somewhat chaotic rabble into a team. Teddy boys, public schoolboys and borstal boys had joined together to try and win the competition for the best platoon. Although many of the corporals were frightful bullies, they had to get their flock into one coherent and disciplined shape within the two weeks. Some of the NCOs were outstanding in the way in which they instilled pride and determination into these young men. Anyone who has served in the British services knows that the NCOs are the key to an effective and disciplined team. 'There are no bad soldiers, only bad officers', it has often been said, but it would be impossible for both officers and soldiers without good NCOs. In fact, the high reputation of the British Army has always been attributable to its non-commissioned officers.

During the six months that I spent in 1951 with the recruits in Aldershot, I met a fellow officer in the mess who had served with the Gurkhas in the Far East. He used to regale us all with the quality and bravery of the soldiers from the high mountains of Nepal, and I remembered that members of my family had served alongside them in the past. It slowly dawned on me that I had to take some decision about my future career, and I had not the slightest idea about what I wanted to do. I was enjoying my time with the young recruits and I had developed a wary mutual respect with the NCOs in the battalion. It therefore occurred to me that I should contemplate extending my time in the Army, but I did not see great prospects in the RASC. I must have mentioned this to my father, who was keen on the Army – not least because he did not want me to join the family firm in the City which he rightly believed had no great future. Quite by chance he told my great-aunt Lettice, the sister of my grandmother; she in turn volunteered an introduction to a friend of hers, John Crocker, who was a keen Church of England evangelical, like the rest of the family.

General Sir John Crocker happened to be the Adjutant General, the second most important general in the Army and the man responsible for all personnel affairs! Chance had played its part on my behalf. In due course, a summons to attend the War Office in Lansdowne House, Berkeley Square, arrived in Aldershot via my colonel commandant, who was naturally astonished that one of his most junior National Service officers should be summoned to see the great man.

I presented myself in uniform to the General, and after a happy exchange about the family we launched into my request. I explained my reasons for wanting to join the Gurkhas: admiration for their bravery and reputation, etc., and the long family connection with India. It helped that Martin Nott, my father's brother, had recently been the last British Chief of Staff to the Royal Indian Navy, decorated during the war against the Japanese but made redundant at the time of Indian independence in '47.

General Crocker reflected over my enthusiasm for this adventure, summoned his military assistant, and asked if this could all be made possible. After a brief enquiry, the military assistant returned to say it was impossible, as the Gurkhas did not take National Service officers. I said that in that case I would apply for a regular commission. The General, apparently impressed by my determination and enthusiasm, ended the interview by saying that I would hear from him.

Not long after – the endless tiers of military bureaucracy must have been bypassed – I received a message that I was to be transferred from the RASC to the 1st Battalion The Royal Scots in Wuppertal, West Germany. The Royal Scots was one of four British infantry regiments affiliated to the Gurkhas – the others being the Rifle Brigade, the 60th Rifles and the Cameronians. There I was to undertake one year's apprenticeship to decide not only my fitness for a regular commission, but more importantly my fitness for the Gurkhas.

I had a great time in Germany. Lt Col Melville, the colonel commanding the battalion, was extremely kind to me – and must have given me a good report at the end of my time there. Initially our barracks were on the hilly outskirts of Wuppertal and nearly all of our leisure time was spent on horseback, the regiment having acquired a whole stable of German cavalry horses. When the regiment was posted to Berlin, we took all the horses with us, and had the added benefit of a large covered riding school at Spandau Barracks, just across the road from the imprisoned German war criminals in Spandau Prison. I was given the responsible task for a second lieutenant of commanding the train that took all the regimental stores, arms, ammunition and horses through the Russian sector to Berlin. Halfway, the Russians stopped the train and demanded my presence in their control hut. Accompanied by two Scottish soldiers, I walked back along the track, head held high, and entered the hut where the Russians closed the door behind me and demanded to see my papers. After a silent exchange, I went to the door to open it – it was locked. I had a moment's horror that I had abandoned the supply train to the Russians. I was wrong, the door opened inwards, and I was free!

Berlin was a fascinating but divided city in 1951. The Berliners had suffered terrible atrocities at the hands of the conquering Russian soldiers in 1945 but, only six years later, it was already a recovering society, active and pleasure-seeking. The main square outside British military headquarters was known to the men of The Royal Scots as 'Gobblers' Gulch', and the most beautiful young German girls were available for a packet of five Woodbines. We young officers raced sailing dinghies on the Wannsee, took part in all the horse shows, and spent several evenings a week on crawls around the proliferating nightclubs, which cost a tax-free half-bottle of gin and had all the vulgarity and perversions in which the Germans excel.

But what really endeared The Royal Scots to me was the character of the Scottish soldiers, whom we called the Jocks. Colonel Melville, at my request, agreed that I should take my platoon on a six-week camp into the Grunewald, the fairly wild park (as it was then) on the banks of the Wannsee. There I subjected my young men to a rigorous training programme during the day, so much so that I was told at the end of it that they were the best trained platoon in the battalion.

Isolated as we were from the rest of the battalion, I got to know the Jocks extremely well. Apart from the NCOs, they were all National Servicemen from Glasgow (although The Royal Scots was an Edinburgh regiment). Most of these young men came from the Gorbals; physically small but wiry and tough, they had an excellent sense of humour but only three consuming interests in life – alcohol, fighting and women. Each evening, although I pretended ignorance of their leisure pursuits outside the camp, they used to get themselves completely plastered before seeking out English soldiers for a fight. If they failed to find their chosen opposition, they returned to the tented camp for a punch-up amongst themselves. By this time I was tucked up in my tent and I ignored their antics. However late and drunk the night before, they were always on parade in time, often bearing the scars of the previous night's affray. It may seem all rather shocking in today's climate of opinion, but these were the immediate post-war days and I admired the fighting qualities of my soldiers. I have always believed that Scottish soldiers are the best for attack, but English soldiers for a dogged defence.

One particular episode at the start of my time camping in the Grunewald would linger long in my memory. I wrote an account soon afterwards, as a would-be short story for publication:

For three days I endeavoured to prevent the faithful band of camp followers from hanging around the camp perimeter but since they had every right to be there, there was nothing I could do to drive them away. The situation was made worse by the fact that they found me a source of constant amusement and I had no doubt that they told dirty stories about me to the Jocks. Discipline was being undermined and the situation was undoubtedly getting out of hand.

One of the few valuable things that my father taught me was that it was no use, and indeed quite fatal, to give an order that you could not enforce. I therefore circled the camp with barbed wire and absolutely forbade the men to bring any of these women inside the camp perimeter. Although it was against my military upbringing and training I then turned a blind eye to the men's absence from the camp at night so long as they were present on parade, spotlessly turned out, by 7 o'clock the next morning.

I may say that it was as much as I could do to maintain my temper. Although I was never so unfortunate as to see any kind of disgusting act of love in progress, the bushes surrounding the camp often echoed with giggles and swear words in the German tongue.

Perhaps I should say here and now that the Jocks respected this concession to their animal impulses and kept their side of the agreement by working hard during the day and appearing slightly pale but well turned out on parade each morning. The sight of their women, however, continued to haunt me (although I must say quite a number of them were agreeably attractive).

About one week after our arrival at this spot I decided to take my jeep out one morning and make a reconnaissance of the edge of the lake in order to find a suitable place to practise a water-crossing exercise. It was a fine sunny day. The lake was perfectly calm and reflected the tree-lined hills quite beautifully.

As I drove along the water's edge on this spring morning I felt contented, for my military training programme was going well, yet somehow incomplete. Although at the time I was ignorant of what I lacked, you will realise that the stirrings of my manhood, buried under a Prussian public school training of 18 years, were beginning to make themselves felt. About three miles from the camp there was a small bay that suited my purpose admirably and I therefore left the jeep on the road and walked down to the water's edge.

As I did so, I passed a small boathouse and saw an old man of about 60 sitting beside it smoking a pipe. Wishing to find out exactly where I had come, I approached him and said in the halting English used quite inexplicably by the British when they wish to be understood by a foreigner, 'Do you speak English?' 'Nein,' he replied arrogantly, in the tone of a proud man who had seen his nation beaten twice by the British but had never admitted defeat. Then turning towards the boathouse he shouted 'Inga', and as a young German girl appeared in the doorway he pointed at me in an ignominious way with the stem of his pipe.

'Aha,' I said, 'Can you help me?' 'I will try,' she said in halting English, with a friendly smile. Now at the time, you must realise, this girl appeared to me to be nothing more than a direction-finder in my efforts to find a suitable place for an exercise. I did not notice her as a woman or hardly as a human being. She might well have been described in an Army pamphlet as a 'local inhabitant of an area' who 'will often prove of considerable value in orientating your position'. Nevertheless, I will describe her now, although most of the details of her features and figure only slowly became evident to me in the two days that I knew her.

Although she must have been of medium height, the impression that remains with me is of a heavily built girl whose figure radiated a considerable voluptuousness. Her legs were strong and her calves were thick and muscular. Nevertheless she had a good waist and large soft feminine breasts that her dress contained with difficulty. Looking back on it her face to English taste would have appeared too full of expression and character. In fact when I showed my sister a photograph of her face she described her as looking like a tart!

I do not believe that I have seen, ever again, such genuinely friendly eyes. They had a watery and greenish depth reminiscent of an alpine lake. Her mouth was large and the lipstick that she wore was a deep red so that it enhanced the roundness of her face.

But more than any other part of her body it was her hair that I quickly noticed, for it was a deep shining brown and it hung in an unkempt and rather stringy manner around her shoulders. I may be wrong, but to this day I look at a girl's hair when I wish to detect her mood. The slightly dishevelled hair of this girl reflected her boredom, her incompleteness and adolescent disharmony with life.

It must I suppose have been the extreme sensuality of this girl coupled with her forthright and completely uninhibited approach that overcame my reserve and shyness. Very quickly we were discussing the beauty of the lake, the islands in its midst and the yachts that lay becalmed throughout its length.

You will understand that any girl that I had ever met before had been as unfeminine and unapproachable as my own shyness had been unconquerable and inbred. Having been brought up at home in an atmosphere of misogyny and educated at an English public school in which the appearance of a maid had appeared unusual, and having understood from my first few weeks from other enlisted men of a different background from myself that women and prostitution were synonymous, my whole concept of the opposite sex was to say the least of it distorted.

On this occasion however I was able to talk and joke with a girl quite freely, and indeed far more freely than my own sense of dignity allowed with my own male friends.

Returning to the camp that night I felt a different man. The feeling of incompleteness that had worried me earlier in the day was gone. As I drove into the camp I passed a group of the men's women who giggled and whispered to one another in an attempt to embarrass me.

My arrogance was however by now complete, since added to the adolescent pomposity engendered by my rank I now also felt an inherent superiority over the Jocks and their whores. Before, although I despised these women and was revolted by their activities, I had no girl of my own. Now I knew a clean, pleasant and wholly attractive German girl who in her looks and conversation was suited to a young officer.

That evening I ordered McDade, my batman, and three other men to blow up the rubber dinghy and to arrange for some sandwiches and a thermos of tea to be ready in the morning. At lunchtime the next day they carried it down to the water for me, and having placed it on the beach they returned and sat on the hill.

At 2 o'clock Inga came to meet me as I had arranged and together we pushed the boat into the lake and set off for a picnic. As I paddled away the four Jocks cheered, laughed and waved, and proud of my conquest I waved back laughingly, understanding how envious they must have been of my good fortune.

After paddling slowly across the lake for an hour I suggested to Inga that we land on a small island and eat the tea that I had brought. She gaily agreed. There for hours I toyed with her, uncertain and hesitant in my actions until she, realising that she was in the hands of a completely inexperienced young man, took control and by suggestion and subtle innuendo indicated the parts of her body that gave her pleasure. However, it was not until darkness came that I could contain my embarrassment sufficiently to explore her buxom body with anything bordering on military precision and even then it would have been difficult to tell who was the more active partner or love's leader.

As the lesson progressed through the gathering darkness, my confidence increased and in the same way that an intangible bond grows up after two Englishmen have sat opposite each other in an otherwise empty railway carriage for four hours without speaking, conversation started and we began to learn about each other and the background to our lives.

'My father and mother were killed by the Russians,' Inga told me, 'when they conquered Berlin and something horrible happened to me. Now I live with my grandparents in Spandau, but they are very old.'

'Do you ever go out in the evening,' I asked, 'with any German boys?'

'There are very few German boys in Berlin,' said Inga.

'You speak such good English – I suppose you learned it at school?'

'Well yes, a little, in fact all. And what about you? You are an English officer and so nice – my grandfather would hate my going out with an English officer. I like the English though and especially the Scottish.'

'Do you know any of them?'

'Oh only one or two …'

It must have been at about midnight that we reached the edge of the lake and I walked up the path past the camp with Inga and on through the trees for a mile to the main road where I kissed her goodbye. And as I wandered back through the darkness I felt weighed down by sympathy for her life and the terrible tragedies of her youth. Yet at the same time the knowledge that she had confided in me, had given herself to me, and had wept at the thought of my one day leaving her, engendered in me a kind of humility that until that day I had lacked. I could no longer feel smug or arrogant because for the first time in my life I had understood and become part of someone other than myself.

Yet as I approached the camp my thoughts were rudely jerked back to the reality of my position and the responsibility that was mine with the men under my command. Sadly I reflected how great could be the benefits that 'my Jocks' might derive from friendship with such a girl instead of their incessant squalid serial acts of physical love in which they indulged with the half-human women of their acquaintance.

Wearily as I reached my tent I sank down upon my bed to find McDade faithfully awaiting my arrival with a mug of tea in his hand.

'Oh well done McDade,' I said. 'My goodness I'm thirsty. How did you guess how welcome this would be?'

McDade just grinned and said, 'I just knew, sir. Oh, how did you find her? A bit of alright, I bet.'

'Yes – jolly good,' I said quite startled. 'What do you mean?'

'Oh only that we reckon Inga's the best bang in Berlin. Until tonight you were the only one in the platoon who hadn't bedded her. Goodnight, sir,' he said and disappeared. My first lesson was complete.

In due course, my time with The Royal Scots drew to an end. The battalion was posted to Korea, a really nasty conflict which was still in progress. My platoon sergeant, who had spent much of his early life in various civilian and military prisons, led a delegation of my Jocks to see me; they made the request that I abandon my transfer to the Gurkhas, and lead them as their platoon commander in Korea. They said it was wrong of me to desert the platoon. It was possibly the most flattering compliment I have ever been paid.

~

After taking a regular commission, and attending an interview with General Sir Francis Tuker, who had commanded the 4th Indian Division in the desert, then the colonel of the 2nd Gurkha Rifles, I was accepted by the regiment and set off for Singapore.

In my diary, shortly after arrival, I wrote an account of the voyage out:

I left the troopship with very few regrets. It had been a pleasant enough journey but travelling through the Red Sea in August with three other people in the same cabin can never be very enjoyable. It was very lucky, for sharing with me were two infantry subalterns and one cavalry subaltern, all with a considerable capacity for entertainment which in its way was not lacking. I had been nominated the ship's entertainments officer and therefore upon me devolved the work of amusing the hideous officers' wives and trying not to be amused with the wholly desirable WRACs who occupied the lower deck amongst a seething mass of the brutal and licentious soldiery. It is no wonder that incidents occur on ships. After many years in the fogs and rain of England, the normal person is thrown into tropical climates in a matter of days and, in addition to this considerable aphrodisiac, the very fact of living on top of women makes them seem infinitely more attractive than their merits warrant.

Travelling as first-class passengers among the 'Orficers' was an unexceptionally stupid young girl who insisted on washing and pressing all our clothes. To begin with this was an embarrassment, but quickly became a blessing since some men, in particular myself, are both clumsy and useless with an iron. Luckily we also had a lady doctor of doubtful age and of Australian extraction who possessed an amazing sense of fun and a wonderful humour. Being the only faintly eligible girl on the whole ship, she spent every evening in the arms of a different subaltern.

Amongst the eccentric males I must include Dr X, a fine example of Scottish dourness. A National Service doctor, he quickly earned the title of the ship's bore. His whole time was entirely taken up in fawning over two RAF wives, most attractive and young, who were quite exceptional in their determination to remain faithful to their husbands. An unheard-of thing on a troopship.

Being in charge of entertainment, I felt that we ought to have a ship's concert. There was plenty of talent amongst the sailors and soldiers and, although I am not much of an impresario, I reckon that there was plenty among the WRACs. The most adequate act for them appeared to be a private performance of the cancan and, therefore, quite justifiably, I felt it producer's licence to sit back and shout 'higher, higher', as they put in their daily practice.

We had a day in Colombo and another in Aden. Driving out for a day's bathe from Colombo proved a great treat. Bathing for the first time in a warm sea with great rollers breaking on the beach was a happy introduction to the East. Aden, on the other hand, could never be a happy introduction to

anything and still vies with Calcutta, in my mind, for the title of the most re-
pulsive place in the world …

I have one other memory of the journey out. It was decided by my committee that we should have a boxing match, but no-one would volunteer. Remembering my past boxing activities at Bradfield, I agreed reluctantly to be
a victim. The deck was organised into a standard boxing ring, and all the
ship's passengers and company attended. The opponent, much larger and
heavier than myself, was quite a thug. Several times he caught me with an
awful clout, but I just about managed to remain conscious and on my feet. I
lost; but as the smaller member of the contest I became the hero of the occasion and received a hearty cheer. Perhaps this was a fitting prologue to my
time on active service in Malaya.

Chapter Three

WITH THE GURKHAS

Worst of all there is no-one to kill; the bandits are too elusive.

(Letter home)

I shall always remember my arrival by troopship in Singapore because, among all the officers on board, I was the only one to be met at the quayside; none of the other officers received a personal welcome and they were simply bussed from the ship to their battalions. The adjutant of the 1st Battalion, Denis Wood, with a Gurkha orderly and a driver, was there to meet me. Years later I was struck by the contrast with Peter Carrington's description of his welcome in the Grenadiers:

> It was the custom in the Grenadiers to make newly joined ensigns sharply aware of their insignificance. This was intended to induce humility, to knock out of the newcomer any false feeling of grandeur or achievement … The salient method was not to talk to him so when I joined nobody talked to me. My brother officers behaved as if I wasn't there.

The 2nd Gurkhas could not have been more different. No-one was addressed as 'sir'; instead, the battalion commander was addressed as 'Colonel' in the mess, where it was obligatory for all other officers to be called by their Christian names. The Guards regiments have a justified reputation, but give me the informal atmosphere of the Rifle Regiment, rather than the hierarchy of the Guards.

In the 1st Battalion, 2nd Gurkha Rifles, I believe that I was at that stage the only second lieutenant. There were around twelve British officers in the battalion, all the platoons being commanded by Gurkha officers, so it was a tightly knit group. Indeed, it was not until 1954 that we were joined by two new officer recruits – John Chapple, who subsequently became Chief of the General Staff and served with me in the MoD, and Digby Willoughby, who won a fine Military Cross in Borneo and has for many years run the Cresta Run in St Moritz. Two

National Service officers, Brian Skinner and Michael Willis, arrived just before my departure – both first-rate officers and good friends.

It is hard to explain the nature of this great regiment; it had probably seen more continuous active service than any other regiment in the Army. The 1st Battalion had fought right through the desert campaign from El Alamein, then on through Italy to the ghastly battles around Cassino and beyond. Hardly had the Second World War concluded, and Indian independence taken place in 1947, than it found itself in Malaya at the beginning of the communist insurrection, followed by confrontation in Borneo. This meant that several of the British officers and many of the senior Gurkha officers would altogether be on almost continuous active service for twenty-five years. This made for a very individualistic, rather eccentric team of British officers, committed more to the Gurkhas and the regiment than to the British Army as such.

It was somewhat daunting for a young second lieutenant to join a group of such distinction, and it was not long before I recognised that it was one of the most heavily decorated regiments in the British Army. Between 1948 and 1994, the last date for which I have a record, the regiment won 3 DSOs, 21 MCs, 43 MMs, 5 DCMs and 189 Mentions in Despatches. Several of the wartime officers, now majors, had an MC and bar – and we had one officer, Peter Jones, who as a very young officer had been awarded an immediate DSO in the desert. There were also several Gurkha VCs, all retired.

The only sensible thing to do was to launch me into active operations with a company, and so I was sent to join 'C' Company under the command of Tony Lloyd-Williams. 'C' Company was based in an abandoned rubber-tappers' hutted camp, not far from a village called Kulai. This area of South Johore had been one of the strongholds of the communist terrorists in the early part of the Emergency but, by the time I arrived, the worst was over. Nevertheless, it was still our role to patrol the primary and secondary jungle in order to hunt down the bandits, as we called them, set up ambushes on the edge of the villages when they came to collect food and supplies, and generally to operate with police and the Special Branch to clear the area completely of the terrorist threat. Johore had remained the most difficult area for operations in Malaya and had become a regular stamping ground of the 1/2 Gurkhas.

'The Company camp is miles from anywhere in the middle of rubber and we are about 30 miles from the causeway into Singapore,' I wrote home:

There are only two meals a day but you find that more is unnecessary. The only food is what the Gurkhas eat which is called Bhat which is mainly Rice with a sort of curry gravy on top. Sometimes you get dried fish sprinkled on the top. It is amazing but we find (British officers) that a small heap of rice, about a small pudding basin full, manages to satisfy you until 9 o'clock at night. The men are perfect simple country gentlemen. You never hear a complaint and there is without a doubt a happier atmosphere in a Company Camp than you will find anywhere.

Tony Lloyd-Williams was an interesting man and we got on well, although he wisely insisted that in the early months I always went out on patrol with him. The British company commanders were a fiercely independent lot; they knew their job through years of jungle operations and were very reluctant to do the bidding of tactical HQ. The commanding officer was called Gerald Rickcord, a delightful and experienced soldier who had won a DSO with the Royal Ulster Rifles in northwest Europe. But Rickcord was not a Gurkha and the senior company commanders did not readily accept an outsider being imposed upon them. He was given a hard time.

Most of the officers were not interested in promotion – they would never have dreamed of sitting the staff college exam – and only wanted to serve in the regiment. They had rather limited time for the British regiments, although socially everyone got on fine. But outstanding company commanders like Peter Richardson never wished to serve elsewhere or on the staff; their ambition was limited to commanding one of the two battalions of the regiment. This exclusiveness, this inward-looking nature of the regiment, although it added to the high quality and achievement of the battalion, did not help it to assimilate easily into the British Army – language being the other problem because, in those days, everything was conducted in the Gurkha language.

Indeed, looking forward some thirty years from when I was with them, it was fortunate that the 2nd Gurkhas had Prince Charles as its Colonel-in-Chief, General Dwin Bramall, a former Chief of the General Staff, as the colonel of the regiment, John Chapple as Chief of the General Staff and the next colonel of the regiment, and myself as a recently retired Defence Secretary. Those British regiments which could not take up all the recruits that wanted to join the Army at that time looked on with somewhat critical eyes at the continuance of the Brigade of Gurkhas. To evoke the spirit of the times, I remember dining in Pratt's Club one night and hearing two elderly Guardsmen complain that it was disgraceful disbanding the 2nd Battalion of the Grenadiers when, instead, it would have been possible to disband the Coldstream Guards altogether! How could we recruit these men from the Himalayas, the British Army asked, admirable and loyal soldiers as they were, when the unemployment queues in England were lengthening and the Army could not take them on? The Brigade of Gurkhas survived, however, in a new form and today fills innumerable manpower gaps in the British Army, at a time when recruiting falls way below the manpower requirements.

Tony Lloyd-Williams, when I came across him, had recently been engaged in one of the classic confrontations of the Malayan Emergency. Major Wimbush, in command of two platoons of Support Company, about fifty strong, stumbled across a jungle camp on a steeply sloped spur occupied by some 250 communist terrorists dug into defensive positions. Wimbush left one platoon to hold the enemy with fire and attempted an outflanking attack through the jungle, followed by a daring charge up a sixty-degree slope. He was shot through the forehead five yards from the first enemy slit trench, the rifleman beside him being killed also.

Due to poor communications, it was not until the next day that a follow-up was mounted by 'C' Company. Lloyd-Williams followed the tracks of the terrorists for several days and eventually came across a hundred bandits dug in around a newly built camp. During the assault on the position, Lloyd-Williams was hit in the back of the head by a bullet from a light machine gun and seemed in a bad way. Tony Wright took command and made a renewed assault on the position of the enemy, who broke off and fled into the jungle. This was one of the worst incidents of the Emergency for the battalion, but happily Tony Lloyd-Williams recovered. I do not recall him ever talking about it on the very many evenings when he and I sat together eating our curry in company camp at dusk.

~

It was not long before the battalion was moved north to a place called Kuala Kubu Bahru. This was a rather mountainous area below Fraser's Hill, where Sir Henry Gurney, the High Commissioner, had been ambushed and killed two or three years earlier. With Lloyd-Williams away on leave or a course, and with me in temporary command of the company, I had my first opportunity to lead

patrols into the jungle. In some respects, the country was easier than Johore because we patrolled mainly in primary jungle which provided a protective tree
canopy and was therefore cooler and less thick than so much secondary jungle
in Johore; this was where the original trees had been felled and re-growth had
occurred.

I found the primary jungle a friendly place, and I think that I was not alone
among my colleagues, most of whom had spent years patrolling, in finding it so.
After a few days in camp, most of us were quite keen to get back on patrol.
There was something primeval, yet rather absorbing and beautiful about it.

A diary account I wrote at the time for my parents gives a good idea of a
typical patrol:

Friday. Left the Camp in transport and went about 10 miles, then got out and
set off into jungle. Marched through jungle for 2 hours, then stopped and
made camp for night. Time about 4.30. Distance covered approx ¾ mile. No
tracks or bandits seen. The going – Average Primary Jungle, slow going –
quite cool – soaking wet with sweat! Got dark 6.30. I was asleep by 8 o'clock.
Average night, bed a bit hard.

Saturday. Left base at 8.30 having eaten, and marched approx 2 miles during
day. Very hilly, almost mountainous. Got lost at 12 o'clock but soon found out
where we were. The going was Primary Jungle, slow and hilly. Reached next
base at 4 o'clock and made camp for night. Very exhausted – marching whole
day – ¼ hour break for lunch only. No bandits or tracks seen.

Sunday. Left previous night's camp at 8.30 having eaten. Marched approx 2
miles during day. No halts. Made Base at 4.30 afternoon. Primary Jungle and
very hilly. Rained for half the day. No bandits or tracks seen. The thickness
and difficulty of the going can be seen by the time it takes to cover 2 miles.

Monday. Kept base in same place, patrolled area during day. Tracks for 2 bandits founds. Half ambushed. No-one came.

Tuesday. Patrolled area. I took section out in afternoon and found good tracks
for 2 bandits on way back. It was getting dark, so returned to base.

Wednesday. Re-supplied with rations and clothing from the Parachute drop. Very accurate. Clothing landed in river nearby but food came down in right place. I took out long patrol of about 4 miles. The going was terrible. Secondary jungle, had to cut every inch of the way. When we were within 100 yards of camp on way back, heard shot. 2 bandits walked into one of our sentries. Both got away. Recovered two bandit hats. We were attacked by a monkey during the day who threw things at us!

Thursday. Moved base camp further South 1,000 yards, are now making camp 3 o'clock. Two Sections out on patrol. No shots heard. Nothing happened.

Friday. Tracks of 2 bandits contacted on Wednesday found beside river. One Section went to investigate. Myself and two men swam crocodile-infested river and patrolled swamp on other side. Saw a lovely tiger very close, a lot of monkeys and crocodiles. Birds absolutely lovely. This place like a lost world – very pretty jungle with a fast flowing wide river in the centre. No trace of two bandits found – returned base at 5 o'clock.

Saturday. This morning waiting for our second airdrop due at 9.15. We received the airdrop and then I joined a different platoon and will stay with them until the operation is over. We left the DZ (Dropping Zone) at 10.15 and went to our new base about ½ mile away. Arrived there at 12.15 and then had lunchtime cup of tea. Two patrols then went out and got back at 4 o'clock. We then made base and it got dark at about 6.30. Nearly put my foot on a centipede which here have a dangerous sting like a snake. It was exterminated with ruthless ferocity by the men around. Received 3 pairs of socks, a towel, 2 vests, 2 pants and a petrol lighter on airdrop, all free. Have so far on this operation worn out 4 pairs of socks and 1 pair of boots. Beginning to feel v. tired at end of day but feel quite fresh each morning.

Sunday. Moved base again this morning. Reached new one at 1 o'clock, having left at 9 o'clock. The first half mile was in jungle but then came into rubber for the first time on the operation – moved then much quicker until we came to Secondary Jungle (10 ft high bracken) which is the worst of all. Had to cut our way through for 300 yards. Had tea on arrival here. 2 Sections are now out patrolling.

Monday. Patrolled in morning and then after tea at midday patrolled through jungle and rubber back to nearest track (about 4 miles) where at 3 o'clock we were picked up by transport and returned to camp.

Had a hot shower and ate big meal. Went to bed early.

I am wiry with considerable powers of physical recovery, but I am not strong and I found eight hours up and down slippery hills, bending and climbing, and wading through streams and swamps with a 60lb pack utterly exhausting. The Gurkhas, short and stocky, were built to carry heavy loads, and from their early youth in the mountains of Nepal they would have had no choice but to carry loads of up to 100lbs for days on end.

It was the Gurkhas' practice to move on a compass bearing, so we needed to cut straight through obstacles rather then go round them along jungle tracks. In this way, the men used to pick up signs of human or animal movement as they criss-crossed tracks. The British battalions were mainly accompanied by Iban trackers, but the Gurkhas were excellent trackers, being true countrymen; they would pick up a print in the ground or a bruised leaf or a snapped twig with considerable skill.

We stopped every hour or so for a breather, having put out sentries, and then on again after ten minutes or so. In this way we covered the ground; but in secondary jungle, with no tree canopy overhead, the leading man often had to cut his way with his kukri through heavy undergrowth, often in great heat with a blazing sun. The secondary jungle was the worst, and there was plenty of it in Johore.

Soon afterwards I tried to describe how I felt going through this secondary jungle:

'I can't go on – I must rest – I must call a five minute halt – I can't go on – we haven't been marching for an hour yet though – we must go on.' Those were the thoughts that raced through my head as in single file we moved through the tall bracken on our way to the next day's camp.

'Why am I doing this? It's sheer hell. I can't go on. I must have a drink of water. Oh hell it's hot,' as the fierce sun beat down on our little party cutting its way through the secondary jungle with no tall trees to give us shade and no flat ground to take the weight of our laden packs evenly on our weary shoulders.

'God, you weed,' I thought to myself. 'Bhimbahadur in front there is carrying more than you and he is cutting the path for the rest to follow. He is doing far more than you, yet he never complains or stops.'

'Oh, heaven! Time for a halt.' I hold up my hand as a signal for a short rest. Like automatons the men wheel out into a fan around me and sit mopping their brows with their ready weapon balanced in their laps.

As my orderly comes silently up to me and hands me a mug of cool water from the jungle stream, the Gurkha officer smiles as if to say 'Tired?' 'No,' I smile back, 'Fine.'

There is no question of sweating; every man is soaking wet as if he has just climbed out of a bath. The sweat simply runs down the body as if it was rain when one is caught in a storm.

'Time to move,' and we are off again. We are moving against the grain of the country up five hundred feet and down to the river. We have now crossed seven ridges in two hours.

'I can't go on – God! It's hot.' My mind races over a thousand thoughts in a few seconds. But we do go on and on and on…

The pain of the day's trek was, however, more than compensated for by the evenings. We stopped in the late afternoon, in order to build camp for the night – and here the skill and experience of the Gurkhas came into their own. As the officer in charge of the patrol, British or Gurkha, waited whilst the signaller tried to establish communication with tactical HQ – never a simple task, with heavy primitive wireless sets and Morse code – the rest went about their business. Some built platforms along the ground by cutting saplings with the kukris and laying leaves on top as a makeshift mattress. Above they strung ponchos to keep out the rain at night. It nearly always rained heavily during the day – and normally at night – so that we arrived in camp soaking wet, smelly and sweaty. It was a time to get the fires going to dry out clothes for the night, get rid of the leeches, have a bathe in a mountain stream and generally to return half-way to normality. The Gurkhas slept collectively on platforms, but the British officer was always given his own bunk, which his orderly prepared for him. It had a poncho above and below over the leaf mattress, and a mosquito net, which was essential.

Over the whole of the three years that I spent with the Gurkhas, I seldom ate European food. While with the men in camp or out on patrol, the British officers, almost without exception, lived on Gurkha rations; we were woken with a cup of tea, had the first meal of curry around 10 o'clock in the morning and a second meal of curry in the evening. All these rations had to be carried. I would be happy to have lived the rest of my life on Gurkha food – and in camp at night, on patrol, that Gurkha curry tasted more delicious than any other meal I have ever had.

It was unusual to see a lot of wildlife, but my contemporary account shows that we did meet up with interesting animals on occasions. There were quite a lot of large pythons, but they made themselves scarce. One Gurkha was famously coiled by a huge python, but his brother happened to be in the same section and cut it off him with his kukri. The most dangerous encounter seemed to be with hornets; on two occasions the leading rifleman stumbled across a hornets' nest, which led to a total collapse of discipline as everyone scattered in all directions. Once I had to evacuate two men by helicopter who had been very badly stung. The other nasty animal was the big centipede, which was very poisonous and had a habit of crawling into warm wet jungle boots at night. We did not put on jungle boots in the morning without checking them for centipedes – and scorpions, too. Never in all the months that I spent on patrol did I sleep on the ground – and this is why we British officers, I suspect, fared better than our contemporaries in the British infantry. Our orderlies looked after us like children and were generally quite wonderful, certainly to me.

On one's first patrol the leeches were a little disturbing, but by the second day they were simply part of life. In the evening it was quite normal to find five or more swollen leeches attached to various parts of the body – they were simply burnt off the skin with a little salt or, more usually, with a lighted cigarette. We were meant to take salt tablets during the day to replace the salt lost in sweat. I never did. We were meant to use sterilising tablets in the water bottle when drinking from mountain streams; it was wise if one ever remembered.

Then, of course, there was the daily dose of Paludrine against malaria; most of us were irregular takers of this pill, but I do not remember anyone getting malaria. The worse afflictions were usually boils and skin infections in that hot and humid climate, but generally we were all extremely fit and healthy.

Just occasionally I wished I was somewhere else. 'I am fed up with this beastly country!!' I wrote to my parents after four months in Malaya:

I object to spending Christmas in a temp of 90°. I object to everyone in the Army other than the Gurkhas. I can't visit Night Clubs, drink myself silly, meet gaytime gals or do any of the more pleasant things in life. There is no time for sailing, fishing, riding or flirting. And worst of all there is no-one to kill; the bandits are too elusive.

~

In fact, I managed to escape from our company camp in Kulai every three weeks or so, and subsequently from the tactical HQ, for what the Americans described as 'rest and recuperation', or was it 'recreation'? 'Recreation' frequently involved tracking down Chinese girls of rather low repute. We had our main headquarters in Singapore, so we used the officers' mess as the base for forays into the low life of Singapore – and there was plenty of it before Lee Kuan Yew turned the whole island into a ghastly sexless concrete jungle. I met Lee Kuan Yew on two occasions when he came to visit Margaret Thatcher in London. As we dined together, I did not tell him or Margaret about the joys of the taxi-girls at the Southern Comfort, the Straits Cabaret and the Seventh Storey.

I am astonished how badly behaved we were in those days. If we had been caught, we would have been cashiered in today's climate of political correctness. Both in Berlin with The Royal Scots, and with the Gurkhas in Malaya, inebriated young officers used to pinch street signs and other mementoes of their evenings out. I was sent once on a young officer's course to the Medical Training Centre, somewhere in southern England. The whole campus was littered with demonstration exhibits of how to keep soldiers on active service in healthy conditions. We were very proud of a big sign entitled 'Deep Trench Latrine', which was removed and fixed outside the personal quarters of the brigadier, Royal Army Medical Corps, who commanded the camp.

I wrote an account at the time of a typical night out in Singapore:

First of all we went to the Southern Cabaret – which was always described as 'a place with atmosphere'. There were a host of beautiful Chinese girls, all looking very enticing and glamorous waiting to be invited to dance. 'David' remarked to me, sitting at the bar, that 6 shillings was rather expensive for two gins, but I said that they were undoubtedly charging us for a bar stool which we had stolen from the same place one month previously. Tonight we had returned as men of peace – and lusted after a beautiful Eurasian girl who was working behind the bar. She took some exception to our comment that she was wearing her backless dress on back to front – and she probably being the girlfriend of the owner, we were asked to move on somewhere else.

The next port of call was the Straits Cabaret where David feasted his eyes on a girl called Jessie who responded with a cold stare which could have passed through three feet of concrete. It registered an emotion which said, 'About time you came back to see me – come along to my house, baby.' She was certainly very beautiful and had recently won a prize as 'Miss Tiger Beer'.

Another evening we went out with a fellow subaltern who was getting married the next day. As he was committing himself to a life of faithfulness he passed on to us a few tips. Among these was that we had to visit the Malaya Bar for lunch at ten minutes to one when we would have the opportunity of meeting the girls from the Singapore telephone exchange. The telephone 'Segamat 99' was, he said, the open sesame to their hearts. What that meant, I do not know. We managed to get away from the wedding reception the next day and, sure enough, met up with two delightful Eurasian girls, one half-Chinese and one half-Filipino. They were wonderful and great fun. Alorette, the Filipino, spoke good English, but her conversation was spiked with American slang. She called the Chinese girl 'a crazy mixed-up kid', yelled behind the car as we went along: 'Excuse our dust', and referred to herself as 'Dynamite'. In spite of her western ways, she was a good Catholic and had to attend family prayers every evening at her home at 8 o'clock. She was my girlfriend in Singapore for quite a time.

My social life in Singapore during these years apparently did not just involve foreign girls. A letter home describes a particularly frustrating episode:

I had an awful evening last night and did not go to bed at all. We arranged to take out two naval officers' daughters and by the time we had picked them up and got back into Singapore it was 10 o'clock; we had a meal then decided to drive out to Changi about 15 miles from Singapore and have a bathe. We bathed for about two hours and it was 4 o'clock when we decided to return. Then one of those idiotic females lost her pearls in the sand and after sweeping half the beach we found them after an hour's search.

When we tried to dress, having found the pearls, we found that all our shoes had been stolen whilst we were bathing. My suede shoes had disappeared and Susie's crocodile high heeled shoes had gone as well. I insisted on backing the car up to shine the headlights on the spot and whilst doing so buried the car in the sand up to its back bumper. We tried everything to get the car out but it was no good until all the Indians who slept near the beach came and lifted us out. By this time it was 6 o'clock in the morning and any enjoyment that I had had was forgotten. Then the last straw which broke my back was driving the women home (about 30 miles). Vivian and one girl were having slap and tickle in the back and Susie the little wretch disapproved of the driver dividing his attentions between the car and herself, and so I had to drive the whole way whilst Vivian whose car it was (he had, conveniently for himself, no licence!) was making whoopee in the back seat. I was livid and have sworn never to drive a car on an evening outing again, NEVER.

Susie is only 17 but has the most voluptuous figure and would make an admirable back seat companion …

Is it any wonder that my grandfather resigned his commission because he could not stand the boisterous nature of mess life, the gambling, drinking and womanising of the young officer class? He had a point.

Altogether, I look back on those days and nights in Singapore with no regrets, just nostalgia. We were on active service in the jungle most of the time, and that is the only excuse I can find for what appears to have been utterly adolescent behaviour.

~

When the battalion moved back to Johore after about a year, Colonel Rickcord (still in command) appointed me signals officer and intelligence officer. They were two separate jobs, but there were not enough officers in the battalion to fill both posts. I was sent to find a new tactical headquarters and discovered a pleasant, traditional-style house on the outskirts of Johore Bahru, the southernmost town in Malaya. The house was a Malay brothel; the institution seemed to be attached in some way to the Sultan of Johore's Palace, which was next door. The Sultan by this time was well into his eighties, but was celebrated by his subjects for the number of children he continued to father. I suspect the brothel was connected, in some way, to his libido.

The remainder of my time in Malaya was spent performing these two important functions, at least until John Chapple arrived to take over as intelligence officer; for a few months we worked together. Gerald Rickcord was, meanwhile, succeeded as commandant by Pat Kent. I had always got on splendidly with my commanding officers, but I did not like Kent, nor he me. Nonetheless, we lived cheek by jowl in headquarters for a year or so, the only other officer being the second in command, Major Jimmy Roberts.

Jimmy was a true gentleman and rather a wonderful man, but some say that, like most Gurkha officers, he was 'quite mad'. He certainly upheld the regimental tradition for eccentricity. He had a great twinkle and saw the humorous side to everything; nearly every evening he had too much to drink. When these drinking sessions were at a pitch, it was Jimmy's habit to get out his shotgun which he kept under the bed, fill it with a cartridge, and with many expletives fire it through the roof. Rickcord and Kent took all this in good heart, but I found this often-repeated experience rather disturbing.

Jimmy was a great explorer and mountaineer. He had opened up many of the most famous Himalayan climbs with Tilman and others. He was made administrative officer, in charge of the Sherpas and the supply chain, in the first successful expedition to Everest under Hunt. He retired, as a much-decorated colonel, to Pokhara (the capital of western Nepal), where he trekked in the hills, bred rare pheasants and founded Mountain Travel, the first and still the best-known trekking company in Nepal. On two separate visits that I made to the high mountains where, in those days, we recruited all our soldiers, Jimmy organised my equipment, Sherpas and porters. Whenever I visited Pokhara, I always called on Jimmy, who used to gather up the soldiers and retired Gurkha officers that had served with me in earlier years. He was, like most of the other senior officers in the battalion, a confirmed bachelor.

At one point, it must have been whilst the battalion was still up north in Kuala Kubu Bahru, Rickcord asked me to join Major General Perowne, GOC 17 Gurkha Infantry Division, as his ADC. Perowne only had four months or so to do before completing his tour in Malaya. I had a most interesting time with him visiting all the British and Gurkha regiments throughout the country. I organised all his travelling arrangements, as well as handling his security and his entertaining. I lived in his house with his wife and daughter. His daughter was a delightful girl, but it is not easy for a young ADC to be living with the General's daughter – a difficult and claustrophobic relationship. This job enabled me to meet Sir Gerald Templer, then High Commissioner, on several occasions, and also General Stockwell, Perowne's immediate superior. The ADCs to generals form a sort of club, gossiping about their bosses, attending all the social occasions, keeping generals' daughters occupied and generally leading a pretty useless sort of existence. The ADC club had the highest opinion of Templer and a pretty low opinion of Stockwell, who was a very good-looking 'lounge lizard' type of man. I met several of that type when I was Defence Secretary.

As my time as Perowne's ADC ended, I received another summons from Rickcord, this time to go as ADC to a much more important man, General Sir Charles Loewen, who was the Commander in Chief Far East Land Forces, based in Singapore. Templer, as High Commissioner in Malaya, was independent of him and was based in Kuala Lumpur. By this time I was getting quite skilled at dealing with all these generals – but I fear the lessons that I learned did not carry over very successfully to the time when I again had to handle their concerns and welfare in the Ministry of Defence, some thirty years later.

Loewen was a Canadian who had served in India before the war and he had requested a Gurkha ADC for an impending official visit to India and Nepal. The real reason for his trip – and it was a good one – was to enjoy the shikar, i.e. the shooting and hunting. After a time in Singapore, again living in Flagstaff House – all generals seemed to live in houses called Flagstaff House and drive around with red plates on their cars carrying stars to represent their rank – we set off shortly before Christmas 1954 in our own aeroplane. Three weeks later, when the trip was over, I sent my parents a detailed account.

After a night in Calcutta, we headed for a city that seemed to take one back to the fourteenth century. Those who know Kathmandu today can see how it has changed since the 1950s:

> The first sight of Kathmandu from the plane is unbelievably lovely as you pass over the mountains and suddenly come into the valley in which Kathmandu is situated. The mountains tower up all around the valley.
>
> The airstrip is perched on the top of a hill and seems most precarious but nothing has ever crashed there since the airport was opened three years ago! On landing you leave civilization and the airport control is in a tin hut with one man who checks the passports etc.
>
> We were met by Summerhays (just knighted) who drove us into the Embassy where we stayed. It is a nice old house with English furniture and food.
>
> The same evening we had two cocktail parties to which all the Nepalese notables were invited. The Prime Minister, B.P. Koirala, and several of his Congress Party members had spent many years incarcerated in the dungeons

of the Rana family but they all seemed to get on famously. Edmund Hillary was also there.

The next day we spent a morning sightseeing. Kathmandu is the most beautiful city I have ever seen. The architecture is superb and the carving on all houses is a work of art. The brick is a beautiful mellowed red. It is a very old city and completely unspoiled by civilization. Cars are few and far between and seem only to be owned by the Maharajahs. It is almost an event if you meet another car on the road and often occupants get out and shake hands in the street. The centre of the town is taken up by an enormous grass parade ground. You can see a market, a caravan from Tibet, an Army parade and a game of cricket all going on there at the same time!

The most interesting visit we paid was to the Defence Minister General Sir Kaiser Shamsher Jungbahadur Rana GCB, GCSI. An old man who is probably the most famous sportsman of the East. His house (about the size of Buckingham Palace) was absolutely piled high to the roof with stuffed tigers, panthers, elephants, every conceivable animal you can imagine. Each one had a story. This one had been wounded by the Prince of Wales and the General finished it off. Another had been presented to him at the shoot by Edward VII and so it went on. Right through the centre of the house ran a cold dark passage which had books lined on both sides. The collection would put the Bodleian Library to shame. When we reached the end of the house we came into a room in which his wife was waiting. An absolutely lovely girl of about 25 (he is 80). Her portrait painted by Graham Sutherland was on the wall and there were a number of Vernon Ward's and Peter Scott's which he had collected while Ambassador in London. We then sat down and his sons (all Generals!) produced three cases of Champagne, one bottle of which he consumed himself.

The next day we left Kathmandu and flew back to Calcutta, so ending quite two of the most fascinating days of my life.

Then, after a trip to Darjeeling where we recruited the Eastern Gurkhas and where we were entertained by Sherpa Tensing, it was on to Lehra, near the other Gurkha recruiting depot in India, for Christmas and New Year:

The camp near Lehra is most attractive and the mess a lovely old country house. The whole place is completely cut off and isolated about 20 miles from the Nepalese border.

On 24 Dec we had a Duck Shoot, leaving the mess at 11.30 and starting the shooting at 12.30. It was the greatest fun and we collected a total of 17. None fell to my gun, but I have never done any of this shooting before. I was also firing from a standing position in a hollowed out tree-trunk which made it extraordinarily difficult to balance. There was a total of 8 guns with numerous boatmen, beaters, etc., so that it was quite a large party.

On Christmas Day we had the traditional Football Match between the British officers and the Gurkha officers. Then the Gurkha officers for drinks in the mess and Christmas Dinner in the evening.

On 28–29–30 Dec we had shooting parties. Two duck shoots for which we got up at 2 o'clock in the morning, both reasonably fruitful. One Snipe shoot and also a crack in the jungle near Lehra after tiger with .303 rifles.

On the 31st Dec there was a buffet lunch in the mess to which all the local planters etc. were invited. Two Tibetan Girls aged about 18 also came and boy oh boy were they honeys. They spoke perfect English, were beautifully dressed and very feminine. A wonderful race the Tibetans. On 1 Jan we set off for Delhi and reached there at about 4 o'clock in the afternoon. We were met by Lady Clutterbuck, the wife of the High Commissioner, and drove in their Rolls to their house.

That evening we were invited out to Dinner and so had quite a late night. In spite of this we set off at 3 o'clock in the morning (the same night) for a duck shoot outside Delhi. We were in position at 6 o'clock standing up to our knees in the coldest water I have ever known. There were plenty of duck there and geese but they were all out of range. And by breakfast at 8 a.m. we were tired, wet and cold with only two duck to show for it. After breakfast however we walked the dry ground around the lake and managed to get 12 partridge; it really was the greatest fun.

Whilst staying at the High Commissioner's residence when we were not out duck shooting, I got up each morning at 5.30 to exercise the horses of the President's bodyguard on the polo ground in Delhi. My boss – General Loewen – was welcomed as a hero, because this was the first official visit by a full British general since Indian independence. We were feted everywhere. My own most enthusiastic hosts were the Sikh officers of the President's bodyguard; hence my early morning rides. It certainly helped that I was a Gurkha officer – implying, I fear rather inaccurately, that I was something of a martial figure myself.

We returned to Singapore on 4 January. One day soon afterwar looking at the Foreign Office telegrams, which came via me on their the General, when I was struck by a sudden flash of inspiration. How ᵤₛ it possible, when I read about these huge and fascinating strategic and foreign policy issues, that I could ever stay in the Army? We were, after all, participating in what Graham Greene described as 'the forgotten war'. The world was so big and so absorbing that I had to be where it was all happening. Where else could that be but politics? I suddenly realised that I had to be in the centre of things – where great issues were discussed, where decisions were made. It had nothing to do with helping my fellow human beings; it had everything to do with intellectual curiosity and the impulse to be where the most important events were taking place.

It is one of my life's ironies that the trigger to go into politics should have been a few Foreign Office telegrams. When I eventually gained ministerial office, I found that Foreign Office telegrams were the biggest waste of the world's trees that I had ever encountered. Without bothering to read most of them, I tipped them into a garbage bag. The *Sun* newspaper had more useful information about the world than all the gossipy Foreign Office telegrams put together.

My father was initially opposed to my decision to leave the Army, and in a long letter towards the end of 1955 I explained to him my reasoning:

1. I have not got the great future that you predict. Perhaps I could reach full Colonel at the highest.

2. My temperament is NOT suited to the Army. I am a rebel by nature. I like speaking my mind. I like free discussion and controversy.

3. I have always ridden near the precipice with some of my superiors whom I consider idiots and tell them so.

4. I have always had good, even exceptionally good reports from my Commanding Officers but they have had no option since, if I might say so, I have done my work well and capably. Some of them, particularly the present one, regard me with suspicion.

5. I abhor the intellectual blight of the Army and its pomposity.

6. I am now earning a lot of money but how many children will I educate on a Lt Col's pay of £800 a year or a pension of £500?

7. I like England, good furniture, a fire, my possessions.

8. I know that I am physically and mentally suited to politics.

Finally, at 23 I have had the best out of the Army, e.g. Travel, Excitement, a wild life. As I get older, I more and more hanker after mental stimulation and the wish to get on and do something for myself instead of rising slowly by age and not ability.

Fortunately I had obtained at Bradfield adequate examination results to qualify me for Cambridge entrance. A fellow Gurkha officer, Roderick Goldsworthy, recommended Trinity College, where he had been himself, so I wrote to the admissions tutor, Michael Vyvyan, asking if I could have a place. Perhaps also influenced by a letter of recommendation from John Chapple (who had also been at Trinity), his charming reply said that the college would welcome a former Gurkha officer. It was all as simple as that – and it was arranged that I should go up to Trinity in the autumn of 1956.

There was, however, the small question of money. I applied for – and obtained – a county scholarship from Kent, as I was deemed as a regular soldier to be independent of my parents. This, together with my Army savings, saw me through Cambridge as a relatively wealthy undergraduate. Those savings almost entirely consisted of my allowance for the purchase of English food, some £1,000, quite a lot in 1956. During my three years, with the exception of the occasional European dish in the mess at Slim Barracks, Singapore, I had lived on Gurkha rations. The rest of my Army pay, I regret to say, had been blown on thrashes around Singapore's night life, and enough has been said about that already.

For what would be my final phase in the Army, I had returned to my duties as signals officer, where things were rather different for me as, mentally, I had moved on. Whilst I was away, the best young riflemen in the battalion had been called together to form a new signals platoon and, on my return, I trained them well in the new smaller wireless sets which had just been issued by the Army. Subsequently, most of my signals platoon became Gurkha officers, and one of them the Gurkha Major of the battalion – that is, the most senior Gurkha. On my visit as Defence Secretary to Pokhara in 1982, half of my old platoon walked two or three days from their homes in the hills to welcome me back to the signals platoon and to Nepal. It was quite an emotional occasion, particularly when a retired rifleman signaller, Gurkha Major

Humbahadur Thapa, presented me with his personal cane bearing a silver band with his name; it is still one of my most prized possessions.

Pat Kent, my commanding officer, did not take my application to resign with a particularly good grace; perhaps he thought that the resignation of a promising young officer was in some way a reflection on him. He expressed astonishment that any soldier would wish to enter politics and was surprised that I had decided to go to Cambridge. By this time, however, the keen and ambitious John Chapple had arrived, and as he had attended Trinity it offered, maybe, some explanation of how these strange young officers behaved.

My departure from the regiment was quite upsetting. I said goodbye to my signals platoon, but I don't think they realised, or would have understood, that a British officer would choose to leave. I did not want to face a gathering in the mess, because I felt something of a traitor. So I sneaked out one night without saying goodbye to anyone. It was hardly the correct way to behave.

~

Reflecting on my Army service, approaching fifty years later, I realise that it was all a great experience. In many ways, I developed a closer relationship with the British soldiers in the basic training depot in Aldershot, and with the men in The Royal Scots, than I was ever able to do with the Gurkhas. If I had spoken Gurkhali more fluently, it might have been otherwise. Although I had passed the language exam – and was paid an overseas allowance and a Gurkha language allowance as well as an English food allowance! – communicating in another language did not enable me to get as close to their interests, concerns and prejudices as I would have wished. It is fascinating to find how well today's young Gurkhas fit into the environment of the Parachute Regiment and other British units of the Army. Times change – and today's Gurkha recruits are rather different from their predecessors.

The foothills below Annapurna which run at around 6,000–8,000 ft have been the traditional recruiting ground for all the western Gurkha regiments. Whole villages like Ghandrung contained families that had produced recruits for the British Crown for over 150 years. These families were the yeomen farmers of the middle hills, prosperous relative to their neighbours, based on the ownership of fertile terraced land – and sustained by Army pensions. These men were tough, resourceful countrymen, retiring eventually as respected headmen of their village.

It is not the same today. Over-population in the hills, more particularly caused by tourism, has destroyed the environment. Trekkers, who have doubled the population numbers in these areas, demand hot meals and water, which in turn requires wood for cooking and heating. The hills have been largely denuded of trees to meet the demands of the trekkers. Landslides caused by deforestation have swept whole areas of terraced land into the rivers. Many of the traditional service families have abandoned the hills and moved to Pokhara, and the plains that border India, partly in order to obtain medicine and schools. Today's young recruits are more easily able to integrate with British troops, but in many cases are no longer the unsophisticated hill soldiers of earlier times. Instead, they will be more demanding, more 'political' in their attitudes and ambitions – but possibly more valuable to the changed British Army of today.

The 2nd Gurkha Rifles no longer exists – except as an old boys' club. The four British regiments were amalgamated in 1994 into the newly formed Royal Gurkha Rifles. I am sure the men are just as fine, resourceful, loyal and upright as they always were. But it is not the same for me. I attended the final parade of my regiment at Sandhurst in 1994. I don't think that I, a mere Gurkha officer of only three years' standing, was the only man there with tears running down his cheeks.

Chapter Four

CAMBRIDGE AND MARRIAGE

This seat of learning needs darning.

(Cambridge Union motion)

I left the Army in the spring, and as there were six months to go before Cambridge I looked around for a job. Eventually I heard of a Frenchman with a big hotel in Menton in the South of France who wanted to send his young son to an English prep school where he would need Latin to catch up with his contemporaries. So I agreed to give the boy two hours of Latin every morning in exchange for board and accommodation. Menton was at its best that summer, but I was lonely in this town of the retired. On the first Sunday I went to the Protestant Church for matins and, as I was looking vacantly at the altar, I had the most extraordinary experience. Alas, it was not a religious conversion but instead a conviction that I would progress fast in politics and retire as Foreign Secretary! If I had ever recited this experience to anyone they would have laughed it out of court and I would have been the subject of derision and ridicule; however, it was real and I saw my political career sweeping before me in a kind of vision of the future. Every part of it came true, except that I did not retire as Foreign Secretary, which was fortunate for me and especially so for the Foreign Office.

As I left the church I saw an attractive girl coming out beside me and we got into conversation. We had coffee and agreed to meet again. She was called Kate and it became my first serious affair. We saw each other every day when she had finished her work as a tour representative and I had finished giving Latin lessons. We bathed, walked in the mountains and sat up at night in the warm air. Menton was truly lovely and it has not changed. I was pretty keen on Kate but I am afraid that when I told her about my political ambitions she responded by sending me a series of poems. These are truly embarrassing, but it would not be all of a piece if I do not publish at least one of them. It is called

'To be or not to be' … oh dear! …

Once he was an Army man but he is that no more
And how he often wished he were, for Menton was a bore.
John Nott he went to Menton town to see what he could do.
He taught the Frenchman of his tongue and taught him Latin too.
But soon to Cambridge he will go, a student wise he'll be.
His aim is fame, that's what it is, not taking a degree.
He hopes to be a famous man, Prime Minister, no doubt.
So that orders he can give and make men run about.
But when in far-off times, I hear his name upon the news
And when the nations come to him and ask him for his views
I'll say that once I knew this man when he was plain John Nott.
That once I helped him on his way when fame was not his lot.
And when I'm poor and down and out, I'll write my memoirs too.
I'll tell the world about Earl Nott and what he used to do.
I'll tell them how his self-control so often let him down.
Of how he said the female race to men should all bow down.
Then when his name's in history writ, at a much later date,
Perhaps like Nelson's Lady H, they'll mention dearest Kate.

~

Cambridge was a bore, unlike Menton. Had it not been that I met my wife there it would have represented the three most wasted years of my life. I was twenty-four by the time I got there, admittedly only two years older than the majority who had completed their National Service, but I had seen so much and done so much. Cambridge seemed to be a closed world – an inward-looking, claustrophobic kind of place. In recent years it has been forced to open up a little. Trinity is a great academic institution, possibly the greatest, but it is too large a college for undergraduates.

Rab Butler, later to be Master of Trinity, used to tell the world that Trinity had more Nobel Prize winners, as fellows of the college, than the whole of France. Maybe so, but I could count on one hand the dons that I met there and, so far as I could see, they evinced interest only in those who were likely to achieve the highest academic eminence. It would have been fun and intellectually stimulating to have enjoyed their company, but that was not to be. Perhaps my failure to get much out of Cambridge reflected the fact that my motive for going there was that it would be a desirable staging-post for politics. To some extent, therefore, I made it worse for myself by seeking to take out of Cambridge more than I was prepared to put in.

I wrote an account soon afterwards of my first visit to my supervisor, a Mrs X:

My Director of Studies at Trinity was a Mr Neild, a Treasury adviser at the time. He told me how difficult it was for undergraduates to grasp the basic principles of economics. 'Your supervisor will be a Mrs X, Nott, and I should go along and see her at the School of Applied Economics some time tomorrow.' I was horror-struck, for an undergraduate's supervisor is his confidante, his form master and housemaster all rolled into one. He corrects and criticises essays and directs every aspect of your studies. I was to be commanded, beaten and criticised by some old harridan from Girton or Newnham.

The next morning, still somewhat disgruntled and considering the whole procedure extremely infra-dig, I made my way to the School of Applied Economics. My foreboding on entering this building increased as I saw bearded intellectual research students hurrying in and out of doors with folios of statistics, algebraical equations and lists of incomprehensible data. Mrs X, that image of bespectacled female horror, lived on the first floor; setting my shoulders, I climbed the stairs slowly and with great deliberation went to the harridan's haven.

'Come in,' said a lilting and extremely attractive voice as I knocked.

Some girl from Girton must be in there, I thought, as I opened the door.

'Oh, I'm sorry to bother you,' I said to the lady that confronted me. 'I was looking for a Mrs X – can you tell me where I can find her?'

'I am Mrs X,' said the lady. 'Come in and sit down.'

'But I … you are Mrs X,' I said.

'Yes, that's right – are you Nott from Trinity?'

My reactions are difficult to describe. Mrs X was about thirty. Tall, slim and with blonde hair falling to her shoulders. She was dressed in a brown blouse buttoned high to the neck and a vivid green skirt that swirled out from a tiny waist. Her complexion was far removed from the sallow features of an economist. In fact she was perfect – a Venus de Milo in the surroundings of a bear garden.

'I'm going to be your supervisor this term so shall we discuss the reading list first of all?' she said.

'Oh yes, yes, that would be a great help,' I replied with a watery smile, looking at the desk at which she was sitting piled high with Government Blue Books on Income and Expenditure, Cost of Living Indexes, Social Welfare Statistics and something that looked like the photographic copy of a schizophrenic doodle.

'Now I suggest that before you tackle the first question here on the National Income you have a look at Meade and Stone. It's an excellent little book and gives you all that you need. Do you think that you can manage that by Wednesday?'

'I'll have a go – yes, yes, I can manage it,' I stammered, colouring slightly at the cheeks.

'Well then, there only remains to settle the time and place of your supervision hours. I suggest that you come round to my house after supper on Wednesdays, it will be warmer round there and more comfortable,' she said with a radiant smile. 'I live at ...'

I suspect Mrs X had leanings towards communism, or at least the political economy of the far left. In this respect she was a fashionable follower of Joan Robinson, Maurice Dobb and others of that persuasion, but she had a stimulating intellect and I really enjoyed my supervisions with her. She was fun, she regarded my developing economic liberalism with rather patronising disdain, but she stimulated me sufficiently to recommend the sort of pamphlets which became the work of the emerging Institute of Economic Affairs; I began to read them with some excitement.

I enjoyed my year of economics before I made the serious error of switching to law for my final two years. I found the law turgid. I am not too sure what I think about the law and lawyers with their outrageous fees, even to this day. An increasingly urgent task is to curb the expanding power of the judges, particularly under the European Court of Human Rights, and to bring their law-making back under democratic control. For all its obvious imperfections, I would rather be governed by the tribunes of the people, and my fellow citizens acting as jurors, than by a clique of overweening judges; there, too, lies my discomfiture at the cultural divide between our continental cousins and ourselves.

I was only kept up to the mark in the study of the law by one of my Trinity colleagues, Dan Goyder, who got a good first. He was supervised with me by a certain Mr Jolowitz. Jolowitz had his rooms beside mine in Bishops Hostel off Great Court, and more than once he burst into my room complaining of the noise from my gramophone. He and I were not a great success together – no doubt because I was lazy, never attending lectures and doing one essay a week, the sum total of my academic effort during my time at Cambridge. 'Bright but indolent' would have been the correct end-of-term report.

My first term at Cambridge was the most interesting and intense of all the time that I spent there because it was the autumn of Hungary and Suez. Both events had a profound impact on me, but in rather different ways. When the Hungarian revolution began, it quickly divided my contemporaries between those who did not care to see an outside event distract them from their studies and their fun, and those who followed it with intense concern. A friend of mine, Charles Owen, and I met every day as the situation worsened. When the Russian tanks moved into Budapest and the newspapers showed pictures of young Hungarians pitching Molotov cocktails at the Soviet tanks, we discussed in all seriousness leaving Trinity, almost before we had arrived, to go and help the oppressed. It would have been a foolish gesture.

Chance then dealt me another lucky break. Visiting the Cambridge Union, in which I had determined to make my mark, I came across a strange character called Robin St John Shurley. He was a friendly, active 'groupie' of the Union and knew the then President, someone called Ken Post. As I poured out my misery about the lot of the Hungarians, he urged me to speak about it. Then to my astonishment I received a visit in my rooms in Great Court from Ken Post himself, urging me to propose an emergency motion on Hungary. I pleaded my junior status, saying that I had not yet spoken in a Union debate – but Post was insistent that he wanted to break tradition by having a freshman under-graduate, particularly one who had served in the Army, open the debate.

The motion I proposed on Tuesday, 6 November was 'this House would risk a Third World War for the sake of a Communist Satellite in Revolt'. My speech began:

During the last two weeks we have seen a series of events in Eastern Europe that is likely to take its place in world history. For the first time we have witnessed the rising of a whole people against a modern totalitarian state. And just as the 1917 Revolution has already been acknowledged as a turning-point in world history, so must this first national uprising be accounted the same.

We must not delude ourselves that other events merit the same significance. The American election [that very day] and our actions in Egypt are indeed matters of some moment. But they will, I suggest, in future times be looked back on as events in history – matters which seriously disturbed the conscience of the world at the time, but which in themselves never diverted the pattern of history from its chosen course. The revolt in Hungary, Sir, short and tragic as it has been, is one of the most significant and momentous happenings of this century.

It is up to this House to decide whether we allow it to become a turning-point in the progress towards world happiness and peace, or merely a heroic story-book stand against a cruel tyranny.

The rest of my thirteen-minute speech placed a lot of emphasis on the word 'risk' – only by confronting aggression, with all the risk involved, would we ever sustain freedom and democracy. According to the press report of this 'serious-minded and often deeply felt debate on the dilemma of the West', my 'poise and general debating skills quickly won the support of the House'. When it duly divided just before midnight, we lost the motion (301–271), but my Union reputation had been established. I went on to become President two and a half years later.

During that time, of course, I spoke in many other debates – but never again with such seriousness as on the issue of Hungary. Instead, I was known not for depth of thought but for delivering witty speeches that made the House laugh. Motions that I spoke for included: that 'Man fulfils himself most fully when uselessly employed'; that 'This seat of learning needs darning'; that 'The Army is the game for me'; and that 'This House has no confidence in Her Majesty's Opposition', a motion I successfully proposed that was seconded by a certain Brigadier J. Enoch Powell. On the other hand, 'This House respects neither a disunited nor a united Church', 'The Country needs a strong Liberal Party' and 'This House regrets that the age of chivalry has passed' were all motions that I spoke against. My last debate, my own Presidential debate, was on 9 June 1959, when I proposed 'That oratory is the harlot of the Arts' – an appropriate motion for an aspiring politician. At the end, 'when the motion was put to the vote, the House after the customary acclamation decided for the motion by the casting vote of the President'.

Back in the autumn of 1956, as Charles Owen and I were exercising our consciences about the plight of the Hungarians and what we could do to help, the French and British governments invaded the Canal Zone. I do not think that we considered whether the Russians would have invaded Hungary anyhow, Suez or not – it just seemed to distract the world and to give them a free run. I was dumbfounded, stupefied, that this could happen at the very time when it was the moral duty of the West to bring military pressure on the Soviets to withdraw from Hungary. I did not quite see the Anglo-French action as an act of unprovoked aggression, as many socialist students did, but rather as an utterly foolhardy exercise distracting the world from the tragedy in Eastern Europe.

Cambridge was in turmoil. Suez galvanised opinion in a way that Hungary had not. Opinion divided mainly along party lines: the young Tories, represented mainly by the public school contingents at Trinity and Magdalene, took a strong anti-Nasser line, whilst the majority of the undergraduates, with their left-wing leanings, regarded it as an act of unprovoked aggression contrary to the Charter of the United Nations.

By the time of Suez, I had become a member of an institution called the Pitt Club. It consisted of two hundred or so rather preposterous young men – a collection of mainly wealthy and well-connected undergraduates of the Alan Clark variety. Most of them travelled frequently to London to attend debutante dances, and some would today be classified as 'Hooray Henrys'. The Pitt Club was founded and run on the principle of a London club, and there was a self-perpetuating committee which presided over the selection of its members. Key committee members in my time included Vere Fane, John Harvey Bathurst and Alistair Pilkington. All three remained acquaintances in afterlife, becoming respectively a head-hunter, the banking director at Lazards under my chairmanship, and the chairman of the family business.

The Pitt Club, meanwhile, was a sort of haven for me away from the dreadful food in hall at Trinity, and I rather enjoyed the slightly louche culture with its emphasis on hunting, shooting and fishing. It was typical of my Cambridge way of life that I was a regular at meets of the Trinity Foot Beagles, where I met one of my greatest friends, Simon Day.

As the controversy over Suez grew, the Pitt Club organised a combined party, led by the Master of the Trinity Foot Beagles, to break up a massive protest meeting about Suez that was being held at the Union on Friday 2 November (four days before the debate on Hungary). The principal speaker was the

Honourable Anthony Wedgwood Benn, as he then called himself, and to the ghastly young members of the Pitt Club he was regarded as a traitor to his class for not supporting Eden's absurd foray into Suez. As for myself, I attended as a protesting member of the Union rather than as a member of the Pitt Club.

Benn's co-speaker was another Labour MP, Kenneth Younger, and Benn's diary entry for that day vividly evokes a memorable occasion:

> The Union debating hall was absolutely packed tight, with crowds round it trying to get in through the windows and jamming the entrance thirty deep. We struggled to reach our places. The UN flag had been stolen and there were wildly noisy scenes and shouts. Great posters hung from the gallery reading, 'Support Eden, not Nasser' and 'We are now committed and must support our troops.' The crowd of students laughing and screaming for war gave me an icy hatred of them. The uproar and noise and jolly funny remarks when the world was on the brink of disaster was completely revolting, disgusting and shameful.
>
> Kenneth Younger's speech was hardly audible, but he persevered patiently and quietly to the end. I decided to take it rather differently, by giving those people who took our view in the Hall something to cheer about and I therefore attacked the warmongers at once. Then I tried to buy silence by promising to answer questions. This was moderately successful though it meant my speech was prolonged to over an hour. My notes were carried away by a rotten tomato and stink bombs, and lavatory paper was thrown all over the place. One did not mind that but it was the flippancy on such a grave issue that was so completely horrifying.

As I recall, it was at a signal from a member of the hunt that the Trinity beagles were released into the debating chamber, accompanied by hunting horns and smoke bombs. Chaos indeed ensued. I remember Benn as incandescent with rage and the meeting being ruined.

I was appalled at the behaviour of the hunting set. To this day, whilst a supporter of hunting, I would do anything to avoid social intercourse with the horsey world and their ghastly noisy and drunken hunt balls. It bothers me to this day that I should have been associated with these ignorant public-school Tories. Possibly I fitted into this kind of undergraduate clique because we had in common a period of Army service. Somehow their company seemed more natural and congenial than that of undergraduates who had not served in the

Army and who, as state school pupils, wisely kept themselves apart. They were known as 'trogs' by members of the Pitt Club and were identified by the fact that they wore college scarves.

Cambridge was thus divided somewhat down class lines, and the incident in the Cambridge Union was indicative of this. It was certainly touch-and-go as to whether I sought my political future in the Labour Party or swallowed my distaste for this section of the traditional Tory Party, something that I was forced to do for most of my subsequent political career. I refer later to Mrs Thatcher's Cabinet. In fact, I joined the Tory Party because it was to become the radical party of the 1970s and early 1980s; and that is where I belonged.

When my younger son, William, came to leave Eton and had obtained a place on his own merit at St Andrew's, I – out of pure fatherly sentiment – decided that he ought at least to consider Cambridge as an option. I telephoned on his behalf and the following conversation took place:

Nott: Is that the admissions tutor at Trinity?

Tutor: Yes, can I help you?

Nott: Yes, I was at Trinity myself and I wondered if there was any chance of my son being able to obtain an interview and take the entrance exam.

Tutor: Maybe, where does he go to school?

Nott: Eton.

Tutor: I'm sorry, but we don't take Etonians at Trinity any more.

Nott: Oh, I didn't realise that, there were a lot of Etonians at Trinity when I was there. Why is that?

Tutor: We don't like them here because they go around in gangs and don't contribute to the life of the College.

Nott: Oh I'm disappointed. William did not get on very well at Eton and rather disliked the place.

Tutor: Well, your son may be interesting – we'll give him an interview and see how he gets on.

William did get into Trinity and had three happy years there, but I have often wondered whether he would have been better off in a rather less academic environment at St Andrew's.

If there had been a committee of privy councillors to examine Suez, similar to the committee which investigated the origins of the Falklands War, two key lessons would have emerged – the need to avoid divisions at the top in Whitehall and the necessity of carrying outside opinion, particularly the Americans. As it happened, the two generals – Templar and Stockwell – under whom I had just served in Malaya were key participants.

In later years I studied the whole episode, and it was very much on my mind when the Falklands crisis blew up. In 1956 Admiral Mountbatten and General Templar, the Chiefs of Staff for the Royal Navy and the Army, had strongly opposing views of the situation. When the invasion force was within four days of arriving at Port Said, Mountbatten wrote to Eden appealing to him 'to accept the resolution of the overwhelming majority of the United Nations to cease military operations' and begging him 'to turn back the assault convoy before it is too late'. Templar's letter to his minister, John Hare, could not have been more different: 'Whether this country was politically right in taking the action it did, is obviously not for me to say, but I can at least have my own personal opinion on the matter. Of course we were right, plum right, and I say it with certainty on strategic grounds.' Ironically, the position of the Service Chiefs at the time of the Falklands was reversed – the Navy Chief was the 'hawk', the Army Chief was the 'dove'. But on both occasions the Chiefs successfully concealed their differences, and courtesies and civilities were maintained.

So great was the muddle and the lack of co-ordination that even at the last moment the Chiefs of Staff, not knowing of the collusion with Israel, were concerned that under the Jordan Treaty we might have to go to war with Israel; accordingly, they were instructing their Air Force commanders to plan 'for air operations at maximum intensity to neutralise the Israeli Air Force'! Indeed, the devious nature of the whole Suez exercise destroyed the loyalty of the civil servants on whom all governments depend.

Above all, what was in my mind in 1982 at the outset of the Falklands War was the memory of an operation twenty-six years earlier involving over 100,000 men being mounted for a war which lasted only a few days – and then being halted as it came within reach of achieving its objectives.

All of these events, of course, were unknown to me at the time in Cambridge, but I read of them subsequently with fascination and some horror.

No-one who has served in the Forces can avoid a certain scepticism about military operations. If you know the Services, you are aware that things go wrong as often as they go right. Every second lieutenant has metaphorically led an armoured division into a suburban cul-de-sac without the ability to reverse, go sideways, or do anything but see the utter absurdity of it all. This is known in the vulgar parlance as GMFU – a Grand Military F★★★-Up, and you encounter many of them as a junior officer.

Suez became part of history. Ted Heath had been Chief Whip, and his memoirs have recently made clear that he was against the whole operation. To be fair to him, in politics you have to judge when to keep your head down and get on with the job. Personal conscience is a luxury to be indulged in infrequently and with discretion, and he is right to say that if the Chief Whip had resigned, it would have destroyed the government. I discovered this kind of political dilemma myself as a Treasury minister during the so-called Barber boom, when many times I wanted to resign – although, of course, the resignation of a junior Treasury minister would hardly have been noticed.

Suez would have a profound effect on me and greatly influence my future thinking. Sitting metaphorically at the feet of Enoch Powell, when I first became an MP ten years later, I came to believe that there could never be a full measure of economic and strategic independence for the United Kingdom unless we rid ourselves of a fixed exchange rate, which made Britain unnecessarily vulnerable to foreign exchange pressure. Even at Cambridge, I used to argue about this long and hard in my tutorials with Mrs X. Since then I have always been a passionate 'floater' – and it remains an important economic argument against joining the single European currency. I am convinced that had we had a fixed exchange rate during the Falklands war, the financial pressures on us would have been very similar to those during Suez.

Suez demonstrated that the world had changed forever. The lingering belief (or was it hope?) that Great Britain could still act as a world power was finally destroyed. The Defence White Paper of Duncan Sandys in 1957 not only ended conscription within three years, but sharply limited Britain's capacity for independent action; decolonisation now went ahead at a more rapid pace. Nostalgia for the days of Empire – great-great-great-grandfather William in Afghanistan, grandfather Lewis in India and Palestine, the protection of the canal as the route to India – was no longer relevant.

The consequences of Suez were different from the predictions of both those who backed the operation and those who opposed it. Thus instead of the American alliance being broken, the British have never since been able to venture on a foreign policy independent of the United States. Instead, it was the entente cordiale with France that was destroyed. Suez was partly responsible both for the end of the Fourth Republic and for the Gaullist diplomacy that twice blocked Britain's application to join the Common Market.

~

During my first long vacation at Cambridge I set off to Canada with a return air ticket to New York. I had very little spending money, so I took a Greyhound bus to the West. By the time that I arrived in Calgary I was down to my last few dollars, but I was told that the park authorities in the Rockies sometimes had summer jobs for students. So, somewhat in desperation, I visited the headquarters of the park rangers in Banff and was offered a job as a fire lookout in a rather remote spot not far from the Alaska Highway, past Lake Louise. It was at a place called Bow Summit. My boss was the local park ranger, an Englishman who had run away from his home in Tonbridge when he was sixteen. He became a good friend. Fortunately it was a wet summer and the danger of fire was remote. His area covered hundreds of square miles of rugged mountains and glaciers in one of the most beautiful and dramatic areas of the Rockies. Most days, and sometimes for a few days at a time, we set off into the mountains on horseback, with a pack-horse in tow, to visit the outlying areas of his kingdom – noting the wildlife, stocking the mountain lakes with trout fry, and catching trout in the lakes and mountain streams for our supper. When we returned to base, I had to climb back up the mountain to my hut above Bow Summit. Climbing up the mile or two in the dusk with a pack on my back containing enough food for several days, I was always nervous about encountering a grizzly bear, for this was the country of the grizzly.

I wrote home on 2 August 1957, sent from 'Bow Lookout, c/o Warden Service, Banff, Alberta':

> I am so much more contented and happy up here by myself than when I am in civilisation. I could never be depressed when I am on my own like this with a pack and fishing rod and a pair of boots. People climb up here and visit me and ask incredulously whether I am not terribly lonely and I look at them and say: 'No, of course not. The only time I am lonely is when I'm with

other people' and they go away scratching their heads. This morning I woke up to find 4 feet of snow outside the hut and the temperature is well below freezing. Beautiful sight with thick snow everywhere. Spent morning repairing telephone lines to Banff; this afternoon have done some fishing but the rivers are swollen as a result of snow but caught a 3–4 pound cutthroat trout.

When I returned to Cambridge at the beginning of my second academic year, I had some magnificent photographs of the Rockies and used to show them at gatherings of the Cambridge University Travellers Club. It was at such a gathering that Miloska, my future wife, first came across me. I now hand over the story to her, which she tells in her own words.

Miloska's Story (1): Marrying an Englishman

I had been in Munich at the interpreters' school, which was headed by Dr Schmidt who had been Hitler's interpreter. When I had finished I went back to Italy and my guardian there said, 'Look, I think you should go to Cambridge. You have all these languages but you don't have English.' So that's really how I came to Cambridge.

The first thing I remember is that we organised for the girls at the language school to meet the English students, and it was one of the most successful balls I have ever been to. The trouble was, there were also a lot of tears because a lot of the English girls lost their boyfriends. Cambridge for me was a sort of funny place, because I was used to working very hard in Germany and it was fifty per cent less when you came to Cambridge.

I had to find a house in Cambridge to live in, and Bill Wedderburn, who was a Professor of Law at Clare, had a room. There were other students there from Girton. I was very fond of Bill and Nina Wedderburn. I think they thought the Italians had made a real bourgeois out of me and they were quite worried. I told everything to the Wedderburns – where I went, everything. Michael Davis's sister was one of the other lodgers. That's how I met Michael, when he visited his sister.

Michael and I got engaged and had a party in York, and then we came back down to Cambridge and another term. Then what happened was that one evening I was picked up by Michael. We had arranged that we would go to see this old film – I can't remember what film it was – at the Arts Club, and when he came he said, 'Darling, I'm sorry we won't go to the cinema, I want to listen to John Nott who's been on the Rocky Mountains in Canada showing some slides.' I wasn't very happy, I was really quite upset, but as a good continental I swallowed my thoughts and followed him. When we got there it was really dark, pitch dark, and John was talking a lot. I didn't follow what he was saying, I didn't particularly look at the slides, but I was fascinated by the voice – such a strong, lovely sort of voice. I mean, being a foreigner, this was a marvellous English voice, and I was impressed. But eventually I got bored and asked Michael if we could leave.

Next day Michael rang me and said, 'Would you like to come to tea with a friend of mine, and John Nott will be there?' By this time I became a bit fascinated, because I really had to meet the man with this voice. So I said 'yes', and we arrived there and I was looking for this big man, strong man, which I had already pictured. So I gazed around the room and tried to think who it could be. I was still trying to find this big man, when Michael said to me, 'Darling, sorry to interrupt, but I want to introduce John Nott.' I turned round and I saw this tall but very slim chap, and I said, 'It can't be you,' or something like that. 'I thought you would be big, and somehow you just don't fit your voice.' I know in retrospect it was a very stupid thing to say, but my reaction was so natural. I noticed that his shoes were in a terribly poor state and the toes didn't quite look out of the hole on the left foot, but almost. I thought, my God, what a strange man, what a funny man. And then I just moved on. I know he did say to me, 'I'm sorry I disappointed you,' when I said it couldn't be him. And the strange thing was that he disturbed me, I don't quite know why – did he disturb me because I thought he was shameless somehow? My peace had been disturbed.

Then nothing happened. Michael was obviously very impressed with this John Nott, because I had to go to the Cambridge Union and listen to John Nott. I can't remember what the debate was, but he made a really very funny speech. I remember laughing. Then I didn't see him for a little while, until suddenly out of the blue I got an invitation to a tea party in John Nott's rooms. One of my fellow students at the language school was called Loretta, so she and I came to tea. I think there was another girl and two men called Julian Grenfell and Mark Roper – boys really, and John was making tea, I remember that. Then the men started to talk about shooting. The whole thing for us was so unbelievably boring, because we didn't know where they shot, what they shot, who shot well, who shot badly and who the people were. I think Loretta was more upset than me. I thought what boring people. Funny really because Loretta married Julian and I married John!

Soon afterwards Michael and I thought it would be very nice if we had another engagement party, this time at Cambridge. So we organised it, and when I saw Michael's invitation list I saw John Nott on it. I really went for Michael and I said, 'Why do you ask John Nott? We don't need to ask him. Why John Nott?' I think I felt a bit of danger. If I had felt immune to John Nott it would have been perfectly all right. Anyhow, Michael was determined to have him. So we organised a party, and John Nott did turn up, and I tried to completely ignore him. There were many people, but I didn't succeed because he approached me and said 'Hello' very cheerfully. And somehow, I don't know what happened, but he was then leaning against the entrance to the room and we started to talk. It was very embarrassing and my behaviour was really very bad. To tell you how nice Michael was, he never reprimanded me; but if I were Michael, I would have said, 'Look, this was our engagement party and you spent half an hour talking to John Nott.' I can't remember what we were talking about much. All I remember is that he said, 'I love you and I'm going to marry you,' and then he went. My party was finished – I couldn't concentrate on anything and all the time I was so angry. I was angry at him. How can he love me when this was only the third time he'd met me? And I just didn't enjoy it any more. I went home, and I wrote in my diary, 'What a cheek, what a conceit, what a presumptuous male.'

Then I didn't see him for a while, until I went to another party and John was there. He came up to me quite aggressively and I was aggressive back to him – we were already fighting, and at the same time I was sort of worried about Michael. I had peace with Michael. Everything was sort of nice and suddenly something was wrong. I just didn't know what was happening to me. My peace was gone and I tried very much to regain it. So I didn't see him for a little while after that.

Then he asked me one day to dinner. I said, 'Order the cheapest thing,' because students don't have money. It was a lovely dinner and it was the first time we started actually to talk about politics and things and had a serious conversation, because up to then we didn't have a serious conversation. Here we were alone and we were chatting. Then I had some suspicion about him, because he wanted to go back with me on his Lambretta, back to Trinity, and

I couldn't remember where I left my bicycle. And he said, 'Are you coming for a cup of coffee?' I thought he had some ulterior motive. Those days the girls 'didn't'. So I was getting quite nervous about the situation. 'Oh, I wonder where my bicycle is, I must go home,' I said. And he became quite aggressive about it. I could read his mind saying, 'Damned girl, I have given her a big dinner, now she won't even …' I suppose it was meant to be a cuddle or something, I don't know, but I just felt I must avoid the danger and go home, which I did. But he was quite rude to me about it. Then a telegram came in the night, 'I love you, I love you and I'm very sorry.' So we had this situation going, although I told Michael literally everything, every time I saw him.

Then one evening – this is the crucial evening – Michael gave a party in his flat. If you were a research student, you were allowed to have a girl friend longer in the room. In fact I helped to wash up. Some corridors at Trinity College are quite dark, and Michael was taking me out of the college just as John was coming in with some friends. This must have been around half past twelve or something, and suddenly we sort of crossed. He said 'Miloska!' and I said 'John!' – and somehow, all the problems started from there. I couldn't sleep when I went home. I couldn't understand why it mattered that he was in this cold dark corridor. I just couldn't understand what was happening emotionally to me.

Then I started to have doubts, that I was not being fair to Michael. It was on and off, but it was always traumatic. When John and I started to talk a bit more about politics, we started to have serious conversations with each other. I started to think about what he was saying. But when he started to tell me that he wanted to go into politics, that put me off. I said, 'My God, no. Anybody who can meddle with politics is going to finish badly, therefore I will finish badly.' I was not conditioned into democracy in the way I am today. He was terribly upset about the Hungarian revolution, and I felt very strongly about Hungary. He really thought so strongly about the injustice of what happened in Hungary, that we let them down. We had all this propaganda in Europe, Free Radio and things, and then we just let them down. And I think that's why he felt so strongly that we should not have gone into the Suez Canal. He became a person to me. His courting for me was absolutely shameless and I have never met anybody like that. I had been brought up very strictly. No man had ever been so impulsive, and that worried me. And nothing was peaceful. Nothing was slow, except when we had a discussion about something serious.

Anyhow, by the start of 1959 my relationship with Michael was getting worse and worse from my side. It was between Michael and me, but John appeared and that became my problem. My contentment, peace and everything went. It was like he turned my life upside-down. And so I thought it was only fair if I told Michael that something was wrong – that I felt that our engagement was not right. And this wasn't easy, because I didn't want to hurt him and I hesitated for quite a time. We were meant to be going to his family for Easter, and I said, 'I won't.' I wanted to break up the engagement, but Michael said, 'Look, don't, give yourself time, you're going through turmoil, this will slow down.' He was really a very faithful person but I knew it was finished. But he wouldn't take the engagement ring back. I decided to stay a few days in Cambridge, and then I would go back to Italy and go on to Yale. I'd finished the course, finished in Cambridge, but Yale had some sort of business course with two or three languages, and I was just applying for visas and things to go to the United States.

The chaplain of Trinity was going to marry Michael and me, and he was very fond of Michael, so he was really upset by the way things were going. Nina Wedderburn was on the side of John Nott, and I was there in between. Anyhow, John bumped into Nina and she told him what had happened – that I had tried to break off the engagement and that I was going back to Italy. So then he couldn't find me, but he left a note in Nina's house, most informal. 'Why don't you come and spend the weekend in an English family? I am sure my parents would like to meet you. Come, and then go to Italy afterwards.' So that's what I did. I don't know why, but I said 'yes'.

Anyway, we had a very unfortunate incident. John took me to see the film *South Pacific* and there was a song 'Once you have found her, never let her go'. I think that is definitely what John Nott did. Now the unfortunate thing was, I had a suitcase for the weekend. I put the best things in and also I had a jewellery box – every time I passed an exam or something, I used to get very expensive jewellery from my family. And I went around with this jewellery box, not insured or anything, all over Europe and it never worried me. Of course, when we came back from the film the suitcase had gone. Somebody broke into the car and it was stolen. So when we got to John's parents, I had no nightie. I had to borrow John's pyjamas. We had to go to a local hotel to get a toothbrush, and literally I had what I had on me. In a way, it was funny about that jewellery, it was as if I had cast off the past. It didn't bother me at all. Unfortunately, Michael's engagement ring was in it.

John behaved completely differently at home. He was nice to his mother – that's the first thing I noticed. He laid the table for dinner. I was amazed, because I had never before seen a man laying the table, and this rather endeared him to me. Then he borrowed the car from his mother, and near the house was Pilgrims' Way – the Pilgrims' Way to Canterbury. So we went out for this drive, and he stopped the car and he said, 'Look Miloska, I'm invited to go to the United States to debate for the university. And you are trying to go to the States. I'm going to chase you all over the States, I want to marry you. Why don't you decide now that you are going to marry me, because this way we can save the money. I won't go to the States, neither will you go to the States, and we'll get married.' You know, I can't even remember what I said.

We came back very quiet and I said I probably wouldn't be able to sleep. John got a half a sleeping pill from his father and I slept. In the morning, when we had breakfast, nobody said anything. Then John's father called me into the sitting room and said, 'I hear you want to marry my son.' I said, 'No, no, no, you've got that wrong, your son wants to marry me.' 'Whichever way it is,' he said, 'would it work?' or something like that. 'You come from the back of beyond, from the woods of Yugoslavia.' I replied, 'While we were already wrapped up in silk, you were still wrapped up in hessian sacks.' He laughed – he had a great sense of humour – and then he said, 'You know, the trouble is that you women from the Continent, you are so beautiful up to eighteen and then you all get fat.' So I said, 'Well, I'll have to try my best not to grow fat.' And that's how we had our conversation, and then he said, 'I have to deal with this myself, I don't know why my son doesn't do it. I shall have to go now to find access to the Bishop of Tunbridge Wells to get the special licence.' This was on the Thursday before Easter, and on Tuesday I was married.

Of course, I had to go back to Michael and tell him I was now John Nott's wife, and that was quite difficult. But anyhow, soon afterwards he married the girl that he broke off for me. He has four children and I thought that was lovely and I heard this years later. But it was so funny because they were all teasing John. They thought we *had* to marry, because why should somebody marry like that? But of course, nothing happened. My God, this was an impulse marriage.

~

Lieutenant, 2nd Gurkha Rifles, 1955

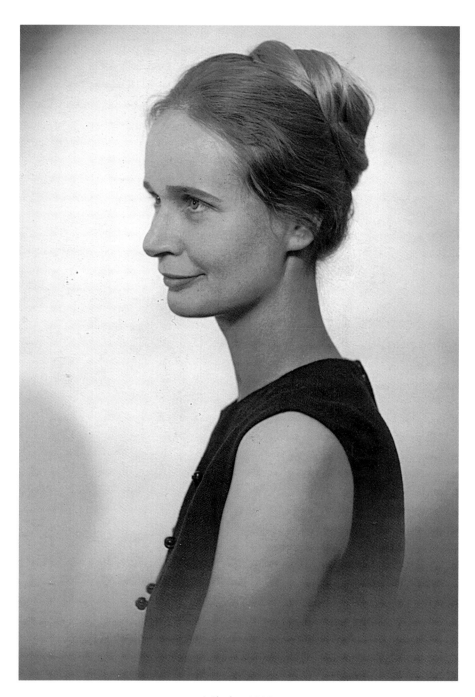

Miloska, 1968

Major General Sir William Nott, GCB

'Encampment of the Kandahar Army under General Nott outside the walls of Kabul on the evacuation of Afghanistan by the British.'
(Published by Hering and Remington, 137 Regent Street, 1848)

Miloska's story is not dissimilar from mine. I was unaware that she had attended my talk on my trip to the Rockies, but when I met her for the first time I was immediately taken with this impish, vivacious child from Central Europe, with a plait at the side of her face. She was full of *joie de vivre* and made every man in the room feel that he was something special, the only one that mattered to her. I made up my mind that I would try and see her again. The next thing I remember is her engagement party. I was captivated almost instantly. We talked and talked. I was aware that I was talking too much to the hostess, and it was noticed at the party and an embarrassment to Michael, but I was so smitten that I did say, as I left, 'I am going to marry you'. And I meant it.

There is no purpose in repeating the ups and downs of our passing and somewhat spasmodic relationship. My fury when I spent more than I could afford at dinner, only to get the impression that all that mattered to her was a wretched bicycle. But our time at Cambridge culminated in my invitation to her to come home for the weekend and my surprise when she accepted. By this time, I was obsessed with this girl. She had completely won my heart. When we came out of the Empire Cinema in Tottenham Court Road after seeing *South Pacific,* and found her suitcase missing, I was devastated. When she said it contained all her jewellery, we went to Charing Cross Police Station, but it was hopeless. The police were hardly interested. Nothing has changed. But I think the incident had some sort of cathartic effect on her and made me feel utterly sympathetic and protective. The feeling that I wanted to look after this insecure waif for the rest of her life was very strong.

By this time, my parents were living in a pleasant house on Pilgrims' Way, at Westerham in Kent, overlooking farmland. It is now near the route of the M25. I did not think that the visit would go well and I knew that my parents would be surprised that I should bring back a Yugoslav girl for the weekend. But it went splendidly and my father, who always had a good eye for a pretty girl, was absolutely charming. The next day we went out for a drive and I stopped at the top of Pilgrims' Way to talk. I knew not just that she had set her mind on going to the United States, but also that she had been engaged, or nearly so, to several lucky men. The only way of capturing her from her many admiring suitors was to move quickly, so I proposed on the spot. She seemed surprised but did not reject me outright. I said that if we were ever to get married we had to do so straight away, within days. Again, she did not demur. All this was very surprising and then I became nervous. What was I doing? I hardly knew her, but already I had crossed the Rubicon and there was no way of going back. The deed was done if not implemented. There was a contract, with completion due the next week.

When we told my mother that we wanted to get married she was very upset. 'What was the rush?' she asked. 'Didn't we want to get engaged and arrange a conventional wedding?' I explained privately to her that my espoused was a skilful escapologist and had spent most of her latter years trying to disentangle herself from an army of admirers – Germans, Italians, Scandinavians and recently the British. I said it could only happen if it happened straight away. We compromised on an engagement which was announced in *The Times* and the *Telegraph* the day before our marriage a few days later.

After the marriage at Tonbridge Registry Office, we had a blessing in church. Bill and Nina Wedderburn were her witnesses. We then set off for a short honeymoon, which took place in a ghastly boarding house at Shaldon, opposite Teignmouth in South Devon. There was so little time. My final tripos was in a few weeks and I was also President of the Union. It was quite a combination – marriage, exams and the Union all compressed within a few weeks.

~

When my father heard that I wanted to marry a girl from communist Yugoslavia (as it then was), he said to me that I couldn't possibly marry Miloska, whom he liked, and also enter politics. I would have to make a choice – politics or marriage. I leave it to Miloska again to tell the story of her early life.

Miloska's Story (2): Childhood and Communism

I was born in Maribor, the second town of Slovenia, about ten miles from the Austrian border. We were very much part of the old Austro-Hungarian Empire. There was a family problem, so I really grew up with my father. But just before the Nazis invaded, I was put on a farm for protection, so that the Germans didn't connect me with my father, who didn't know if he was safe with the Germans or not. He would come and collect me, and we would spend weekends together.

I loved the farm. I was freer, I could run about; they didn't dress me up in stiff collars and things. I have nothing but very happy memories of it. The family had four boys, who were all older than me, and one daughter. We were completely self-sufficient there – the only things we had to buy were coffee and sugar. They killed all their own pigs and cattle and preserved meat for the winter in pigs' fat. They had a small vineyard and made their own slivovitz. I still remember all the ways that we fed ourselves – I could survive today on our farm in Cornwall if we ever had to go back to subsistence agriculture; but I don't know how the urban population of this country, which has lost its knowledge of basic farming skills, would ever survive.

When war broke out, the Germans came to the farm quite often, although there were no roads up to it. My hairstyle had to be changed because I had a fringe, and that would have shown that I was not a farmer's daughter. So I had to have two plaits, to make it appear that I was their daughter. I think the boys started to believe that I was really their sister. Every day I walked to the village school, which was several miles there and back. And in the winter there was a lot of snow. Slovenia is very cold in the winter.

My father's family had a lot of land and they had a lot of businesses. My grandfather had made a lot of money – he had provided the grain and fed all the horses for the Royal Yugoslav Army. My father loved music, and he didn't really work for his living. He had a hotel in Maribor, and the Gestapo and SS would come to eat in its restaurant. And so the waitresses always knew who was due to be deported – they apparently had a tunnel under an old cemetery, and so people were smuggled away. As well as my father, there was a professor and some other people who dug this tunnel. They would hide the people who were intended to be deported to concentration camps for three or four days in this tunnel – and when the Germans stopped looking for these people, then they would get them up to the Pohorje Mountains, and they were safe there because you couldn't find anybody at all in the mountains. So this went on until around 1944, and then the professor was caught, and apparently he was tortured and mutilated by the Gestapo, and people think he gave my father away. I don't know exactly what happened when my father was taken to Dachau in 1944 – nearly at the end of the war.

In Dachau people had seen him. But they had so many stories. Some say that when the Americans bombed Dachau he was running with some other people over a bridge and this bridge was bombed. Then the other story, which is persisting still, is that he survived and that he came as far as the border and then the communist partisans killed him. They killed many people who came from the old 'capitalist' families in Slovenia. And they killed a lot of people returning from concentration camps because they did not understand how they had survived the Germans. But we have no proof, we don't know where he died, and there are many stories.

After the war I finished elementary school and wanted to go to further education. So I walked to Maribor by myself – it was about ten miles from the farm. I was nearly ten years old; the Nazis had gone and the communists had taken over. I had no family to go to – my father was dead and my aunts were in concentration camps in Croatia – so I was taken to a privileged sort of students' home where some of the children were orphans and others were from famous heroes of the resistance to the Nazis. It was run by the communist Party. I can't remember how I finished there. I was taken to an office and told that I could sleep the night there. I told them who I was. Also that the farmer's wife who had looked after me during the war had died and that the boys were coming back from war but now they were grown up. And then I had some sort of intelligence test and I was allowed to stay.

At this school I was brainwashed completely into communism. I was made into the most enthusiastic eleven-year-old communist that you could find. I gave a bouquet to Tito when he visited Maribor – funnily enough, Tito was a distant relation of my family.

Our patron at the school was the Red Star Army, the Yugoslav Army. We got everything from them. We were very privileged. It was rather like a communist Eton in a way, and I was very happy there. We had a political afternoon, but basically our education was the same as anybody else. Once at New Year – we didn't have Christmas ourselves, because we were communists – we had to recite partisan poems in the officers' house, and the interesting thing was that the heroes were always Serbs. Drago, a schoolboy friend of mine, and I were invited by the Army officers to play the guitar and sing partisan songs. Evidently Drago had said somewhere 'the officers are eating like pigs and the people are still queuing for bread'. Then a few days later I got called by the Secret Police, saying 'Did you tell anyone what Drago had said, did you tell anyone outside, and what else was he saying?' and they went on and on and on. And for the first time I got frightened about the Secret Police. I actually got frightened of the system. I got worried. I had switched off from my own background. I wanted to be either a peasant's daughter or a hero's daughter; one thing I did not want to be was from the type of family that I came from, because that was shame. We had in this school a big picture of a fat, fat capitalist with a boy who was begging for food, and this capitalist takes a whip and he's going to hit him but not give him the bread. Every capitalist was bad; there were no good capitalists. Everything in the Western world was exploitation. One per cent of the population was very rich, that's how we were taught, and the rest were all poor and starving. Of course, I believed every single word they said. You were not really a private person, you were the child of your country, and they were preparing you for your country.

I had never known my mother because of the family dispute. Eventually I found a relative of hers who said that she remarried in '43 – that she went to Split and was an interpreter because she spoke a lot of languages, and that then she married this chap from Rome and had gone to Italy, and that she knew how to find her. So I went to Zagreb to see the Italian consul. The school said that I could go to Italy to find my mother – the director rather liked me, he was very nice and he let me go.

I had not seen my mother since I was two months old, so it was quite difficult. I wrote to her and I got a very strange letter back, rather a cold letter. And I then remembered that I needed a passport. Somebody told me that a friend of my father was now Minister of Culture in Tito's government, I think, and he would see me. By this time I was sixteen and a half. He gave me a passport. He organised a passport for two weeks during my school holidays.

So then I wrote to my mother and said I'm coming. She said she would wait for me in Milano at the station, which she did. When I got there I can remember thinking, 'Oh my God, not her.' This beautiful looking woman, very tall and dark-haired – and I'm not dark-haired, I'm fair. And I looked exactly like my father, and she looked – because she's Hungarian originally – quite different. I just didn't want her to be my mother. And I think she was equally disappointed that I hadn't got her colouring, she had a sort of olive complexion. A really good-looking woman. Anyhow, I looked like my father. We went home. And my mother just went out. The maid looked after me and my stepfather was kind to me, but she was never there. I was there two months and I wanted to escape.

I did escape – I escaped to the Yugoslav consul in Milano. And he brought me back because I was a minor. And then I escaped again three days later. But I remembered that the Italian consul in Zagreb had said something funny – he must have known that my mother didn't really want me to come. The Italian consul had said, 'I want you to take this address. If you have any problems, ring.' I rang this person, who said, 'Come to Como, and somebody will be waiting for you.' This was a princess, an old lady from an Italian royal family, and she talked to my mother and said, 'This girl will go back to communism if you are not interested in her.' That was the last time I saw my mother.

The Italian princess became my guardian; she was very religious and, as a passionate Catholic, she wanted to save me from communism. From that time on I never wanted for money or anything. She arranged for me to attend a convent school in Milano. I had a private tutor for the Italian language. I started at university. I really wanted to read medicine, but because I knew so many languages I thought the easiest thing was to read languages. I wanted to take Russian again, but I had already done Russian for seven years, so she organised the Italian ambassador in Germany to arrange that I go to the Goethe Institute.

What I have not mentioned yet is that I had a terrible problem. When I came to Italy, I was looking for all these poor people and I couldn't find any, and everything that I was told by the communists was a lie. And now I couldn't understand how these people that I had trusted so much, who were more than my parents, who were everything to me over all those years, how they could lie so much. Also, some nuns in the convent school were not much different from the communists, although they were good to me. They were also trying to brainwash me. There was a priest who was continuously telling me that I should talk on the radio against the communists. But I had this fear of the communists and what they could do to me, even outside Yugoslavia. I wouldn't talk against communism. Anyhow, I felt the nuns were similar to the communists – they were both trying to ruin me. And I developed a high temperature and loss of weight. They started to send me a very attractive Jesuit. At this time I was seventeen, he was around thirty-five. He was always sitting at the bottom of my bed, and one day he said they were confiscating some books on philosophy or something that I'd bought. He said to me, 'Miloska, forget the nuns, forget the brainwash of the nuns, you have enough in the communist system.' Also all this religion they were pumping into me. And he said, 'Love is God and God is Love.' And that I think is what cured me in the end. Because if you have any love for humanity, it's OK; and if God exists, and has love for you, you will have love for him. It was so simple.

Anyway, after leaving the convent, I had a very intensive course at the Goethe Institute. Then I went to an interpreters' school in Munich, where I was for nearly three years and I passed my exams there. I found it very difficult in Germany, because I could still remember the people who had died and the people who had been taken away. I remembered how on the farm next door to ours, the Germans took all the animals out and killed them, because the farm had clandestinely killed their pig and you had to have permission to kill a pig. Of course all the villagers talked about the people who had vanished under fascism. So it was difficult, and I have to say that, although I speak German reasonably well, I don't like the German language.

Two incidents happened to me in Germany that I remember well. One is that I had a lecturer who had lost an arm in the war and he was continually saying, 'If we didn't do this or that, we would have won the war.' I hated him really, just for that. The other thing, which was so characteristic of the Germans, is this. We were all worked up about what was happening in Hungary, and we had a meeting of students from all around. There was a young German student, probably about twenty-five, and he was speaking and there wasn't a murmur. If a pin had dropped you would have heard it. And this sort of impressed me. And I think if he had said, 'Let's march now,' everybody would have followed him. Another thing that struck me in Germany was young mothers beating their children excessively – I had come from Italy and we don't beat our children. And then there was Hofbräuhaus, the beer house, I thought that was the most vulgar thing I had ever seen. Just to see an Oktoberfest – I have never, ever seen so much vulgarity. And people were so drunk and they were manhandling you, I never did go again.

So, there are certain German characteristics which I dislike. I can't generalise that every German is like that, but I also had a separate resentment because they had occupied my country. So it was difficult …

~

Miloska has told the story of her early life, but I have always seen it from a rather different perspective. For the first thirty years of our marriage, she would not talk about her early life at all and I, respecting her privacy, never sought to enquire about the war and her family. It was never discussed. When I became a Treasury minister in 1972, a creepy little man from MI5 came along to interview me, as was the custom in those days. He had a frayed collar and a nervous tic. I had to help him through the interview. Perhaps his embarrassment about it all was just a clever technique for capturing my confidence, but I don't think so. He was definitely incompetent. There is undoubtedly great talent in the security services but, being a closed world, it must also be a home for an army of civil service passengers. I assumed that a promising young minister with a Yugoslav wife brought up by communists had to be seen as a high risk – indeed, as a potential 'sleeper'. If you make your career in the turgid world of security, you have to dream dreams; suspicion and invention are your bedfellows.

No doubt my wife's background had already been investigated. Indeed, when in Cambridge she had been apprehended by two incompetent communist recruiters from the Yugoslav Embassy, she had reported it to the police. Two Special Branch gentlemen had produced an album of photographs and she had identified them readily. In 1972 they would have opened her file, and mine. Neither then, nor at any moment thereafter, even when I was handling daily the most highly classified material at Defence, was Miloska ever mentioned. No doubt they intercepted and investigated our lives with some frequency, they would not have been doing their job if they had not. But at least it was done discreetly. The idea that ministers involved with security – namely the Prime Minister, the Home Secretary, Foreign Secretary and the Defence Secretary – are kept informed about these things is, of course, a well-publicised myth. They are much too busy to enquire into, or follow, the activities of the security services, and the fundamental 'need to know' principle protects ministers if challenged and gives MI5/MI6 a wide area of discretion.

I spent much of my time at Defence dealing with security issues, particularly with defence intelligence, and I learned to treat security briefings with the utmost caution; many of them had as much complicated stuffing as the insides of a clock (as Napoleon said of the despatches received from his marshals). All western security agencies have an agenda, and that agenda takes them nowhere unless they can capture the imagination and attention of their masters. It means that all these agencies, in particular the Americans, are prone to speculation, pessimism and exaggeration. As a minister you have to aim off. Once after leaving politics, I was approached through the Foreign Office by some overdressed lounge-lizard from MI6 who wanted me to report to him personally on any suspicious money operations, including money-laundering, that I had encountered in my capacity as the chairman of a merchant bank. I said that I would do this anyhow as a matter of course and I did not need access to a private telephone line at MI6. I said that I did not wish to appear on one of their lists as an 'informer'. A year later I was approached by the man's successor, who told me that he wished to continue with the arrangement. I said there was no such arrangement and I complained most vigorously. It shows the other-worldliness of such people that they had the impertinence, for such it was, to ask a former Defence Secretary to act as an 'informer'. Who do they think they are?

To go back to my own story. Here was I in 1959 – a child of the Empire and, like my family, pretty ignorant and oblivious of the history and affairs of Europe – marrying a girl from communist Yugoslavia, albeit one who had been brainwashed by Italian nuns and had lived in Italian bourgeois luxury. Africa, India, Egypt, Malaya were all familiar places in my family history; Europe, and Central Europe in particular, were not. By the time I had arrived at Cambridge I had travelled much of the world, but because of the war and Army service I did not know my own continent, nor was I particularly interested in it. The headmaster of Bradfield, Colonel Hills, a former commander of the Eton Corps – we called him 'the overdressed waiter' as he stalked around with a mortar board and white tie and tails – had tried to teach me history. Hills was obsessed with nineteenth-century Balkan history and he had a particular fondness for the Austro-Hungarian Empire. Colonel Hills and Lord Salisbury, our late-Victorian prime minister, may have understood the intricacies of all these races and nations with their strange names and chaotic happenings, but I did not. Now I was marrying a child of the Austro-Hungarian Empire from a wealthy Slovene father and a Hungarian mother. Perhaps my distress in 1956 at the Soviet invasion of Hungary was an omen that I would fall for a Slav. I can now, almost fifty years later, understand why my headmaster was obsessed with Balkan history. It has a special fascination for Englishmen.

I have steered pretty clear of politics since I left Parliament in 1983. You are either in that game, or out of it; there is no half-way house. But I did get emotionally involved (as I did over the plight of the Hungarians whilst I was at Cambridge) when Bosnia was invaded by the Serbs and the arms embargo removed the Bosnians' right of self-defence against a vicious aggressor. The response of the European Union was pathetic – with its coalition governments, can it ever be anything else? Miloska, who speaks their language, did wonderful charitable work over several years for the Bosnian Muslim refugees, who were the victims of the most frightful atrocities. No words that I can find can fully express my contempt for the manner in which the Major Government handled the Bosnian crisis. The man in charge was Douglas

Hurd – and it was proof that no Foreign Office official should ever be made Foreign Secretary. Whilst thousands of innocent people were being herded into Nazi-style concentration camps, tortured and slaughtered in Europe's own backyard – Sarajevo is not much further from London than Rome – Hurd prattled on about allowing diplomacy to work; memories of Halifax and Chamberlain. History will record the holocaust of the Bosnian Muslims and our appeasement of Milosevic as one of the most shameful episodes in British post-war history.

When I first heard the full story of Miloska's early life, I became still more proud of her, even though we had already been married for more than twenty years. Soon afterwards she was persuaded to return to Slovenia by their deputy ambassador in the Yugoslav Embassy in London, who was also a Slovene. Her memory of her father, with his unknown but tragic early death, is intense and detailed. When we visited the family's country home, now utterly dilapidated but still occupied by ten different families, she pointed out where all the trophies from the hunting parties used to hang on the walls, where she sat when friends came to stay, how her father used to take her riding in the hills. I found northern Slovenia to be the most beautiful part of Europe that I have seen. We visited the farm where she was deposited by her father – it is still a working farm, about fifty acres in the hills with its own vineyards and milking cattle. Her family, as she calls them, is still there struggling to make a living. It is a wonderful spot, and the stories about the war and the atrocities of the Nazis are too numerous to mention – how the sons of the farm, made citizens of the Third Reich by Hitler, were forcibly recruited into the German Army, but somehow they all survived.

Our marriage was a high-risk adventure. For Miloska's part, she was prepared to marry a penniless undergraduate and a non-Catholic and cut herself off from the financial support of the Italian princess who had effectively adopted her. We had a financial struggle throughout my time in politics, but she never complained once about that. It has been a good marriage because of her. She has been a wonderful wife – loyal, hard-working and a good mother. Of one thing all my contemporaries are agreed: John Nott has the lowest boredom threshold that you can find. But I have never been bored with Miloska. Marriage across different races and backgrounds carries disadvantages, but because of the surprises and the differences in attitudes and cultures, somehow it keeps the marriage fresh. Miloska was brought up with a rigid code by communists and Catholics alike, while I have had a more free-wheeling, liberal approach to life. She is a true conservative, whilst I am a radical. It has caused problems but we are still together after forty-three years. Why? Because although the marriage contract was sealed in days, both of us meant it to last for life.

~

So my Cambridge days came to an end. Near the start of this chapter, I described them as three wasted years. At the end of it, having recollected the events of Hungary, Suez and the Cambridge Union, all of which substantially influenced my later career, I would still feel that I found the whole undergraduate experience quite tedious and unsatisfactory. But, had it not been for Cambridge, I would not have married an exceptional young lady – so perhaps it was not such a wasted time after all.

Chapter Five

WARBURG: THE CITY REVOLUTION STARTED

Warburg is certainly clever, but you know it's not the sort of firm where you should start your career.

(My father's advice)

In 1958 finding work was not the nightmare for undergraduates that it subsequently became. In the late autumn of that year, I read in the *Observer,* a newspaper that has no place in my affections, of a right royal punch-up in the City of London.

It was the battle for control of the British Aluminium Company, which was to divide the City down the middle. The City establishment had backed an offer by Alcoa of America; but another consortium put together by the upstart house of Warburg, acting for Reynolds Metals and Tube Investments, had entered the fray – and were eventually to emerge victorious. All my instincts were to support an upstart against the might of the City establishment.

I was not totally ignorant of the City because my father was a partner in a family commodity broking firm, H.M. Bell & Co., that had been founded by his uncle towards the end of the nineteenth century. It was based on the shipping that came into the Pool of London and the large international commodity business surrounding Mincing Lane. H.M. Bell & Co.'s principal business before the war had been in rice. In the 1930s this was a pretty prosperous international trade and my family lived well. When the war came and my father joined the Services, my mother continued to draw an income from H.M. Bell & Co., which was kept going by a delightful Polish refugee called Mr Pollock. After the war, commodity markets were in a parlous state – indeed, many of them did not reopen until the 1950s – and so my father steered the firm into animal feeding stuffs; he eventually became chairman of the English Cattle

Food Trade Association. His most important customer was Unilever, which provided animal feeding stuffs to much of British agriculture.

In 1946 my father was asked by the British Government to go to Egypt on its behalf and buy rice for the starving British people. (I was also starving at the time – on Bradfield food.) During a holiday from Bradfield I made my first visit abroad. I flew out on an Imperial Airways flying boat from the Solent, stopping overnight at Catania in Sicily to refuel; those flying boats were furnished like suites in the Dorchester, they were enormously comfortable and bore no resemblance to the aeroplane discomforts of today. I spent three or four weeks in Alexandria and had a wonderful time, glimpsing for the first time how British reserve and upright behaviour are changed, even transformed, by a bit of sun. After my father returned, the firm tottered along, I suppose until about 1975, when he sold it for a pretty knockdown price. Ironically enough, as I later found out, after H.M. Bell & Co. had abandoned the Mincing Lane area it took offices in King William Street – the very same offices that I was later to occupy as a trainee in Warburg.

There was another, less obvious reason why the City was somewhere on my radar as I looked ahead to life after Cambridge. A year earlier, in the autumn of 1957, an enormous row had broken out when two non-executive directors of the Bank of England – Lord Kindersley of Lazard and W.J. ('Tony') Keswick of Mathesons – were accused of making money for their firms through their knowledge of the government's intention to raise bank rate. This was the so-called 'bank rate leak', an issue pursued with great vigour by the shadow chancellor, Harold Wilson, thereby earning him the undying enmity of the City. Eventually the Macmillan Government reluctantly agreed to appoint a tribunal of enquiry, which spent most of December taking evidence at Church House, Westminster. Many prominent City figures gave evidence – much of it unintentionally hilarious, as they referred to each other by their nicknames and described taking key decisions while shooting in Scotland. 'I thought the Attorney General [Sir Reginald Manningham-Buller, widely known as 'Sir Reginald Bullying-Manner'] went out of his way to be offensive about the Governor,' Kindersley privately wrote after one session. 'If he was the next gun to me tomorrow I would certainly use my cartridges in a different direction to the pheasants!!!' An especially celebrated remark was when Kindersley said of Lord Bicester, the chairman of Morgan Grenfell: 'Rufie is not very bright but we all like doing business with him.'

The proceedings of the tribunal were widely reported in the press, and I was sufficiently intrigued to travel from Cambridge to Westminster to see what was happening. I thought that many of the City figures on parade at the tribunal were tremendous stuffed shirts, pompous and rather stupid, and it encouraged my not very latent radicalism to seek an institution that might put them down. Warburg fitted the bill admirably.

I had also been to the Cambridge Appointments Board and they had suggested that I try for a job in the City. They told me that the two best opportunities that they had on offer were a traineeship either with Glyn Mills, then seen as a highly prestigious bank, or with the Blue Funnel Line in Liverpool. I had no intention of emigrating to the provinces, so I put my name down for an interview with Glyns. 'We think there are great opportunities there,' they had said. They also offered me an interview with Michael Verey of Helbert Wagg, who gave up his time by talking to ambitious undergraduates, and he strongly endorsed the opportunities at Glyns – 'the best possible place to start in the City', he said. Glyns had taken one Oxford and one Cambridge undergraduate each year, and it was the training ground for City luminaries like Jeremy Morse.

It was while I was waiting for my interview with Glyn Mills (things moving with majestic slowness in the marbled halls of Lombard Street) that fate played its part and I read the *Observer* article about how this relatively new merchant bank called S. G. Warburg & Co. was at odds with the City establishment. The article inspired me to write to Siegmund Warburg himself, asking if I could have an interview with a view to joining his firm. Ronnie Grierson, subsequently a director of Warburg, says that I emphasised in my letter that I was a gentile and that I hoped this would not tell against me if I joined a Jewish firm. I am sure that his anecdote is untrue, as I have never been entirely stupid! Ian Fraser, in his memoirs, claims that Warburg called him into his room and showed him my letter, which according to Fraser went like this: 'Dear Mr Warburg – You are the most distinguished banker of your generation and I am the most distinguished undergraduate of my generation. We ought to meet.' Also quite untrue! But it is clear that my letter must have caused some interest in King William Street for these anecdotes to persist.

Almost certainly my letter contained some praise of Warburg, and flattery – as I came to discover – was Siegmund Warburg's secret weapon. Anyhow, to my astonishment I got a reply almost by return, saying that 'I was most interested to receive your letter and I'm very flattered to feel that you would like to join my firm' – I'm sure that was the phrase he used, because he used it to almost everybody – 'and I am arranging for my associate, Mr Ronald Grierson, to call on you in Cambridge because I understand that he is visiting Cambridge on the weekend of so-and-so and he will make contact with you.'

So I waited to hear from Grierson, who when he wrote to me included the gratuitous information that he was coming to Cambridge to visit a well-known academic figure, Professor Rostow. I came to realise that name-dropping was another weapon in the Warburg armoury and that there was in fact almost nobody in the world that Ronnie didn't know. In due course he arrived at my rooms in Bishops Hostel and, again characteristically, he was in an enormous hurry – if there'd been mobile phones he would have taken four or five calls whilst he was talking to me.

I am reminded of a much later meeting that I was to enjoy with the chairman of the *Daily Mirror,* in his penthouse suite, one Mr Robert Maxwell. In the middle of our talk he was called away by the butler to talk on the telephone to 'Mr Gorbachev'. On his return, he regaled me with the advice that he had offered to the First Secretary. I am sure that the whole performance was invented to impress his visitor. This would have met with approval in the Warburg book of banking skills.

Ronnie Grierson was very charming, and he entered the essential note of flattery by saying, 'Well, you're obviously going to be President of the Union, that is a major post.' The conversation went smoothly enough and he suggested that I should travel to London to meet Warburg.

A few days later I donned my suit and travelled up to King William Street, where I was ushered into the great man's presence. Beaming at me in a very charming way, he said: 'I'm glad you've been able to come, and I'm very pleased that you should want to join my firm. I don't understand why you would wish to do so.' I mumbled something about how interested I had been in the British Aluminium battle. Then Warburg went on: 'If I was in your position I would certainly want to go into politics.' To which I replied: 'Well, yes, Mr Warburg, I would like to go into politics one day, but I want to make a career first and I don't think …' 'Ah,' he said, 'well, someone who wants to go into politics is just the sort of person I'd like to have in my firm. And indeed, you know, if I hadn't got a German accent, I would certainly want to go into politics myself.' Today, anyone seeking a job who admitted that he might want to go into politics would be shunned immediately. A week or so later I received a letter offering me a job at Warburg, at £700 a year. It wasn't a fortune, but it was a perfectly decent salary. I accepted, with a view to joining in the early autumn of 1959.

My father was shocked when I said that I wanted to go to Warburg, as he much preferred the infinitely more respectable, infinitely more prestigious Glyn Mills. I asked him why. He explained: 'Warburg is a very new business, they don't have a very good reputation in the City, they're regarded as being very sharp. They are certainly clever, but you know it's not the sort of firm where you should start your career.'

To this day I am astonished that a letter from an unknown undergraduate seeking a job should have provoked an immediate reply from the chairman. Siegmund must have judged me, perhaps correctly, as being rather different – an 'original'. Warburg, in those days, never recruited anyone who would have been regarded by the outside world as being wholly normal, i.e. conventional. The Warburg recruitment policy was eccentric – and when I joined the firm in 1959 it was full of 'originals'. Hardly any of its people would have fitted in anywhere else. Warburg changed, and became in due course a conventional City firm.

~

I did not realise at the time I started work in King William Street that the City of London was at the beginning of a long revolution – a revolution that would take over a quarter of a century to complete and was in large part inspired by the vigorous, unsentimental, meritocratic example of Warburg. In many ways, the Luftwaffe's bombs notwithstanding, the City of the 1950s was not so different from the City of half a century earlier or even a century and a half earlier. It comprised a dense web of self-contained, specialised markets and types of activity, in turn populated by a myriad of small- and medium-sized firms like my father's firm. This intense specialisation – often involving rigid if unspoken demarcation lines – was in effect a latter-day equivalent of the medieval guild system. The City was not yet the almost wholly financial centre that it later became. It was also a very intimate place in which almost everyone of any significance knew each other, a method that for many years worked well. 'My word is my bond' had long been the City's justifiably proud boast, a major source of strength in relation to other financial and commercial centres. The problem was that it was an ethos that derived largely from the City's distinctively club-like character – and a club, in a world that was starting to change quite rapidly, was no longer an appropriate model.

No-one could have described the City of the 1950s as a competitive, hard-working, hungry sort of place. Among the merchant banks, the top names had hardly changed since the late nineteenth century, as they enjoyed the considerable privileges that went with membership of the Accepting Houses Committee; the big five clearing banks operated as more or less a closed-shop cartel; the discount houses in the money market were protected by the Bank of England from the consequences of risk; and on the Stock Exchange, there was not only a strict division between brokers and jobbers (the latter not allowed to have anything to do with the public), but also a system of minimum commission that made it impossible for brokers to compete on price. The less than taxing hours of work also helped to make the City a way of life fit for gentlemen.

In retrospect, the pervasive complacency – and hostility to new ideas – was astonishing. Edward du Cann may not have been my favourite Tory politician, but I must pay tribute to the persistence with which as a young man in the mid-1950s he toured the City with an increasingly dog-eared prospectus looking for backers for a new unit trust management company. This was based on the idea of popularising share ownership, against the background of an increasingly affluent society. 'If this is such a good idea, Mr du Cann, pray tell us, why has no-one else thought of it before?' was the typical response he got. It would, in fact, be almost impossible to exaggerate the old City's deep-dyed resistance to innovation – and the Bank of England, in particular, epitomised this negative conservatism.

In the 1950s it was still the great dynasties that largely ran the City's top houses, above all the merchant banks. Lord Kindersley of Lazard was in his eighties by the time he retired in 1953, when he was succeeded by his oldest surviving son; his grandson, Hugo Kindersley, was still in Lazard when I joined it in the 1980s. At Morgan Grenfell, Lord Bicester stayed firmly at the helm until his death at the age of eighty-nine. At Rothschilds it was not until the 1960s that a non-Rothschild became a partner, while at Morgan Grenfell there was a similar block in the 1950s on 'players' (as opposed to 'gentlemen') advancing to directorship. The cult of youth was not yet even on the distant horizon. In 1955, when Andrew Carnwath was about to take charge of the new issue side at Barings, that bank's Lord Ashburton felt compelled to reassure the Deputy Governor of the Bank of England that the new man was 'young but very highly thought of'. Carnwath had recently celebrated his forty-sixth birthday. Last year, I am told, one American investment bank dismissed all its traders over the age of forty-eight because they were too old! In another bank, apart from management, there are no corporate financiers over the age of forty-five.

There was, however, one outside element that – by dint of sheer ability and dogged, thick-skinned determination – had been able to penetrate the City's higher echelons. They were the foreigners, often German Jews, of whom the great exemplar was Nathan Rothschild in the first half of the nineteenth century. He came from Frankfurt via Manchester (where he was a textile merchant) and rapidly established himself as the City's dominant figure. Another German Jew was the great international financier Ernest Cassel, who despite enormous prejudice and backbiting made himself so indispensable to the British establishment that he became financial adviser to King Edward VII.

These were the City's golden years – the period up to 1914 when it was a truly international financial and commercial centre, perhaps the greatest the world had ever seen – but during the next, much less glorious forty or so years there was a distinct tendency to close ranks and make it much harder for foreigners to gain entry to the inner circle. This was still the case after the Second World War, to judge by the steer that the Issuing Houses Association received in 1948 when considering an application from Walter H. Salomon of the firm of that name:

> Mr Randell of Bank of England says he is a very pushing individual – German Jew – who established himself here in 1938. They don't know a lot about him, but think it would do no harm to let him cool his heels a bit more ...
> He knows all about foreign exchange business but they 'haven't caught him out yet' ... His office is full of foreigners ... Mr Bull [also of the Bank of England] quoted the old saying, 'I do not like you Dr Fell, the reason why I cannot tell' ...

I knew Walter Salomon and he was rather an impossible man but he had the thrusting determination of the immigrant. He was generally regarded as being rather tiresome – even by Siegmund Warburg – but he at least had energy and drive.

When I joined Warburg in 1959, London was showing precious few signs of being able to mount a serious challenge to New York as the world's leading international financial centre; the City needed a fresh injection of outside talent as perhaps never before. Exchange control was still in place; sterling was prone to sudden collapses of international confidence; and London's once paramount role as an exporter of capital barely functioned. The elderly and complacent City establishment was never going to lead the charge for a return to the City's glory days. Realistically, such a return would happen only if there emerged another Nathan Rothschild, another Ernest Cassel.

In so many ways this turned out to be Siegmund Warburg, supported by his brilliant colleague Henry Grunfeld. As a young man in the 1920s, Warburg had set out with M.M. Warburg & Co., the family bank that was based in Hamburg; but being Jewish, he felt compelled to leave Germany not long after Hitler came to power, taking up permanent residence in England in 1934. The Warburg family was, however, powerful in the United States and well known in financial circles; one member of the Warburg clan had been a founder of the Federal Reserve and Siegmund himself was later a partner in Kuhn Loeb, one of the most prestigious houses in Wall Street. In the autumn of 1934, with help from Rothschilds and the blessing of the Bank of England, he formed the New Trading Company, operating out of three small offices in King William Street. Much of its early business was barter. Warburg took his measure of the City and spent much of his time enabling Jewish families to get themselves and their money out of Germany. Indeed, he took directly under his wing in King William Street three immigrants – an Austrian, Eric Korner, and two Germans, Ernest Thalmann and Henry Grunfeld. In the long run the most important of the trio was Grunfeld, who after a gruesome encounter with the Gestapo in 1934 had already established himself in the City before being recruited by Warburg in 1937, becoming his utterly trusted right-hand man. The four German Jewish immigrants were known in Warburg, by the rest of us, as 'the Uncles'. Frank Smith, the clever senior Englishman, called them 'the Germans'.

Despite some friends in high places (notably Rothschilds), Warburg's personal relations with the City establishment as a whole were at best prickly. In 1956 he noted bitterly that 'one of the dominant attitudes in the City is tolerance towards mediocrity'. The City returned the compliment, snickering at Warburg as upstart 'bond-washers' and 'dividend strippers'. Both were practices that did much to establish Warburg's financial reserves in the early days; it was a practice also indulged in by other firms and basically consisted of turning income into capital where taxes were lower. Moreover, for all Warburg's success in acting on behalf of medium-sized companies, what the firm had not yet managed to achieve by the late 1950s was the acquisition of a clutch of blue-chip companies as corporate clients. These were still very much the days of 'relationship' banking – American-style notions of 'transactional' banking were not even a distant gleam on the horizon – and Warburg prior to the closing weeks of 1958 was far from a well-known name. The 'Aluminium War' changed all that.

The 'Aluminium War' was unquestionably a watershed episode. Not only did it establish Warburg's reputation as a master financier, but it dealt a severe blow to the prestige of the City establishment. Moreover, the whole atmosphere of the City now started to change, becoming altogether more competitive. Change did not happen overnight, of course, but City people older than myself are agreed that – for better or worse – things were never quite the same again. I joined Warburg soon after the 'Aluminium War' was concluded. It could not have been a better moment.

~

As it happened, I had a brief interlude between leaving university and starting at Warburg. I had spent the last two years at Cambridge reading law and had also fulfilled my quota of dinners at the Inner Temple. This was after I had been seen there by a man called Trevor Reeve, who was a relation of ours and subsequently became quite a well-known judge. Offering to propose me for the Inner Temple, he then uttered a word of caution: 'You must understand what the Bar is like. Next door to me in my office I actually have a woman barrister – we even have a woman barrister in my chambers!' (Gasp.) I remember one other part of our conversation very well. 'You must join the Inner Temple,' he said. After I had asked what was wrong with Lincoln's Inn, he explained: 'It's full of black men. At least in the Inner Temple we've managed to keep most of the black men out.' I became a barrister, but by that time I could not afford to practise, because it was a two-year grind before it was possible to earn any money.

It must have been about November 1959 – a few weeks after Harold Macmillan's 'we've never had it so good' election triumph – that I began work as a management trainee at Warburg. Conscious of being already in my late twenties, I found the first year or so incredibly tedious and frustrating, as I was sent around the bank learning the ropes. This included spells of several months in each of the main departments – banking, documentary credits, foreign exchange and investment – of which the investment department was by far the most congenial, being at least halfway to civilisation. There I learned how to read companies' balance sheets and profit and loss accounts; my bible – without which I could never have survived in Warburg – was a book called *Beginners Please* by Harold Wincott, the celebrated financial journalist whose strongly pro-markets column each Tuesday in the *FT* was compulsory reading for almost everyone in the City. The investment department was run by two gentlemen called Mr Robinow and Mr Rosenbaum. They took no notice of me, but there was a smattering of statutory Englishmen who looked after prestigious private accounts like those of Anthony Eden. Eden telephoned almost every day to discuss the movements of the market; it was sad. He was a rather lonely and poor ex-politician by this time, the Earl of Avon.

I was also dragooned into something I had hardly bargained for, which was organising the firm's move to new premises. The offices in King William Street were becoming too small, and so the decision was taken to move in 1961 to an ugly, functional, modern, mauve building in Gresham Street, located directly opposite one of Wren's most beautiful churches, St Lawrence Jewry, behind which was Guildhall. It was the first time that a leading merchant bank had located itself to the west of the Bank of England, and naturally this caused a huge fuss. Although the building was only 100 yards from the Bank of England, 'the Uncles' went into a complete neurotic state about whether it was *'haute banque'* to move in that direction, as opposed to towards Bishopsgate. Roll on Canary Wharf!

By my second year in Gresham Street I had become a little more established and, in a minor way, even started to become a business-getter. For a time they placed me in a sort of investment research corner, from where I bombarded Siegmund Warburg himself with a series of ideas for mergers and new business. He replied scrupulously, by memorandum, to every one of my daft ideas. I was then annexed to what was known as the 'Syndicate Room' – this was really the engine room of the bank and handled everything that 'the Uncles' dreamt up. I got involved in everything from export finance for Standard Telephones to endless prospective mergers. Under the tutelage of Frank Smith I did various rights issues, and a few mergers for the National Coal Board.

My most difficult client, whom I handled alone but with occasional reference to another key Warburg director, Geoffrey Seligman, was the famous Isaac Wolfson. He obviously enjoyed dealing with a green young banker, and he and I negotiated many mergers in the wool textile industry, such as Aire Wool and Whittingham. Isaac Wolfson was a delightful rogue. He was completely unscrupulous in negotiations; he used to agree a deal and then use that agreement to salami-slice his opponent by opening up the transaction again, sometimes two or three times over. But I enjoyed him – and I learnt a lot.

In February 1964 I was largely responsible for launching something called 'yearling bonds'. Knowing that our *raison d'être* at Warburg was inventing new business, I had discovered, to my surprise, that there existed no security in the market between the short-term local authority deposit and the long-term local authority stock – at a time when the local authority market as a whole was growing rapidly. So I went up to Manchester to see the city treasurer, a man called Harry Page, probably the best-known treasurer of the time and the first to have taken his pension fund into equities. Together we cooked up the yearling bond, though in fact it had a life of between one and four years. Typically, the Bank of England didn't like the idea and tried to stop it, but fortunately Page had such an outstanding reputation that in the end it felt unable to resist him. By the time I left Warburg in 1968 this new market had grown into many hundreds of millions of pounds.

The creation of yearling bonds was not one of the great turning points in the City of London's history. But the first Eurobond issue – done by Warburg in July 1963 – undoubtedly was. This was a $15m loan nominally for the Italian toll motorway company Autostrade. I remember all the dramas surrounding its introduction as, by this time, I was acting as Siegmund Warburg's personal assistant. Normally such a financing would have been procured from the New York foreign dollar bond market, but by the early 1960s the worsening US balance of payments position was making the American financial authorities increasingly reluctant to encourage New York as an international capital market. Accordingly, the idea was conceived – with Siegmund Warburg playing a leading part – of initiating an offshore international capital market in dollar-denominated bonds. One of Warburg's many European banking friends was Guido Carli, governor of the Italian central bank, and this directly led to the Autostrade issue. It proved an immensely complicated flotation to organise, and much of the hard work was done by two of my British colleagues, Ian Fraser (who had joined Warburg from Reuters) and Peter Spira (who had come from the accountants Cooper Brothers). For tax reasons, most of the coupons had to be cashed in Luxemburg, while partly because of Stock Exchange obscurantism most of the secondary market lay outside Britain.

Even so, it was a profoundly important turning point for the City – in effect, the start of London's long road back to becoming something like the world-beating international capital market it had been before the First World War – and barely a fortnight later the issue's importance was confirmed when President Kennedy announced the Interest Equalisation Tax, involving a 15 per cent tax on the purchase by Americans of foreign securities from foreigners' stock. 'This is a day that you will remember for ever,' the chairman of Morgan Guaranty in New York is reputed to have announced to his colleagues. 'It will change the face of American banking and force all the business off to London.' The Eurobond market could only have been started by a determined visionary – and not even his worst enemies ever denied that Warburg was that.

My years at Warburg coincided with the firm's great take-off. When I arrived there were less than a hundred staff; by the time I left there were well over three hundred. (When Warburg effectively collapsed in 1995 it was employing 6,500 worldwide.) Increasingly the firm was recognised as the powerhouse merchant bank – although its reputation was far higher in the international field than in the domestic market, where the old-fashioned merchant banks still had a strangle-hold on the big UK companies. However, by 1964 or so major UK companies started to transfer to Warburg for financial advice; no-one in the mid-1960s was any longer raising an eyebrow if an ambitious young man chose to go to Gresham Street to cut his teeth in the City.

From Siegmund Warburg's point of view, the only real dilemma for his growing bank was the American situation. Since the 1950s he had also been a partner in the long-established, upper-class Wall Street firm Kuhn Loeb; but by the early 1960s he was increasingly disenchanted with them, regarding them as rich, useless and never bringing enough business to Warburg. There were also increasing personality clashes, with a diametrical contrast between the aggressive, go-getting Warburg and their much more laid-back approach, reflecting the fact that they had quite enough business already without needing to break out in a sweat.

It was probably in late 1964 that I accompanied him on a trip to New York. Training young men and giving them experience were at the very centre of Warburg's way of doing things. Warburg had telephoned David Rockefeller, with me listening to the call, and asked whether he could 'rely on you, David, for my visit to New York'. Rockefeller: 'Siegmund, you know I will lay everything on for you.' Siegmund: 'David, have you got any premises?' Rockefeller: 'Yes, you can have the Chase building in Park Avenue.' This was for three of us! So we arrived to find an empty first floor of a huge building in Park Avenue, with a desk, a couple of messengers and a secretary. I sat in the outer office, with nothing to do while Warburg tried to sort out his Kuhn Loeb problem, in effect by ending his firm's formal connection with them. What Warburg had in mind was to try to cut a deal with the far more go-ahead Lehman Brothers, so I started going down to Lehmans every day. There the senior partner, Bobby Lehman, was extremely kind to me – not least in showing this very insignificant young man around his private art collection, now the prize exhibit in the Metropolitan Museum.

~

What sort of place was Warburg in the 1960s? Over the next few pages I will try to give some idea, based not only on my own recollections but also the excellent, already published accounts by Ian Fraser, Peter Spira and Peter Stormonth Darling (who joined the firm in 1963, starting a distinguished career on the investment side).

Fundamentally, the atmosphere was that of a German bank; it was very un-English. It certainly bore no resemblance at all to what one today thinks of as merchant or investment banking. Almost everybody was there to dream up business, there were no hard-and-fast demarcation lines between people and departments, and the prevailing climate was entrepreneurial and fast moving. There was a separate investment department but it held inferior status. Everyone turned their noses up at the investment business which was to become Mercury Asset Management. Warburg in later years even tried to sell it to Lazard for a nominal sum – and Lazard turned it down. It was to become far more valuable than Warburg itself. There was an aristocratic contempt for stockbrokers, who were thought to be people without any brains, incapable of doing anything else. The fundamental emphasis was on brains, not money – indeed, Warburg had a profound mistrust of giving corporate financiers access to capital, which he knew they would only waste. How right he was.

Desks at Warburg were occupied by nine in the morning and often after seven in the evening – almost unheard-of hours, earning 33 Gresham Street the nickname of 'the Night Club in the City'. Lunches were abstemious (beer, cider or mineral water were the only choices of drink with the meal – this at a time when wine was served at lunch throughout the City). Ascot, the Lord's Test and Wimbledon were still time-honoured points in the City calendar, but 'it was frowned upon in Warburg if we took the day off for such occasions', in

Stormonth Darling's words. 'Holidays were permitted, with some reluctance, on condition that you left a telephone number where you could be reached. All business travel had to be at weekends whenever feasible, so as not to miss any working time.'

Warburg was famous in the City for its lunches – jokes were told about them wherever you went. There were several lunches held at 12.30 p.m. and several at 1.30 p.m. If you were asked to the 12.30 lunch, you knew that you were considered to be of junior status, or a visitor of passing interest. Sometimes 'the Uncles' attended a 12.30 lunch if there was someone they wanted to meet, but invariably they found some excuse to leave at 1.15 so that they could attend the more important lunch. If Warburg was entertaining himself, he invariably invited a number of junior members of the firm to speak up. It was never a monologue. I cannot remember a day at Warburg when I was not invited to one lunch or another. It was also Warburg's practice to swap juniors around other City lunches. He often called me in and said, 'Nott, I would like you to go to lunch with Kit Hoare of Hoare's,' then a very leading stockbroker, or 'Nott, I have arranged for you to go and lunch at Schroders, let me know what is discussed.'

These lunches really set the tone of Warburg, and none can describe it better than Ian Fraser. I include two extracts from his autobiography:

> One day our new client, the Canadian television magnate Roy Thomson, said he would like to buy *The Times* from Lord Astor who, he believed, was finding the continuing losses too much of a burden. Ronnie Grierson, who knew everybody, said he would bring Lord Astor to lunch in the office without Thomson being present, so that Warburg could throw a fly over him. A couple of weeks later, Lord Astor arrived for lunch and the party consisted of Warburg, Grierson, 'Uncle Henry' Grunfeld, Peter Spira and myself.
>
> Warburg started by laying on the flattery with a trowel, one of his favourite techniques. The conversation went something like this:
>
> 'You know, Lord Estor, your femily has a lot of edmirers in this country and I am one of them.'
>
> Lord Astor said it was very kind of Mr Warburg to put it like that.
>
> 'For several generations now, your femily has a tredition of public service, which sets a vonderful example to the young.'
>
> Lord Astor agreed it was very important to set a good example to the

young. He hoped that his family had always tried to do so.

'Your femily, if I might say so, has always had a vonderful business sense and you have been so successful in everything you have done. Good menegement is the secret, don't you agree, Lord Estor?'

Lord Astor said he had always been very careful about choosing his manager.

'And of course you are lucky in owning your own source of raw materials. You always buy your stock from your subsidiary in Canada, I understand. So you know your stock position very well.'

No, said Lord Astor, there Mr Warburg was wrong. He never bought any stock in Canada, he only bought the best British Herefords.

Ronnie had got the wrong Lord Astor. Warburg tried hard not to look like thunder. Uncle Henry looked at the ceiling. Spira almost did the nose trick. I said something in the general conversation about Aberdeen Angus being my favourite beef beast. Warburg recovered his balance and explained to Viscount Astor of Hever Castle that he too had been brought up on a farm and was very interested to compare notes. I do not think that Bill Astor noticed a thing. After a decent interval Grierson brought Baron Astor of Hever, Bill's uncle and the real owner of the newspaper, to the office and we bought *The Times* for Roy Thomson.

Korner invited a stream of business people to lunch. One day he asked Bickham Sweet-Escott, the treasurer of British Petroleum, to the early lunch. Bickham was a well-read person and had written books himself about his activities in the spy service during the war. Suddenly Korner asked him: 'Mr Sveet-Escott, hev you read Yenkins on Eskvit? We have ze grendson in ze Haus.'

Our guest looked puzzled and when Korner repeated the question said, 'Yes, Mr Korner, absolutely,' hoping that this was a safe response. He looked at me to interpret and, when Uncle Eric was called away to the telephone for the third time (a normal occurrence at his early lunches), I explained that there had been a question and a statement. The question was, 'Have you read Roy Jenkins' book on H.H. Asquith?' and the statement 'Asquith's grandson, Raymond Bonham Carter, has just joined us here at Warburg.'

The next day, the treasurer of Unilever, Jasper Knight, came to lunch and the same exchange took place. But Knight had been warned, I suppose by me. Korner said proudly that he had drawn the attention of Sweet-Escott to the book, adding 'You know, British Petrole [sic] are our clients.' This was quite untrue but Knight was impressed. Korner was nothing if not even-handed and when Sweet-Escott next came to lunch he told him that Unilever was a client of Warburg.

There was a great stress in the firm on internal communications, with Warburg and the other 'Uncles' deliberately encouraging an open-door, partnership approach. Every meeting had to be recorded by a memorandum, and the inner circle of directors was expected to arrive by half-past eight so that they could read all the incoming mail, all the outgoing mail and the office memoranda of the previous day. I was made the secretary of the 'Mail Reading', so that for two years, every single morning, I encountered Uncle Henry, Geoffrey Seligman, often Warburg himself, and Frank Smith when he felt like turning up. This was rather a tiresome start to a long day.

Could it fairly be described as, overall, a happy place? Certainly, for most of the younger generation such as myself, working at Warburg in the 1960s was memorable and in its way formative; but the atmosphere was not very congenial because Warburg believed in generating competition within the firm – as well as towards the outside world. At any one time, rather as in a medieval or renaissance court, one was either 'in' or 'out' – and for those who dropped out of favour, not invariably for reasons that were easy to understand, there was sometimes no way back. For others (of whom, broadly speaking, I was one) it was a valuable experience, combining hard and purposeful work, intellectual stimulation and a sense of being in an elite team getting new business and trying to do it in new, high-quality ways. 'Warburgs was indeed an acquired taste,' Stormonth Darling rightly remarks. My colleague Peter Spira obviously lapped it up. I don't think Peter Darling, Ian Fraser or myself really ever signed up to the Warburg way of life.

As I had already discovered, one of the great ways the firm differentiated itself from the City establishment was in its imaginative recruitment methods. The experience of Martin Gordon (a future corporate financier) in 1963 was typical. Following Harrow, Oxford and two years in the Army, he applied for a job at various merchant banks, but to his exasperation found that every interview included a question about which school he had been to – until at last he went to Warburg, where there was no such question. Inevitably, I had no shortage of interesting colleagues, of widely differing type and background. There was, for example, Milo Cripps (nephew of Stafford Cripps) – eccentric, very clever, somewhat frenetic – who in my time was taken out of the investment department and put into the syndicate room. Siegmund Warburg's son, George, a really delightful and clever man, was there. But he didn't get on with his father and he eventually departed, with Milo Cripps. Milo had left behind in the investment department not only Mr Robinow and Mr Rosenbaum, but also another excellent Jewish character, Bob Arnheim, who used to run Warburg's own personal investment account. Bob was very kind to me when I was learning the ropes. I remember it. Then there was a wonderful man called Mr Sharp – Charlie Sharp – who despite being of German-Jewish origin was for some reason, I never quite knew why, bullied and generally treated extremely badly by 'the Uncles'.

A sometimes underestimated business-getter, and also a good man, was Geoffrey Seligman (Warburg had taken over Seligmans, a sleepy accepting house, two years before my arrival), for whom I worked quite a lot. I also spent a fair amount of time with Ronnie Grierson, who was always rushing around the world, dumping hired cars in ditches everywhere and causing chaos with the airlines. It was a nightmare working for him – he never sat still for more than two minutes – but he knew everybody and was therefore useful to the firm. I have to say of Ronnie, a well-known City character, that he was always great fun – and he had a good English sense of humour. One day, though, we had a massive row. After he had asked me to do something and then been quite aggressive and rude, I shouted at him and said, 'You terrible man, I'm not going to work for you any more!' This took place in his office, with Ronnie getting red in the face at this insignificant young fellow telling him where to get off. He stormed off to Grunfeld's office and demanded that I be sacked. Grunfeld, who I'm sure often found Ronnie a trial, clearly sympathised with me and managed to calm things down. 'I hear you've had a "disagreement" with Mr Grierson,' he remarked when he next saw me. To which I said, 'Yes, I'm afraid I did. I lost my temper with him.' To which he replied, 'Well, it would be better if you didn't do that again. End of story.'

Two other people who stick in my mind, for quite different reasons, were Billy Straker-Smith and Gladwyn Jebb. Billy was married to Robin Jessel's sister, the daughter of Sir George Jessel, quite a significant figure in the old City. Billy's own family had been wealthy shipbuilders and had a big estate on the

Tweed opposite Alec Douglas-Home. He was a lovely man, very amusing about 'the Uncles' and about Warburg, but sadly as the years went by he spent too much time in White's and in the end gambled away the whole of his family fortune. Everybody loved him – even Siegmund, who was exasperated by him but enjoyed him too. Gladwyn Jebb by contrast was one of those people who came and went without making an impact. He appeared to me to be the most pompous, useless, Foreign Office stuffed shirt – God knows how Siegmund ever got hold of him. He had, of course, been a famous ambassador at the United Nations and in Paris. He used to sit around in his office all day, with nothing to do, and made no attempt to understand the business or learn the tools of the trade; and, of course, no-one ever went near him or the other Warburg dignitaries like him. Presumably they were there for their 'connections'; but in practice, connections outside the banking world, however grand, don't count for anything unless they actually bring in business.

Everyone treated the two key women in the firm with the utmost respect. One was Miss Meyer, who apart from being the wife of Manny Shinwell, the former Labour minister, was connected to the big timber business, Montagu Meyer. She was the person who every day used to go through all the memoranda and produce the daily summary. She was a very important lady, whom you did not dream of offending, because you knew that if you offended Miss Meyer you were offending 'the Uncles'. Like them she was a German-Jewish refugee. The other pivotal woman was Doris Wasserman who, some time after I'd arrived, became Siegmund's secretary. She proved to be the ideal person to control him, because although he would shout and yell at her she took it all in good heart and was utterly loyal. Doris Wasserman was lovely to everybody and, still alive, remains the guardian of the flame.

At the heart of the firm, of course, were 'the Uncles'. There was always a fair amount of humour going round among the Englishmen, because they were really very brilliant but also quite funny. It was extremely bad taste to joke about their German accents, but we did – sometimes you couldn't understand what they were saying. Eric Korner's pronunciation was perhaps the most baffling. Stormonth Darling was once asked by him to take care of some of his clients in his absence. There took place what was, to the Englishman's ear, an incomprehensible conversation:

Korner: Darling, I'm going on holiday next week, I'm going to Essen.

Stormonth Darling: Mr Korner, you can't be going to Essen for a holiday, no-one goes to Essen for a holiday.

Korner: (Impatiently) No, Darling, not Essen. Essen.

Stormonth Darling: Why on earth do you want to go to Essen, Mr Korner?

Korner: (Even more impatient) Not Essen, Essen – where zey have ze Parsenon [Parthenon].

Another holiday destination sounded to Stormonth Darling as if it was Pakistan, and they went through a similar routine – it turned out to be Bad Gastein.

'The Uncles' were highly suspicious of Jewish immigrants who changed their names on naturalisation. 'You see,' said Korner to Fraser one day, 'they all have personality problems: they do not know where they belong.' Fraser observed that a lot of them had been very brave in the war, when the British Army had insisted that they change their names in case they were captured. 'Ah, yes,' Korner said, 'that is different. But they should have changed their names back again when the war was over.' He liked to have the last word.

One of his theories was that everyone had a Jewish ancestor somewhere but kept quiet about it. One day Sir Brian Mountain, the head of the Eagle Star Insurance Company, came to lunch in the office with Uncle Siegmund. Korner and I were there. Afterwards Korner told me, 'Zis Mountain, he is Jewish. He talks about shooting and fishing so as to hide it.' I said I did not think so, I believed the Mountains to belong to the old English squirearchy. 'You are wrong, Siegmund says he is Jewish. The real name is Berg.' The next day I turned up with a copy of *Burke's Peerage* and pointed out to Korner the Mountain entry: the first Mountain was living in Norfolk in the early eighteenth century and the wives of his descendants all bore solid Anglo-Saxon names. 'Zis book is not right; Siegmund is right,' came the reply. That was the end of the conversation.

Korner was a thoroughly engaging, extrovert, larger-than-life figure. Basically, Uncle Eric was a trader, with an outstanding gift for selling useless things to customers. He specialised in buying up old South American railway stocks, until eventually he got stuck with something called the Peruvian Corporation and couldn't get out. But in the end he did get out – and everybody lost a lot of money, except Uncle Eric. We all suspected that Korner went in for insider dealing in a pretty big way – based on advance knowledge of a client company's forthcoming announcements.

Uncle Eric and I did share a memorable experience. It began when he came one day (in 1962 or 1963) into the syndicate room where I was working:

> Nott, I would like you to help me form an investment trust. I have an idea we can make money out of forming a new investment trust.
>
> What sort of investment trust, Mr Korner?
>
> I think that we should form an investment trust for energy.
>
> Yes, that seems a good idea, Mr Korner.
>
> Yes, for energy, and we will get all the best investors into this investment trust and we will make a good initial commission.

So the lawyers were called in and they constructed a new investment trust to invest in European energy. One of the principal shareholders was to be Rothschilds in Paris. So, acting on this occasion as Korner's bag-carrier, we went off to Paris for a meeting with the French Rothschilds followed by lunch.

The meeting was optimistically scheduled for 12 noon, and eventually they drifted in, in dribs and drabs. Korner, frustrated by the lack of discipline about the calling of the meeting, was looking increasingly impatient even before it started. The second Rothschild man there was Elie de Rothschild. He was the owner of Château Lafitte and he played a major part in the life of Pamela Harriman. On my frequent trips to New York in future years I could not be unaware that he was one of the three great high-life womanisers of the time, along with the Shah of Persia and Giovanni Agnelli. It was well commented upon that all three of these gentlemen were known to the most famous and beautiful girls in New York.

Not surprisingly, banking was of rather less interest to Elie de Rothschild than women and wine – and certainly he was not even remotely interested in Uncle Eric's investment trust. That was for sure. Indeed, it was only out of loyalty to Warburg that the Paris Rothschilds had agreed to invest in it, and throughout lunch Elie talked about nothing else except women. It was a thoroughly enjoyable lunch, with the best wines and the best conversation. Elie de Rothschild said that France was going to the dogs, absolutely going to the dogs, to which Uncle Eric said, 'And why would that be, Elie?' To which Elie replied, 'Because, you know, when I was a young man, Paris was full of the most beautiful women who were freely available to people like me. And now, there are no beautiful courtesans any more.' Uncle Eric was very shocked by this, but it did not stop the new investment trust from going ahead.

The most puritanical of 'the Uncles' was Uncle Henry, whereas Siegmund wasn't a bit puritanical but only pretended to be. It is chronicled that Siegmund had a long affair with a beautiful Russian ballet dancer, Alexandra Danilova. The two men were superbly complementary. I was privileged to spend a year or so as Warburg's PA, effectively his private secretary – reflecting his great admiration for the private office concept of the British civil service, with which he had become familiar during the war. I sat in a room between Warburg and Grunfeld, and several times each day I would be called into Siegmund's office to hear his telephone calls with the great and the good of the banking community around the world. I would write the note on his conversation with Jacob Schiff in Wall Street or with Hermann Abs, chairman of Deutsche Bank and the man more than any other whom Warburg courted. I needed my wits about me, but it was a great introduction to the world of international finance. In retrospect I find it in a way astonishing that I wasn't thrown out of the place, because they were quite impatient with people they didn't think were going to make it.

Perhaps inevitably, few anecdotes have attached themselves to the austere Uncle Henry, who beneath the Prussian-style correctness of his manner with people was in fact a really wonderful man. Unlike Warburg, he wasn't remotely a bully, but intellectually he could be quite intimidating. He was remarkably clever – in fact, I think he may have been the cleverest man I have ever met. It was always very interesting attending meetings with Grunfeld and Arthur Winspear, a Yorkshireman who had come to Warburg after writing about the Aluminium War for the *FT's* 'Lex' column. Winspear was extremely bright and knew the business backwards, but he was quite ponderous and long-winded, and it was a wonder to see the two men working together. Grunfeld, with his astonishingly quick brain, would streak off in all directions, looking at a balance sheet or a profit and loss account and instantly knowing every single corner of it. 'Mr Grunfeld, I think you've got that wrong,' Arthur would say. 'I've got it wrong?' Grunfeld would reply. 'I haven't got it wrong, Winspear.' Occasionally he had got it wrong, and he was always intellectually honest enough to admit the fact.

Of Siegmund Warburg himself, I would have to say that overall I respected rather than loved him. He was an extraordinary mixture: on the one hand a Jewish aristocrat who knew everybody in the banking world that mattered, having got to know them all from his pre-war days banking in Germany and having kept in contact with them; on the other hand, an archflatterer and intriguer akin to an old European diplomat like Talleyrand. 'My father confessor,' he was wont to call the Bank of England when talking to the Governor or Deputy Governor; yet beneath the cajolery he never developed any great regard for the Englishmen running the City, or indeed the country, after the war. Almost everybody was, to quote his favourite word, 'useless', and he would spend a fair part of the day storming around the corridors saying that X and Y were useless. There was no great venom about it – it was just the way he talked.

The people who were particularly useless were the other key merchant bankers. The chairman of Lazard, the chairman of Morgan Grenfell, the chairman of Hambros were statutorily useless because they were part of the old City. He especially despised Lord Kindersley of Lazard, whom he considered to be a very stupid man as well as being anti-Semitic. In fact, he was negative about much of the English way of life. Country houses, London clubs, sporting activities – to him they were all senseless diversions from business. Skiing was the worst sin of the lot. After recklessly admitting once that I'd been skiing on my way back from the United States, he exploded, 'Skiing? Why do you want to go skiing? It's a dangerous sport, you'll break your leg like Mr Grierson and you'll be out of action for a month. You should never go skiing. I thoroughly disapprove of it.' He also had a great 'down' on the English sense of humour, which both he and Uncle Henry found detestable. Occasionally I'd make a flippant remark to Siegmund, and he would instantly cut me down: 'That's a typical English remark … There's nothing funny about that. You can't make flippant remarks.'

Arguably they never really understood the English. They couldn't conceive why all Englishmen wanted to become owners of country estates. They couldn't understand country sports. They didn't understand club life. They thought the English were fundamentally lazy, which of course they are; they saw the country in decline and wanted to do something about it. Unfortunately, they kept on encountering civil servants and politicians (assiduously courted by Siegmund) who seemed passively to accept that Britain would never return to its former greatness. This irritated and infuriated them.

There was a time – during the year and a half or so before the October 1964 general election – when Warburg thought that Harold Wilson might be the man to head a national renaissance. Although thereafter he continued to maintain friendly relations with Wilson and the rest of the Labour government (including George Brown, who used to show up quite often at Warburg), that hope rapidly faded during the rest of the 1960s – notwithstanding

Siegmund being duly honoured by the knighthood that Wilson gave him, and that the Bank of England tried to block, in 1966. (It is really a City scandal that Grunfeld was never recommended for an honour by the Bank of England.) The 1970s, for Warburg, was a decade of complete disenchantment with politicians, but by 1980 he was privately praising Margaret Thatcher for her 'outstanding valour and fortitude in making it clear that after successive Conservative and Labour governments had encouraged the country to live far beyond its means this reckless course of self-indulgence is long overdue for a radical change'.

Curiously, not long before his death in October 1982, I ran into Siegmund, standing in the corridor at No. 10 outside Margaret Thatcher's study. He was due to go in after me, presumably with some great scheme for saving the world and saving the country. When I saw Margaret again, later in the day, I asked, 'What were you seeing Siegmund about, Prime Minister? I didn't know you knew him.' 'Oh,' she replied, 'yes, I know Sir Siegmund.' So I said, 'He's a bit of an old rogue.' To which she said: 'Oh, you think he's an old rogue, do you John?' – in other words, implying that I was a bit of a rogue too. She didn't tell me what they had been talking about, and it was the last time I saw him.

For all his stress on dedication and on thinking about business at all hours, I am not sure that Siegmund was all that interested in money as such. Certainly I never saw him look at a balance sheet or at a profit and loss account – that wasn't his world. Siegmund would open the door and come in, walk across my room into Uncle Henry's office, and say to him something like, 'Do you think that ICI is creditworthy?' Uncle Henry would reply, 'Well, let me have a look at the accounts and I'll let you know.' For Siegmund, banking was about something quite different – people and contacts and making connections between finance and the outside world. He was similarly indifferent to investment and had the deepest contempt not only for stockbrokers but for the Stock Exchange itself. 'How's the market?' he would ritually ask Stormonth Darling in the investment department, but his only interest in the answer was to see whether the young man knew. 'If I told him it was up when it was down, he was in no position to correct me; nor did he care.'

Siegmund also had an obsession with minor detail, and he was passionate if he saw a letter going out of the bank with a grammatical error or a punctuation mistake – this was a subsidiary reason why every document and meeting had to be meticulously copied and minuted. He found it almost impossible to let go. On Christmas Day 1964, just after noon, the telephone rang at Stormonth Darling's home:

I do hope I'm not disturbing you.

Oh no, Mr Warburg, not at all.

Well, it's about your note dated 22 December on the American stock market. Do you have a copy in front of you?

Er, no, I'm afraid my copy is in the office.

Well, let me remind you of your second sentence in the fifth paragraph …

I think there should be a comma after the word 'development' …

Siegmund's obsession with graphology – an obsession not shared by Uncle Henry – was probably part of the same syndrome. Everyone had to endure it. Not only was an analysis of one's handwriting a mandatory part of being interviewed for a job at Warburg, but on the frequent occasions that he thought that his colleagues were completely useless, he used immediately to send off a specimen for a further check by his expert graphologist (a certain Mrs Dreifuss, I believe a cousin of Siegmund's). Nor was her analysis just confined to members of the firm – more than once, she was asked to scrutinise the prime minister's handwriting. I well remember Siegmund on several occasions walking along the corridor waving a letter from Harold Wilson in his hand and saying, 'Zactly what I thought.' For myself, reading the analysis as it came in, I never could quite see what the excitement was about, because according to Mrs Dreifuss nearly everybody was neurotic and unstable. These were two terms that Siegmund used to light on with particular relish – despite (or perhaps because of) the fact that he was quite unstable himself and definitely neurotic.

These were serious flaws, but I must emphasise that there was far more good about Siegmund than bad. He had enormous charm. He was genuinely interested in people, with a strong paternalistic feeling for his staff. He was particularly good with his young men, paying them far more attention than would be normal today and deliberately setting out to train us in the ways and values of *haute banque*. We all had to be properly dressed, we all had to behave well, we all had to treat our customers and guests with a high degree of deference. He also drummed into us that the redeeming sin of merchant bankers is arrogance – a conviction that they know all the answers, when in fact they don't. He liked to say that the most arrogant thing that a banker can do is to go and visit a factory, because if he goes to a factory he'll tell them what they're doing wrong.

So you must never go and visit a factory. Still more fundamentally, he taught us the virtues of pessimism – a pessimism that came partly out of the long-suffering Jewish heritage, partly out of his memories of the slump of the early 1930s, and led him both to shun unnecessary risk-taking in business and not to depend on the durability of relationships. These were lessons I have tried never to forget. I believe in maximum liquidity; cash is king. Years later, I would try to put them into practice at Siegmund's old adversary, Lazard.

The sadness is that Warburg itself, after Siegmund Warburg's death, became the most arrogant institution in the City. The arrogance was quite offensive, and also very English. I had to sack Warburg as the stockbroker of a company that I chaired. It had bought in all the English arrogance of the Stock Exchange represented by Rowe & Pitman and Akroyd & Smithers. Siegmund Warburg also believed in keeping his firm small – it only got out of hand when he was gone. He often regaled us, individually and collectively, not only about the banker's besetting sin of arrogance but also about the inevitability of another crash. He saw that each generation disregarded the experience of their predecessors, and he believed that disaster would strike again from some totally unexpected quarter. He was right, of course, and it is a lesson totally ignored by the so-called bulge-bracket investment banks of today; they too will go the way of Warburg, leaving banks like Lazard to pick up the position which they have temporarily vacated.

I left Warburg after I became an MP as a result of the general election of March 1966. Uncle Henry, however, wanted me to stay on as a consultant, so as to retain and further build up the local authority bond business. I didn't particularly want to, but the money was good – about £10,000 a year, as far as I can remember, at a time when there wasn't any proper salary in politics. After about two years, by when Warburg had made a lot of money out of these bonds but I'd done nothing since becoming an MP, Uncle Henry suggested to me in the nicest possible way that the consultancy arrangement did not really make much sense. I agreed, and my relationship with Warburg ended in a very friendly way in 1968. I have no regrets about the seven years I spent there. Where the Warburg experience was above all valuable was in giving me the knowledge that if ever I ran into trouble with politics – a notoriously insecure trade – there would be no difficulty in finding a berth in the City should I need it. That reassuring knowledge gave me a sense of independence in my political life – not financial independence as such, but the psychological underpinning that allowed me to maintain an independent outlook. Of course I value my time at Warburg for other reasons, but that for me was the single greatest benefit.

~

My active life in politics really began while I was still at Warburg. I took three weeks' holiday – I think Warburg knew what I was doing – to help Charles Morrison fight the Devizes seat in the October 1964 election. I canvassed all over the constituency with his wife Sara and the very young Michael Ancram, still in the political maelstrom, and it was an enjoyable time. She was great fun, but subsequently I lost contact with both Charles and Sara, as they moved to the far left, liberal wing of the Tory party, with people like Ian Gilmour and Peter Walker. But in the 1960s I used to go and stay on the family island, Islay, and so got to know old man Morrison (Lord Margadale), who until the 1964 election was chairman of the 1922 Committee and therefore a great power in the Tory party. In the way things were then, to be seen as a friend of the Morrison family was an enormous help to getting on in the Tory party.

Soon after the 1964 election I had another stroke of luck. Wilson's majority had been so small that it was obvious to everyone there was going to be another election before long, and the Tories launched immediately into finding their candidates. All the best chaps found themselves marginal seats, but I was out of the picture – partly because during some of the crucial weeks I was away in New York with Siegmund Warburg. By the time I came back most of the marginal seats had been taken. In the event this proved very fortunate. The narrowness of Labour's majority meant that everyone in the Commons was having to keep extremely late nights – as a result of which, over the next year or so, many of the old colonels and knights of the shires in the Tory party either died of exhaustion or, more often, got fed up with the whole thing and announced their resignation. In the months leading up to the March 1966 election, this led to a dozen or so safe Tory seats becoming available – a doubly attractive proposition at a time when it was pretty obvious that Labour was going to be returned at the next election with a thumping majority, as indeed proved the case.

Sometime in 1964 I got myself on the candidates' list, and the first seat I put my name in for was Hove. Not surprisingly, since this was the second safest Tory seat in the country, two or three hundred other people also put their names forward. I managed to get on the short list of four, of which the other three were all ex-MPs. The main reason why an unknown City banker got this far was that Hove was a very Jewish seat, with its selection committee headed by a Jewish retired colonel. He rather liked the idea of a young man from War- burg – at that time riding very high – as well as the fact that I had been Presi- dent of the Union at Cambridge and had been in the Gurkhas. Although I lost the selection at three o'clock in the morning – after balloting and reballoting and transferring of votes – Central Office now decided that I was a coming man. I was subsequently shortlisted for three safe seats: St Ives, Holland with Boston, and Canterbury.

Canterbury was obviously the most convenient for London, but Miloska and I agreed that I was not in a position to pick and choose, so we decided to try for the first one of the trio to come along. This turned out to be St Ives. I'd never been to West Cornwall, so we drove down two days before the meeting – all part of the Warburg training – to read the local newspapers as well as to meet at least one of the editors and the chairman of the National Farmers Un- ion. By the time I got into the meeting I knew quite a lot about the area. I was already aware that local selection committees aren't a bit interested in one's views on economic policy or what's going on in the world, but instead what they want to know is whether the aspiring candidate is interested in their local politics. I'd done my homework – motivated further by the beauty of St Ives on a day when the sea was an absolutely transparent bright blue.

During these days I was much helped by Miloska, who was looking par- ticularly good and, although a foreigner, charmed the pants off all the wives and old ladies whom we had to meet. As always, she was the popular one – people just about tolerate me, but they want to have her around. I became the Member for St Ives on 1 April 1966. It was just over a decade since I had read those life-changing Foreign Office telegrams.

Chapter Six

TRAUMAS AT THE TREASURY

So long as the price of anything is fixed, it will nearly always be wrong; for everything in the real world is changing all the time ... So we borrowed huge sums to keep up the fiction [of a fixed exchange rate] and accepted government interference in our lives in all directions.

(Enoch Powell, 1969)

Every fortnight, as the Member of Parliament for St Ives in Cornwall, I conducted my constituency surgeries in one of the local towns; they were one of the most satisfying and worthwhile aspects of my whole political career. Sometimes I made a difference, often just by listening like an old-fashioned doctor. When I became a Cabinet Minister, these surgeries became something of a burden because I returned to London with a voluminous correspondence about a host of personal problems – sorting them out had to take priority over such insignificant issues as the modernisation of the nuclear deterrent!

One of the crosses that all Tory politicians have to bear is being patronised by businessmen, particularly stockbrokers. The City is full of experts about what the man on the Clapham omnibus is thinking. After seeing twenty or thirty constituents each weekend about a multiplicity of little problems, it is quite hard to suffer these businessmen. 'Politicians are out of touch' – one hears it daily, but they are in fact much more in touch than businessmen can ever know; and the City is, of course, living in a cloistered world all of its own with no real contact with ordinary people and their concerns. The arrogance of most bankers, particularly investment bankers, combined with their ignorance of real life, ensures that there can never be a meeting of minds between politicians and bankers.

St Ives (with no air service) was the most distant constituency, in travelling time, from Westminster – and quite another world from the shire counties and towns of England. Every Thursday night I caught the night sleeper to Penzance, and each time I felt during my seventeen years in politics that I was visiting a foreign country; far more so than on any trip that I ever made to capital cities around the world.

In spring 1972, I was interviewing, at my Penzance office, a certain Mrs Curnow about her blocked sewers. Her case had received scant attention from the Penzance council at the time. Two-thirds of the way through this important and rather critical interview, I was interrupted by my constituency secretary who, putting her head around the door, said, 'Excuse me, John, the Prime Minister is on the telephone.' 'Oh,' I said, my heart jumping slightly, 'I will take the call.' Mrs Curnow was temporarily shown to the door. After a number of false starts from the Private Secretary at No. 10, Ted Heath was on the line.

'I want,' he said, 'to appoint you to my government but, as you disagree with most of our policies, I'm not sure that you would wish to accept.' It was a rather typical introduction from the PM.

'Oh, Prime Minister,' I said, 'I don't disagree with all the government's policies; it depends which particular policy you mean, you have not told me which department you are thinking of.' I should perhaps add that, at that particular juncture, I was earning a considerable sum of money outside politics working for US multinationals operating in Europe and I had also started my own company with a friend making high-pressure umbilical hoses for the sub-sea extraction of oil – it later went bust – and I would not have given it all up to serve as Parliamentary Secretary to the Minister of Works; and indeed, ambitious as I was for office, there were only a limited number of jobs that I would have wanted. It is good advice to aspiring ministers to take whatever is offered; but the advice, whilst sound, is nevertheless inconvenient if you are leading an independent life on the back benches, earning a very good income outside politics; which was anyhow necessary for me because my parliamentary salary in 1972 only amounted to £4,500 per annum.

Ted Heath said, 'I had it in mind to offer you the job of Minister of State at the Treasury – the Economic Secretary's job – in the place of Terence Higgins.' I replied, 'Prime Minister, there is no other job in the government that I would like more than that; as you know, I am very interested in Treasury issues, and it would be a real privilege to take that particular job if it were offered to me'.

'Well,' said Ted Heath, 'I had understood that you were not in favour of the government's exchange rate policy' – which was true. He had heard from somewhere that I was in favour of a floating pound whilst he was very much a fixed-rate man; in fact, sterling was to be floated only a few months later.

At that moment, however, fresh from a discussion of Mrs Curnow's sewers, I did not think it appropriate to engage in a discussion with the Prime Minister about exchange rate policy, so I replied, 'Prime Minister, I do not think that I necessarily have any disagreement with the government on these issues, and I would be very delighted to accept.'

'Well,' he said, 'Tony Barber will get in touch with you to discuss it further.' So that was the way that I was introduced to ministerial office. I do not believe that Ted Heath really wanted me – and, like most other junior ministers, I do not think that he spoke to me more than once in the next two years, although I saw him often at meetings. I owed my promotion, I am sure, to the urging of Francis Pym, the Chief Whip, and to Tony Barber, the Chancellor, with whom I had always had a good relationship.

So began the most arduous two years of my life. I can say that it was intellectually the only occasion in my entire life when I have been really stretched to the limit. I could not do it again. How then had I come to this, just six years after winning my seat?

~

The greatest moment in most political careers is the day that a newly elected MP enters the House of Commons for the first time. The place is large, empty and quite awe-inspiring, and I felt that I had – at last – arrived. I was shown by the attendants a red ribbon on which to hang my sword, and I was allocated a locker in one of the corridors to hold all my constituency and parliamentary papers. The luxurious offices and high remuneration of today's MPs were not even contemplated. Few of us had desks of our own, let alone an office, so we dictated letters from benches in the corridors. I did not mind. I had undergone the tedium of Cambridge and the indignities of Warburg to achieve my ambition. After a time on the back benches, I was keen to acquire ministerial office; but, if that had never happened, I would still have felt that it had all been worthwhile. I was in the centre of things – unimportant maybe, but full of self-confidence about the future.

I had been selected as the National Liberal and Conservative candidate for St Ives in 1965 – not the Conservative candidate, I should add. I was told by the local association that St Ives could not be won by a Conservative – but that as the

National Liberals supported the Conservatives and had done so since 1931, I should not fret about the label. In due course, along with David Renton, the MP for Huntingdon, I became one of the last National Liberal MPs. The two of us, with undue generosity I thought, gave the accumulated funds of the National Liberal Party (around £50,000) to the Conservatives – who, of course, blew it in an afternoon on some futile advertising campaign. Sadder still, David Renton conceded one of the best rooms in Parliament, overlooking the Thames, for allocation by the Tory Chief Whip, so I was never able to live in the splendour of fine offices as my status entitled me as the last National Liberal member. In my third election, the ghastly miners' strike election in February 1974, I dropped the National Liberal label and suffered a small fall in my majority.

We bought a cottage in the constituency, and every parliamentary recess my wife drove the young family from London to Penzance in a red Mini. The journey took her nine hours, loaded up with two children and an au pair girl. I worked very hard in those early back-bench years from 1966 to 1972 before I became a Treasury minister. There were seven local authorities in the constituency, and each of them had an annual feast day parade and a church parade; then there was Remembrance Sunday. I was always parading through the streets for one festival or another, preceded by the town band. I worked the constituency every Friday and Saturday, attended endless events and conducted my surgery. The local newspapers were very good to me and reported all my speeches, supporting local industries and hammering the government for neglecting Cornwall. The good will engendered in these early years really carried me through until my retirement in 1983. It became difficult when I was in government because I could no longer publicly blame the government for everything – and that was the surest way to the hearts of my Celtic constituents.

At general elections I doubt if I had a large personal vote, but my wife had a great following. She was a natural canvasser and her charm, good looks and naturally flirtatious style swung considerable numbers my way, particularly on the council estates. She always did a deal with the municipal workers, and the dust carts carried the Conservative label around the constituency until the local council officers intervened. We had a well-organised canvassing team at elections – and the only thing that I dreaded was visits by leaders of the party who did not understand the peculiarities of far-flung west Cornwall. They put their foot in it and invariably made hard-hitting political speeches, whilst my wife and I hardly mentioned party politics during a general election campaign – except, of course, when we were speaking to Conservative Party workers. We simply covered the ground congratulating the locals on the state of their gardens, their pretty houses and handsome children, chatting about the weather, and deploring all the backbiting in the campaign upcountry. I stood flagrantly as a local candidate, interested in local issues, and avoided the national campaign as much as possible.

Recently, reading Andrew Roberts' biography of Lord Salisbury, I was much amused to come across Salisbury's justly celebrated letter to a friend written in 1861. This was when he, Salisbury, was first required to dirty his hands by fighting an election on the hustings. He did not enjoy the experience:

> Days and weeks of screwed-up smiles, the hearty handshake of the filthy hand, and the chuckling reply that must be made to the coarse joke; the loathsome, choking compliment that must be paid to the grimy wife and sluttish daughter, the indispensable flattery of the vilest religious prejudices, the wholesale deglutition [swallowing] of hypocritical pledges ...

I never felt like this, but it is indicative still of the underlying superciliousness and paternalistic disdain of a certain class of grandee politician – now, fortunately, largely extinct.

Twice a year I made a 'state visit' to the Isles of Scilly, part of my constituency. Whilst I was a substantial figurehead as the local MP on the mainland – far more so than would have been the case in the English constituencies – I was treated as a distinguished visitor on my trips to the Scillies. The Chairman of the Council and the Chief Clerk met me at the heliport when I arrived, and there was always an official lunch, preceded by a discussion of local needs and wishes.

I had two rather unusual constituents, Harold and Mary Wilson, and we got on like a house on fire. Harold was prime minister and I was a lowly backbencher, but we used to drink together in the pub, 'The Mermaid', beside the harbour. I liked Harold Wilson very much and found him much easier than Ted Heath; Harold was generous and fun and never talked politics except to endlessly rib me about the failings of my leader. Ted hardly acknowledged my existence. Harold Wilson was insistent that Mary, his wife, voted for me, and not the Labour candidate. All part of the fun.

On one occasion we were crossing to the Scillies on the *Scillonian*, and Harold Wilson and Ray Gunter were on the same boat. Suddenly a young man attached himself to my wife and asked her a raft of questions. Subsequently she was chatting to Harold in the Scillies. 'You know, some time ago,' he said, 'when we were both on the *Scillonian* together, I sent my Special Branch detective to discover "who is that attractive girl, with long hair, find out all about her".' Harold had an eye for the ladies.

Ted Heath did not. On another occasion a conversation between my wife and Ted went something like this. Miloska: 'We have just had two weeks in China [just after the Gang of Four was denounced] and I was shocked at how little freedom they have – and how even their fashion and hairstyles are controlled by the state.' Heath jumped on her, saying with great enthusiasm: 'They have an aim, I respect them, they know where they are going.' Somebody who grew up under communism could hardly have welcomed this eulogy to the Chinese bosses. When we were in China, the Minister of Culture said to my wife that 'Mr Heath is a good friend of China and we remain loyal to our friends – we do not change old suits for new ones.'

My other eccentric constituent was Tom Dorrien-Smith, the lessee of Tresco, in the Isles of Scilly. He could be charming, but his bucolic personality, arrogant behaviour and attitudes reminded me rather of Randolph Churchill. When I visited Tresco, Tom used to send his yacht across to St Mary's flying the White Ensign. We landed normally at Old Grimsby – a landing stage – where I was met by a retainer in a bowler hat, and we trotted across the rough ground in a sort of farm cart up to the entrance of Tresco Abbey. On the first occasion when my wife and I were invited for lunch, we rang the doorbell and it was answered by a very glamorous young lady whom we mistook as the daughter of the household. It was Tamara – Mrs Dorrien-Smith – a Russian lady of youth and beauty. I fear that Tamara must have found her husband and this isolated existence all too much, and she eventually departed for the mainland and another marriage.

I really enjoyed those early years as a constituency MP in West Cornwall. I felt that I was doing good for the locals, and they responded by greeting me in the street and increasing my majority at each election, with the sole exception of February 1974. In so many little ways, I did more good as a constituency MP than I was ever able to achieve as a minister. Being an MP is a privilege and an opportunity. I am glad that I retired as a Cabinet Minister; but those MPs who never obtain high office (like my successor in St Ives, David Harris) do a great deal of public service of a very special kind.

~

The parliament that I joined in 1966 bore no resemblance to the House of Commons of today. On the Tory benches, there were a substantial number of large landowners – such as Harry Legg-Bourke, Robin Turton and Charles Mott-Radclyffe – and the majority of Conservative MPs had fought in the war. Many used their military rank and were called by the Speaker accordingly: 'Major This, Brigadier That, Admiral So-and-So'. There was a smattering of younger members who had entered the House in the late fifties and early sixties, particularly at the 1964 election, but the tone of the Tory Parliamentary Party was unideological, loyalist, traditional and disciplined. Most of the members seemed happy to vote in accordance with the dictates of the Party Whips, and they appeared to have limited political ambitions – although this may have been a false impression. The term 'knights of the shires' has gone out of fashion, no doubt because such creatures no longer exist, but it was a good description which embraced an attitude and a position in life which was very much of the time.

I encountered my more elderly colleagues on the back benches overwhelmingly during the debates on the Finance Bill, which was then taken on the floor of the House, not hidden away in a committee room upstairs. Following the budget in April, the time of the House of Commons was dominated, right through to the summer recess, by these debates. In opposition, it was easy for a younger member to shine on such occasions, because the House was always well attended and went on late at night. Although there were several well-known Finance Bill characters, such as Gerald Nabarro, Douglas Glover and Nigel Birch, it was a genuine free-for-all; and quite unlike today, when the frustrations of an enforced silence are intense, it was quite possible for younger, unknown members to get called to speak on the floor of the Chamber of the House. I hold the unfashionable view that the decline of the House of Commons, which should be a sounding board for the views of the nation, began with Norman St John Stevas' introduction of a raft of all-party specialist committees. Nowadays the floor of the House is empty whilst MPs sit on these committees and pose as experts, cross-examining in a self-important way the witnesses that come before them. All of this is excused by the phrase that Parliament is 'calling the executive to account'. In practice, it does no such thing. It is the theatre of Parliament that matters.

A brief intervention on the Finance Bill Committee evokes something of the flavour, when in June 1968 I followed the splendidly moustachioed MP for South Worcestershire:

Nabarro: It is drivelling rot to say that a camera should be taxed at 50 per cent, but that the Savile Row suit I am wearing should be taxed at 9 per cent.

Nott: If my hon. friend was wearing miniskirts he would have to pay no purchase tax at all.

By this time I had already experienced what was to prove one of the more satisfying episodes of my whole parliamentary career. It had nothing to do with a Finance Bill. Instead, it occurred in February 1968 when the Labour government (with Jim Callaghan as Home Secretary), supported by the Tory front bench, sought to rush through legislation in order to remove the British passports of the 200,000 Kenya Asians who were being persecuted and ejected from their own country. I have never opposed immigration controls as such. I see their desirability, but this measure was a breach of faith to stateless persons. A promise to a Jamaican or an Indian should be just as binding as a promise to an Englishman, and to renege on a promise at just the moment when it was most desperately required was a despicable act, condoned by both political parties and the vast majority of the House of Commons.

Opposing this disgraceful but highly popular measure led to difficulties with my constituency party. There was a very fierce and divisive debate in Parliament – the people who now call themselves New Labour almost wholly supported this measure. So did the Tory Party. The second reading of the Commonwealth Immigration Bill was passed by 372 votes to 62. Only seventeen Tories voted against the measure. We were led by Iain Macleod (who was Shadow Chancellor), and my fellow-rebels included Michael Heseltine, Terence Higgins, Nicholas Scott, Ian Gilmour and Norman St John Stevas – all of them in a seldom-to-be-repeated ideological alliance with me. On the Labour side, apart from Michael and Dingle Foot, we were joined by Reggie Paget, John Mackintosh and Brian Walden, who later was to save my bacon at the time of the Falklands. Sir Cyril Black, well known for his extreme right-wing views, also joined us. It was quite a famous cross-party alliance.

Duncan Sandys, the principal Tory advocate of the Labour government's bill and a fierce opponent of immigration, was sitting in front of me when I made my speech. It finished with this peroration:

This is a bad bill. I think that it is a racialist bill, but that is not the burden of my argument. It has been the natural law of nations since Roman times that countries have an obligation to look after their own citizens. Maybe we did not intend that these people [the Kenya Asians] should become our citizens in 1962. Maybe it was all a horrible mistake, but it arose, and we have this obligation to them, whether we like it or not. We cannot abrogate this moral obligation, and the British government should recognise this if they intend to go through with this bill tonight.

Quintin Hogg (who was leading for the Tories as Shadow Home Secretary) and I had several rather bad-tempered interventions. When I sat down, Sandys turned around in his seat and said, 'I did not agree with what you said at all, but it was a very good speech, well done.'

I think it was extremely courteous for a Tory elder statesman to say such a thing to a newly arrived colleague of a different generation, but the House of Commons was very like that in the 1960s. Indeed, the respect and friendships between the Labour and Conservative benches – between the old-fashioned, died-in-the-wool trade unionists and the knights of the shires – were varied and many. I remember Marcus Kimball whipping in several Labour MPs, including Reggie Paget, in support of hunting and other country sports. Both major parties in those days were also united in their contempt for the Liberals, who appeared to appease every prejudice and interest group. I believe it would today be called the politics of the 'focus group'. Find out what people think today – not yesterday or tomorrow – and act accordingly. The 'focus group' culture is the curse of all political parties today – it is the death of personal conviction in politics.

The Labour government of the late 1960s was overwhelmed with immigration problems – it was not just an obsession on the part of Enoch Powell. My own speech referred to the 'problems in our great cities'. In fact, it was only a few weeks later that Powell made his infamous 'rivers of blood' speech – a speech that I deplored less for its content than for its tone. Immigration was at the time a major issue in Enoch's Wolverhampton constituency in the West Midlands, and I well understood the grievance of the working-class families who saw themselves being displaced by a swelling volume of immigrants. Ted Heath was right to sack Enoch from the Shadow Cabinet, but it was sad that he became a pariah as a result of a single, emotionally charged speech. He was the first victim – but deservedly so in this case – of 'political correctness'.

More than thirty years later Powell's speech, in its entirety, merits sober study – not that it will get it; he prophesied the dangers to a 'united' kingdom from 'multiculturalism'. A more recent article by the *Sun's* brilliant right-wing commentator Richard Littlejohn put the unfashionable view very well:

Multiculturalism means always having to say you're sorry … it is a one-way street … it means worshipping all cultures and traditions rather than those of the majority.

Powell's peroration was interesting when he held up to critical scrutiny the legal weapons that politicians and opinion-formers have created to promote tolerance and restraint. Some of them have gone too far and contribute to the resentments that they were designed to prevent.

We have reached a rather pathetic state in the Tory Party when it is seriously suggested that the party whip should be withdrawn from Tory MPs if they are politically incorrect and offend a 'focus group' or shifting media opinion. Such authoritarian action removes the most important function of the House of Commons, which is to represent all views, however distasteful to fashionable opinion of the time. The latest manifestation of this trend is to ban MPs from being members of the Monday Club. I would never have anything to do with this absurd reactionary body, but the Conservative leadership must recapture its self-confidence by standing up against the media, rather than slavishly submitting to its prejudices.

Ted Heath himself had telephoned me in 1966 the day after I had entered the House. I had not met him. He asked me whether I wanted to share a secretary with him. He told me that Sir Richard Thomson, Sir Donald Kaberry (a successful Yorkshire industrialist) and he all used the services of Rosemary Bushe for their constituency mail. I knew immediately that it was a bad deal for me because I would inevitably be the tail-end Charlie whenever I needed Rosemary's services. But I could hardly say 'no' to my leader, even before I'd met him. My worst fears were realised. I contributed my share of the cost for much less than my share of the work!

My reputation as a successful young man from the City must have been reported to Ted, and became quite quickly known to the knights of the shires, in the way that these things used to work. Everyone was kind to me. I had a lovely Whip called Jasper More from Shropshire. He was a charming gentleman, and it made my constant rebellions very awkward (although he was to resign himself when he voted against entry to the Common Market). Jasper handled me very well, implying, but never saying, that gentlemen did not rebel against the party whip – it was simply not the done thing. The Chief Whip at that time was William Whitelaw, and he and I had several arguments about my voting intentions: we never got on.

Ted Heath singled me out and was very good to me – and I never knew quite why. I suppose he felt that I might become a sort of bright young thing, attached to his Private Office. He asked me to several of his personal parties, such as his annual carol service in the Albany; but somehow I could never go, primarily because of my commitments in Cornwall, and travelling problems in getting there. Unfortunately, his confidence in me was misplaced and did not last long, because quite quickly I became one of the awkward squad. My relations with Ted Heath have been rather inadequate ever since.

The crucial fact to grasp about the Tory Party in 1966 was that the key men – such as Heath, Macleod, Reginald Maudling and Robert Carr – had all been junior members in Harold Macmillan's Cabinet or government (1957–63). With the sole exception of Enoch Powell, they took a paternalistic, collectivist, consensus view of the Tory mission. Generally, they passionately rejected unemployment and believed in expansionary policies, including low interest rates. They were not ill-disposed to incomes policies and opposed them only because they were advocated by the Wilson Government. Fundamentally, they were under the sway of the corporatist orthodoxies of the 1960s – orthodoxies epitomised by the way in which fashionable policy-makers looked reverently to the French model of indicative planning, finding a British echo in 1961 when the Macmillan Government introduced a pay pause and established the National Economic Development Council ('Neddy') to bring together government, industry and the unions. It was early into this descent into collectivist, corporatist politics – as early as 1958 – that three ministers (Peter Thorneycroft, Enoch Powell and Nigel Birch) bravely resigned from the Treasury in protest against what they saw as excessive public expenditure. Macmillan at the time famously dismissed it as a 'little local difficulty', with no inkling that this episode would come to be seen in later years as the beginning of the counter-revolution within the Tory Party.

By the 1960s a group of younger MPs, which included myself, was becoming increasingly disenchanted by this corporatist, statist orthodoxy. Some of us were very much under the intellectual sway of Enoch Powell. And, remarkably, when the party leadership in January 1970 thrashed out its policy for the election expected later that year – at a conference held at a hotel in Selsdon, near Croydon – the economic thrust was far more free-market than might have been expected. 'Selsdon Man is not just a lurch to the right,' Harold Wilson opportunistically declared, 'it is an atavistic desire to reverse the course of twenty-five years of social revolution. What they are planning is a wanton, calculated and deliberate return to greater inequality.' In their hearts, it is unlikely that any of the former members of the Macmillan cabinet that signed up to these 'Selsdon' policies believed in them. But for an anti-collectivist backbencher like myself, this was an encouraging breakthrough. 'There was no case for a socialist budget,' I declared in the Commons soon afterwards, in March 1970. 'The best way is to restore consumer choice and stimulate growth through the encouragement of market forces.' And two months later: 'Sovereignty should be returned to the individual, so that instead of a benevolent state paternalism under which the government spends large sums on behalf of the individual, the money is left in the individual's pocket and is spent as he pleases.'

Perhaps as a reward for having established clear blue water between the Tories and Labour, Heath unexpectedly won the June 1970 election. I stayed on the back benches, but later that year was asked to join the One Nation Dining Club, whose nine founding members back in 1950 had included Heath, Maudling, Macleod and Powell. 'Recruits must be both clever and congenial,' *The Times* reported at the time I was asked, and the other two invited with me were St John Stevas and Marcus Kimball. We met over dinner in the House of Commons, and each week there were fierce arguments, especially between Powell and Angus Maude on the one side, Carr and Maudling on the other. Keith Joseph was a regular attender, but was often quite ambivalent in those early years of the counter-revolution, and it was quite difficult to place him. He seemed to be working out in his tortuous way the intellectual route to follow. I am amused today by the way in which the left of the party describe themselves as 'One Nation Tories'. The famous Dining Club and its earlier book on which the name was based was in no way unanimous about the direction of Tory policies, and its debates over dinner were dominated by a brooding and intellectually aggressive Enoch.

In a broader sense, he was not alone. For example, few people now remember Richard Law, the son of Andrew Bonar Law (the 'unknown Prime Minister'), who as early as 1950 published *The Return from Utopia*, which strongly urged the Tory Party to turn its back on the Keynesian-Beveridgean 'utopia'. He also condemned the Macmillanite notion of 'the middle way' in politics and had this to say of the so-called floating vote: 'The floating vote lives up to its name. It floats with the tide: and whoever must influence it, must first influence the tide. You attract it not by angling for it, and changing your fly from pool to pool, but by convincing it that you yourself are convinced.' It was Richard Law and Diana Spearman, a colleague of Enoch Powell in the Conservative Research Department, who were at the forefront of the original fightback against the collectivist policies of Macmillan. They were joined by the influential Institute for Economic Affairs and by academics such as Lionel Robbins and Michael Oakeshott.

But it is to Enoch Powell that the modern Tory Party, indeed New Labour, owes a significant intellectual debt. 'He was the Tory intellectual who came to the rescue when socialism seemed invincible,' a friend, Richard Ritchie, justly wrote after his death in 1998. 'He was classless, impossible to compartmentalise, and undefeatable in debate. He moulded a new political generation …' In the 1960s he embraced economic liberalism at a time when it was deeply unfashionable. If he had any mentor, it was Hayek. But I do not think that Enoch's views of life stemmed from economics. Nor, of course, was Hayek's great wartime work, *The Road to Serfdom*, ultimately about economics. What Enoch most wanted was (again in Ritchie's words) 'an England not necessarily powerful, but self-confident and independent'. Economic policy was simply a tool to support an independent sovereign country – an independent sovereign England. He was not fearful to talk of England; today, in spite of Scottish and Welsh devolution, it is politically correct only to talk of Britain. How pathetic! 'British this, British that.' There is no such race as the British – we are all Scots, Welsh, Irish or English. I hope that devolution will destroy this passion for Britain – and we can all boast again of being Englishmen!

In economic policy, Enoch believed that at the heart of upholding a self-confident and independent England was the need to free sterling from the straitjacket of fixed exchange rates, as embodied in the Bretton Woods system that had been established in 1944. A quarter of a century later, in September 1969, there occurred the first crack in the fixed-rate system, when Germany – in spite of its undertaking otherwise within the Common Market – floated the Deutschmark. Powell, speaking at a National Liberal Club dinner, was exultant:

It's happened, it's happened, it's happened. Without so much as a by-your-leave to anybody, let alone to the other members of that wonderful, indivisible, glorious political unity, the European Common Market – 'splash!' The German went overboard, protesting he did not mean to do it at all but could not help it …

Come on, let's all join Fritz in the water. Like those Magnificent Men in their Flying Machines, 'We'll go up, tiddley-om-pom, we'll go down, tiddley-om-pom'; but the main thing is: we'll float. The long nightmare of deficits and surpluses on the balance of payments, of repression and controls and 'squeezes' and all that nonsense, will be over at last. Our nation will turn again to face the world and tell the facts about itself and its money – 'Supply and demand', the Germans called it; did you hear? We shall have the truth and daylight to do our work by.

Soon afterwards, still rejoicing, he addressed the Conservative Party conference at Brighton:

There is no secret about the cause of the 'cycle of stagnation, restriction and debt'. For a quarter-century we have been taught to believe that our livelihood depends on a pretence, on pretending that the £ is worth more in the world than it is. So we cling desperately to a fixed exchange. But so long as the price of anything is fixed, it will nearly always be wrong; for everything in the real world is changing all the time. The result has been either a surplus or a deficit and increasingly often a deficit. So we borrowed huge sums to keep up the fiction and accepted government interference in our lives in all directions. Once you have a wrong price fixed for anything, there is no interference by government that cannot be justified.

This being the cause, the remedy is plain. We have to do what we were on the verge of doing after 1951 but unhappily did not. We have to set the rate for the pound free to behave like any other price and keep supply and demand in balance. A fortnight ago this would have sounded like theory. For ten days now it has been fact. The pound has been floated, at least against the mark, and, contrary to expectation, the world has not come to an end …

The truth is better; the truth is safer; and the truth is freer. In this, as in so much besides today, our fears are our own worst enemies. Let us dare to face reality: it is the road to freedom.

In retrospect, it is a pity that Nigel Lawson was not paying sufficient attention;

for Nigel was responsible for the shadowing of the Deutschmark in 1987–88. It is hard to remember how economic policy in those days, before we floated sterling, was dominated by the balance of payments, when in truth it hardly matters. As Economic Secretary, I spent an inordinate amount of time each month trying to massage the figures – an expert Treasury skill – and then excusing them in the House of Commons.

As it happened, my education in liberal economics extended throughout my time as a Treasury minister, as I was publicly forced to advocate policies of a totally contradictory kind. Nicholas Ridley had formed the Economic Dining Club in 1972, the year that I joined the Treasury. It was limited to twelve members and met monthly in colleagues' homes. I was one of the original members, together with John Biffen, Michael Alison, Jock Bruce-Gardyne (one of my principal tormentors, along with Nick Ridley, in the House), Cranley Onslow, Peter Hordern and John Eden. Nick Ridley later stated that his purpose in starting this group had been that of 'trying to anchor Enoch Powell in the Conservative Party'. That objective was not achieved, but all of our monthly discussions in the early years were dominated by Enoch's intellect. I had quite a difficult time, as a minister and a recipient of the government's internal secrets, to be dining among a group of predators who increasingly held the Heath Government's policies in contempt. I did not attend when internal differences within the government or external events became intense.

Enoch was merciless in debate and took no prisoners; he was aggressive and pugnacious to the point of rudeness. He did not sparkle in any discussion unless he could dominate it. This was not too difficult for him, because there were few subjects in which he did not excel intellectually. He fixed his opponents in discussion with a beady stare, almost with a look of contempt; yet we all enjoyed his stimulating company. I think he mistrusted me, not because I failed to resign as a Treasury minister – he understood that – but because of his dismay at the way I voted for entry into the European Economic Community. I was one of the last Tory backbenchers to be persuaded for the European Community Act in 1972, because I partly foresaw, under Enoch's influence, the consequences for our independence if we joined this club. But, in the end, I confess that the influence of other friends and colleagues got me through the lobbies behind the government. Among those in the Economic Dining Club, only John Biffen voted with Enoch against the Act of Accession.

During these early years we discussed whether we should ask Margaret

Thatcher to join us. But we were uncertain, at that time, whether she was 'one of us'. Margaret was Education Secretary, and wisely kept her head down as a junior member of the Cabinet. The majority also took the view that 'she talked too much'! She and Keith Joseph were the two big spenders in the Heath cabinet. She eventually joined the Club in 1977, after she became leader of the party, and was a regular attender. I do believe that the direction that we wanted to go in government, should we win an election, was hatched in the Economic Dining Club quite as much as in the much better-known Centre for Policy Studies. We discussed every aspect of economic policy, and we set the course for what has become known as 'Thatcherism'.

I dislike the word 'Thatcherism' for two reasons. First, it implies that Margaret was the author of the philosophy that became associated with her name. She was not. It required, of course, her determination and will to see the policies implemented – a much more difficult task. Like a good leader, she fastened on to the ideas of others and took them up as her own. Secondly, and much sadder in my view, was the fact that she never acknowledged the true author of her economic policies: Enoch Powell. This was partly because it was difficult to acknowledge publicly someone who had become a pariah in many Tory circles, but partly also because he never deferred to her, nor indeed to anyone. She did acknowledge the debt which we all owe to the Institute of Economic Affairs – to Ralph Harris, Arthur Seldon, John Wood and others – but never to Enoch Powell. You can search her memoirs to find some hint of that debt, but it is not there. Instead, she praised the work of the Centre for Policy Studies, which she jointly founded with Keith Joseph. It was her creation, and therefore had to be presented as the true iniatator of Thatcherism, but in fact it was not. Napoleon once said: 'A man to be really great, no matter what order of greatness … must have improvised a portion of his own glory, and shown himself superior to the events he has brought about.' It was true of her and the economic policies that bore her name.

The economic policies of the Thatcher years were first forced on the Tory Party, against all the instincts of the Macmillan inheritance, by backbenchers during the period of opposition between 1964 and 1970. They were resisted by Heath, Macleod, Maudling, Carr, Whitelaw, Carrington and the rest – almost right up until the 1970 general election, their resistance being temporarily suspended at the Selsdon conference, in the election manifesto, and in the 'Quiet Revolution', Heath's best-ever speech at the party conference that year. As it turned out, the Heath Government was an aberration, with its so-called 'U-turns'. Margaret Thatcher's policies were founded, I believe, on the early period in opposition in 1964–70 – not, as she would say, in 1974–79. And the true author of 'Thatcherism' was Enoch Powell.

~

I joined the Treasury in the spring of 1972. I was given two tasks, the job of Economic Secretary and the Financial Secretary's responsibilities for the Inland Revenue. I succeeded Terence Higgins as Minister of State. He kept responsibility for Customs and Excise, and became the chairman of the Cabinet committee dealing with prices and incomes policy. Patrick Jenkin moved up to Chief Secretary. There were, therefore, three junior ministers, where there are now four. The burden on me was very great – too great. Within six weeks of being appointed, I had to help Patrick and Terence steer through the committee stage what amounted to the most radical post-war changes to the tax system.

Throughout my time in the Treasury, I was responsible for the Inland Revenue, and I had to comment upon and agree on a flood of highly complex tax issues. The quality of the briefing was outstanding, but the concentration needed, as a newcomer to tax matters, was very great. At one o'clock at night, I used to leave my red boxes and go to bed, rising four hours later to complete the previous night's work. My first introduction to this business was the new corporation tax, which I was expected to see through the committee stage of the Finance Bill, faced as I was by a number of accountants on both sides. One particular schedule baffled me. I had a succession of briefings from Revenue officials, and I sat up late trying to master it. Eventually, this schedule passed through the committee at four o'clock in the morning, on the nod, and was never debated!

Another time-consuming aspect of my work in these months concerned the labyrinthine subject of what was and was not to be zero-rated for VAT purposes. Hearing aids, lifeboats of less than fifteen tons, natural fruit juices, 'the commemoration of the dead' (not only tombstones, headstones and mausoleums, but even 'trees and shrubs in a cemetery') – all these were matters of parliamentary moment. On one occasion there was even what I dubbed 'the fish and chips debate', concerning the proposed zero-rating of food consumed off the premises, which inevitably raised the vexed question of whether this applied to take-away food that the consumer started to eat on the premises.

VAT was generally a contentious issue, and in November 1972 I had a brisk exchange with a well-known Labour firebrand:

> Joan Lestor: How will the price of food not go up, bearing in mind that the packaging on food is subject to VAT? How can you buy packaged food unpackaged when the package is already around it? (Laughter.)

> Nott: Miss Lestor still doesn't understand how VAT works. She must repeat constantly to herself: 'I must remember to deduct my inputs.' (Loud laughter.) Let me explain. (Renewed laughter.) Any VAT payable on packaging and tins can be fully reclaimed by the food manufacturers so that the final product including the packing and tins will be zero-rated.

In all fairness, I must add that a Conservative colleague, Hugh Fraser, then piped up: 'Mr Nott must control his output. (Laughter.) Some of his figures are misleading …'

The 1972 Finance Bill also contained ambitious proposals to bring together the taxation and social security systems into what was called the 'Tax-Credit Scheme'. This meant that everyone from millionaire to pauper would receive a weekly cash payment which was just sufficient to fund a family on welfare. Everyone within the tax system, above the starting-point of tax, would have had their cash payment clawed back in extra tax, in what was called a negative tax system. This would have avoided what has since become the conventional approach – namely, the means test, which not only involves a massive administrative bureaucracy and the invasion of privacy, but creates a major disincentive to work and produces marginal tax rates for those coming out of welfare of up to 100%.

Naturally, the Treasury, with its blinkered approach, has always favoured the 'cheaper' means test; but on this occasion, it had been persuaded by Arthur Cockfield (our tax adviser and a former Commissioner of the Inland Revenue) to look at the wider social, administrative and political advantages of such a radical reform. Agreeing the details of this huge project was almost a job on its own, yet it formed only a part of my responsibilities. Eventually, the tax-credit scheme fell by the wayside partly as a result of a minor mistake on my part. I had been advised by the Revenue that the credits should go to the head of household, i.e. the taxpayer, as in those days there was no separate tax assessment for wives. Barbara Castle, Shadow Social Security Secretary, took this up as a feminist issue, ranting against the iniquity of the scheme. She turned the

Labour opposition against the whole project, and when they became the government in 1974 it never saw the light of day.

The gulf in understanding about how to tackle welfare reform is surely one of the greatest dilemmas in modern politics. A few years ago it led to the resignation of Frank Field, even though reputedly he had been charged with 'thinking the unthinkable'. I believe the problem will never be solved whilst the Treasury remains obsessed by cost rather than by value. The Treasury, I fear, was at the vanguard of Great Britain's decline, with its special brand of puritanical negativism. Today, regrettably, the Conservatives are no less hooked on the means test than is New Labour.

As a newly appointed junior minister, I was greatly privileged to receive copies of all the key internal papers – both on economic policy and on the principal public expenditure dilemmas – which pass across the desk of the Chief Secretary. The Economic Secretary may not be a very senior post, yet there is no better vantage point from which to observe the machinery of government in action. When Tony Barber was otherwise engaged, I sometimes took his place at meetings of the Economic Committee or the Overseas and Defence Policy Committee of the Cabinet, both chaired by the Prime Minister. It was here that I first gained an insight into defence issues.

I recall one very fraught meeting at No. 10 between Ted Heath and the military Chiefs of Staff about how we were to deal with the Cod War. Because we were unwilling to declare open war against Iceland and sink their gunboats, few in number, we were losing the ability to fish within the Icelanders' newly declared 200-mile limit. The Royal Navy was there in some force, but was unable to prevent the Icelanders harassing our fishing fleet. The PM got utterly exasperated with the Chief of the Naval Staff when he explained, quite rationally, how powerless our ships were to protect our fishermen. Exploding, Ted complained bitterly that we were spending huge sums of money on the Fleet and now he was being told that the Royal Navy could not defeat the actions of one of the smallest nations in the world. A decade later, when I really wanted to provoke the Board of Admiralty during my time at the Ministry of Defence, I used to ask, tongue in cheek, 'Admiral, what is the Royal Navy for?' The answer always came back, 'Secretary of State, to protect British shipping around the world. I am surprised you asked the question.'

The tension between the Treasury, No. 10 and the Ministry of Defence is almost institutionalised. Tony Barber used to complain continuously to his

Treasury ministerial colleagues of how Peter Carrington, the Defence Secretary at the time, was quite unwilling to make his fair contribution to reductions in public expenditure, which were so desperately needed. The problem always is that those responsible for other spending ministries – education, health, welfare, roads – are quite unable to accept that defence, in those days one of the largest spenders of the lot, should be placed in some kind of special position, as it tends to be in Tory governments.

My main *bête noire* in the Treasury was Alan Bailey, the Chancellor's Principal Private Secretary; he went on to become, as most Treasury officials did, a senior mandarin as Permanent Secretary to the Department of Transport. The other departments had more practical, less intellectual civil servants, but they always seemed to be overridden for senior positions by the Treasury's grip on the Whitehall machine; the preference granted to Treasury officials in the promotion stakes has been damaging to the cause of good government and administration. Whitehall works at several levels. At the top is the group of senior Cabinet ministers who head up the most powerful departments and who are represented on the key policy-making cabinet committees – the Economic Committee and the Overseas and Defence Policy Committee. There is also a similar grouping among the key Permanent Secretaries, under the chairmanship of the Head of the Civil Service: they see themselves as the ultimate custodians of constitutional proprieties and the co-ordination of departmental activities; basically it is a negative and conservative force in moral contradiction to the excesses of the politicians. Then there is a sort of informal network of the Principal Private Secretaries to the senior ministers, who work closely with the Prime Minister's Principal Private Secretaries – these are the men who make things happen and initiate action in Whitehall.

Alan Bailey was a member of this informal club. As Economic Secretary, I responded constantly to internal Treasury memoranda on key policy issues by minuting my boss, Tony Barber, with opinionated comments and suggestions on the issues of the day. Alan Bailey, like all good private secretaries, set out to lighten Tony Barber's red boxes and I became convinced that he withheld my memoranda from those boxes – at least until they had lost their moment. My comments were often critical and questioning of government policies, and no doubt Alan Bailey saw them as adding to the burdens of his boss. The senior Treasury officials tended not only to develop an arrogant disdain towards other, weaker departments; but they all, more than other departments, regarded the junior ministers as being something of a pain and a distraction from their own role as advisers to the Chancellor. Perhaps this is all in my imagination, but I fear not. Treasury junior ministers were not regarded with the same respect as in other departments, although the officials could not have been more courteous in responding to requests for information – and indeed, making themselves available for meetings.

The Treasury – albeit a collectively arrogant institution towards the outside world and, of course, to other departments in Whitehall – nonetheless operated internally a very democratic and flat system of management. The quality of the memoranda was outstanding, if not always relevant to the real world outside, which Treasury officials did not understand and which they held in some intellectual contempt. Every key issue was thoroughly considered, initially by a relatively junior official, and then as the papers moved up the hierarchy, other seniors added their views – including, I may say, the views of the Economic Secretary! Very often the junior paper was the most imaginative and interesting, and the sheaf of opinions was circulated widely. The Chancellor was always shown the papers prepared by junior officials, with senior comments added. In other departments, it was well known that the Secretary of State was normally presented with the distilled wisdom of the department, often under the signature of the Permanent Secretary.

I think the Treasury practice was excellent, and it would have helped me in the Ministry of Defence because the junior officers often held the most stimulating opinions; but that, inevitably, was impossible in the most hierarchical department of all. Could you imagine the Chief of the Air Staff wanting his political master to see the radical ravings of a junior flight lieutenant? The most preposterous hierarchy of the lot was in the Bank of England, where every opinion had to be filtered through the Governor. He was the sole spokesman, particularly towards the Treasury, of the Bank of England's view. This process was known in the Treasury as 'the Everest Problem', because everything had to emerge from the top.

I was involved in an extraordinary incident that reflected this state of affairs – and also the inferiority complex which the Bank felt in dealing with its senior cousin in Whitehall. One evening I met Charles Goodhart, who was an adviser on monetary policy to the Governor, Sir Leslie O'Brien. As I was the junior minister in the Treasury dealing with monetary policy, I suggested that we meet informally for lunch. A week later, I had a call asking if I could go along the corridor and see Tony Barber. When I got there, he had a wide grin all over his face and said that he had been instructed by the Governor to reprimand me. I was slightly surprised, because I saw the Governor quite frequently at meetings in Tony's room and he had never appeared to be anything other than very friendly. Tony then performed his charade:

Barber: I have had a letter from the Governor, expressing his grave concern at your behaviour. The Governor is really shocked about your bad manners and the way in which the Treasury is behaving. I understand that you invited Charles Goodhart to have lunch with you.

Nott (rather surprised): Yes.

Barber: Well, the Governor says that if you want to have lunch with one of his officials, you should follow the correct procedures and apply to me, the Chancellor, asking if I would approach the Governor to see if that was acceptable to both of us.

We both dissolved in laughter.

On joining the Treasury, one of my duties was to supervise the team that policed exchange control regulations. These were the days when private individuals could only purchase overseas assets by buying their currency through the so-called dollar premium. This sold at a premium of 10–30 per cent above the official rate of exchange. There were draconian penalties for breaching these rules. Not surprisingly, people who could acquire overseas currency independently of this foolish system tended to do so. There was a team of former CID inspectors who had been recruited by the Treasury and the Bank to track down criminals trying to avoid the exchange control regulations. They reported to me. Every so often, I received a visit from these detectives bearing evidence that so-and-so was advertising a villa for rent in the South of France or wherever, and that he had not purchased it through official channels. I received one minute after another about these overseas villas, and frankly I did not care. I detested exchange control and all the petty officiousness and bureaucracy that went with it. Even in the traumatic early 1970s, as we abandoned the sterling area and our reserve currency status, we would have been better off without it. Of course, sterling might have been lower, but it could also have been higher; and once we had a floating currency, that then much-feared concept of 'supply and demand' would have acted as a self-correcting mechanism.

One day I called together the leaders of the team of former police inspectors and Treasury officials and suggested to them – indeed, instructed them – to divert their expensive efforts away from villas and towards the invoicing practices of the multinationals. I stated (with some knowledge) that every single day transfers across the exchanges, through somewhat artificial invoicing by the multinationals, exceeded many thousand times over the amount lost by purchases of villas. What absurdities civil servants can get up to – in a regulated environment. The Bank of England had an army of officials working on the minutiae of exchange control. Hurrah, they are all gone.

~

All of us who served in Ted Heath's administration try to be fair to him. I confess, after all these years, to a sneaking respect for the old man. After all, he gave me my first job in politics. He is straight, very intelligent and, on some occasions, when casting off his general air of boredom and detachment, can show flashes of considerable charm. Sometimes, however, like most people I have suffered from his most boorish behaviour. In November 1971, for instance, I was selected to move the motion on the Queen's Speech. (Kenneth Clarke, incidentally, seconded the motion.) This is a considerable honour for a back-bencher, and by tradition he dines at No. 10 the evening before the debate and sits on the right hand of the Prime Minister. It was a terrible experience, as multitudes of similar sufferers would confirm. I tried to be pleasant and struggled with a whole gamut of observations – music, sailing, pictures – all to no avail. He did not deign to utter one single word to me from the beginning of the meal to the end.

The truth about Ted is, I am afraid, that he is corporate man incarnate. He passionately believed in saving the country from its long decline, but he saw it as a task for management. 'Action not words' was the slogan of the 1970 Conservative election manifesto. It suited him admirably. Was Ted a leader? Perhaps; but his skills would have been best deployed as head of the civil service or as chief of staff to a famous general. He would have been a brilliant chief of staff to one of Napoleon's marshals, counter-balancing the inspiration and genius of his master with dogged determination in the field and using the kind of skills that he deployed as Chief Whip after the Suez debacle.

The Heath administration faced extraordinary international difficulties, many of which were not of its own making. Following the abandonment of the gold guarantee backing the dollar in August 1971, the United States was pumping out dollars – unbacked by gold – into the global economy, creating inflation everywhere. At one stage, world commodity prices were rising at 30 per cent a year. Attempts were made to achieve a realignment of world currencies, and sterling was fixed at $2.60 to the pound – an unsustainable parity as soon as the balance of payments began to deteriorate. The world was about to change for the worse, especially from the autumn of 1973 with the Yom Kippur war and the oil embargo. It is undeniable that Ted Heath faced an infinitely more difficult time than Margaret Thatcher, not least because there was no public mood to tackle the nation's problem; the whole British establishment was inured to the politics of decline. Ted fought this mood with courage, but he was simply defeated by it.

Domestically, however, it has to be said that in 1970 he inherited from Roy Jenkins' chancellorship an improving economy. Unemployment was stable and had changed very little over the past three years. Consumer prices had recovered after devaluation in 1967 and were rising at about 5 per cent per annum. The public sector was in financial surplus, with a negative borrowing requirement. The money stock had increased by less than 3 per cent (it was to grow to over 30 per cent) and the balance of payments, after a long series of deficits, was in increasing surplus.

By 1974, when the Conservatives were defeated at the general election in February, only unemployment was below the level at which it had started in 1970. Almost every other economic indicator had deteriorated disastrously. So bad was the economic situation inherited by Labour in 1974 – in stark contrast to the favourable domestic position inherited by the Conservatives in 1970 – that it would have been a miracle if the Wilson and Callaghan administrations that followed had been able to correct it in a short five years. By 1975, for instance, wage claims of up to 40 per cent were being submitted – and, following the oil price increase, the current account deficit reached nearly £3.5 billion.

Perhaps Margaret Thatcher owes her election victory in 1979 to the appalling mess left behind in 1974 by the Tory Cabinet – of which she was a member. And what was the principal cause of such failure? It was simple. Ted Heath and his senior colleagues had, as I have already argued, inherited this fear, this detestation of unemployment from Macmillan. It assumed such a central position in policy-making that it negated every other necessary economic counter-measure.

Interestingly, however, the first year of the Heath Government went quite well. The tenets set out in the manifesto and in Ted Heath's speech on the 'Quiet Revolution' at the Conservative conference in 1970 were maintained. Tony Barber's first mini-budget in 1970 made no attempt to influence aggregate demand. Even in his spring budget in 1971, he thought it 'irresponsible' to take action to reduce unemployment by boosting consumer demand 'until we get a substantial reduction in the level of pay settlements'. He then proposed limited tax cuts to allow output to grow at 3 per cent per annum instead of 2 per cent. In fact, output at the end of 1971 was only 2 per cent higher than it had been eighteen months earlier, and unemployment was about to hit the emotive one million mark – a level that had not been reached since the Second World War.

It was at this point that all caution was abandoned – a panic about unemployment set in. Ted Heath in his typically unapologetic autobiography describes the meetings with Tony Barber in early 1972 to review economic policy. He notes that Tony and the Treasury were very cautious about a highly expansionary budget – but did not resist. As a result, a diktat came down from No. 10 to the Treasury saying that unemployment should be halved within a year – an absurd and dangerous notion. There is no doubt that the Treasury was astonished and, whilst it knew how to devise a budget in 1972 that might achieve this result, it was equally aware that there were serious dangers attached to such a policy. Nonetheless the Prime Minister's diktat was followed and the Budget that March set out a programme to achieve 10 per cent growth over the next two years. At 5 per cent per annum, this was twice the rate of the economy's productive potential. Perhaps inevitably, the economy overshot, and in 1973 (the climax of the 'Barber boom') growth rose by 7 per cent – a wholly astonishing, unsustainable level for a developed economy at that time.

The 1972 Budget was the most expansionary since the Second World War. In his speech, Tony Barber declared: 'I am not one of those who look to unemployment as the cure for inflation … A further boost to demand is required.' This apparently sanguine belief that higher growth could go hand in hand with lower inflation represented a complete reversal of his budgetary caution a year earlier and, I suspect, of his own instincts.

The arguments in favour of this gamble on growth were advocated by the Cambridge School, then headed by a tiresome man called Wynne Godley. But there were people in the Treasury – Sir Donald MacDougall, the Chief Economic Adviser, being among the most influential – who were also out-and-out expansionists. The central political argument for this course was that the performance of the British economy had been so poor in comparison to our European competitors that radical action, even risks, had to be taken to 'break out' of the spiral of relative economic decline – not least so that we could hold our head high when we joined the European Economic Community at the start of 1973.

The economic arguments were sophisticated but, in retrospect, were hopelessly wrong. Industrialists claimed that higher growth would reduce unit costs, but economists talked more about the 'real wage push theory'. It went something like this:

> The job of the Treasury is to use the instruments at its command to make the real economy grow faster, thereby bringing down unemployment and delivering real wage increases. Following the Jenkins deflation of 1968–69, workers have received no increase in real take-home pay for three years. If growth delivers real wage increases, workers will restrain their wage demands and, as they restore their share of rising output, inflation will fall.

Economists were confused, because they had been educated to believe in a very simple economic principle – namely, that if you lower unemployment, you risk raising inflation and vice versa. But by the beginning of 1972 inflation and unemployment were both rising rapidly, and this baffled the theorists.

A whole set of explanations arose to explain the rise in inflation. It was alleged that fundamental social changes were taking place in society, inflation was a sociological and political phenomenon, not a monetary one – some even talked of 'Swinging London' as a symbol of this change. The unions had acquired a whole new generation of militant leaders, Scanlon, Jones, McGahey and the rest. In short, all these non-economic factors were contributing to massive wage push inflation. So it was felt by some insiders that, if faster growth did not deliver lower inflation, the only course was to resort to the law – in other words, a statutory prices and incomes policy. This is what indeed happened before 1972 was out.

But it is important to an understanding of the Heath Government to realise the thinking behind the policy. Basically it was corporatism gone mad – the belief that intervention could deliver a fair and reasonable basis for proceeding. In the lobbies, backbench opponents of this approach disparagingly referred to Ted as 'Mussolini'. And Ted certainly believed that government could 'make the trains run on time'.

The idea was that you brought about a bargain between the government, the unions and industry – a bargain in which the government said, 'If you, the unions, will moderate your pay claims, and you, industry, will moderate your prices, we, the government, will give you 5 per cent growth'. And how could anyone complain? Hey presto, the problems of governing with consent were solved just like that. Embodied in this concept was the idea that growth was generated by the government, handed out like chocolates to children. But the unions were not, at that stage, prepared to contemplate pay bargaining with the government; they had suffered from it too much under Roy Jenkins' chancellorship during the previous Labour government. So in the course of 1972 we moved inexorably to a statutory prices and incomes policy.

In the chapter of Ted Heath's memoirs fittingly entitled 'Tripartism on Trial', there is a telling example of the nonsense which was being disseminated about inflation and growth, in this case on 19 June 1972:

> Reggie Maudling produced another thorough and logical paper for Cabinet on 'the economic problem'. The most serious difficulty we faced, he argued, was inflation, which was fuelled by the cost-push created when incomes grew ahead of productivity increases. Our policy of expanding demand was essential to growth and employment and, therefore, broadly non-inflationary, on which basis inflation resulted largely from wage settlements … Maudling's conclusion was that 'we can only hold the spiral of cost inflation on the basis of some agreement with organised labour … The basis of any such agreement must be an acceptance of a norm, which in effect means what the economy can bear in the way of general incomes inflation.'

Reggie Maudling, who retired from the Cabinet a few months later, had always been in favour of a prices and incomes policy.

The consequence was that a fiscal expansion, a monetary expansion and a world boom were all combined. Consumption boomed, public expenditure boomed, only industrial investment was stagnant. Ted Heath raged up and down the country criticising industrialists for not investing. But the industrialists were quite right; no responsible businessman believed that such a boom would last. And many of them, who did invest, went out of business in the severe recession which followed in 1974 and 1975. By then, of course, the political dance had moved on.

~

Looking back on our rapidly worsening economic plight between the summers of 1972 and 1973, three episodes stand out strongly in my mind: the floating of sterling in June 1972, the extraordinary Health/Brandt *démarche* on currencies nine months later, and the initiative I took that led in the autumn of 1972 to the abolition of the bank rate.

The story of how we came to float the pound in June 1972 was fascinating. Just as Suez marked the end of Britain's imperial pretensions, so the floating of sterling signified the abandonment of the sterling area, our status as a reserve currency, and the ending of our close financial links with the Commonwealth. In many respects it was a symbol of our country's shift from Empire to Europe, or from the Commonwealth to the European Economic Community.

Our move into Europe was against a background of protracted turbulence on the international exchanges. As a result of the currency chaos following Nixon's decision in August 1971 to abandon gold and impose a 10 per cent import surcharge, most currencies were allowed to float. But on 19 December 1971, at the Smithsonian Institute, currencies were realigned and the US surcharge was withdrawn. At the end of April 1972 the six members of the EEC took what they regarded as a step towards European Monetary Union by limiting fluctuations in their currency relationships to 2¼ per cent either side of parity. This was known as 'the Snake'. It was part of the Werner Plan, which had set out a series of steps to achieve complete European economic and monetary union by 1980. Britain joined the Snake on 1 May and for nearly two months was a member of this primitive exchange rate mechanism.

In the meantime, the domestic financial position in the UK was deteriorating. The balance of payments – that perennial obsession of the Treasury before we floated – had become very weak in the early part of 1972, wage settlements were rising to around 12–14 per cent, sterling had been set high at $2.60, and export prices were estimated to have risen by at least 10 per cent above those of our competitors abroad.

Ted Heath describes in his memoirs how he called a series of meetings at Downing Street to discuss the deteriorating situation, and the rapidly gathering outflow of foreign currency. The Treasury and the Bank of England urged a raising of bank rate. They said that if no action was taken, it would be widely assumed that the government was not intent on defending the exchange rate. Even at this critical stage, on 21 June, Heath said that he remained doubtful about the argument for raising bank rate to stem the increase in money supply.

He argued that the increased lending to consumers was in line with government policy. He asked, reasonably enough, whether the Bank of England could not reintroduce some form of quantitative control in order to avoid the rise in bank rate. But the Bank replied that, under the recently introduced monetary regime (known as 'Competition and Credit Control'), there was a limit to the measures that it could sensibly adopt. Eventually, it was reluctantly agreed that bank rate should be raised next day, the 22nd.

Meanwhile, as the reserves diminished, I joined in a series of meetings in the Treasury to decide whether to devalue or float, should emergency action be forced upon us in the next few days. Against floating were the Community arrangements for narrowing margins in 'the Snake' and our obligations to the IMF. But in terms of confidence, a temporary float, leading eventually to fixing a new rate, would be different from abruptly going down a step in one move. It was also said by officials that a devaluation would carry little conviction unless it was combined with some definite action on inflation, implying quite incorrectly that action on inflation was less urgent with a float. In the event, in spite of repeated urgings over the next two years from No. 10, Tony Barber resisted all attempts to re-fix the parity, and Heath left office with a floating pound – a great boon to a future incoming Conservative government under Mrs Thatcher.

The decision to float was taken on the 22nd. I attended a meeting in the Commons between Barber and Heath which triggered the decision, and thereafter two meetings took place with members of the Cabinet to brief them on the reasons underlying it. So the £ was floated before the opening of business on 23 June. Tony Barber's statement to the Commons that day contained a passage that was eloquently indicative of the government's broader policy:

We have set our national economy on the path of a 5 per cent rate of expansion, more than twice as fast as the rate we have achieved over the past decade. Recent statistics, especially those showing the very big reduction in unemployment, confirm that we are well on course. There is still room in the economy for considerable further development without straining either capacity or the labour force or pressing on demand. The general growth in exports will not therefore be impeded by limitations on capacity and, unlike on some previous occasions, it is not necessary or, indeed, desirable to introduce restrictive measures.

It was, of course, a lot of nonsense – restrictive measures were essential.

Reflecting on this whole episode, it is clear that many mistakes were made. Unless the government was prepared to clamp down heavily on the emerging boom by a major increase in interest rates, the fall in the value of sterling was bound to worsen inflation. Because of booming world commodity prices, the fall in sterling's value raised import prices to a very high level; but the priority was to go for growth, so no restrictive measures were taken. In the internal Treasury meetings, I was an enthusiastic voice for floating and not inclined to suggest that it should be temporary. By this time, under Ted Heath's leadership, our policies were heavily influenced by Community interests, and his private determination to launch the United Kingdom into economic and monetary union overlay many of his attitudes. He knew that we needed to return to a fixed parity if we were ever to rejoin 'the Snake' – the Community currency arrangement. Indeed, I have always thought that he showed great courage in agreeing to a float as opposed to a devaluation, given his overriding concern for our relations with the Community.

Meanwhile, in the international field, my Euroscepticism was increasing. I had been not only to a number of meetings of the Council of Ministers in Brussels, but also (as Barber's deputy) to several other international gatherings, especially meetings between Barber, Schmidt and Giscard, respectively the finance ministers of Britain, Germany and France. The discussions barely concealed naked national wrangling, but more sickening was the posturing of Giscard and the behaviour of the French. Schmidt was as arrogant as Barber was modest – perhaps that represented the relative strength of the two countries – but Giscard's conceit was nauseating. He ensured, even in those early days before he became an overweening President, that he made an 'entrance' at every meeting, however small. It became a sort of joke, much emphasised by Connally, the Texan US Treasury Secretary, that every meeting was preceded by a long wait whilst the assembled delegates awaited the ceremonial entry of the French, led by Giscard. At every available occasion, the French set out to rile the Americans.

By floating sterling, Ted Heath must have felt that he had damaged the cause of 'Europe' – even before we had entered the Community, which was due to take place on 1 January 1973. He kept in particularly close touch with President Pompidou and Chancellor Brandt. Assuring them that these events had in no way diminished his wish to make progress in European monetary co-operation, he asserted that 'even a soundly based currency is vulnerable to confidence movements which have no objective justification'. Surely he could not have believed that this applied to us. The French, less courteous than the Germans, claimed that they had entered into an agreement with the British two months back on 'the Snake', and that this decision 'had blown it sky-high'. They wanted to know when we would be returning to a fixed parity and what scale of devaluation we were anticipating. Pompidou emphasised to Heath his utter conviction that fixed parities were an essential prerequisite to European monetary union. The Americans, meanwhile, were more in favour of a float than a downward adjustment and said that they had been expecting it.

Of course, with a stern monetary policy it might have been possible to discipline the financial system had we devalued in June 1972 instead of floating; you can't have a floating currency and a weak monetary policy or, at that time, no monetary policy at all. If, instead of floating, we had devalued, say from $2.60 to $2.40, a loose monetary policy would have been impossible; for this would have caused a further outflow of the reserves and interest rates would have forcibly risen in order to protect them – a rise that was vitally necessary if inflation was to be checked.

Less than a year later, after we had entered the Community, a remarkable sequel arose in this interplay between the requirements of currency management and Ted Heath's personal obsession with the European experiment. On 2 March 1973 I was sitting in my office in the Treasury when I saw the most extraordinary telegram from Bonn. The whole episode is recorded by the then British Ambassador in Bonn, Sir Nicholas Henderson, in his autobiography. The telegram, which bore his name, described a summit meeting the previous day between Chancellor Brandt and Prime Minister Heath. The telegram revealed a sensational proposal to use the continuing currency crisis (the day before the meeting, the Germans had accepted an inflow of no less than $2.7 billion) as a springboard for a major advance to the goal of economic and monetary union. The only way of achieving progress towards Community objectives, they agreed, was to adopt a Community solution. This, they said, should take the form of, first, a fixing of EEC parities in relation to each other, and then a collective float against the dollar with mutual intervention in EEC currencies.

Brandt expressed a willingness to make funds available for intervention (effectively to the Bank of England), without interest and with no obligation to repay. In other words, he was prepared – in order to make a leap forward to achieve the common goal of economic and monetary union – to initiate the pooling of Community currency reserves of a kind that would be central to eventual EMU.

I found these proposals astonishing, not least because of the repeated assurances by Ted Heath, not long before, that our entry into the European Economic Community would have no adverse consequences for our sovereignty. It was this assurance that had persuaded many Conservative MPs to vote for entry to the Community. I do not believe that even Tony Barber – and certainly no other member of the Cabinet – was aware of where the discussion between Brandt and Heath might lead. In many respects, even if you disagree with them, these ideas were exceptionally bold and courageous. Here was the opportunity for a massive leap into economic and monetary union, effectively political union, as early as 1973, which even predated by seven years the 1980 target set out in the Werner Plan as the destination for a political Europe. If carried out, it would have taken Europe further towards a single integrated political unit than anything that has been achieved since – and we are now in 2002, nearly thirty years later. Ted Heath quite rightly believed that such a move could only happen as an act of political will.

Although I would have been deeply opposed to such a move, I still admire the determination which led to an agreement between the two men. What is also interesting is that the two leaders agreed that a leap forward into a political Europe could not be achieved without the enlargement of the Community budget to provide the necessary resource transfers to rectify the consequential economic imbalances that would result. Today the single greatest economic weakness underlying the introduction of a single European currency is that no such provision exists. This must lead to one of two things: the political collapse of the project, as different regions suffer economic decline as a result of a single interest rate; or, less likely, a huge expansion in the European budget, making essential a unified fiscal and financial framework with a single authority – a single political entity – to control it. That can be nothing other than a single European government. As Dr Otmar Issing, the chief economist of the European Central Bank, has observed, there has been 'no example in history of a lasting monetary union that was not linked to one state'.

When the Cabinet met to consider the international monetary crisis, and to hear from Ted Heath about his talks with Chancellor Brandt, Tony Barber reported on the meeting of the Community finance ministers, who had gathered to take forward the Heath/Brandt agreement. He said that opinion had been divided. Schmidt, the German finance minister, had not been in favour of the central plank in the Heath/Brandt agreement – made in his absence a few days earlier, namely, the pooling of reserves. Barber said that the overall view of the finance ministers was that if Britain wished to pursue these ideas, we should take the initiative.

In the following days, Ted Heath tried to revive the agreement between himself and Brandt, but got nowhere. The worst outcome, he thought, was to do nothing because the £ might simply decline further and make the handling of the counter-inflation policy almost impossible. Tony Barber said that we should be thinking about a timescale and conditions for our rejoining a Community scheme. However, he explained, it was difficult to fix on a date unless the government was prepared to contemplate drastic economic action; it was impossible to fix a parity with the UK industrial situation in its present state; he thought that if the counter-inflation policy was successful, we might be able to fix one by the autumn. But he stressed that it would be disastrous to enter a Community arrangement and be forced out of it again. In the end, despite Heath's urging, we never did fix the parity.

Ted had been defeated. He believed his plan for a great leap forward for Europe had been sabotaged by the Treasury. From this moment, I am sure, he held the Treasury in complete contempt. More and more he came to rely on the advice of William Armstrong, head of the civil service and a former Permanent Secretary at the Treasury, and on the political and moral support of Carrington and Whitelaw. It was a disastrous combination. In fact, the agreement between Heath and Brandt had been sabotaged not by the British Treasury, but by Schmidt and the Bundesbank. Understandably, they saw no reason to make Germany's hard-won currency reserves available to help the profligate British. Over the following few months in 1973, as almost all the key UK economic indicators steadily worsened, they can have had few regrets.

Back in 1972, long before the Heath/Brandt *démarche* on economic and monetary union, difficulties at home over domestic monetary policy were accelerating. I was the Treasury minister who had to explain and defend this monetary expansion in the House of Commons. The fiscal expansion was well established, interest rates were being held down to further economic growth and a major structural change in the arrangements for controlling credit was adding to a monetary explosion. This structural change was called 'competition and credit control', which abolished the 'rationing' of the volume of bank advances and hire purchase agreements.

Unfortunately, the short-term implementation of this very desirable policy proved disastrous. One of the reasons why the money supply rose so fast from late 1971 was that once the banks were free to reshuffle their balance sheets, they expanded like crazy their advances to companies, advances being one of their most profitable activities. This new policy enabled the banks to expand their lending by 33 per cent in 1973. Nevertheless, government itself was the main culprit. Having provided the means whereby bank lending and the money supply could grow rapidly, and having taken away from the Treasury a traditional way of rationing credit, it then demonstrated itself either unable or unwilling to do its bit by controlling the price of money. It was simply in opposition to the government's drive for expansion.

In fact, it was increasingly obvious that the suddenly unrationed demand for credit had got completely out of hand. As the 1972 Finance Bill was put to bed that July, I had more time to consider the state of the economy. It was deteriorating rapidly: inflation was rampant; hourly wage rates were increasing at an annual rate of some 14 per cent; and, for me most worrying of all, the monetary indicator M3 was rising fast. Between the first quarter of 1971 and the first quarter of 1973, it rose by about 44 per cent. Although some of the younger Treasury officials, in particular the younger economists, were aware of the new monetarism being advocated by Milton Friedman – and increasingly pushed by the IEA – the senior officials believed that demand governed prices and that the quantity of money was more a symptom than a cause of changes in demand. There was little sympathy for Friedman's conviction that 'inflation is always and everywhere a monetary phenomenon' – as yet, the simple notion that money would lose value the more of it that there was in circulation had few supporters among the mandarin class.

But anyway, and much more pertinently, the cardinal fact was that Ted Heath would have none of it. He had set the economy on a course of expansion in the 1972 Budget and would not hear of measures to slow that expansion down. Moreover, he was in a dialogue with industry and the unions, and neither side would contemplate a rise in interest rates to curb the rise in the money supply.

I had many meetings with an excellent Treasury official called Frank Cassell. He was in charge of monetary policy in the Treasury, but his voice did not carry a lot of weight. I am sure that Tony Barber and the Governor (O'Brien) pressed for high interest rates, but neither had sufficient clout at No. 10. By this time Ted Heath had acquired – *de facto* – Sir William Armstrong as 'Deputy Prime Minister' (as the TUC's Vic Feather dubbed him). It became a very unhealthy relationship. Armstrong increasingly carried more weight than almost all members of the Cabinet, certainly more weight than the Treasury officials whom Ted had come to despise. When Ted had disagreements with his Chancellor – and such disagreements are commonplace between all Prime Ministers and their Chancellors – he tended to call in Carrington and Whitelaw in support. This quartet of Heath, Armstrong, Carrington and Whitelaw – with the latter two having no feel for economic issues – became the key figures in the government, and Tony Barber could make no headway. I often saw Tony depressed after his meetings at No. 10. He was an excellent man – and could have been a very good Chancellor – had he not suffered from one serious defect. As a former Whip and friend, he saw his loyalty to Ted and the government as paramount. I don't think that would have been the case with Iain Macleod.

By August 1972 I had become aware of the urgency of raising interest rates, but equally I saw that the Prime Minister was a major obstacle. By this time, mortgage rates were becoming an obsession at No. 10, because of their impact on the retail price index and hence on wage demands. Mortgage rates became the latest excuse to hold down interest rates. I wondered if perhaps we could disguise rises in the government's own interest rate – namely bank rate – by abolishing it altogether. If we could somehow allow interest rates to find a natural, market-related level, without the overt influence of government, they should rise significantly of their own accord.

I therefore sent the following internal minute to Tony Barber on 24 August:

The key role of Bank Rate in dictating the level of interest rates generally has clearly diminished in the last ten years. Yet the Press, and consequently Ministers, still seem to accord it a reverence more in keeping with its traditional pre-war role.

I find this unfortunate. If we are to avoid a return to selective controls we must educate the Establishment and general public to regard changes in interest rates as a normal occurrence.

Can you tell me why we have to have 'Bank Rate' at all? Of course we need a Rate at which the Bank acts as a lender of last resort etc. But why do we need to call it 'Bank Rate' and go through all this Thursday ritual with the

Government Broker moving portentously in and out of the Bank of England in a silk hat?

I think that we should aim at making it less embarrassing and difficult for Governments under the new credit policy to act promptly as and when financial and economic conditions require.

Such a radical proposal coming from a junior minister was, of course, an act of *lèse-majesté* in the eyes of the officials who should have dreamed it up as a recommendation from themselves. As with any change of course in Whitehall, it took an inordinate time to be implemented. In particular, the Bank of England put up a host of objections. Some were rational, such as that there could be occasions when the government needed to lead markets with an indicative move, but there was a more emotional motive at work. The 'Thursday' announcement was the Bank of England's big moment each week. It reminded the City and a wider audience of the importance of the Bank. The Government Broker in his ludicrous uniform – the uniform of all the discount brokers when I was at Warburg – was a symbol of the importance of the City, and a weekly reminder that here was a creature of the Bank's authority.

The announcement ending the 270-year rule of bank rate was made in October 1972. 'It has been decided to relate the last resort rate of the Bank of England to the actual level of rates prevailing in the money market,' explained Tony Barber's official statement. 'It will normally be at ½ per cent above the average rate at each Friday's Treasury Bill tender … This will give the rate considerably more flexibility than it has at the moment …' The statement's concluding paragraph was the most revealing:

Interest rates generally have risen in recent months, as was only to be expected at a time of very strong demand for credit … In this context, however, I want to make one point clear beyond doubt. The totality of economic indicators is consistent with a rate of economic growth of 5 per cent a year which is about twice the rate we achieved over the past decade. This is the only sure means of securing a faster improvement in our national prosperity and I do not intend to be deflected from pursuing the policies necessary to achieve it.

That final sentence, although I cannot prove it, suggests the inimitable hand of Sir William Armstrong and No. 10. Thereafter, in any event, interest rates rose quite fast, and reached a peak of 13 per cent in December 1973.

Nevertheless, there was still the larger problem. Although I was in principle an enthusiastic supporter of the new monetary regime, I fretted about 'competition and credit control' and wanted to suspend it. But the Bank of England resisted a return to quantitative controls on credit, which they saw as a defeat. And the Treasury, in the person of Douglas Allen, the Permanent Secretary, was also reluctant to take on the Bank. The fencing between Douglas Allen and Leslie O'Brien was a notable feature of those days. As a result, by the time the policy was more or less abandoned *force majeure* in December 1973, with the imposition of the so-called 'corset' (penalising the banks and finance houses if they allowed their sterling deposits to grow too fast), the fatal damage had been done. Fiscal laxity, a weak monetary policy, and a floating currency – it was a lethal cocktail.

In the Commons, I continued to soldier on, defending an economic policy in which I had ever less faith. 'We are going for a policy of growth, and one month's trade figures can be misleading if looked at in isolation,' I riposted after the Shadow Chancellor, Denis Healey, had highlighted in April 1973 the recent bad trade figures. The following month, claiming that the money supply figures were looking more under control, I struck an optimistic note: 'There are grounds for saying that we are now moving into an investment- and export-led boom of the type which we all wish to see.' And in July there was this exchange with, of all people, my economic mentor:

Nott: The recent National Institute of Economic and Social Research review pointed out that the Government's counter-inflation policy had met with considerable success …

Powell: When have you known the National Institute to be right? (Loud Labour laughter.)

Nott: I have every hope that on this occasion the more optimistic forecast of the National Institute will prove correct. (Renewed laughter.)

It was not, all things considered, a comfortable time.

~

By the autumn of 1973, the critical symbol of progress or otherwise was not the balance of payments and, in consequence, the defence of the currency reserves. This had no longer quite the same priority, as we were floating. Instead, what seemed to matter most was finding ways of holding down the retail price index to satisfy the trade unions, which were under pressure to reduce their wage demands. A search was made to find candidates for subsidy – using public expenditure to hold down key elements in the RPI. Tony Barber, knowing that public expenditure was already out of control, tried to resist subsidies on mortgage rates (Heath was obsessed by keeping them in single figures) and the main constituents of the shopping basket – but the search was widespread.

The meeting of Commonwealth finance ministers and the World Bank meeting were to be held that autumn in East Africa – in Dar es Salaam and Nairobi respectively. A few days before the Treasury delegation was due to depart by British Airways, the security services reported a plan by Black September, the terrorist group, to attack the World Bank meeting in Nairobi. We were all allocated an RAF VC10 and a team of Special Branch detectives to defend us.

We had an interesting refuelling stop in Aswan, where we visited the Egyptian sites. Whilst we were wandering around, I made contact with the two detectives who had been allocated to me. One of them came from Newlyn, the fishing port in my constituency. I asked them what they had been doing before they were diverted to this task, and they told me that they had both been investigating Tony Lambton's activities, prior to his resignation for being caught in bed with two high-class call girls. They spoke with some pleasure about all the interesting clubs and other dives that they had visited.

When we got to Dar es Salaam, I found that there was very little role for me, so my two detectives and I spent many pleasant hours on the beach. They were both good swimmers, and often I sat on the beach with their machine gun between my legs whilst they went swimming.

In Nairobi there were a number of incidents. One was when a finance minister's bodyguard became so exasperated with his boss that he shot him. The World Bank meetings are, of course, a ludicrous annual jamboree. On this occasion I was fully occupied; but each morning I had a debriefing with my Special Branch detectives who, every night, tracked down Black Mommas in the Nairobi nightclubs – not, I fear, a very healthy occupation. Ten years later, I was in Kenya once again, visiting British naval vessels off Mombasa during their period of rest and recreation from the Gulf patrol. I was shocked to find that the young sailors were allowed to stay onshore, away from their ships at night – and this was in the days when AIDS had been discovered.

Then a major political crisis erupted around us. Tony Barber and I were staying in the High Commissioner's residence. The High Commissioner was Sir Anthony Duff, an excellent man with a good sense of humour, who subsequently became the security services co-ordinator in the Cabinet Office – the leading link between MI5, MI6, Cheltenham and the government.

A telegram arrived for Tony Barber from Ted Heath informing him that, in his absence, the Cabinet had met and agreed further economic measures, each with substantial financial consequences, in order to bolster the statutory prices and incomes policy. Tony was shocked. There had been a Cabinet meeting before his departure when a series of additional measures had been agreed in his presence. He had no notion that any further changes were foreseen in his ten-day absence. He subsequently told me that one of the new proposals was to place a subsidy on bread. The flour millers had reported that the sterling price of hard wheat was escalating, and there were suggestions that a standard loaf might have to rise from 11.5 pence to 15.5 pence. It was, however, a very expensive move for the Exchequer. The idea of a subsidy on bread, which was seriously considered, shows the state of desperation which the government had reached in its mission to hold down the RPI.

I was not privy to the telephone conversation which took place between the Prime Minister and his Chancellor, but Anthony Duff and I were in little doubt that Tony Barber had said that it was intolerable that such matters should be considered in his absence. As a result, Downing Street proposed that Douglas Wass, the senior official in the Treasury dealing with economic affairs, should be despatched secretly to Nairobi in order to explain to Tony what was happening. Because the sudden appearance of this well-known Treasury official at the World Bank meeting, when he was not part of the Treasury delegation, would have raised major suspicions among the British financial journalists present, Douglas had to be smuggled out of the airport and kept in hiding in the High Commissioner's residence whilst the Bank meetings were in progress.

Over the next few months there was not much else to smile about. The Arab oil producers, reacting to the Arab–Israeli war which started on 6 October, raised their price by 66 per cent only ten days later (they were to double it from 1 January 1974), and decided to cut production by 5 per cent per month. At the same time, the miners and electricians threatened a strike. The miners rejected an offer of 7 per cent and began an overtime ban, while the electrical power engineers started a strike at the end of the month which was settled at the end of the year.

In November the government declared a state of emergency – various restrictions were imposed on heating, lighting and supplies of oil, with a speed limit of 50 mph for vehicles. By early December the mood was increasingly apocalyptic. Front-page headlines from the *FT* on Monday 3rd convey something of the darkening atmosphere: 'Bid to avert all-out coal strike'; 'Tight situation in power industry'; 'Fighting flares in Golan Heights'; and 'Sunday drivers left stranded'. A few days later I was interviewed on BBC2's 'Money Programme'. Quoting me as saying in best 'Corporal Jones' style that 'there is absolutely no cause at the present time for panic', *The Times* reported that 'Mr Nott emphasised the Government was ready to act, but said it would carry on its policy of growth at the highest level possible in the circumstances.'

Things soon got even worse. On the evening of the 13th, a sombre Heath announced the start of the three-day week; by the close of trading the following day, the *FT* Index had fallen by almost a third in barely a month. An emergency mini-budget on the 17th at last saw Barber retrenching (including large public expenditure cuts), but it was far too late. The miners in the new year ruthlessly took advantage of the oil situation and announced on 5 February a full-scale strike to start five days later. On 7 February, Heath called a 'Who governs Britain?' election, to be held on the last day of the month.

As Economic Secretary during these desperate months, I was in receipt of all the latest economic information. By November 1973 I could not envisage anything other than a further serious deterioration in the economy in early 1974. I thought that we had no choice but to go for an early election, and that was the view of all the ministers in the Treasury.

Accordingly, at some point before the Christmas recess, I went up to the Prime Minister in the lobby whilst we were voting (he was talking to Christopher Chataway at the time). I said, 'Excuse me, Prime Minister, would you mind if I had a word with you privately after the division?' Turning to me, he replied brusquely, 'If you want to resign, put it in writing.' I was momentarily taken aback, as this was the first time I had really approached him personally in two years. He must have realised that I was shocked at his rudeness, so he agreed to see me in his room.

I did not know that Peter Carrington, as Party Chairman, was urging him likewise, but I explained to him that I believed we were facing a rapidly deteriorating situation. Of course, I stressed, 'the decision was only for him,' but I hoped he would consider an early election. He did not react – or speak. I would not have expected him to do so.

Would we have won the general election if we had held it, say, a month earlier? Conventional wisdom – after the event – seems to be that we might have done so. I am not clear, however, how a Tory government would have tackled the ensuing financial and industrial crisis. Perhaps it was right for the country that we lost. If this chapter is critical of Ted Heath for what I see as a series of major errors of economic policy, I would certainly not criticise him for his hesitation in the calling of an election. At the best of times it is a difficult decision for any prime minister; in the midst of a major constitutional confrontation with organised labour, it was a fearsome decision to take.

I returned to West Cornwall to fight the election. It was very hard. As a member of the government, I had not been able to speak on any local issue for nearly two years; I was seen as a supporter of the three-day week and everything that went with it, but I won with a reduced majority. It was a bad February.

When the election stalemate was declared – the Conservatives gaining more votes, but the Labour Party more seats – I was appalled that we did not immediately surrender office. The idea of doing any deal with the Liberals was anathema to me. I had a call from my admirable Private Secretary, Diana Seamen, who had been a great supporter through all these traumatic times. She said that the Prime Minister had requested that all ministers should return to their desks whilst the Cabinet considered the constitutional position. I refused to return to London. I had had enough of my own government and had no intention, whatever the result of any deal with the Liberals, of remaining as a minister. Nevertheless, I did feel sorry for Ted Heath. He had tried hard, but he was finished.

Chapter Seven

THE FIRST THATCHER GOVERNMENT

An outsider to her party cannot know what she has put up with.
(Matthew Parris on Margaret Thatcher)

I felt a great sense of release when the Conservatives lost the election, and in-deed, although I shall always vote Conservative whilst it remains a Eurosceptic party, I had the same sense of relief when John Major lost in 1997. On both occasions the country needed a change of government, but for very different reasons. It was Ted Heath's obstinacy, combined with his mission for economic growth, that had destroyed his government; whereas it was John Major's prevarication and lack of any sense of direction which had led to the catastrophe of 1997.

If I was a modern historian, rather than a pluralist who flits from one activ-ity and one career to another, I would place some Labour leaders higher in the history books than their Conservative counterparts. I would place Attlee, Blair and Callaghan – the latter inheriting impossible conditions – higher in the pantheon of prime ministerial talent than Eden, Macmillan, Home, Heath and Major. Taking all these individuals together, only Attlee and Thatcher stand out as the great post-war holders of that office.

Blair is an interesting phenomenon. He might have been a candidate for that hall of fame, but I suspect that hubris will lead to his premature demise; the British system has a remarkable capacity for toppling the over-mighty subject (as it did with Thatcher) and Blair is looking vulnerable. He thinks that he can do it all himself – how wrong he is.

It was March 1974, and I had no job other than my constituency and back-bench duties. This was something of a problem, because I had given up all my outside business interests when I became a Treasury minister two years earlier. By this time my children were embarked on expensive private education – Summerfields in Oxford for the two boys and subsequently the dreadful

Cranborne Chase for my daughter. But more expensive still was my small estate in Cornwall, which I had purchased in 1967 out of the fulsome earnings that I was generating at that time. In fact, the farm (which I write about in the final chapter) proved to be our financial saviour. I bought it for £300 an acre and took out successive mortgages on it, as the price of high-quality land rose to £2,500 an acre. This kept me solvent – or rather, financed; the substantial assets only marginally exceeding the liabilities in the years up to my retirement from politics in 1983.

Although it might have been possible, I did not want to return to some non-executive role in the City. I could see that part-timers were held in very limited respect; to do it well, investment banking has to be a single-minded obsession, and I was still a politician. So I telephoned a Cornish acquaintance, Nicky Williams, the chief executive of Burmah Oil, and asked him if he had anything that I could do. I was duly appointed a financial adviser to Burmah. I travelled once a week to its headquarters in Swindon. This was in the interregnum between the spring and autumn elections in 1974, which were both won, the first without an overall majority, by Harold Wilson, my Isles of Scilly constituent. Ted Heath was still the Tory leader.

My short experience with Burmah was interesting for two reasons. One, which nags me still, concerns the treacherous behaviour of the Treasury under Denis Healey and of the City, backed by BP – 21 per cent of whose shares were held by Burmah. Let me explain.

By 1974 Nicky Williams was within reach of creating a 'third force' in the UK oil industry, alongside Shell and BP. Burmah was the principal shareholder and operator in the Ninian Field in the North Sea and also had a stake in the Thistle Field. It had useful shares in the Gulf of Mexico, and a large oil trans-shipment terminal in the Bahamas off the east coast of the US. It had a profitable industrial division, including Castrol. Unfortunately, Nicky Williams' fatal mistake was not to allow his fellow directors – and in particular his finance director, Bill Gage – to get involved with Elias Kulukundis, who ran Burmah's tanker division out of New York. Ironically, given that I was an outsider, he encouraged me to visit Kulukundis to talk about his operation. For the previous two or more years, Kulukundis had made a real killing in the tanker market. I suggested to Nicky that he should insist that Gage, a dour but effective Scottish accountant, get involved – but Kulukundis would not have it, and Nicky Williams did not press the case. When, like all unsupervised traders, Kulukundis got into trouble, he tried to buy his way out of it. It was fatal. Late on New Year's Eve 1974, with the *FT* Index closing the year at a miserable 161.4 (less than half what it had been at the start), it was announced that Burmah Oil was going into liquidation.

The real problem had been the jealousies that Nicky Williams generated in the City. He had abandoned Barings (who were the trustees of the Burmah loan stock) as his principal advisers, and instead was using Chase Manhattan to do his deals. This was in the days when the leading City merchant banks dominated financial advice in London – and the Americans were considered upstarts. When the tanker losses and the fall in the value of Burmah's holding of BP shares in the bear market of that time breached the conditions of the loan stock, Barings went to the Bank of England to discuss the default, and Burmah had few friends.

In retrospect, it would have been quite possible to bridge Burmah's difficulties with a support operation. But it was not to be – the predators wanted to break up Burmah. The Bank of England took the BP shares for £179 million, raising the government stake in BP to 68 per cent. I remembered all too well how Douglas Allen, the Permanent Secretary at the Treasury, and other officials there had spent an inordinate amount of time on BP, the excuse being the government's large holding of BP shares. It was obvious, however, that the top Treasury officials loved dabbling in the affairs of a fascinating private-sector enterprise; it was one of their few windows on to the real world. The temptation to rid BP of the Burmah shareholding was great, and there were no City merchant banks pressing the Bank of England for a rescue. The BP shares doubled in the months after the Burmah default, and the ultimate value of the Burmah holding when BP shares were eventually sold by the government was over £4 billion. It was daylight robbery – nationalisation with inadequate compensation. It was a mistake, because Burmah could have been a major asset for this country.

The other main interest of my brief time at Burmah was that one of its directors was Denis Thatcher, and we had several prophetic conversations about the state of the Conservative Party. We were all appalled when Ted promoted the cause of coalition government in the period leading up to the October 1974 election. Without any consultation with his party, he vigorously advocated an all-party solution to the nation's problems. The Tory parliamentary party, fortunately for party management, has certain sheep-like qualities and can be driven through all sorts of ideological hoops; the number of politicians that feel strongly on matters of policy being quite limited. The party was reluctantly prepared to accept the prices and incomes policy, and the corporatist direction that it involved, but it was horrified at the concept of a coalition with socialists and Liberals. As early as July 1974, I was reported in the press telling my constituency officers in Penzance that 'in the current mood of a divided nation talk of a national coalition was self-delusive'. Eventually it would become clear that Ted Heath had played Russian roulette with his party, and that the gun had fired, triggering his political suicide.

Accordingly, as early as that summer, I remarked to Denis Thatcher at Burmah in Swindon that his wife might shortly be among the candidates to succeed Ted. 'Never,' said Denis. 'What a ghastly thought!' I have always thought that Denis, protesting at his wife's great triumphs, was privately intensely proud of her achievements – and so he should have been. This may have been one of the first occasions that an outsider had speculated in this way; after all, there were several other senior members of the former Cabinet who had a far greater claim. She had a very outside chance in 1974 – seemingly no chance at all.

After Ted Heath lost the October 1974 election (during which it was rather pointedly emblazoned across the front of my election address that 'Your vote is for an MP to represent this constituency – not just for a national party and its leader'), a leadership contest became unavoidable. I was invited to join the Opposition front bench as a junior to Margaret Thatcher, who had been appointed as the shadow Local Government Minister. I visited Ted in his Commons office. He had a glass of whisky in his hand and did not get up when I went into his room. He said that the Whips had suggested that I should rejoin the front bench, making it clear that it was not a proposal of his own volition. I turned it down for two reasons. First, because I wanted to be free to choose a new leader in any forthcoming contest, without any obligation; and second, because I wanted time to replenish my bank account by taking outside jobs. It was a fortunate decision. I was almost alone, among all Ted Heath's former ministers, in having no sense of obligation to vote for him on the first ballot of the leadership contest in February 1975. Margaret Thatcher emerged as his main opponent. All the principal candidates, particularly Whitelaw, felt inhibited by a sense of loyalty not to stand against their leader. If Ted had resigned after losing two elections, which he certainly should have done, the history of the Conservative Party and the country would have been different. Whitelaw, I believe, would have won on the first ballot – an unmitigated disaster. A successful manoeuvrer, extrovert and popular, he would certainly have followed the consensus policies of Macmillan, and there would have been no determined and radical attempt to solve the nation's problems. The management of decline would have suited William Whitelaw very well.

Keith Joseph withdrew as the obvious champion of the radical right, and Edward du Cann, as chairman of the 1922 Committee, did not stand. The way was clear for Margaret Thatcher. Her lead over Heath was so substantial on the first ballot (130 votes to 119) that Whitelaw stood little chance of catching her in the second.

I canvassed for Thatcher throughout the two ballots – at one point helping Norman Tebbit to try and persuade Michael Heseltine to vote for Thatcher in order to give Whitelaw a chance in any second ballot. I do not know whether we succeeded. I found the behaviour of some of my colleagues rather sickening. They kept their heads down, failing publicly to declare their colours in the first ballot when it was thought by many that Margaret Thatcher could hardly poll more votes than Ted. Then, when she emerged the winner, you might have thought that those colleagues had supported her all along.

Thus did the political world change.

Another summer, after Margaret Thatcher had been elected leader, we all spent a holiday as guests in the Morrisons' house on Islay. The idea – cooked up by Peter Morrison, Charlie's brother, whose approach to politics I shared – was that I would keep Margaret amused in the Highlands by sitting up half the night talking politics with her; however, I failed hopelessly in my duty as a guest. Every morning, John Morrison rallied his guests for the day's sport; and having spent all day stalking, I came back from the moors exhausted and went to bed after dinner, leaving Margaret bereft. It was not an auspicious start to my forthcoming ministerial career; however, Margaret and Miloska struck up a friendship and used to go walking on the moors by day.

On Margaret's victory, I agreed to rejoin the front bench as Shadow Chief Secretary and as deputy to Geoffrey Howe, the new Shadow Chancellor. Geoffrey is a delightful man, highly intelligent with all the right economic instincts. But, like all good lawyers, he can support any brief, whatever its merits. We always had a good relationship but we did not warm towards each other. I was too instinctive and maverick for Geoffrey; he was too much of a ponderous lawyer for me. Sometimes Geoffrey lacked cutting edge and ruthlessness in debate – and no-one ever said that of me. It became invidious when people compared our debating skills – Denis Healey, the Chancellor, cruelly described being attacked by Geoffrey as 'rather like being savaged by a dead sheep' – and it made our relationship uncomfortable. Geoffrey's meetings, moreover, would go on and on, bogged down in detail; for all his qualities, he did not possess the businessman's talent for the despatch of business. However, he became a courageous and successful Chancellor, under the determined leadership of Margaret Thatcher, the First Lord of the Treasury. No-one can ever explain the blind faith which many intelligent men feel for an integrated political Europe, but that apart, Geoffrey has served his country well.

I was asked by Margaret Thatcher to join the Shadow Cabinet in December 1976. Alick Buchanan-Smith had had a disagreement with his colleagues about Scottish devolution, which he favoured, and had resigned; Teddy Taylor took his place, and I inherited Teddy's Shadow Trade portfolio, with Cecil Parkinson as my deputy. I knew Cecil well because he had served on successive Finance Bill Committees, together with Nick Ridley, David Howell, Peter Rees and Nigel Lawson. I had been in charge of our team which harassed Labour Treasury ministers late into the night. Often I tried to persuade my colleagues to curtail the Committee towards midnight, as I like early nights, but it was to no avail. Peter and Nigel, in particular, made brilliant, entertaining speeches right through into the early morning. I suppose it made some sense, but I have always been in favour of sensible working hours in the House of Commons, so that MPs can have a vestige of family life.

My principal role at this time was to wind up economic debates in the House at nine o'clock in the evening. It is quite a tricky task summing up the day's debate whilst making it light enough to entertain the troops. I established something of a reputation as a witty House of Commons man, and on occasion even managed to induce my colleagues to leave their dinner parties and their clubs to hear my speeches.

My other task, as Shadow Trade spokesman, was to get around the country persuading businessmen that the Tory Party had their interests at heart. It also involved listening to their views. Unfortunately, a substantial minority of businessmen ruined these occasions by showing off to their colleagues. Every gathering followed a predictable pattern: the shadow minister made his speech and then a vulgar, tanked-up businessman launched an attack on politicians generally, the

Tory Party and its leader. At that time, no luncheon party avoided the ritual claim that the Tory opposition was hopeless – and its leader, Thatcher, so incompetent that we could never hope to win an election. The same was said when Ted Heath was in opposition, and Iain Duncan Smith will now suffer from the same nonsense, particularly from the advocates of European integration. It is extraordinary that businessmen, who often crave some input into government, so often exclude themselves from the whole process by their ignorance of the necessary compromises and realities of political life. Why should an intelligent businessman believe that politics, or even government, has any affinity with business? It has none at all.

An episode from Cecil Parkinson's memoirs illustrates both these points:

John and I spent a lot of time meeting representatives of various organisations and interest groups. One of our earliest meetings was with Freddie Laker. We went down to Gatwick by train and were ushered into the presence of the great man, who then launched into a half-hour-long harangue about governments and politicians. He was clearly out to intimidate us, and when he had finished he said to John Nott, 'Well, have you any questions?' 'Yes,' said John, 'what time is the next train back to London? We didn't come here to listen to that kind of drivel, we came to learn about your airline, and if we're not going to, we might as well leave.' Freddie was not used to being spoken to in this way, and I waited for him to explode. To my surprise, after a moment's pause, his face broke into a broad grin, and he said, 'You and I are going to get on.'

Cecil also describes me in Parliamentary action:

An unusual feature of John's speeches was that he enjoyed teasing Mrs Thatcher. On one occasion, during a debate on prices, he talked about people appointed by the government to represent the consumer interest and argued that the views of what he called the 'statutory female aggravator' should not be exaggerated. The Labour Party was slow to catch on, but after he had repeated the remark, the Labour front bench started to point and jeer at Mrs Thatcher who was sitting alongside him. He pretended to be surprised and looked at where they were pointing. 'I realised that there was a possibility that some honourable Members might point in the direction of my right honourable friend the leader of the opposition, but she is one of the boys.' The whole House, including Mrs Thatcher, burst out laughing.

It was during these years, the mid-to-late 1970s, that Keith Joseph came into his own; he led the philosophical fight-back after the Macmillan/Heath years. He made a series of speeches around the country which echoed the economic principles enunciated by Powell and others in the 1960s. His courage in the face of intellectual and even physical abuse from left-wing students – and from the fashionable intelligentsia of the soft centre – was considerable. He treated with disdain the so-called 'middle way', which was and still is the chosen mantra of the Tory left. 'We must not abandon the centre, etc., etc. …' The middle way, argued Keith, 'moved continuously to the left by its own dynamics'. Far from achieving social harmony and strengthening the centre, 'it has created resentment and conflict'. His speeches echoed the claim of Richard Law, ten years earlier, that the task of politicians was to influence the tide, not embrace it. The strong fish swims against the current.

Keith recruited two radical businessmen, John Hoskyns and Norman Strauss; but as with Alfred Sherman, they had less influence on the overall direction of policy in the first Thatcher government than is often suggested – a fact partly attributable to their expressed contempt for politicians, the civil service and the political process. Although they had considerable personal influence on Mrs Thatcher, I doubt if Whitelaw and Carrington and the rest of the senior ministers of the Heath era were aware of their existence. At Margaret Thatcher's request, they wrote in 1977 an aggressive and doom-laden tract, *Stepping Stones*, about the state of the country, arguing strongly for the destruction of the power and privileges of the over-mighty trade unions. Without a root-and-branch attack on the unions, they insisted, nothing else was possible. Their principal target, as Shadow Employment Secretary, was Jim Prior, who was all in favour of a softly-softly approach to trade union reform. Hoskyns and Strauss tried unsuccessfully to get him moved.

However, the main influence on Jim, who fought a relentless war against Hoskyns, Strauss and Sherman, was the course of events. First, in 1977, there occurred the violent picketing at Grunwick, with unforgivable abuse against the workers who wanted to carry on with their jobs; and then in 1978–79 came the infamous 'Winter of Discontent', with rubbish piling up on the streets and the dead being left unburied. Reluctantly, I believe, Jim Prior moved towards the necessity of some form of legislation.

Geoffrey Howe had a good relationship with Hoskyns and Strauss, and on one occasion assembled us to discuss policy over Sunday lunch in his house in Lambeth. But all the wise and apolitical words of this policy-making gathering were obliterated for me by the behaviour of Quintin, Geoffrey's Jack Russell. As soon as we had finished our meal, Quintin was allowed to lick the plates clean; I was so disgusted that I could not thereafter contribute a single pearl of wisdom to the gathering. In the meantime, work went on in Geoffrey's Economic Reconstruction Group, which included David Howell, Nigel Lawson, Peter Rees, Nick Ridley and John Biffen as well as myself.

The Shadow Cabinet was an unsatisfactory forum. Margaret, being an outsider by instinct and a woman to boot, was nonetheless anxious not to alienate the old guard; nearly all the key members of Heath's Cabinet, even Reggie Maudling, had moved effortlessly into the Shadow Cabinet. Margaret was too careful, and certainly not strong enough, to take them on. There was little doubt that they believed she would fail; and if they stayed around for long enough, sanity would return in the form of another consensus candidate of whom they might approve. I suspect they felt it would have to be a man – a man with a proper sense of traditional hierarchy, with the correct sense of how things should be done, with an understanding of the limitations of the political process and with an aristocratic disdain for activism in any form.

When I later joined the Cabinet in 1979, the first Thatcher Cabinet, it was divided. I call it a division between the traditional Whigs and the radical Tories, but these labels are rarely used and understood today. The radical Tories, of whom there were probably only five or six out of a Cabinet of twenty-three, were determined to meet the problems of the country head-on, but the Whigs eschewed confrontation. Their approach was best represented in the honourable character of Peter Carrington. Some phrases in his memoirs are revealing. 'One should not precipitate these things …', 'Adjustments take time …', 'I thought we could improve the atmosphere'. This is the politics of diplomacy, not of government. But it was also the politics of Macmillan back in the 1950s and 1960s: under his premiership, government was about 'the management of decline' – and the avoidance of conflict with organised labour which under the Heath and Callaghan Governments nearly brought the country to its knees.

The journalist (and former MP) Matthew Parris, referring to Mrs Thatcher, has expressed the situation well: 'Nobody could have fought through the spoken and unspoken prejudices of the '50s; the giggles and sneers of the '60s; and the concealed male resentment and subtle male condescension of the '70s and '80s, without bearing the scars. An outsider to her party cannot know what she has put up with.' She was to get her revenge in due course.

Although, as always in the Tory Party, the proper courtesies were maintained, there were already two camps influencing policy. On the one hand there was Keith Joseph and his allies, who had the ear of Margaret even though she was very careful not to give them any special status or public support; on the other, there was the Conservative Research Department under the direction of the left-wing Chris Patten and including characters like Michael Portillo, who used to work for me. I used to sit at the Shadow Cabinet table opposite Chris Patten, who attended in the margins. Very much an ally of Ian Gilmour, Peter Walker and the rest, he would sit there with a perpetual smirk on his face, as Margaret and her allies tried to sharpen up policy, normally failing in the face of opposition from the old guard. I really disliked Chris Patten's politics at that time and still do – he only partially retrieved himself, in my eyes, with his courageous stand for democracy in Hong Kong.

Accordingly, the Shadow Cabinet roughly divided into two camps: Carrington, Gilmour, Pym, Prior, St John Stevas, often supported by Heseltine and Hailsham, taking one view, and Joseph, Angus Maude, Sally Oppenheim, Airey Neave and Thorneycroft taking another. Geoffrey Howe, the ultimate reasoning lawyer, straddled the two groups with his long-winded ambivalence and his evolving diplomatic skills. Whitelaw always pretended to support the Leader, but pleaded consensus, thereby making progress on policy-making virtually impossible. The Shadow Cabinet was divided. All of this found its true expression in the cautious Tory manifesto on which we fought the 1979 election; with only minor exceptions, it could have been written by Ted Heath. The first draft was in fact written by Chris Patten, which amounted to much the same thing.

The Callaghan Government had survived only as part of the Lib-Lab Pact. The political and economic climate was very unstable, and Callaghan was continually held to ransom by the unions and an endless series of unofficial strikes. The appalling economic situation that the Labour government had inherited from the Tories in 1974 had led eventually, under Healey's chancellorship, to the appointment in 1976 of the IMF mission, which had helped to restore some stability. But the dying Labour administration could only contain the wages explosion by appointing Professor Clegg to undertake a study of public sector pay. His report was eventually to cause immense difficulties for us. In March 1979, Callaghan lost a vote of confidence and named 3 May as polling day.

I was not a public figure; indeed, as a junior member of the Shadow Cabinet, I was hardly known. It was not in my nature to wield the mace about my head like Michael Heseltine, which might have helped my reputation, or otherwise. So I was not called upon to play a prominent role in the campaign and confined my speaking engagements to the West Country, where I had a higher profile. However, as always during an election campaign, there was a moment of panic – and I was asked by Tim Bell of Saatchi & Saatchi to do a television take for a party political broadcast. I protested about my inexperience and lack of ability in this medium. But they insisted, and so I was helicoptered from my front lawn in Cornwall to London, where after much coaching and several retakes my contribution was duly 'canned' on account of its inadequacies. In the new era of television politics, I was never going to meet the performing skills required – a world of sound-bite politics, where style is all.

Two days before polling day, Ferdinand Mount looked ahead in the *Evening Standard* to a Tory victory. After referring to me in passing as 'a particular favourite of Thatcher's' – not necessarily true – he went on to point out that the majority of the Shadow Cabinet 'still belong to the liberal, moderate or wishy-washy wing (choose your own adjective), the sort that believes in incomes policy and proportional representation and not being too beastly to the unions'. And he warned: 'For all Mrs Thatcher's own messianic spirit, the danger remains that a Thatcher Government will do too little rather than too much.'

~

The Conservatives won with an overall majority of forty-three. In my own constituency, I obtained, like many of my colleagues, a large majority – the greatest that St Ives had ever had – and I remained on the farm to have a couple of days' rest, not knowing, of course, which job might come my way. I was hoping very much that I would go to Trade. I had held the job in opposition; I was familiar with the issues; and I liked my team. The only other possibility, for a relatively junior member of the Shadow Cabinet, seemed to be to return to the Treasury as Chief Secretary. I had worked alongside the Chief Secretary in Ted Heath's Government and it was a job of great importance within Whitehall, particularly if it was in the Cabinet. But I wasn't sure that I would work very easily with Geoffrey Howe and, secondly, I wanted my own department. In fact, John Biffen was made Chief Secretary, which delighted me.

It was on the Saturday after the election that the new PM telephoned me:

John, I have been thinking about it and I would like you to stay at Trade.

PM, I would be delighted. I assume it will be in the Cabinet.

Oh yes, and I have also decided to combine under you and Trade, the Department of Prices and Consumer Affairs. It will, of course, be a powerful department, a major economic one since Prices and Consumer Affairs and Trade together will form a major economic policy unit.

There is no job, PM, that I would like better. I am most grateful to you. Perhaps you would be so kind as to let me know who you think of appointing as my junior ministers I will wait here in Cornwall until I hear from you.

Yes, I will ring you back.

In due course, another call came from No. 10:

John, I've been thinking about your junior ministers – would you be prepared to have a lord?

Well, if you insist, Margaret, I will have a lord, but there are no political lords that I know very well and none that I would particularly want. I would much prefer it if some other department had a peer.

Well, I may have to come back to you on this subject, but for the time being let's leave that on one side. Do you think you could possibly have Norman Tebbit? He's worked extremely hard and he was a very vigorous member of the opposition, I'd like to find him a slot somewhere.

Yes, I would be happy to have Norman Tebbit in my team. I think the natural thing for Norman would be the aviation job [Aviation and Shipping were then part of the Board of Trade] since, as an ex-British Airways man, he knows that field very well indeed.

I agree with you, let's do that. The other man whom I had in mind is also a pilot, and he is a peer [Lord Trefgarne]. Would you be prepared to have him too?

Look, Margaret, I honestly think that one pilot is enough – can we leave it there?

And so, in an hour or two, my team was settled – a very good one too. It consisted of Sally Oppenheim and Cecil Parkinson as the Ministers of State for Consumer Affairs and Trade respectively, and Norman Tebbit. Finally, towards the end of the formation of the administration, I had another call asking if I would be prepared to have Reg Eyre as my other Parliamentary Secretary. Reg had served in earlier governments. He was a delightful man, a solicitor, a person upon whom one could absolutely rely. So Reg joined the team and I gave him the task of overseeing company law. We worked well together as a team and Trade was a happy department with a very considerable *esprit de corps*. I was also fortunate – as I was in all my ministerial departments – in having a quite outstanding Permanent Secretary, Sir Kenneth Clucas. He had been the Permanent Secretary at the Department of Prices and Consumer Affairs and made the transition from Shirley Williams, and then Hattersley to Nott, with patience and good humour!

I had already seen sufficient of the workings of government to know that, as a cabinet minister, my red boxes would not dominate me in the same way that they had done in the Treasury. I remember very clearly indeed the first paper that had been placed for me in that box. It was an extremely well-argued piece containing many underlying memoranda, all of which I read with care, recommending that I should not rush into any hasty conclusions about the Price Commission, which the Labour government had inherited from Heath. The paper agreed that it needed reforming and, in accordance with the Conservative manifesto, required substantial changes to its composition and powers; but broadly speaking, the advice was that I should tread warily, and perhaps an opportunity might present itself for a serious review of all the options as soon as I was in a position to call a meeting.

On my return to London, I called my first ministerial meeting in the department, which included Ken Clucas, the Permanent Secretary. We discussed the Price Commission, which had a major institutional function to perform in a climate where the prospect for prices was very poor – not least due to the pending report of the Clegg Commission on public sector pay. Sally Oppenheim led the call for the abandonment of it, root and branch. She was echoed by Parkinson and Tebbit. For my part, I was not sure that I could persuade the new Prime Minister to take such a brave step, as I had seen her own caution in Shadow Cabinet and in the ambivalence we had expressed towards price control in our manifesto; however, I decided that it was now or never. If the Price Commission survived our first few months in office, I could see there being a hundred foolish reasons given, as prices rose, for not getting rid of it. I therefore recommended to Margaret Thatcher that we should announce the abolition in the impending Queen's Speech, the first occasion for setting out the proposals of the new government. With some courage – and I am sure against the consensus of Whitehall advice – the Prime Minister agreed to its abolition.

I am happy to say that, whilst the abolition of statutory price, dividend and wage controls caused considerable pain, as all the economic indicators moved in the wrong direction between 1979 and 1981, this step laid the foundations for the prosperity and economic freedom of the later Thatcher years. Together with the abolition later in 1979 of exchange controls – for which bold, controversial step Nigel Lawson and I were the greatest proponents – it established the United Kingdom as an open world economy, based on the liberal economics that I had espoused since my undergraduate days at Cambridge.

Meanwhile, the department strongly urged that I should attend the meetings of UNCTAD (the United Nations Conference on Trade and Development) in Manila, regarded by the Trade officials as of the highest importance. I refused, and sent Cecil Parkinson in my place. I did not intend to be stuck for a week on the other side of the world whilst the new government was settling in. Indeed, I wanted to be a somewhat land-based Trade Secretary, able to attend the important Cabinet Committee meetings, and accordingly I left most of the travelling whilst Parliament was sitting to Cecil. Even so, it sometimes felt during Parliamentary recesses as if I was covering half the world.

The officials used to bring me a proposed list of travelling destinations twice a year. I noticed that they always excluded South Korea, a country of growing consequence for our trade. 'Why not South Korea?' I asked on several occasions, but received only a sort of blank look in return. Eventually, I called in Ken Clucas to nail it down:

Well, we do not recommend it because of the problems encountered by one of your predecessors. The Foreign Office would not want a similar incident to be repeated.

What was the incident?

Well, one of your predecessors was taken to a party with lots of girls in attendance and, when one of them put their hands on his thigh, he walked

My parents' marriage, 1930

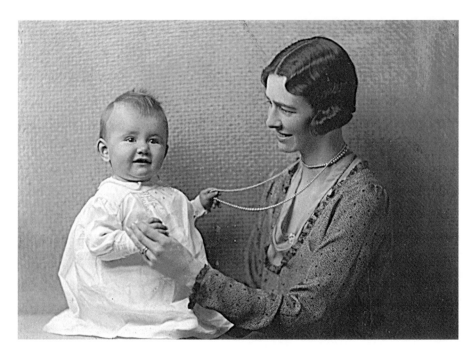

My mother and me aged 10 months

Grandfather and great-grandfather Francis outside Bridestowe Rectory on Dartmoor, 1910: 'A hunting parson and his son'

Signals Officer, 1/2 Gurkha Rifles, Malaya, 1954

Defence Secretary, presenting sword of honour, Sandhurst passing-out parade, 1982

Captain Narbir Tharpa, 2nd Gurkha Rifles, the first Queen's Orderly Officer

2nd Lieutenant, 1st Battalion the Royal Scots; escort for battalion train to Berlin, 1951

My scout car with signalman, Malaya, 1953

Rifleman Bhimbahadur Gurung with kukri and patchet gun

Family photo for election address, 1970: with Julian, William and Saša

Miloska, daffodil fields

William and Thomas Nott, mackerel fishing off St Michael's Mount

Another grandchild: Saffron Swire with Lillie

Admiral Fieldhouse, Commander of the Falklands Task Force,
and myself during the campaign

Caspar Weinberger, US Secretary of Defense, and myself in a Tornado
just before the Falklands crisis

Trewinnard, 1835 – our home in Cornwall. It is still like this today

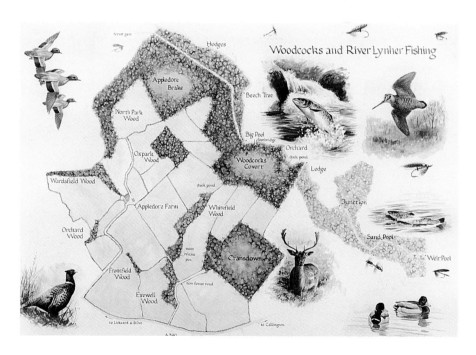

Woodcocks – our small sporting estate in Cornwall

out in disgust. The South Koreans were deeply offended, and it caused quite a strain in Anglo–Korean relations.

That settles it. I am going – it sounds just the place for me.

When I got there, I found that my Korean hosts in Seoul had arranged a similar Keesam party for me; and, accompanied by the British ambassador, we arrived at this high-class place of entertainment. There was a collection of the most beautiful girls in traditional Korean costume. My host, the elderly chairman of Korea's largest conglomerate, Hyundai, took the most beautiful girl as his partner. I was given the second most beautiful, the British ambassador the third, and so on. We sat around a low table on cushions, and our partners chose the delicacies for us and steered them into our mouths. I had a most enjoyable evening, not dissimilar from my earlier parties in Singapore. In due course, my partner's hand strayed under the table and she started stroking my thigh. I knew instantly that this was a country with which we must intensify our diplomatic and trade relations – the visit was a success.

Less happily, Carrington as Foreign Secretary breezed through Baghdad one day, saw Saddam Hussein, and agreed that efforts should be made to re-establish more friendly diplomatic and trade relations between our two countries. I was the fall-guy sent out to handle this unenviable task. My host, the Commerce Minister, was the most disgusting thug; he wore khaki uniform throughout and exhibited a revolver at his waist. He drove me around Baghdad in a car with accompanying outriders and sirens blazing and with curtains over the windows – and for three days we hardly spoke, except very formally at meetings through interpreters. I met many of Saddam's senior ministers, without exception equally brutal thugs. On the final evening, I was taken to a famous Baghdad restaurant, where suddenly my host embraced me and began drinking large quantities of hooch. A back-slapping, cheerful evening resulted. I am ashamed that I joined in the fun. It was, however, the most unpleasant trip of my entire political career – they were a nasty bunch. Nonetheless, we did do business with them.

On another trip, I was returning from Brazil to visit Nigeria. As the Varig aeroplane approached Lagos, we were told that we were being diverted to Accra in Ghana due to a strike. When we landed in Accra, I was instructed not to leave the plane until the British High Commissioner had come on board to see me. A nervous, perspiring figure, he said that my diversion to Accra was a disaster. 'Why?' I asked. 'Because you, Secretary of State, have cancelled all flights from Ghana to the UK from tomorrow, because the Ghanaians have refused to pay their landing fees at Heathrow.' I had forgotten, but it was true. 'Do you want to come to my residence, and I will see if we can discreetly ask one or two members of the government to meet you?' In due course, the knowledge that this dreadful British minister was in Accra spread around the town – and by lunchtime, half the Ghanaian government had encamped at the High Commissioner's residence.

The Ghanaians are lovely people, easier than the south Nigerians, and the ministers were a delight. They did not seem to hold my authoritarian behaviour against me, and we sat down to discuss how I could assist their economy, and how I was going to get out of Accra on the last Ghanaian Airways VC10 flight back to London that night. It proved an expensive diversion, as in instant discussions over the faltering telephone line with the Trade and Foreign Offices in London, I managed to divert several million pounds of extra aid their way. They were delighted, and I was released from house imprisonment and escorted by half the chattering cabinet to the airport to bid me farewell. I never found out how we resolved the question of their unpaid bills at Heathrow, but I have been in love with the Ghanaians, with all their dreadful problems, ever since.

Another African episode, later in my ministerial career, also had its moments of frisson. On a Defence trip, I was supposed to be going on to Indonesia from India and Nepal, but at the last minute this was cancelled by the Indonesians. So instead, I decided to take our RAF VC10 to the recently independent Zimbabwe, where we had a military mission. Halfway there, I received a message from the Foreign Office to the effect that Mugabe's people were torturing some white Rhodesian air force pilots (claiming they had blown up half the air force) and that the Foreign Office wanted me to see Mugabe and remonstrate with him. Accordingly, I arranged to have breakfast with him the next day. He was all charm, and in my most tactful way I asked him if he would either bring the pilots to trial or release them. Unfortunately, this was the cue for Mugabe to go ballistic – and the breakfast ended hurriedly, without any mutual professions of undying friendship.

Appropriately, given all this time in the skies, my greatest blow for free trade occurred in the airline business. First, in July 1979, I announced the government's intention to privatise British Airways. It was the first privatisation announcement of the Thatcher Government. I had been part of Geoffrey Howe's and Nick Ridley's study groups to make the process really happen – in contrast to the failure of the Heath Government, when only the Carlisle pubs and Thomas Cook left the public sector. I was glad that we were first over the privatisation fences, especially as over the next few years the privatisation process helped to transform the economy. Unfortunately, British Airways became embroiled in an anti-trust suit in the US and it did not actually join the private sector until much later, when Lazard Brothers, under my chairmanship, brought it to the stock market.

I was also responsible for the appointment of John King as chairman. I had inherited Frank McFadzean, the former chairman of Shell, but he wanted to retire. Rather unwisely, I succumbed to the pleading of BA itself for an internal candidate and agreed to the appointment of Ross Stainton – a good man, but not the ruthless businessman required. When the time came, I was at a loss to find a successor to him – until one day Ken Clucas came to my office, said that he had just met John King at lunch, and wondered whether he would be a candidate. I knew from my City days of John King's rise from humble beginnings to build a very successful bearings business, and I was attracted to the idea. One day he arrived to see me after a good lunch, with a long wet cigar sticking out of his mouth, and I thought to myself, 'God, what am I doing?' I introduced him to Norman Tebbit and, although we had our doubts, I agreed to pass the appointment across the Prime Minister. 'John King, why do you want him?' Margaret asked rather aggressively. 'Is he really the right man?' 'I cannot be sure,' I replied, but I persisted that we should give it a go. John King has told the world ever since that he was appointed by Margaret Thatcher. If that pleases the tycoon, who has become very grand in his old age, it is all right by me! He turned out to be a brilliant chairman, and transformed the airline's prospects.

British Airways was notorious, in the days before John King's surgery, for its unreliability. This was particularly evident in its bad service to Hong Kong, where it had a British monopoly position and where its record of unpunctuality was such that Lufthansa was taking more and more of the Hong Kong traffic. Not surprisingly, I was pressed to put another airline on the Hong Kong route. The negotiation of bilateral air service agreements took up a lot of time; the Americans were always greedy and unreasonable on the transatlantic route; they would not let our airlines service their domestic cities. Hong Kong, however, was a British colony and, for the first time, we had freedom to make a choice. I was pressed to allow Cathay Pacific, which described itself as Hong

Kong's 'own' airline, to run a service to London. Freddie Laker, meanwhile, was trying to open up a round-the-world ticket, while British Caledonian was always griping at the preference given on routes to British Airways.

I called in the experts and was told, with the exception of one dissenting junior Board of Trade lawyer, that I could put only one extra airline on the route. The Act was very clear, I was informed. I only had the power to award a route if it was 'economic' – and clearly more than one airline, in addition to British Airways, would make it 'uneconomic'. 'Why?' I asked. They looked at me as if I was daft. How could three, let alone four, airlines be 'economic' if they were sharing out the traffic now held by only one? I persisted, and the junior lawyer, Robert Ayling (who subsequently became chief executive of BA), took my side against his peers, arguing that the law was there to be interpreted in a favourable way for the client, me.

In the end, I gave rights to Cathay Pacific, Freddie Laker and British Caledonian, which all joined British Airways. The civil servants muttered; their negativism had been overridden. Making the public announcement, I said that I had been convinced 'by the Laker argument that there is a large untapped market for air services' that were 'safe, efficient and cheap'. This turned out to be the case. Competition on the route intensified, the fares came down, the traffic vastly increased, and it has become an 'economic' route for everyone. The consumer, the poor passenger, now has choice – so British Airways has to run on time.

Only one incident of consequence arose in the field of company law. The officials had prepared a companies bill, which became the Companies Act, 1980. I was consulted about insider trading and resisted the request that it should be made a criminal offence. I contended that it was better that it should be a civil offence, enabling injured parties to sue more easily for losses incurred. The officials joined the Bank of England in insisting that it should be a criminal offence; the City wanted it, not least to answer the political charge that the City was rife with insider dealing. I surrendered to the City with misgivings – and over twenty years later, I think it is very hard to say that I was not right all along. Very few criminal charges for insider dealing have been successful, whereas civil suits would have had much greater success.

Not long after I had arrived in my office, I had a delegation from the Stock Exchange, insisting that we should remove its reference to the Restrictive Practices Court which had originally been made by Shirley Williams. I believed that the whole of the City was rife with restrictive practices, and I have described them in an earlier chapter. In any event, I did not see how we could apply one law to capital and another to labour, given that we were about to launch an attack on the restrictive practices of the trade unions. Some of the leading Stock Exchange firms had been major financial contributors to the Tory Party and, whilst no-one ever said so, it was clear that the concession they wanted from me was seen as a *quid pro quo* for their support. I was very unpopular in the City for refusing to exempt the Stock Exchange (the chairman, Nicholas Goodison, publicly condemned a 'weak political move'), as was my equally obdurate successor, John Biffen; but I think that by doing so, we did something to force that institution's reform – eventually leading, for good or ill, to the 'Big Bang' that followed Cecil Parkinson's agreement with Goodison in 1983.

All during my time at Trade, of course, the domestic economic situation was worsening and unemployment was rising sharply. We were besieged by demands to restrict imports of cars, textiles and electronic goods, particularly from Japan, where we had a large and growing imbalance of trade. I visited Japan to protest at their illiberal import policies, but it was no good. Although trade policy was in the hands of the European Community, Margaret Thatcher was determined to find some way of handbagging Japan – they certainly deserved it. At several meetings, I tried to explain to Margaret that trade was multilateral, not bilateral, in its impact. For example, the volume of our exports of manufactured goods to Australia was in part dependent on Australia's exports of primary products to Japan. If we took action against one country in the loop of international trade, the consequences of generally lower international trade would come back at us; with 30 per cent of all our gross domestic product going into exports, we had an interest in widening free trade, not restricting it. Margaret Thatcher never believed in liberal economics – it is a complete misreading of her beliefs to depict her as a nineteenth-century Liberal. Cecil Parkinson and I used to argue free trade with her, but emotionally she was an authoritarian and a protectionist.

The situation was most acute in the textile industry. As the money squeeze tightened, and sterling rose, textile imports flooded into the country. Delegation after delegation came to see me as unemployment in the North and the Midlands rose dramatically. In 1979 the textile industry employed nearly 1½ million workers, by 1982 the numbers had virtually halved – at least another half a million were added to the dole queues. I felt devastated for these people. Eventually I surrendered to the pressure and persuaded the European

Commission to impose anti-dumping duties against cheap textile imports. It was a foolish mistake. I had imagined that meeting the urgent request of the textile lobby would bring them some relief, but the opposite was the case. An equally large section of the textile industry was dependent on these cheap imports, which were then recycled into exports of finished goods. I learned a solid lesson: governments tamper with free trade at their peril.

~

Throughout the first Thatcher Government the internal atmosphere was poor. This was caused not only by genuine disagreement over philosophy and policy, mainly in the economic domain, but also by indiscretion and background press briefing. Both sides were responsible for disloyal and indiscreet comments to the vultures in the parliamentary press lobby. But the principal responsibility for the bad blood created by leaks and gossip undoubtedly lay with No. 10 Downing Street.

Politics being the life-blood of Margaret Thatcher, she had an insatiable urge to gossip among her immediate circle about her ministers – their attitudes, their failings, and what she could do about them. It was extraordinary how so many disagreements over policy were personalised and found themselves into the pages of the press. Forthcoming reshuffles surfaced there with regularity, usually accompanied by suitable canards about the intended victims. To some degree, these stories were simply generated by background briefings from No. 10, but rather worse was the extent to which a small coterie of her immediate friends and political allies traded on her friendship by gossiping around the clubs and dinner parties of London. Much of the gossip came from several unelected political allies of Margaret from within the public relations profession. I am afraid that for anyone who inhabits this world, the leaking of gossip and inside knowledge, presented in an interesting way, is the irresistible fast track to popularity, reputation and success.

I suffered much less from background gossip and political malice than many others, because in these early years of Thatcher's premiership I happened to agree with the broad thrust of what the government was doing and was therefore seen to be 'one of us'. But towards the end of my time I had some serious disagreements, and almost instantly No. 10 was briefing against me, and articles appeared in the press criticising me personally. This practice was a major stain on the first Thatcher administration, and the denial that No. 10 ever had anything to do with it is, of course, untrue. If one compares the unending flow of press tittle-tattle and malice flowing from inside the Thatcher government, with the Heath and Major administrations where it was virtually non-existent, it is clear where the responsibility lay. This inability or unwillingness to curb the practice, must, I am sure, have been a contributory factor to Margaret Thatcher's downfall.

There was another extraordinary practice, whereby Margaret Thatcher, whilst not openly disagreeing with her ministers, made it clear by gesture and body language when she did so. It seemed as if we lived in a world where collective responsibility lay with us, but not with her. There was a well-known episode when she was seen applauding vigorously as the audience at a Conservative conference jeered at a section of Whitelaw's speech. It is extraordinary how she felt able to preside over a government which she was seen to criticise. I suspect that from 1983 onwards – after my departure, and when Margaret had a Cabinet more amenable to her mastery of affairs – this habit diminished. But if there was any practice that turned me against the later Thatcher Governments, it was this behaviour, exemplified by the occasion when Ingham briefed against John Biffen, calling him 'a semi-detached minister'.

During the first Thatcher Government, I was fortunate enough to be a member of the key committees – 'E' Committee and 'OD', i.e. the Economic and Overseas and Defence Policy Committees – two out of the three decision-making bodies of government. Although perfunctory exchanges of view about economic policy took place in full Cabinet, virtually no decisions were taken there. Instead, much of its time was (and no doubt is) taken up with hearing from the Foreign Secretary about various irrelevant happenings around the world and in deciding the following week's parliamentary business. I remember only one full Cabinet meeting to decide the following year's public expenditure; and I suspect, after my early departure from politics, Margaret Thatcher was never so foolish ever to refer again any matter of consequence to a body invariably numbering well over twenty ministers.

Indeed, during my tenure as Trade Secretary (or President of the Board of Trade, as Michael Heseltine characteristically preferred to call the job when he did it), I spent more time on E Committee and OD Committee than I did in the department. Each of these committees, chaired by the Prime Minister, numbered between eight and twelve members, depending on the subject under discussion. To my enormous benefit, I had at Trade a dedicated and expert team, set up by Ken Clucas, to brief me for every meeting of the E Committee and OD. It was formed out of the nucleus of experts who had been in the Department of Prices and Consumer Affairs, and they had briefed my predecessors (Shirley Williams and Hattersley) in that now collapsed department. When I attended meetings – often on widely varied subjects, sometimes four or five times a week – I was reasonably well briefed on the arguments. Moreover, I had an excellent private secretary called Tom Harris, who was succeeded by Stuart Hampson, who had also been Hattersley's private secretary. Stuart is now the chairman of the John Lewis Partnership.

By contrast, when I arrived at the Ministry of Defence, I had no such briefing team. The MoD was simply not interested in the affairs of other departments, and I could hardly ask for a briefing team when I was cutting back quite drastically on the civil service numbers in my own department. I reduced the size of the civil service by about a third during my two years at Defence. So, although I remained a member of E Committee, I ceased to be fully briefed for all the meetings. My private secretary simply produced papers on sometimes complicated issues, with a top paper saying, 'There is no Defence interest in this subject'!

OD was the main Foreign Office battleground on such subjects as our contribution to the European budget, preparations for a succession of pointless summits, our stance towards the Common Agricultural Policy, and European affairs generally, as well as most matters concerned with defence and defence procurement.

Britain's contribution to the EEC budget saw Margaret Thatcher at her most determined and the Foreign Office at its most feeble, appeasing self. The final deal on the budget was not concluded until 1984, but I participated in the early discussions in OD about our negotiating tactics and saw the interim agreement which resulted. Instead of the Foreign Office accepting from the outset the gross inequity of the British position, putting all their efforts into getting it right, they fought a continual rearguard action with the Prime Minister, lest our forthright demands caused some offence to our European allies. Given their priorities, they would have sought a pathetic compromise long before the going got tough.

I have never been able to understand how a collection of such intelligent, pleasant and well-meaning men can be seduced by the gutless culture of this institution. After I left politics, several of the leading ambassadorial posts were filled by my former friends from Cambridge; it was sad to see how such good men had succumbed to the appeasement, and indignity, which goes under the name of 'diplomacy' Of course, foreign relations have to be a game of give and take, but why is it necessary so often to be embarrassed about our national interest and so reluctant to offend those who are nakedly asserting theirs?

Ian Gilmour was in immediate charge of the negotiations on the budget, and Ian is an archetypal Foreign Office man. I do not think that Ian was quite such a passionate European as Geoffrey Howe or Ted Heath – passion is not one of his characteristics. But he disseminated a high degree of scepticism in response to Margaret Thatcher's aggression; as her determination to get her way increased, so his languor intensified. Peter Carrington normally attended the meetings, and their combined superciliousness towards this 'impossible' woman was an interesting aspect of this particular contest.

Peter Middleton, who had been Tony Barber's press man and whom I had always liked during my time in the Treasury, was in charge of the numbers, which were obscure. No-one quite knew what the British contribution would turn out to be. But it was clear that the structure and size of British agriculture, together with our reliance on traditional imports from outside the Community, would combine to make our net contribution as high as that of the Germans, and much more than that of the French, at a time when both these countries had a gross national product far in excess of our own. We published our estimate of the British contribution and the Commission published theirs. Armed with the Commission's numbers, Margaret Thatcher then set out on a public crusade to reduce our net contribution to nil. She came up against the solid phalanx of Schmidt and Giscard, then Chancellor of Germany and President of France respectively, and of course the Commission itself. She had no friends, except for the British Treasury and a few allies like myself on OD.

The Foreign Office, as an institution, was clearly appalled at the damage she was doing among our friends and allies; it was desperate for a compromise – in other words, for diplomacy to be allowed to work, as usual against our national interest. Carrington and Gilmour came back to OD with a suggested package of trade-offs: North Sea Oil, agricultural exports, in fact anything to stop this damage to our reputation as good and faithful subscribers to the European ideal – an ideal, I have to say, that was not much in evidence when it came to the interests of France and Germany.

The Dublin summit in November 1979 passed with a minor improvement of the British position, but no agreement. A series of ministerial meetings, proposals and counter-proposals came before OD, all culminating in the Luxemburg summit in April 1980 where the Europeans agreed to double their original offer of £350m to £750m. Margaret Thatcher turned it down, because of the short-term nature of the offer. Britain's relations with her European partners were in a state of collapse, but the Foreign Office eventually, at the end of May, achieved a minor improvement on the Luxemburg terms. When Carrington and Gilmour brought these new terms to OD for agreement, there was a total impasse. I supported Thatcher, but I was beginning to have my doubts about the wisdom of fighting further. Why, the following week, Thatcher backed down, with bad grace, I do not know; but I wonder if Carrington and Gilmour, unbeknown to the rest of us, had threatened resignation. They were probably right to do so, because the row had gone on long enough – and, as all of us learned in our several ways, Margaret when hyped up on one of her missions became an extremist.

The Economic Committee tended to be less controversial, because most strategic economic matters were decided outside the Cabinet committee structure – and anyhow, unlike OD, Margaret Thatcher had a majority of like-minded colleagues with her, namely Geoffrey Howe, Keith Joseph, John Biffen and myself. Most weeks the four of us met over breakfast in the Prime Minister's flat to plan our position on economic issues in the week ahead. The idea was that we would form a solid phalanx against the 'Wets', who wanted to reverse the economic policy. We therefore dominated E Committee, where the Prime Minister also had the backing of Whitelaw. He always supported the Prime Minister – in spite of his consensus inclinations, whatever the subject – regardless of whether she was advocating nonsense or not.

E Committee was, however, the main forum for vigorous punch-ups between Jim Prior and Margaret on the subject of trade union reform. Here I must interpolate my praise for Jim. He was far and away the most candid and vigorous spokesman for the 'Wets', but unlike the rest of them, Jim Prior was no 'Wet'. He gave as good as he got. The rows between him and Thatcher were a delight. Margaret never lost her cool, but was often outrageously aggressive and rude; Jim was never rude, but he grew more and more red in the face as the row raged across the table. In his very human behaviour and overt exasperation, he was the exact opposite of Carrington and Gilmour.

Jim was not without allies on the Committee, and it is a very false reading of history to suggest that Margaret's natural allies were always on her side. Indeed, every meeting was preceded by an opening shot from Margaret stating the conclusion that we should reach. This just provoked controversy unnecessarily, and many meetings began, as a result of her poor handling of the Committee, with her finding herself in a minority of one. She was an absolutely rotten chairman. Indeed, she saw herself as a chief executive and was constitutionally incapable of sitting on the fence until she saw the moment when she could swing the debate her way. This is the way that all skilful chairmen behave, and it was a skill honed to perfection by the mandarins; however, the times required a chief executive, not a chairman, so there is no criticism of her for that.

A story from a year or two later captures perfectly the Thatcher style. Towards the end of the Falklands campaign, in early June 1982, President Reagan attended a G7 summit at Versailles and returned via London. In due course the normal meeting between Prime Minister and President took place at No. 10, with Pym and I attending. Margaret had been given a list of world-shattering issues which she wished to raise with the President; and with her list in front of her, she started on a detailed harangue without once drawing breath. Reagan sat opposite, doodling on a pad, and smiling at her very sweetly. Still she battled on. Reagan said nothing. Indeed, it would have been impossible to interrupt. After half an hour or so – no dialogue having taken place – she beamed across the table and said, 'Ron, what would you like to say?' 'Oh,' said Reagan, 'I don't have anything Margaret, but it was very interesting.' And wholly unfazed, he got up to go. I might add that I made a move to gather up his doodle; but as Meese, his chief of staff, reached the door, he turned back and hastily picked it up. Thus was I denied an interesting historical document.

On the thorny issue of the unions, Jim Prior started from the position that we needed their co-operation, although he was always clear that they could not be allowed to be an arm of government, as they had become during the Heath Government. He was cautious about the place of the law and wanted to ensure that whatever was passed met with at least the reluctant acquiescence of the unions. He was often supported by Quintin Hailsham (the Lord Chancellor) in this view. Geoffrey Howe was a hawk and seemed to me to have a wholly exaggerated expectation of how the law might work, in spite of the abject failure of the Heath Government's Industrial Relations Act, which he had drafted. Insofar as I had a position, I often supported Jim Prior, to the disquiet of Thatcher. In 1979–80, although the public was coming our way on the need to curb the unions, I felt that a stage-by-stage approach had the best chance of success.

The main area of dispute, particularly between Prior and Howe, lay in the abolition of the closed shop and more rigid laws against violent picketing and secondary action. Jim was pushed further than initially he would have liked, but gained a Pyrrhic victory with his Employment Act of 1980. His approach did not survive the appointment of Norman Tebbit in September 1981 to succeed him. I view trade union reform, together with the sale of council houses and privatisation, as the key successes of the Thatcher years, but it took the whole of the first parliament to get trade union reform implemented. I believe that the containment and then near-elimination of trade union political power was more the consequence of high unemployment, brought about by a fierce monetary policy and the high price of sterling, than it was of legislation; but undoubtedly the law had its place.

I must now briefly tell that larger economic story. In the crucial first six months after the May 1979 election, there were several key moments. One was my decision (and Thatcher's willingness to back it) to end the Price Commission. Another, soon afterwards, was Geoffrey Howe's first budget. In opposition, we in the economic team had all agreed that, come what may, we had to make a bold switch from taxes on income to taxes on expenditure. It was a difficult moment to do so, but Geoffrey courageously grasped the nettle and reduced income tax, financing this by a major increase in VAT, to the then unthought-of rate of 15 per cent. This, coupled with an increase in nationalised industry prices as a means of holding down public expenditure, caused some fury in the TUC and the first protest from Jim Prior and his like-minded colleagues. We were already going in the opposite direction to the Heath Government, and none of the 'Wets' had been consulted on the economic direction that we were taking.

Much less happy was an unwanted legacy from the Callaghan Government. When we assumed office, one of the central problems was what to do about the impending Clegg award to public sector workers; in the election campaign itself, there had seemed to be just too many public sector voters to deny them in advance this highly inflationary award, which directly led to a 25 per cent increase in the public sector wage bill. I think Margaret Thatcher seriously considered abandoning her pledge, no doubt urged on by the Treasury, but I argued strongly for keeping to the commitment. I did not see how we could break our firm electoral promise within a month or two of giving it. The consequences of Clegg, however, were grim, with the public sector borrowing requirement rising above £9 billion and inflation forecast to hit 18 per cent. There were only two alternatives: to follow the Heath recipe and impose an incomes policy; or to let a monetary squeeze, coupled with a rising petro-currency (minimum lending rate was already at 17 per cent), force inflation out of the system. The problem was the time lag in embracing the latter policy – and for a long time there was no sign of the monetary squeeze having much effect on inflation.

It was not just Clegg to blame. The persistent rise in sterling was devastating in its impact – a rise largely explained by the fact that the North Sea was then one of the few active and prosperous parts of the economy, thereby according us the doubtful accolade of being possessors of a petro-currency. Still, there was a major incidental blessing to sterling's excessive strength. I do not know whether some bright spark in the Treasury felt that the abolition of exchange controls might in some way weaken sterling; but in any case, to my surprise and delight, Geoffrey came forward with this proposal at our breakfast gatherings – and, no doubt, in private meetings between himself and Margaret Thatcher. I had long been a strong advocate for abolishing exchange control. In opposition, Thatcher, Howe and I had made frequent visits to the City; there we found no support for such a policy. It was opposed by the Bank of England for being too risky – and the commercial banks were in favour of freedom for themselves but not for everyone else. Nigel Lawson was a strong supporter within the Treasury, but that summer and early autumn I had to press hard in our private meetings against the very natural nervousness of Margaret and Geoffrey. It was a very brave move for them, in difficult times, but I consider that abolition – announced by Geoffrey on 23 October 1979, the very day of my refusal to let the Stock Exchange off the hook – was possibly the single most important measure that we took in all our time in government. It made us a genuinely open economy for the first time since the war. Of course, the sudden revelation only the day before that we were about to abolish all exchange controls was taken by a sullen majority of members of the Cabinet as another sign that the government was in the hands of a crazy cabal.

Over the next two years, as prices rose, profit margins shrank and output withered, unemployment climbed steeply. During the Heath Government the rise in unemployment to one million had led to the famous U-turn; but this time round, as the jobless total rose towards three million, there was no such U-turn.

Were we right? Yes. There was no alternative, except for a return to the prices and incomes policy which had destroyed the previous Tory government. The pressure on government revenues of unemployment and low activity was severe, and in both 1980 and 1981 the Treasury, with the strong urging of Margaret Thatcher, brought in big reductions in public expenditure to try and hold the rise in the Public Sector Borrowing Requirement. I supported every one of Geoffrey's budgets, but was one of only five or six members of the Cabinet who did so. On each occasion, I spoke up firmly in his support – and saw in the demeanour of most of the other members of the Cabinet the contempt which they felt for what they saw as my toadying attitude.

I have praised Jim Prior for standing up to Margaret Thatcher, but I cannot say the same for his ideological allies in the Cabinet. Admittedly, several of them were placed in an unenviable position, partly because it was against their instincts to argue vigorously with a woman. Margaret, of course, used her femininity as a weapon and was charming, even mildly flirtatious, with her opponents – and whilst a few of them must have actively disliked her as a person, others disliked her politics and aggressive behaviour, but not her personally.

When the economic going got very tough, with virtually every indicator heading in the wrong direction, there was remarkably little overt opposition in Cabinet to the policies. Few of the opponents piped up with an alternative set of economic proposals. The gentlemen among them, like Francis Pym, put their heads down and looked quite miserable, saying nothing – their upbringing had not prepared them for heated arguments with a hectoring and aggressive woman. But the majority were just rather pathetic. Apart from Jim Prior and Peter Walker, who occasionally spoke their minds, they sat there listening to a catalogue of economic woes (rising unemployment, high inflation, high interest rates, booming sterling) with a supercilious smile upon their faces – as much as to say, 'We told you so, you ignorant band of mad monetarists, you are destroying the country and the tolerance and fair-minded views of the British people.' Apparently this was also the view of the Palace. This was the stance, if not the expressed view, of Carrington, Gilmour, Soames, Walker, Stevas, Pym, Heseltine, Carlisle; the worst of them was Stevas, who always had a flippant aside calculated to gain a cheer from his peers. Margaret was right to get rid of him in January 1981. Resenting my support for these economic policies, I used to read in the press that he referred to me as 'John Nitt'. I had been through preparatory school, so it did not bother me; in return, I referred to him privately as 'St John Stevarse'. When he received his life peerage, he called himself Lord St John of Fawsley – that says it all.

I am sure I am right to be so critical of the Cabinet opponents of the economic policy for not speaking up more forcibly and openly – after all, never was there greater scope for a well-argued critique of how the policies in 1979 and 1980 were working out in practice. Even so, I do acknowledge that most of these opponents were temperamentally alien not only to what was being proposed, but even more to what was happening in society. After the Macmillan era, it was necessary, in my view, to popularise the Conservative Party – to make it acceptable to the aspiring working class, in other words to allow the symbolic Essex man and woman to feel part of society's mainstream and to better themselves, without feeling that they were being patronised. These people were never going to want centrist policies. Centrist policies were about the support of the status quo – and that offered little for them.

The celebrated phrase 'We've never had it so good' gave the show away. Macmillan meant 'You've' – 'you' were a different class of person from 'me', Macmillan, a millionaire publisher, married to a duke's daughter. One of the glories of English society through the generations has been the ability of successful men to move up in the world, through money made in trade, first into land and eventually into the aristocracy. Macmillan himself was a case in point. After two world wars and penal tax rates, the aspiring middle and working classes were taking control of their destiny through greater security and prosperity; they were usurping the position of the upper classes who had ruled so long – too long.

When I joined the House of Commons, the Tory parliamentary party was dominated by public-school men (up to half the Macmillan Cabinet had been to Eton), which meant that those ambitious souls, like Ted Heath, who came from a more modest background, had little choice except to join them. I suppose I am puzzled that the likes of Ted Heath and Peter Walker felt more at home with a Carrington or a Gilmour than with a Thatcher or a Tebbit. Why weren't they of a radical disposition, finding their natural home among Tories who stood for small business, small farming, strong personal independence, rather than with Whigs who were hooked on stability, even the 'management of decline', and the success of big business? It is a truly major divide between personal independence on the one hand and corporatism on the other. Why is

Michael Heseltine, whom I like and respect, such a great corporatist? He comes from roughly the same background as I do; the only difference I can detect between us being that he is very rich and I am modestly well-off. But why should our politics be so different? It is a puzzle.

Recently (January 2001), I came across in *The Times* an interesting view on this question by Anthony Howard, not only a journalist and commentator of considerable experience, but the co-author of Michael Heseltine's biography. Wondering whether they learned the habit from Macmillan, he points out that 'today's "Wets" have always given the impression of liking to pose as patricians even when they lack the attributes and qualifications to do so'. He sees this as a fatal mistake:

> Of course, it was funny when Julian Critchley described the overthrow of Edward Heath in 1975 as 'the Peasants' Revolt', and I admit to having laughed out loud when in one of his books he recommended his readers to write to 'Margaret Thatcher, c/o Dickins & Jones'. But all this – and his jibe about the contemporary Conservative Party consisting entirely of garagistes and second-hand car dealers (mostly from Essex) – must have represented a deliberate effort to position the Tories' liberal wing so that it could adopt a condescending attitude towards the new populist regime …
>
> It did not help either that some of the solid upholders of the 'One Nation' tradition within the Conservative Party not only genuinely were 'toffs' (Ian Gilmour, Francis Pym, Peter Carrington) – but, even when they were not, raised equal hackles by being ostentatiously wealthy (Michael Heseltine, Peter Walker, Tim Sainsbury).
>
> The conclusion seems to be irresistible: other things apart, the heirs of Rab Butler, Iain Macleod and Edward Boyle in today's much rougher Conservative Party have allowed themselves to be mugged as out-of-date supercilious representatives of an ancient and snobbish regime …
>
> Naturally, this class analysis cannot provide the whole story – but, if only because their backgrounds have led the 'wets' to be a good deal gentler and politer than their right-wing populist opponents, it still must provide a substantial part of it.

I cannot agree with all of this, but it is a telling commentary on the defeat of the liberal wing of the Tory Party, which could have fought back in the first Thatcher administration but signally failed to do so. Twenty years on, it has not yet learned its lesson. The election of Kenneth Clarke would have destroyed the Conservative Party. The left still prattles on about capturing the 'centre'. The centre shifts from one moment to another; the Tories cannot hope to capture the position so successfully occupied by the social democratic government of Tony Blair. It has to start where the Tory radicals of the 1960s began – by taking risks with public opinion – because to lead, and influence, is to risk. The politics of the focus group are as futile as the politics of consensus. The Tory fish must learn to swim against the stream.

All that said, it would be inaccurate if I gave the impression that I was invariably a supporter of the economic policies in the early 1980s. Hugo Young, in his biography of Thatcher, refers to me as a 'double-dyed monetarist', but the truth is more complex. In particular, I had (like John Biffen) little sympathy with the impossibly rigid Medium-Term Financial Strategy introduced – largely at Nigel Lawson's behest – in the spring of 1980. My position was also more ambiguous during 1981, an extraordinarily difficult year, before at last the economic position began to look up.

Around the time of that year's budget, which caused grave concern within the Cabinet because of its obstinately deflationary nature, the mood within the economic team became uncertain. Geoffrey and the Treasury began to have some doubts about whether the squeeze was going too far – and even the monetarists among them started to argue that further cuts in public spending were unnecessary. Poor Geoffrey was in a dilemma. Shortly before, in January, Margaret Thatcher had made one of the great mistakes of her premiership – she had appointed Alan Walters as her personal economic adviser. It was comparable in its consequences to the appointment of Sir William Armstrong as Ted Heath's principal economic adviser in the early 1970s. The creation of tensions, of a personal kind, between No. 10 and the Treasury is always a mistake. Several years later it led to the sad and unnecessary resignation of Nigel Lawson as Chancellor, in an astonishing set of circumstances, when Margaret Thatcher behaved disgracefully by taking the side of her indiscreet adviser against her own Chancellor.

Before we won the election in 1979, Alan Walters was well known and respected by all of us. He was a provocative but expert monetarist. I think it was Walters who defined an economist as 'a politician who does not have to seek election'. Like John Hoskyns he had little respect for politicians, even less for the Douglas Wass contingent in the Treasury. He had been an enthusiastic visitor and advocate in the Centre for Policy Studies; so he was no stranger. But his intervention at this stage was unhelpful. For political reasons, I believe that he stiffened the sinews of the Prime Minister, if that was ever necessary – first into agreeing the deflationary budget in March and then in July bringing forward yet another proposal, this time to cut a further £5 billion off public expenditure in 1982–83. This led to the historic Cabinet meeting on 23 July 1981, later described by Thatcher as 'one of the bitterest arguments on the economy, or any subject, that I can ever recall taking place at Cabinet during my premiership'.

It was the night before that I saw the Treasury paper for that Cabinet – and I was surprised at its poorly argued case for further cuts. The argument went roughly like this:

> Some 48½ per cent of the income of a married man on average earnings is now taken in tax, as against 45 per cent when the Conservatives came to office. If we want to reduce taxes, we have no choice but to reduce further the burden of public expenditure. Given that the Medium-Term Financial Strategy has set out a declining public sector borrowing requirement (as a proportion of GDP), we have no choice, in spite of the recession [which was, of course, raising rather than lowering the PSBR] but to cut £5 billion more out of public spending *than we planned earlier in the year.*

I have taken the opportunity to look at all the arguments again, and it is clear that the Treasury authors did not believe what they were advocating. My criticism of the paper had nothing whatsoever to do with the fact that I was now in a big spending department – the argument simply did not make the case for its conclusion.

I read the Treasury paper again the next morning, and showed it to my private secretary. But he smiled sweetly, as much as to say, 'This is your subject, Secretary of State, not mine.' I may have been influenced – it would be hard not to have been – by the fact that riots were breaking out in several cities. Indeed, the night before had seen renewed violence in the Toxteth district of Liverpool. I therefore arrived at the meeting in a state of some uncertainty.

When Geoffrey Howe introduced the paper, he did so without conviction. And I suddenly thought that it was intolerable that Cabinet should be treated in this way. I felt as the 'Wets' must have felt on several previous occasions – namely, that the Treasury was simply assuming that, because it would have the support of the Prime Minister and her economic cabal, its advice would go through anyway. Several spending ministers and opponents of the economic policy spoke up against the proposals for yet further cuts in public spending.

I then spoke very critically about the Treasury paper, saying it was completely inadequate in the circumstances; I did not speak against the proposals as such. Much to my surprise, John Biffen then forcibly attacked the proposals, saying that the public spending cuts had gone far enough. I have to say that John had a longer track record as a monetarist than Margaret Thatcher. Such was the nature of the meeting. Margaret was appalled. The economic team – her cabal – had disintegrated, and she adjourned the meeting. 'All at once the whole strategy was at issue', she wrote subsequently about this memorable occasion.

> It was as if tempers suddenly broke. I too became extremely angry. I had thought that we could rely on these people [Biffen and Nott] when the crunch came. I just was not interested in this kind of creative accounting that enabled fair-weather monetarists to justify an about-turn …
>
> I had said at the beginning of the government 'give me six strong men and true, and I will get through'. Very rarely did I have as many as six. So I responded vigorously in defence of the Chancellor …

Let me also quote from Geoffrey Howe's version of what took place:

> Among the most significant and scornful defectors were John Nott and John Biffen. They had both been long-time sceptics about the Treasury as an institution. John Biffen felt liberated perhaps from his previous uneasy loyalty, as a result of his move to the Department of Trade. And John Nott had probably been at the Ministry of Defence long enough to absorb something of their big-spending culture. Certainly his attitude revealed no trace of the very generous tribute he had paid to my Budget only four months before.

I fear that Margaret's expressions 'creative accounting' and 'fair-weather monetarists' justifying 'an about-turn' give the game away. The control of the money supply is not, as Ian Gilmour amusingly described it, 'the uncontrollable in pursuit of the indefinable'. But it does require the exercise of judgement about what the indicators mean. I had come to the conclusion that 'monetarism' dictated an easing of restraint. I may have been right, I may have been wrong, but it had nothing whatsoever to do with 'an about-turn'. It was a judgement on the margins of policy, and I was going to speak the truth as I saw it.

This episode no doubt explains Margaret's charge against me in her memoirs:

John is a mixture of gold, dross and mercury. No-one was better at analysing a situation and prescribing a policy to deal with it. But he found it hard, or perhaps boring, to stick with the policy once it had been firmly decided. His vice was second thoughts.

I am afraid that Margaret had been up against the majority of her Cabinet colleagues for so long, and had been so infuriated by their supercilious disdain for her performance, that she had come to regard it as a holy war of the just against the unjust. Everything had to be either a victory or a defeat. She was on a mission, this time urged on by Walters; and her mission had been arrested by those whom she saw as her friends – Biffen and Nott. Only Howe, Joseph, Leon Brittan (the Chief Secretary) and Willie Whitelaw ('the non-playing Captain of the "Wets"') supported her.

It was about this time that a Tory MP reputedly compared the progress of the government with the Crimean War – but with one difference: 'Florence Nightingale is leading the Charge of the Light Brigade and Lord Cardigan is tending the sick and wounded.' Unless you can laugh in politics, you can have a miserable time.

~

Around the end of 1980, long before this famous row occurred, I had decided that I would like to move on from Trade. Perhaps it was my low boredom threshold – but it was more, I think, that most of the policy objectives that I had set myself there had been achieved. The Board of Trade had been a pleasant and enjoyable department – and ministerial colleagues had also provided me with plenty of stimulation. Sally Oppenheim, Norman Tebbit and Reg Eyre were all good ministers and fun to work with. I had gained a lot of respect for the understated ability of Cecil Parkinson – or the late Mr Parkinson as we called him, since he was incapable of ever being on time for any meeting.

Looking around the options, only Defence seemed to be a possibility. It attracted me too because, having started my career as a regular soldier, the idea of completing it in Defence had great appeal. As a member of the Overseas and Defence Policy Committee, I had attended many discussions on defence policy, and my political memory stretched back to 1973 – to the time when Peter Carrington had successfully blocked Tony Barber's attempts to get some reductions in Defence expenditure. Unless Defence is seen to make an effort at economy, none of the other spending departments can be expected to suffer their share of pain. Like other politicians, I had my prejudices against Defence, which appeared to be lavish, extravagant and lacking in any reasonable financial control. My colleagues and I looked across at the great white building beside the Thames and saw the 'brass hats' driving around in their black limousines (actually Ford Granadas) with all those batmen and servants at their beck and call.

In late 1980, Francis Pym had brought forward to 'OD' a very full paper which sought to justify the four pillars of our defence policy: nuclear defence, our maritime commitment to the Eastern Atlantic, our contribution to NATO on the Central Front in Germany, and home defence. He successfully argued, supported by the Foreign Office, that we could meet these wide commitments only if we upheld the NATO obligation for 3 per cent annual volume growth in defence spending, without having it undermined each year by the Treasury's cash limits. These cash limits were calculated to resist the tendency for defence inflation (mainly in equipment escalation) to exceed by far the general inflation rate. Francis, in short, was not coughing up any cash – and Margaret Thatcher was unhappy.

Going back to Treasury days, and the pleading of Douglas Allen, the then Treasury Permanent Secretary, I had long been convinced that the Plowden system of volume control of public spending (known in the Treasury as 'funny money', because it discounted inflation) had to be supplemented by stringent cash controls. Otherwise, a department like Defence could see its cash expenditure (real money) far exceed its volume expenditure ('funny money'). More recently, in the early period of the Thatcher Government, I had been a hawk at our breakfasts in No. 10 on two subjects above all – the abolition of exchange control, and the imposition of cash limits. Geoffrey had a difficult time with Douglas Wass and the Treasury officials because they argued, reasonably enough, that there were also dangers in cash control. What happened if you overestimated inflation and set the cash limits too high? It would be a recipe for excess spending by departments. Similar difficulties of control arose with the so-called Medium-Term Financial Strategy, advocated by Lawson and Howe but strongly opposed by Biffen and myself. Inevitably, events made a nonsense of the numbers, as real-life unpredictability intervened. Similarly, in mitigation, there was always an argument between cost-plus contracts, the traditional means of pricing equipment orders, as against fixed-price contracts. But where, with highly sophisticated equipment, were you to set the price (perhaps with a forward estimate of cost-plus)? And what did you do on a five-year contract if your contractor was going bust? Did you abandon the project and write off the development costs?

No doubt Margaret Thatcher understood all these arguments, which every-one in the spending departments grappled with day by day, but she was not in-terested in them. Simply wanting public expenditure cut when it was seem-ingly getting out of control, she was impervious to Pym's line of reasoning and resented it when he won his case. Then, quite quickly, external conditions made Pym's life impossible. With the recession deepening, the defence contrac-tors became desperate for funds and started delivering defence equipment early – an unheard-of event. The Prime Minister and the Treasury foresaw, because of the cash-flow profile, the likelihood of a substantial Defence overspend. A moratorium was imposed on all defence expenditure, and Francis was asked to find £200m from somewhere within his budget.

Although I have sounded somewhat critical of Francis as one of the 'Wets', he was a good politician and an upright man. When he was being abused by the Prime Minister during the Falklands, I often tried to give him some moral support. I wonder whether he realises it; probably not. Francis was an outstanding Chief Whip in Ted Heath's days; then he became ill, left for a time to recover, and never quite had his original edge on his return, or so I thought. Anyhow, I was approached by Ian Gow, the Prime Minister's Parliamentary Private Secretary, and indirectly asked on two occasions – at least once over lunch at the Cavalry Club, a favourite haunt of Ian's – what job I would like to do next. I said 'Defence', but it was already taken so I hap-pily soldiered on at Trade.

Shortly before the reshuffle in January 1981, I was asked to visit the Prime Minister in her flat at No. 10. When I got there, I was surprised that Denis Thatcher, Ian Gow and Clive Whitmore were also present. The atmosphere was very friendly and informal, and I was offered a drink – about as different from being offered a job by Ted Heath as you can imagine. It still seems a little odd to me that it was not a private meeting with the Prime Minister alone. I was delighted at the appointment, but said that the announcement would have to be delayed because I was setting off the next day to Indonesia as Trade Secre-tary to try and solve a mighty crisis. This involved a ban on some £800m of British exports to that country, which I had jeopardised by slapping anti-dumping duties on some Indonesian T-shirts, whose value could not have exceeded a few million pounds.

I also asked Margaret whether she 'excluded a radical look at the Defence programme'. 'Oh no,' she said unhesitatingly, realising perhaps, at this early stage, what political discomfort a radical look at the Defence programme might involve. 'No, by all means you can have a radical look at the Defence programme, and I hope you do.'

Next day I set off for Indonesia, laden down with white papers on defence and other briefing material provided by the House of Commons Library, as I could not reveal my pending move from Trade. I spent three days in Jakarta and returned via Singapore, where I spent the weekend at the High Commissioner's residence doing my homework. Together with the defence papers that I had seen in 'OD' and 'E' Committees, I was reasonably well-briefed on my return to London. The house which the High Commissioner occupied was where I had lived as a young subaltern whilst acting as ADC to the Commander in Chief in 1955. It was no longer called Flagstaff House.

The trip to Indonesia was my final fling as Trade Secretary. I could not have done a lot in that capacity, but the ambassador tipped off President Suharto, himself a general, that I was about to take the post of Defence Minister, a post also held by him. The atmosphere was transformed. I had a long and friendly talk with the President about defence; trade was hardly mentioned. Not only did I sort out the problem of all those Indonesian T-shirts and get the embargo against our exports lifted; but also, when I departed, the Trade Minister came to the airport to see me off – and, on the instructions of the President, handed me a list of further military equipment, including Hawk aircraft, which Indonesia wanted to buy. Yes, my time at Trade was interesting, relaxed and enjoyable; my next department was to be rather different.

~

When I showed this chapter to my elder son, he told me that I should be very careful about explaining Margaret Thatcher's treatment of her Cabinet colleagues in terms of her sex. 'Somehow', he said, 'this just isn't compatible with the spirit of our time.' But as her sex was the key to everything, how can I avoid it?

I realise, of course, that many of my recollections are politically incorrect – but how can anyone of my generation tell a vivid story of his times in the more cautious language of today? This book is not a civil service communiqué. The world has changed, and educated liberal opinion has got a hold in most parts of the media and particularly in institutions like the BBC. Men and women do behave differently – why try and hide it? To me, Margaret Thatcher was always charming and considerate, except when we had a fierce disagreement on a policy issue – and then of course I read about it, with appropriate canards, in the press. As a person I have always liked her very much, but I think that I might have been, among her Cabinet colleagues, in a minority.

Her attitude towards her colleagues, and her behaviour towards them in meetings, was dominated by her passion to get her way. Often she was dismissive and aggressive if someone's reasoning was different from her own. She would constantly interrupt and challenge. But if the victim did not hold his corner intellectually, she could be scathing. This did not endear her to her more timid, or should I say more gentlemanly, colleagues. Privately, outside the processes of government, I believe that she treated even her most dedicated opponents with considerable courtesy and friendliness. She has many admirable qualities.

Those outside the world of politics often do not understand that it is a passionate profession. Most people who enter politics feel deeply, often emotionally, about key issues. Those uninterested and detached from politics – the vast majority of educated people – cannot understand the heat that it so often generates.

I noticed, long after I had left the hothouse world of Westminster, how if a former minister made some minor, even constructive, criticism of her government, the lobby briefing in response implied that the minister in question was a 'disappointed man'. In other words, the assumption was that politics was all that mattered in life. That passion for politics, and belief in its primacy, was the motive force of Margaret Thatcher's great achievement.

Chapter Eight

UPSETTING THE NAVY

The Naval art and the Military art are both in a state of transition; the last discovery of today is out of date, and superseded by an antagonistic discovery tomorrow. Any large accumulation of vessels or guns is sure to contain much that will be useless, unfitting, antediluvian, when it comes to be tried. There are two cries against the Admiralty which go on side by side: one says, 'We have not ships enough, no "relief" ships, no Navy, to tell the truth'; the other cry says, 'We have all the wrong ships, all the wrong guns and nothing but the wrong ...'

(Walter Bagehot, 1867)

On my arrival in January 1981 at the Ministry of Defence, I invited each of the Chiefs of Staff of the three Services to come and have a chat. I wanted to establish a useful working and personal relationship with each of them from the outset. I was surprised at my first meeting with the Chief of the Naval Staff when, by implication, he was critical of Francis Pym. It was my first meeting with Sir Henry Leach and occurred long before there was any suggestion of reductions in the forward naval programme. It left a bad taste in my mouth and I remember saying at the time to my Private Secretary how surprised I was that a Chief of Staff could criticise the Secretary of State's predecessor at the first meeting with his new boss.

Although I had become somewhat exasperated with what I had seen, in Cabinet Committee, at Francis' unwillingness to get some grip on Defence expenditure, I liked Francis with his obvious integrity, and I admired his determination to fight for the MoD in the corridors of Whitehall and in Cabinet. In fact he destroyed his future relationship with Mrs Thatcher, and his long-term political career, by fighting his corner on behalf of the Services. Not much good did that do him.

I realised within a few days of my appointment, as a result of this incident and joking about it with my Private Office, that in the last resort the Secretary of State was just another expendable front-line soldier, to be disposed of where necessary, in the battle for more money. He was judged by his ability to 'win' against the Treasury. Francis Pym did not deliver, as Henry Leach saw it, and he was happy to see him go. Sir Henry himself recalls in his memoirs (*Endure No Makeshifts*) the situation as he saw it by the end of 1980:

> In the Ministry of Defence there was a certain edginess abroad but on the whole the more important programmes had survived. Francis Pym, convinced now of the imprudence of further defence cuts, was (just) holding his corner in Cabinet with some effect. At which point it was announced that Nott (from Trade) would replace Pym early in the New Year.
>
> 'What do you think of the impending change of Secretary of State, sir?' asked Brian Brown, my excellent secretary.
>
> 'Well,' I replied, 'at present we have a charming man but one to whom decision making does not seem to come easily. I know nothing about Nott but it must be a change for the better.'
>
> How wrong I was.

Elsewhere in his memoirs Sir Henry wrote: 'Francis Pym was not perhaps the strongest ever Defence Secretary. Small decisions were an irritating inconvenience to him; big ones were more difficult and he preferred to avoid them.'

I say some very complimentary things about Henry Leach later on, but he did not create a good impression on me at our first meeting.

~

Before embarking on this story, it is worth noting one startling fact. When I joined the Ministry of Defence we were spending vastly more – nearly 60 per cent more – in real terms on the Royal Navy in 1982–83 than we were in 1950–51 just after the Second World War, when we still had a very large Navy with many more ships. The table illustrates not only this remarkable fact, but also how the Navy's share of the total defence budget had risen over the years.

For the rest of the 1980s, in the period for which I was responsible, we planned to spend more – in each year, in real terms – on the conventional Royal Navy (i.e. excluding the nuclear deterrent) than was spent in 1978–79, when we first came to office.

The reason for the apparent paradox of more money and fewer ships lies in

	Naval budget in £ million at 1982–83 prices	Navy's percentage of total Defence Budget
1950–51	2564	25
1960–61	3612	25
1970–71	3602	27
1978–79	3607	28
1982–83	4047 (excluding Trident)	29

the fundamental point that the Navy had to increase its expenditure on ever-more elaborate and sophisticated weapon systems if it was to meet and match constant shifts in technology and the Soviet threat. To illustrate this dilemma, the torpedo programme alone was worth £2,000 million, equivalent to the capital costs of purchasing an additional 10–15 frigates. The principal dispute between the Royal Navy and myself concerned the number of surface ships in the Fleet. But the money saved on ships was not going elsewhere – it was devoted to upgrading the Navy's weapon systems and its submarine fleet.

Although at the time it was felt inappropriate to say so publicly, the fact was that the Navy lost six ships in the Falklands War, against an opponent possessing fewer than ten modern Exocet missiles. The Soviets had hundreds of missiles and launch platforms that were far more sophisticated than anything in the Argentine armoury. The Falklands showed the severe vulnerability of the surface ship against a sophisticated and determined enemy – and even before that event, it was clear that something had to be done about it.

It is quite hard in retrospect, following the collapse of the Soviet empire and when for the last ten years we have been engaged in a series of low-intensity conflicts around the world, to remember our concerns in the early 1980s. Even making allowance for the exaggerations and inventions of the intelligence community, there was every ground for believing that the Soviet Union, with its Warsaw Pact allies, was overtaking the Western alliance in the volume and quality of its equipment; it already had a vast superiority in manpower on the continental land mass of Europe. The United States with its reinforcement capability was a very long way away.

I do not believe that many of us thought, in a nuclear world, that the Soviets were likely to risk an assault on the front line in Europe. Nevertheless, almost all their exercises, which we followed closely, were predicated not on the defence of the Soviet Union but on an armoured attack, with chemical weapons, across the plains of Germany; often across the Hanover plain, the location of 1st British Corps.

The reason for the prevailing pessimism was that whilst the Soviets were pouring more and more money into their defence military establishment, the United States (under the Carter administration, with its dithering and uncertainties) had been marking time. Only in the nuclear area had any positive changes been made. The NATO alliance was going through a period of uncertainty too, with a wholly inadequate force contribution from the smaller countries, hostility outside the tent from the French, and a very political West Germany dominated by a coalition of Social Democrats and Liberals – typified in the characters of Foreign Minister Genscher and a much more objectionable Liberal called Count Otto von Lambsdorff, an antagonist of mine when I had been Trade Secretary. The United Kingdom, with some 5.4 per cent of its gross domestic product in defence, was the only European NATO country (with the exception of Greece, which had armed itself against its NATO ally, Turkey) making a proper contribution towards agreed NATO targets. It was impossible to foresee at this juncture that the huge boost to defence brought about by the incoming Reagan administration would eventually cripple the Soviets and precipitate the collapse of the Warsaw Pact.

The Chiefs of Staff, quite correctly, saw the threat as being very real and that it was their duty to forestall it by a continuing real improvement in our capability. They are to be complimented for that. It was not their job to concern themselves overmuch with economic issues; that was for the civil servants and the politicians; however, between them all – no doubt encouraged by the ethos of the Defence Department and Francis Pym himself – they had placed unbounded faith in the aspirations of the incoming Conservative administration for strong defence. Indeed, the Tory election manifesto had declared that 'while we seek value for money in defence expenditure as elsewhere, we will not hesitate to spend what is necessary on our armed forces even while we are cutting public expenditure on other things'. Of course, an apprentice in the workings of democratic politics might have suspected that such a commitment was misleading – if it was taken to mean that defence alone would be immune when it came to the competition for funds against education, housing, health and welfare. Worse still was the notion that, with inflation rising at 15 per cent, defence, with its escalating equipment programme, could alone be isolated from economic reality.

I was keen then, though it took another ten years for it to happen, to give the soldiers, sailors and airmen their own cash budgets right down to the operating units, so that from the bottom up there was an understanding of how equipment and maintenance and pay were all tied in with the money available – the simplest principle in private industry. The individual Services had their budgets, or 'target headings' as we called them, but their programmes had priority; and if they exceeded their budget, it was the job of the Secretary of State to sort out the problem. In many ways individual budgets for each of the three Services was the wrong way of looking at it. We would have been better with a sea/air budget and a land/air budget, thereby expressing the real nature of our capability.

Compared to the acceptance of the simplest budgetary principles in the outside world, there was something of a yawning gap in understanding. Field Marshal Bramall, in his excellent book on *The Chiefs*, puts it very well:

Nott was obliged to rescind some of his measures before the Falklands crisis broke, but the overall impact of his review [of defence expenditure] was to reduce the real growth in Defence Expenditure to about 7 per cent over the three years since the general election. This rose to 8 per cent the following year instead of the 12 per cent hoped for under the NATO 3 per cent annual growth commitment.

What, of course, upset the Chiefs was that the annual 3 per cent real growth target was not what it seemed. Every year the Treasury allocated cash limits which eroded the real volume, resulting in an out-turn which was less than the NATO commitment. In 1981–82 the volume of defence spending, at 1980 prices, was £9.7 billion – but the real cash spend was £12.3 billion. As a great protagonist for cash limits, I could hardly complain if real money, cash, took precedence over 'funny money' volume.

I was faced by a group of highly intelligent men feeling that real growth in expenditure of 7 per cent over three years was a disappointing let-down, and this at a time when the economy was hardly growing at all and unemployment was rising to three million. In relative terms the military was basking in the Elysian fields, but they could not accept it. 'Ah, but the Soviet threat,' they would say – as if there was not a different threat to the country in poor schools and hospitals, and the riots which were being exacerbated by high unemployment.

What happened in practical terms was this. The aspiration for strong defence, enunciated by the incoming Tory administration, led to the defence programme being assembled on an annual (volume) growth of 3 per cent over the entire forward ten year life of the so-called 'long-term costings'. No one in the government when I joined the MoD had suggested that the 3 per cent annual growth target might last beyond 1983–84, yet public commitments to the equipment programme were being given on the assumption that 3 per cent volume growth would continue until 1989–90. It was pretty clear that compound growth of 3 per cent in volume terms, given that defence costs invariably rose faster than inflation, would have bankrupted the Exchequer long before the target had been reached.

I remember Admiral Lygo, by then Chief Executive of British Aerospace, telling me quite openly about the internal politics of the Ministry of Defence. If, in competition with the other two Services, you could get a new ship or a new weapon system into your published programme, it would be a source of intense political embarrassment ever to get it out. The game was to get it into the programme – and announced. It was then for the Defence Secretary to sort it out.

The Royal Navy had played this game with skill. Its share of the total defence budget had risen from 25 per cent to 29 per cent over the years from 1950 to 1982. Leaving nuclear expenditure on one side, its budget was the most over-extended of the three Services. The conventional naval programme rose in volume terms by £500 million between 1979 and 1983, and my Defence Review did not affect this in any way. But the Navy's commitments to its forward programme bore no relation to the likely availability of money in the later years. Indeed, the outcome of the Defence Review confirmed an increase in the volume of defence expenditure of 3 per cent for a further two years until 1985–86, but thereafter I set it at 1 per cent. In cash terms the programme was to grow by 21 per cent between 1978–79 and 1985–86. It was the cutback in the later years that caused the pain – but the pain was self-inflicted. In retrospect I was far too optimistic about the future, and in the final years of the ten-year survey, long after I had left the MoD, defence expenditure actually declined in real terms.

I return to the memoirs of Sir Henry Leach. According to him:

January 1981 saw the start of increasing unease and uncertainty within the Ministry. Nott assumed office with preconceived ideas that the Navy needed to be cut back, the Air Force needed to be built up and the Army was about right. The origin of these preconceptions was never discovered but they persisted throughout the usual round of initial briefings – in which many questions were asked but scant heed paid to the answers – and beyond.

Did I arrive at the MoD with some prejudice against the Royal Navy, as Leach has so often suggested? I am not sure how I could be prejudiced against a great British institution when so many of my family had served as sailors. My great-grandfather, Captain Stephens, died off the coast of South America whilst commanding HMS *Thetis* and its flotilla; my great uncle was a captain, Royal Navy; my uncle, Rear Admiral Martin Nott, was the last British Chief of Staff of the Royal Indian Navy. They all went to Dartmouth. Even my father went to sea in the Second World War as an aircraftsman, when he could not join the Navy due to his age. I have lived half my life in the West Country surrounded by the sea – and the ethos of the Royal Navy. The Royal Navy is different from the other Services, hardly surprisingly. It is somewhat detached from the real world because it spends so much time at sea; but if I had to choose, I would say it is the greatest of our three Services. All in all, although it is true that the Navy bore the brunt of the reductions in the forward programme, it is complete nonsense to suggest that I started off with some prejudice against it.

Indeed, had NATO been prepared to introduce a degree of specialisation among its members, I would have found it sensible to re-weight the British contribution to NATO more heavily in favour of a maritime role and away from our commitments to the central front in Germany; however, for reasons which I shall explain and after I had examined this very option, such a shift became impossible to contemplate because it would have been against our Brussels Treaty commitments – and the determined position of our allies. Clearly such a shift towards a more maritime strategy appealed to the 'deep blue' instincts of Admiral Lewin, the Chief of Defence Staff, a former First Sea Lord; but I believe that even he came to see the political road-blocks to taking such a course. I was not a defence expert, nor did I need to be. There were 3,000 serving officers and men in Whitehall and a large civilian staff to advise me.

I have often been asked whether my time in the Army helped me when I arrived at the Ministry of Defence. I have thought about it quite a lot. With a mere six years of service I certainly did not learn anything of military strategy or tactics – but I did absorb at that time the attitude of Service people: the way they think of each other, the way they think of politicians, their general prejudices towards the outside world, and more particularly the sense of rank and hierarchy, which is much less strong now than it was then, but is still very evident even today. I think that I had a reasonably good feel for the Services when I arrived and I was certainly very conscious that I should show respect to the Chiefs of Staff. I had no intention to come barging in laying down the law; the senior officers had spent forty years in the Service and risen to the top, and I hope my respect for their position communicated itself to them. Generally, I had a good relationship with the admirals, generals and air marshals – and they were certainly very courteous to me.

I had spent much of my time in the Army on active service and I did arrive with one prejudice: however low the level of the conflict, you are still very conscious of the fact that your life depends on the effectiveness of your weapons. If you are spending weeks hacking your way through the bloody jungle, you are very aware too whether or not your equipment is serviceable and whether you have sufficient ammunition to sustain combat. You must never let the ordinary naval rating or soldier down by skimping on his ammunition, his kit, his training and his food – this became a simple but relevant issue once the Defence Review began.

When Francis Pym was moved sideways to be Leader of the House of Commons and I was appointed in his place, there was no doubt that I arrived under grave suspicion. I look rather like an accountant, if there is a way that accountants look, but all my business colleagues would agree that I am as far removed from an accountant as you can get. Nevertheless, I was caricatured in the press as a sort of hatchet man, a Treasury stool pigeon. All the expectations were that, as a former banker, I would be mainly interested in controlling the cash. But I quickly made it clear that I wanted to look first at the strategic choices, matching resources to commitments – something that the Chiefs had demanded repeatedly in all their submissions to the earlier Cabinet Committees that I had attended when Trade Secretary. I never saw my role as purely that of controlling the money.

I suspect that the Chiefs did not really feel that it was legitimate for a Secretary of State to crawl over the details of the actual programmes. It had not happened in this way since the days of Denis Healey in the 1960s. In their unstated view, questions relating to the size and shape of the Armed Forces were a matter for them, not ministers. Their repeated request for commitments to be matched to resources was reasonable enough; but they must have known that we were locked politically into our NATO and other commitments, so in reality it was another way of asking for more money. It was like their unanimous request for 'balanced forces' to meet the unexpected. I would have liked 'balanced forces' to meet any contingency, but there wasn't the money to achieve it. All we could do was to design a force structure to meet the main threat to the United Kingdom – and make that force structure sufficiently flexible to meet the unexpected.

The Chiefs of Staff were always scrupulous in accepting my authority over the MoD; but they expected me to come along on behalf of my Cabinet colleagues and say, 'Here is a situation [for instance Belize]; how do you defend it? Please tell me, Chiefs of Staff, the way to do it.' And without doubt, if I had asked this question, I would have received a very professional answer. This is where our military leaders are first-class. I remember Frank Cooper, the Permanent Secretary at Defence, saying to me, 'John, what you must realise is that war is really about getting men and equipment from A to B and they can be brilliant at it.' We were to find that out quicker than any of us realised at the time. Field Marshal Rommel also made a similar comment when he said, 'Before the battle proper is fought, it is decided by the quartermaster.'

The Royal Navy took it as the unquestioned view of their role that they were to reach out worldwide, performing the traditional 'blue water' role of safeguarding British interests and British shipping all around the world. They saw their principal wartime function as the convoying of US reinforcements across the Atlantic and the support of the American carrier battle group which was to move into the Greenland, Iceland and Norwegian waters to contain the Russian naval threat in the Atlantic. I wanted to understand the logic of this strategy because, unless I did so, it was hard for me to have any feel about the forward Naval programme.

I had a series of briefings from the Naval staff but they always seemed to me to be unsatisfactory. It was not until I went in early March to Norfolk, Virginia, with the Chief of Defence Staff, Admiral Lewin, to visit Admiral Train, the Supreme Allied Commander Atlantic, that I began to grasp the true scenario. Sensibly it involved a series of hectic, dispersed single sailings to avoid the Soviet submarine threat, rather than Second World War escorted convoys. The briefings that I received from the staff at SACLANT (Supreme Allied Command Atlantic) were of a much higher intellectual and practical quality than anything that I obtained from the Naval staff in Whitehall. Again and again I saw that I was being briefed in a way that fortified the traditional naval interest without getting down to the real nitty-gritty of the problem. We were a country trying to reconcile budgetary constraints with the optimum degree of conventional deterrence. It was a tricky task.

What was needed was fresh and original thinking to meet the Soviet submarine challenge; I got none. I was forced to seek proposals elsewhere and impose my own priorities within the growing naval programme. In the end, we agreed to an expansion of the submarine programme at the expense of the surface fleet.

I had two difficulties. The first and most important was that I could never get a clear recommendation from the Chiefs of Staff as to how we were to solve the financial problems. I also had to tell the Cabinet that we would require at least an additional £300 million a year above the NATO 3 per cent real increase if we were to sustain existing programmes – and there was no way that this was forthcoming from my colleagues, let alone the Prime Minister. The Chiefs could not agree on how to share out the pain involved. Although the Chief of Defence Staff was a man of exceptional stature, Admiral Lewin had not at that stage been made the principal military adviser to the government. Terry Lewin was in a difficult position as he was merely responsible for tendering the collective advice of the Chiefs to the Secretary of State. I cannot do better than give Dwin Bramall's retrospective description of the position:

> As a recent First Sea Lord, steeped in the naval tradition, Lewin could hardly be expected to ignore the naval case, nor could he expect Bramall [the senior soldier] and Beetham [the senior airman] to give Leach [the senior naval man] more than qualified support. There was unanimity amongst the Chiefs that there was little operational justification for naval cuts, but, if something had to go, CGS [Bramall] and CAS [Beetham] felt that some trimming in the numbers of vulnerable surface ships was not illogical in a purely NATO context, in which the Navy's primary role was anti-submarine warfare in the Norwegian Sea and Eastern Atlantic.
>
> With the Chiefs reluctant to come to any unified conclusion, Nott turned for advice to the two other centres of power in his ministry – the Permanent Under-Secretary, Sir Frank Cooper, and the Chief Scientific Adviser, Sir Ronald Mason – and to the Foreign Office.

Let me also quote from Admiral Richard Hill's excellent biography of Terry Lewin:

> He [Lewin] was getting no help from the single-service staffs, and neither was Nott. The studies set in train … soon became bogged down in the Central

Staffs when single-service inputs proved incompatible. Lewin, with his own very small staff of briefers, confessed later to feeling 'both impotent and frustrated'. Nott became increasingly impatient.

Quite so.

As soon as the Defence Review was concluded – and very fortunately before the Falklands – Terry Lewin came to see me with a proposal that the Chief of Defence Staff should be made the Principal Military Adviser to the government with authority over his own tri-Service central staff – and, more especially, authority over the Chiefs of Staff Committee. I agreed this vital reform. It was vigorously opposed by Henry Leach, and less vigorously by Michael Beetham, but it was implemented on my recommendation – and endorsed by the Prime Minister. It is recorded in Terry Lewin's papers, 'Fat lot Nott did!' It seems a little harsh, when I implemented his proposals with alacrity! But perhaps I did not take his side overtly against the opposition of Leach and Beetham. Maybe if Terry Lewin had held the authority which the Chief of Defence Staff holds today, things would have been different in the Defence Review – but I doubt it. The outcome of the Defence Review had a logic which it would have been very hard to deny, even by a 'purple' admiral (i.e. one that had discarded his naval skin for a broader defence approach).

My other problem was that, after several months of dialogue, I had lost confidence in the Admiralty Board. There were two excellent members: the Controller of the Navy, Admiral Lindsay Bryson, and the Chief of Fleet Support, Admiral William Pillar. Pillar was faced by the huge task of reducing the size of the Royal Navy's support infrastructure, and he conducted this exceptionally emotive and difficult assignment with great courage, and as much humour as any man could muster in the circumstances. Lindsay Bryson, reputedly the first naval engineer ever to be appointed to the Admiralty Board (and that says something about naval tradition), was also a highly skilled and intelligent man. Keith Speed also deserves praise as the Under-Secretary for the Navy, but I shall say more of him later.

Unfortunately the high quality of these naval members of the Board was not equalled by their seniors. I did not see much of the Second Sea Lord, Admiral Cassidi, but when I did he just scowled at me, so my judgement on his talents has to be suspended. The man that I saw the most was the Vice-Chief of the Naval Staff, Admiral Staveley, who subsequently became First Sea Lord. He was the front man put up to argue the naval case with me, and I encountered him several times a week. I liked him as a person – he was charming and courteous – but I quite quickly lost my respect for his intelligence, as I received one inadequate briefing after another. I was asked to accept ideas which even a layman like myself could see were nonsense, and in all such meetings I had other independent people with me.

There were, apart from the outstanding Admiral Lewin, several other admirals whom I respected. Admirals Fieldhouse and Eberle were both excellent men, the latter something of a politician, but both had the high intelligence and wide experience which rightly brought them to the top. Neither of them, however, was on the Admiralty Board at the time.

So I come to my antagonist, Sir Henry Leach, the First Sea Lord. In his deservedly acclaimed account of the Thatcher years, *One of Us*, the distinguished political commentator Hugo Young has this to say of our relationship in the immediate wake of my Defence Review:

> Roaming freely round Whitehall and Westminster, calling it 'the con trick of the century', Leach was unsparing in his dissection of his minister's personality … Although the Defence Secretary had never fought in a real war – 'a few months in Borneo', Leach snorted to anyone who would listen – he presumed to know what the defence of Britain required. In more reflective moments, surrounded by his aides, he would muse, 'I don't think I actually hate John Nott – but then perhaps I am not a hater.'

Actually, I don't think he hated me – and I certainly didn't hate him. I rather liked the man. In spite of our fundamental disagreements, I don't think that we ever had an ill-tempered word. Henry Leach always treated me, to my face, with respect and courtesy. It may have been rather different when he left my office, but I always found him charming and considerate in my presence. I realised from my first meeting with him that he had a contempt for all politicians – but that is not an unusual trait among sailors and I took it in good part. I cannot give him greater praise than to say that he was a fighting admiral, in the Nelsonian tradition, and I would have been happy to have served under him as a junior officer. But, alas, that was not to be the nature of our relationship or of our respective roles. Henry Leach was a naval traditionalist; the Royal Navy, and good for him, was his life.

He saw our differences so emotionally, and that was part of his problem.

After all, he could have argued his case, been seen to have fought his corner on behalf of the Navy, and then accepted the decision. Moreover, the decision was never mine alone; it was based on a range of tri-Service and civilian advice which I received from the Central Military Staffs and from the senior civil servants, who understood the issues quite as well as he did, not least because they had lived with these dilemmas for most of their working lives. I don't think Henry Leach ever appreciated that I had a job to do – to get the budget back on course – and that it had nothing whatsoever to do with any prejudice in favour of one Service or another.

Again, I resort to Bramall's version of events. He describes the advice I was getting from other than the Chiefs:

> The Permanent Under-Secretary's Department [i.e. at the MoD] were realists, who knew that it was no use carping about the Treasury's methods in setting the financial targets because there was, in truth, a fundamental mismatch between the existing weapons programmes and the slice of the national cake likely to be considered reasonable by the electorate for allocation to Defence. The Scientists [i.e. also at the MoD] had sound reasons for doubting the validity of the naval programmes. In their view, too much was being spent on hulls [i.e. ships], or platforms as they called them, and too little on the weapon systems to go into them. They also favoured increasing resources devoted to submarines at the expense of surface units; and they believed that the Air Staff were right in their claims that greater use should be made of maritime aircraft in the defence of the Eastern Atlantic. The Foreign Office was clear that Britain was now primarily, if reluctantly, a European power, and that land and air defence of NATO's Central Front should take priority over maritime commitments.
>
> With so much advice outside the Chiefs of Staff Committee pointing the finger at the Naval programmes, Nott, with the courage of his own convictions, made his judgement of Solomon.

It is a good summary of the position. Nevertheless, it was not a judgement of Solomon, because I eschewed the easy answer of equal pain all round. Instead, the harshest reductions in the forward programmes – or 'cuts', as the victims called them – fell on the Royal Navy.

~

I had written to Sir Frank Cooper from the Board of Trade before I departed on my trade trip to Indonesia, to say that I would like to see him as soon as I returned. My relations with Sir Kenneth Clucas at the Board of Trade were excellent and I knew that Frank also would be a key man for me, especially if I needed to attack budgetary issues. Ken Clucas gave me a good run-down on Frank Cooper and he sounded just the man for me. Clucas said he was tough and experienced, which proved to be true. Always an admirable supporter, and sometimes a tactful critic, Frank was just the source of strength that I needed; however, being 'a good civil servant', he was not the man to wield the hatchet to the Service programmes – that he left to me.

I suggested to Terry Lewin, the Chief of the Defence Staff, that he might like to organise an away-day with all the Chiefs, the Permanent Secretary, the Chief of Defence Procurement and the Chief Scientific Adviser. We held it in Terry Lewin's quarters in Greenwich Naval College, and it took two days. This was about a fortnight after my arrival, and we covered every aspect of defence policy. The theme, if it had one, was 'What is the strategy?' It went rather well. The Chiefs suspected that I intended to have a go at the budget but money was not discussed. Nevertheless, there was an underlying concern – principally about the Prime Minister, because although she always talked about strong defence, she had consistently backed the Treasury against Francis Pym. It puzzled them. They did not realise that Margaret Thatcher was an expert in facing both ways at once.

During the early months of 1981, before I launched the Defence Review, I spent most of my time (apart from visits to the three Services) on nuclear policy. This was an area of huge importance, fascinating intellectually, but highly controversial.

I have always been in favour of an independent nuclear deterrent. What I had never considered, because it was not my job, was whether we would need to modernise the existing deterrent, Polaris. One Thursday morning at the regular meeting of the full Cabinet, whilst I was still at Trade, we were simply informed by the Prime Minister that a decision had been taken in conjunction with the Americans to modernise the deterrent with the introduction of Trident. I was shocked that the Cabinet had neither been given any facts nor consulted on the issue. I protested. I said that I thought it was an unsatisfactory way of conducting the government's business, not least because this was a matter of fundamental national importance. I do not recall anyone else supporting me.

The Prime Minister explained that it had happened in this way because the discussions had leaked out in Washington, much to the embarrassment of the Carter administration and ourselves, and she had no choice but to announce it. The whole matter took up about ten minutes of Cabinet time. We then spent a rather greater length of time discussing whether there should be a two- or a three-line whip on the West Wolverhampton Local Authority Bill or some such subject. Such are the ways of Cabinet government.

When Margaret Thatcher offered me the post of Defence Secretary, and no doubt remembering this incident, she asked me whether I was 'sound' on the nuclear deterrent. I said 'Yes' – but I wanted to examine the background to the decision.

I resolved that if, as Defence Secretary, I was ever in a similar position I would organise a full briefing for my Cabinet colleagues. A year or so later, when we abandoned the original Trident decision for a different project which I call Trident II (Trident D5), I persuaded a somewhat reluctant Margaret Thatcher to agree to such a meeting. Having obtained the permission of the Americans to pass on some very delicate information, we explained to the Cabinet how much we knew about Soviet nuclear, biological and chemical capabilities, where their command and control bunkers were situated, and how the development of anti-ballistic missile defences bore down on the requirements for a credible deterrent. This was in an era where the extent of satellite photography and electronic and signal intelligence was not much known to those outside a small circle. I think the briefing was worthwhile. My colleagues were fascinated; but the Chancellor had come from a good lunch and slept during the briefing.

My education into nuclear theology in the Ministry of Defence was mainly conducted by Michael Quinlan. Michael was a key man in my life because he held the crucial post of Deputy Under-Secretary (Policy), perhaps the most important job in the department. He had a brilliant brain and was an outstanding draughtsman and later became the Permanent Secretary before being appointed as Director of the Ditchley Foundation. Michael was intellectually fascinated, almost obsessed, by nuclear theology; and he and Arthur Hockaday, the Second Permanent Secretary, spent a great deal of time with me. Although both of them had been closely associated with the nuclear debate for a long time, I found them very moderate on the issue. We discussed the moral and ethical issues involved – we were actually human beings – and whether what was described as the seamless web of nuclear response, strike and counter-strike was in fact more of a tangled web full of holes. I formed the view that whilst our nuclear deterrent was the first and most important of all our defence capabilities (we are truly independent; the Americans hold no veto over us), the whole nuclear debate had become stuck in a rut. It would need Reagan and Gorbachev to break down the barriers to a saner world.

It is nightmarish to speculate about what might have happened had some madman gained control in the Kremlin. Lying at the heart of the Defence Review was the appalling fact that, at that time, our forces on the Central Front had less than one week of ammunition stocks with which to resist a high-intensity assault by conventional forces over the German plain. My whole thrust was to rebalance the programme, so that we transferred resources away from ships, tanks and aeroplanes into weapon systems and into missile and ammunition stocks. In the Falklands campaign, a very minor skirmish compared to what we would have seen on the outbreak of a Third World War, we actually consumed almost the whole of our missile stocks. The shortage of ammunition stocks to meet a high-intensity conflict was a disgrace, partly brought about by cheese-paring at the margins each time the Ministry of Defence was asked to reduce expenditure. One budgetary economy after another, imposed too late, had led to reductions in training – one hour of Tornado-flying cost somewhere in the region of £3 million – and a reduction of stocks, spares and ammunition.

If the Warsaw Pact had ever crossed the line and launched an assault on NATO forces, we might have held them for a time. But unless we had been able to interdict successfully the second echelon of their forces – and that was primarily a job for airpower –it would have been nearly impossible, in my view, to stop them reaching the Channel ports, such was their conventional superiority over NATO in tanks and men. Would we have released battlefield nuclear weapons? Who can say? We certainly did so in our exercises, and fortunately the Russians were aware of our intentions. But the world of exercises is different from the real world. The dilemma was: how in a real conflict would you stop nuclear escalation from battlefield to tactical to strategic nuclear weapons? The United States had no cause to defend Europe if that threatened the destruction of their own cities by a strategic strike from the Soviet Union. This was partly why our nuclear deterrent provided added security for Europe. But would we have chosen to defend Germany or France with nuclear weapons if the consequence was the nuclear destruction of the United Kingdom? I did not hesitate to say in every debate on nuclear weapons that we would release them, because that was what deterrence required. But would we have done so in the event? Fortunately for our survival, none of us were ever put to the test.

I re-examined with Michael Quinlan and others alternative means of modernising the deterrent; submarine-launched Cruise missiles being the only other possible option. But for a variety of reasons, more particularly because the range of Cruise was short, it made no sense. When Trident II came into service we could launch missiles to within a few yards of a designated target and launch them from almost anywhere in the oceans of the world. The deterrent is only real if the ballistic missile submarine is invulnerable to discovery. Trident provides that requirement.

Just as I was putting the Defence Review to bed, the new Reagan administration announced that they were abandoning the existing Trident I infrastructure and going to Trident II. This presented us with a serious dilemma. We did not wish to be on a different system from that of the United States; it would have meant us keeping production facilities going in the States at huge risk and cost. Trident II was, however, much more expensive than Trident I – where were we to find the money? An equally dramatic turn of events arose when we discovered that the existing Polaris system, which still had fifteen years to run, needed a substantial upgrade costing something like £300 million if it was to remain credible to the Soviets. This was also hugely expensive at just the wrong time. Fortunately, by reshuffling cash flow we were able to fit Trident II into the programme and also upgrade Polaris. It was one of the trickiest decisions that we were called upon to make in my time at Defence.

I think that Trident makes our country safe and independent for at least the next twenty years. It is only part of our defensive structure, but it remains the ultimate guarantee of our freedom.

I conclude this nuclear saga, about which I could easily fill a whole book, by recording how the Trident decision kept on intervening as we conducted our examination of the conventional programme. Frank Cooper came to see me about where the cost of Trident should fall. It involved more than just the missiles and control apparatus. We wished to install a new pressurised water reactor (PWR2) in the Trident submarines, a quieter and more efficient propulsion system than PWR1. Also, there were plans for a substantial upgrading in sonar capability, possibly the crucial area which gave us superiority over the Soviet submarines. Understandably the Naval Staff asked for the cost of Trident to be spread equally over the three

Services. I rejected this request and it subsequently became another source of Naval grievance.

I did so for several reasons. First, the Royal Navy was responsible for the operations and running cost of Polaris, the existing deterrent. Secondly, as a pure question of financial control and responsibility, it had to be part of a single budget. We could not have the Royal Navy running Trident – and then the Army and the Air Force carping about the management and the cost. Thirdly, the nuclear deterrent had always been a single-service responsibility – the Air Force being in control of the early air-launched deterrent. And finally, as Trident was the United Kingdom's most valuable defence resource, I wanted the high quality and management dedication of the Royal Navy to continue; I would not have had the same confidence in the Army or the Air Force.

Of course, I could have fudged the issue, given the other two Services a larger slice of the cake, and then taken it away from them again as a contribution towards Trident; but the outcome for the conventional programmes of the three Services would have been no different.

~

After spending my first two months visiting units of the three Services, meeting all the key people and debating the nuclear options with this small group, I was ready to try and get to grips with the Service programmes. Endeavouring to solve the £200 million overspend which I had inherited from Francis Pym, I had already learnt my first lesson about Defence expenditure. Up to 90 per cent of the programme was already committed, and mainly contracted, up to ten years ahead. The Tornado programme exceeded ten years. This was the reason why the ten-year long-term costings were the vital annual re-examination of the budget. I found that – apart from food for the Forces, the training budget and stocks of ammunition and spares – there was nothing to cut back in the short term. The Treasury, with its annual nightmare of reconciling expenditure and revenue in the annual PESC review, was fond of looking to Defence with its £12 billion budget to fill any shortfall. How could it be difficult to find £100 million savings out of a £12 billion budget? Its attitude was supported by Margaret Thatcher. When Defence lost the annual punch-up with the Treasury, it had no choice but to stint on training expenditure and stocks. This was the reason underlying our inadequate ammunition stock on the front line of NATO. It was an utterly demoralising and damaging process. It had become worse in my time because of the foolish self-imposed corset – Nigel Lawson would have called it discipline – of the Medium-Term Financial Strategy.

I never found the savings to recover the £200 million overspend; but as the outside industrial contractors found that their non-defence work began to recover with the easing of the recession, so the cash demands on the MoD eased, and the problem solved itself. But I learnt that I had to get much deeper than I would have liked into the whole process in order to free up the long-term programme. The MoD is like a huge supertanker. It takes a long time to turn it in another direction and years to reverse it. At constant prices the defence budget today is about three-quarters of the size that it was in my day. It would have taken much longer to have achieved the so-called 'peace dividend' after the end of the Cold War had I not insisted on 1 per cent volume growth in the programme from 1986–87.

I must have started the meetings on the long-term programme in March 1981, when I returned via Bermuda from a meeting in Washington with Weinberger, the US Defence Secretary. The note – drafted by Michael Quinlan and which came to be called 'the Bermudagram' – that I sent around the Ministry on my return launched a radical review of the long-term programme. It began:

> The Defence Programme needs to be revised for two reasons. Firstly the latest Ministry of Defence long-term costing has confirmed that, even if the current programme were ideal in relation to the growing threat, it is overfull by any reasonable standard of what we can sustain. The Force structure is too large for the means likely to be available. Secondly the rapid advance of military technology exploited by massive Soviet spending calls for changes in our priorities.

I had no intention of conducting a Defence Review as such – a high-profile public exercise which was completely unnecessary. The very title raises emotions of doom among the Services and excitement with the journalists, who can sniff the friction and controversy involved. The MoD's annual examination of the ten-year costings was a perfectly adequate mechanism for doing everything that was necessary; that is why the joke around the Ministry was that it was 'Nott a Defence Review'. However, the Royal Navy took fright and leaked out that I had become engaged in a Defence Review, with all the emotive connotations that this involved. By making the exercise high-profile and public, the Navy ensured that everyone took positions. They sought to use the strong naval lobby to stop it in its tracks —which forced me, in return, to get the final decision through my colleagues and Parliament before the summer recess.

I called in Michael Beetham of the Royal Air Force and some of his subordinates. I remember Air Marshal Hine and Air Marshal Harding very well. They were altogether of a higher intelligence and quality than anything the Naval Staff had to offer at the time – or anyhow, they made more sense. Knowing that all I could expect from the Chiefs of Staff Committee was a feeble consensus, the lowest common denominator of inter-Service rivalry, I adopted a free-wheeling, exploratory approach and decided to question the underlying principles and assumptions upon which the plans had been set. I was provocative.

I have often wondered, in retrospect, whether my deliberately challenging approach – based on a series of questions which the civilian staffs and scientists prepared for me in advance of every meeting – was counter-productive. Subsequently, I asked those most qualified to give me an honest and critical reply. But the message I received was that the Ministry of Defence was such a bureaucratic and lumbering monster – tribal in its attitudes and rivalries – that only by provocation had I the slightest chance of opening up the debate. This was the view of the senior civil servants and scientists led by Sir Frank Cooper.

Accordingly, I asked the Royal Air Force what they were doing in Germany. Would it not be more cost-effective if they kept some forward airfields in operation but withdrew most of their planes to the UK, where they would have more hope of protecting them – and also of protecting the UK airfields – against a first strike? I questioned the balance between the strike attack Tornado and the defence version (Tornado ADV). I agreed that we would negotiate the purchase of Tristars owned by British Airways, in order to give us greater air flight refuelling capability and more troop lift.

I asked also why the task of the German Tornado squadrons at that time was to perform a maritime role in the Baltic, whilst we were charged under NATO tasks to interdict the Soviet second echelon in Germany. It seemed more logical that we should pursue a maritime role protecting the Atlantic bridge and our ships patrolling it, leaving the Germans to take responsibility for the central front.

Michael Beetham was surprised at first by my questioning of Air Force strategy, but he learnt to take it all in good part. He did not feel that I had some special prejudice against the Air Force. He instructed the admirable Air Marshal Hine among others to answer this foolish politician. Of course, the

RAF had a low opinion of the Royal Navy – and the Royal Navy a high degree of contempt and snobbishness towards the RAF. Each of them, with their long-standing disagreement over almost everything but particularly over tactics, offered me useful questions to ask the other. I wanted more savings in the later programme years from the RAF, but the tri-nation Tornado programme, which was more costly even than Trident, was virtually set in concrete and the Harrier, Nimrod and other weapons upgrades were all contracted; there was less room for manoeuvre than with the other Services. Moreover, we were woefully short of aircraft to defend the home base. There was virtually no air defence available to protect our Polaris base in Scotland, nor the dockyards in the South. In the meantime the Soviet Backfire bombers out of the Kola Peninsula were growing in numbers and sophistication. I discovered that we were spending far more on the air defence of surface ships at sea than we were on the air defence of the United Kingdom's key defence installations on land.

Towards the end of my time, I made one of the more feeble decisions of my tenure. The Royal Air Force had their strike attack bomber, the Tornado, but they had no fighter, except for the less than agile Tornado defence variant and some very ageing Phantoms. Although we managed to buy some more Phantoms from the United States, supplementing them with some additional Hawks, none of them would have been a match for the Russian threat. We had put into the forward programme the funds to develop a new Rolls-Royce engine for a fighter, but there was nothing on the drawing board for the aeroplane itself. I was visiting Wharton, British Aerospace to discuss this issue on the very day that we intercepted the Argentine order for the invasion of the Falkland Islands.

To the distress of the Royal Air Force, I resisted the building of a UK fighter aircraft. For one thing, I did not think, if we were to advance specialisation within NATO, that it was our task to engage with a new fighter in dogfights over Germany – this was for the Germans. We wanted aircraft that could stay in the air for long periods and which had air-flight refuelling, the most sophisticated long-range air-to-air missiles, and better radar. This was to meet the threat from the Backfire bombers out of northern Russia. I wanted to put the money into weapons systems and not into new platforms. This also seemed the perfect case for buying from the Americans the F16, which was a tried and tested aircraft of great sophistication. In all this questioning and analysis, as with everything, I had the support and briefing of Michael Quinlan, the scientists, the procurement specialists and the tri-Service and civilian Central Staffs.

However, I had recently been responsible for hazarding the parliamentary seats of several Tory MPs in the Thames Estuary by my decision to close Chatham Dockyard; and I was uncomfortably aware that if we did not give some new development work to the aerospace industry, it would wither away quite quickly. Again, many constituencies were involved, mainly in the north of England. I surrendered to the RAF for industrial and political reasons: not because I accepted the rationale for developing a new fighter aircraft, but because of its impact on British industry and politics. I therefore agreed to the building of a demonstrator aircraft, leaving it to my successor to decide on the main programme. Michael Heseltine did so and, as a result, we now have the European fighter aircraft.

The Army embraced a rather different set of problems. Its equipment programme was nowhere near as costly as that of the RAF and the Royal Navy, but even in those days it was manpower-deficient. The Army was living cheek by jowl with the Germans, and 1st British Corps, commanded by General Bagnall, was part of Northern Army Group under the leadership of a German general, von Senger. The Army was always in a twitch about German criticisms of its equipment. The German and British forces were overwhelmingly the best-trained, but there was great competition between the two nations' forces. The Germans never failed to make snide comments about the Army's tanks and armoured cars, which back in London always got under the skin of the Army Board. Moreover, until General Bagnall with great skill and persistence had persuaded von Senger to agree to some changes in the disposition of our forces, the British Army of the Rhine was strung out in a long thin line along the Forward Area, providing a political tripwire but little coherent defence. Furthermore, the British Army in Germany was subject to the most tiresome German politics – and the German generals were intensely political, always referring everything back to Schmidt and Genscher, the leading lights of the coalition in Bonn. With the politicians for once mercifully keeping out of it, Bagnall managed to get von Senger to agree to a rather different battle formation, allowing 1st British Corps more mobility to fight effectively. But the whole episode demonstrated the German obsession with holding every inch of German soil, whilst regarding the British forces ultimately as a political tripwire.

It was as I was examining the Army programme that the defence journalists whom I saw frequently approached me to say that they had learnt from the naval staff that some 40 per cent of the entire defence budget was consumed by the British Army of the Rhine and by RAF Germany. Sir Henry Leach recalls in his memoirs how he told the Prime Minister, to whom he rightly made his protests, that his 'alternative' to reductions in the naval programme was to take £2 billion out of the Army budget by bringing the Army home to the UK. I knew that this would be strongly opposed by the Foreign Office, as spokesman for the Germans, and even more fiercely opposed by the excellent General Rodgers, the US Supreme Allied Commander, Europe (SACEUR); but it gave me the opportunity to delve deeply into this option and the facts.

I asked Edwin Bramall, the Chief of the General Staff, to cost out for me a two-, three- and four-division option for the British Army of the Rhine. This provoked a similar reaction to Beetham's – quite fierce protest but taken in good part; however, I was not prepared to accept just like that that it was contrary to the Brussels Treaty and, therefore, was not worth examining. A very great deal of useful staff work was undertaken by the Army and the civil servants, which made it clear that far from saving £2 billion or anything at all it would have added substantially to the budget. Whilst there was a complete infrastructure for the Army and the RAF in Germany, there was insufficient barrack accommodation and very little training ground in the UK. The naval staff then briefed the journalists about the cost of Germany in foreign exchange; the pound was floating and the foreign exchange issue was a complete red herring. Sterling was much too strong anyhow.

In the end, General Bagnall, to whom I am in debt, reduced our divisions from four to three; by doing so he saved a substantial sum in headquarters and support costs. He also produced, as I have said, a far more effective plan of battle. He had a very good brain and a strong tactical and strategic grasp of issues. It is a pity that he was never Chief of Defence Staff. Maybe it was his red hair and occasionally fierce personality that failed to project him to the very top! However, he did become a field marshal, along with many others.

At this time, just as I was trying to understand what was the most effective anti-submarine weapon – was it a surface ship or another submarine? – so I was debating the tank. Was the tank the most effective anti-tank weapon or would this function be overtaken within the next ten years by the anti-tank helicopter? It was important to look far forward because of the huge time lags in procurement.

The programme for the Challenger tank and, more particularly, for the new armoured personnel carrier was coming forward at great cost. Each MCV80 (as the APC was called) was costing nearly £1 million and I asked the Army why they could not have two less MCV80s (there were some 200 on order) so as to re-equip the Territorial Army! I am afraid that the regular Army has never really supported the Territorials. It will always be a difference between the politicians and the Army Board, who at that time wanted to pour more and more money into Germany the better to equip our regular divisions in 1st British Corps. Too much money, in my view, was going into Germany – where, frankly, our divisions might not have survived a battle – and far too little was going into the second- and third-line Army reserves. It was the Army that was making its forces inflexible, not me.

This was the background at the time that I made a visit with my wife to General von Senger. He had fought on the Russian front and was a brave and distinguished soldier. We had a very good day of briefing, and Miloska and I stayed the night with him and his wife. At dinner, wisely or not, I reflected over my wine how things were going to look in ten years' time. I suggested that the most natural role for the British was to act as SACEUR's (Supreme Allied Commander Europe) strategic reserve, and with that in mind we should equip our forces in a more mobile role with shorter lines of communication back to the UK and not string them out as the first line of resistance along the FEBA (Forward Echelon Battle Area). With more specialisation in NATO, this function, I said, should develop over time into the main role of the German Army. I also ruminated on how the British and German air forces had had their natural roles reversed, as well as how I wanted more specialisation in the maritime role. There was, I explained, a serious overstretch in our commitments: we still had responsibility on the northern flank in Norway, we had the principal European maritime role in the east Atlantic, and we still had obligations in Belize, which the Americans were determined we should not change. I did not mention the Falklands. The British could not do everything, although we had the largest defence budget in relation to our GDP in Europe. Altogether, we had a very civilised and friendly discussion, and von Senger joined in the dinner-table talk with his own views.

I had already agreed with the Army Board, after some resistance, that we should look to equip at least one brigade of 2 Division as an air-mobile force, using Chinooks and Wessex helicopters. The Navy at that time was planning to make the Wessex redundant and to replace it with the new Sea King helicopter. Predictably there was a row with the RAF as to who should fly the Wessex, but that was par for the course. The Americans had an air-mobile division in southern Germany and it was a good example of what I wanted to be examined. In the event, following the Falklands, the Navy decided that, after all, they wished to keep the Wessex for the Royal Marines. I only mention this thwarted initiative because it accurately reflects my preoccupation at that time about how we could recover as much of the British Army as possible should disaster strike in Europe. Perhaps it is my memories of Dunkirk that have always led me to be concerned that, in the last resort, our Services exist to defend these islands, not to act as a world policeman. Still, if we have a standing army in times of peace, I can see the argument for keeping it occupied. I touch later on the strategic rationale for our forces in the changed conditions of today.

Anyway, after my visit to von Senger I returned to London to find that the Foreign Office had gone berserk. Clive Rose, our Ambassador to NATO, a good man but a flapper, had sent a telegram to London about our discussion over dinner. Von Senger had gone straight back to Bonn about my purely intellectual musings over dinner, implying, I suppose, that the British were contemplating withdrawing from the FEBA. I was asked to put it right by sending an explanatory letter to Bonn and to Bernie Rodgers (SACEUR). My wise Private Secretary, and others who had been with me over dinner, supported me when I said it was a complete nonsense and that I intended to do nothing at all.

It was a typical incident of those times and explains why the Germans gave me so much trouble over the Falklands and Trident. They were basically neutralist and feeble – and they still are. I suppose that is the nature of Social Democrats and Liberals and, even more so, of coalitions based on half-baked electoral systems, as they have in Germany, which give unnatural influence and power to minority parties. The Liberals, although supplying the foreign and other senior ministers, had only about 6 per cent of the total vote. If we ever abandon our first-past-the-post electoral system, you can be sure that we will never again have strong defence; nor can we do so if we ever enter a single European currency. We could find ourselves held to ransom by a minority party, like the Greens, who had polled about 5 per cent of the electorate.

This chapter may be called 'Upsetting the Navy', but I hope I have shown that I also upset the Royal Air Force and the Army! However, because they reacted intelligently and unemotionally, we were able to do useful business together.

~

I have already given a feel for the development of my differences with the Navy, but I must return to it before concluding this saga – intellectually the most absorbing of my time in politics. It was not as hard and exhausting as my time in the Treasury or as relaxed as my time in Trade or as difficult as my position during the Falklands, but I could not have chosen a more interesting experience to conclude my political career.

I was pressed by the Central Staff, which included officers of all three Services, to examine the cost-effectiveness of our naval assets in the war against the growing Soviet submarine fleet. Not only were these Soviet submarines (some hundreds in number) moving faster and diving deeper, but they were also being equipped with anti-ship missiles of increasing sophistication and range, targeted by satellite, which could be released by the Soviet submarines from under the sea. Clearly these missiles posed a very great threat, when coupled with the Backfire bombers, to our surface ships in the North Atlantic. This raised the whole question of whether we should not put more emphasis on our submarine fleet. Missiles and satellite targeting had created an entirely new world to that prevailing at the end of the Second World War.

I pleaded with the Naval Staff that several of the relevant scenarios should be studied by our operational analysis unit at West Byfleet – the MoD's in-house scientific study group. The Naval Staff steadfastly refused to listen to anything that came out of West Byfleet, so I had to resort to the Chief of the Defence Staff's resources within the Ministry. After what seemed an interminable length of time the Deputy CDS, General Maurice Johnston, produced an agreed tri-service paper – one of the few I remember receiving – of outstanding quality categorising the effectiveness of different naval assets against the Soviet submarines. The carriers were placed in the fourth category of effectiveness, near the bottom of the list. In fairness, it should be said that, in a crisis, it was proposed that the British carriers should join the US Navy's battle fleet in the North and would, therefore, have benefited from the much greater protection of the US northern battle fleet.

Had I been Defence Secretary in today's climate following the collapse of the Soviet threat and that of its navy, which is now largely tied up in port, I would happily have endorsed a three-carrier fleet – two in service and one in refit. I have never had any doubt about the value of carriers in a climate of low-intensity warfare or in meeting local crises around the world. My predecessors at Defence had fought the carrier battle with the Royal Navy on earlier occasions, with Healey losing his Navy Minister and his First Sea Lord in a comparable situation. But I did not see how we could afford three carriers in planning for a high-intensity war against the Soviets, nor how at that time we could afford to equip ourselves, in priority, for an out-of-area low-intensity war – not least because the protection of the carriers required a flotilla of supporting frigates, of which we had few in number anyhow. Indeed, all the advice – outside the Naval Staff – supported me. The carriers were hugely expensive in maintenance, refit costs, helicopters, Harriers and men, and in escorting frigates. With no pleasure at all, because I realised how controversial it would be, we therefore decided on a two-carrier fleet.

The discussion on *Invincible*, one of our new carriers, was protracted; but when the Australians wanted to buy her for her cost price, together with a shopping list of other British defence equipment, I decided that she should go. It was also a great opportunity to open up the Australian defence market and entice them away from the Americans, at a time when we needed defence sales urgently to cover the overheads of our defence industrial base. However, although under pressure from the salesmen to sign on the dotted line, I held back from formally signing the contract with the Australians. I was clear that *Invincible* could not go until *Illustrious* and *Ark Royal*, two new carriers, were in operational service. On several occasions I asked the Naval Staff whether they wanted to put any resources into simple platforms – cheap container ships with a deck that could temporarily provide a sea platform in an emergency for the naval and Air Force's Sea Harriers – but the idea was rejected. In fact, we sent many Harriers to the Falklands on the deck of the ill-fated *Atlantic Conveyor*. The Navy felt, maybe correctly, that whatever platform was used by the Harriers it needed the full panoply of electronics, command and control, and support services afloat. When I saw the plans for building a replacement for the *Atlantic Conveyor*, I diverted significant funds from the Defence budget to strengthen her decks, so that the new ship could be converted to carry Harrier aircraft should some new emergency arise.

Just as I was departing for my constituency one Thursday afternoon in November 1981, Henry Leach asked to see me about *Invincible*. I said to my Private Secretary that I had already had many, many meetings on the carriers and there was nothing new to discuss. I said that I would see Henry Leach on Monday. I certainly did not intend any discourtesy. I had an open door for the Chiefs of Staff. I arrived in Cornwall to stay the night with Julian Williams at Caerhays Castle, the famous Cornish garden. Julian was, at that time, Chairman of the Cornwall County Council and possibly the most widely respected and liked member of the Cornish establishment.

When I arrived my Private Secretary telephoned to say that the Ministry of Defence was in uproar, because the Naval Staff was saying that I had refused to see Sir Henry Leach. I said that I could not return to London due to my engagements in Cornwall, but if Sir Henry had any new points to make and was prepared to travel to Caerhays, I would see him there. I was somewhat distraught when I heard that bad weather had prevented Henry flying down in an hour or so to RAF St Mawgan or RNAS Culdrose. Instead, he was coming on the train, which takes an age. I have done it for nearly forty years and it takes it out of me every single time.

It must have been around eight o'clock in the evening when he arrived at Caerhays. With his sleeper due to depart from St Austell at midnight, I wanted to give him plenty of opportunity to go through all the arguments for the umpteenth time. But Julian Williams, revelling in the presence of a First Sea Lord in his kitchen, opened bottles of champagne and then took us through the history of the Williams family and their several naval exploits. Henry and I, as good-mannered guests, did not wish to interrupt him.

Eventually he and I adjourned to the library, but as there was only an hour or so left for the discussion (during which Henry trundled out all the same old arguments that had been advanced in favour of the carrier ever since the Healey review in the mid-1960s) I offered to drive with him to see him off from St Austell station. It was beastly cold on the station and I had no coat. The Wren driver got hopelessly lost on the way back to Caerhays – I must have been there a hundred times, but I can easily get lost – and I got back some time after two o'clock, exhausted and chilled to the bone.

I confirmed to Henry Leach in the morning that I could not change my decision on *Invincible* – but it was characteristic of the determination of the man, and I admire him for it, that he made this dash to Cornwall, although in practice it was quite unnecessary.

Two factors influenced me in seeking reductions in the surface fleet. The first was the increasing vulnerability of surface ships to Soviet submarine and air power, proved conclusively in the battle for the Falklands. The second is well explained in Richard Hill's biography of Lewin:

> At the heart of the strategic debate, when this was conducted (as it was) within the straitjacket of NATO scenarios, lay a conundrum. Rightly or wrongly, whenever a battle on the central front was 'gamed' by NATO, by the Defence Operational Analysis Establishment [at West Byfleet], or by the Staff Colleges, given the accepted intelligence assessments, the situation within seven days or so was so desperate for NATO that they were forced to initiate the use of tactical nuclear weapons. If this conclusion was correct, it meant that reinforcement by shipping across the Atlantic, which was a main plank of the naval case, would be too late to prevent a catastrophe. It also meant, if it was correct … the likelihood of a short war.

The short-war versus the long-war scenario became one of the most contentious areas for discussion that I had with the Naval Staff. They said, wholly reasonably, that no war turns out as predicted – and they could provide excellent examples to prove their case.

The long-war scenario led me to insist on building up more stocks, particularly of ammunition, in Germany; and a protracted debate arose within NATO about the pre-positioning of more US equipment reinforcements in Europe to avoid the huge delays and uncertainties of transatlantic resupply, but the Germans, inexplicably, were obstructive to this policy. However, my visit to Norfolk, Virginia, for briefing by SACLANT did not support the Naval Staff's Second World War type convoying proposals, even if the war turned out to last six months rather than a week. Modern targeted sub-sea missiles and nuclear weapons had transformed deterrence; it required more radical proposals about how we would prepare for a short/long war in the late twentieth century. I wanted to have an open debate with the Royal Navy about these issues, but they stuck to the long-war thesis on the basis that this justified the traditional naval role.

One of the documents that I read when I was wondering what on earth to do about reducing the forward programme was a very good study by my ministerial colleague Keith Speed, the Under-Secretary for the Navy, who chaired the Admiralty Board. He was a pleasant man, and although he caused me some difficulty – no more so than I caused him – I found him a useful colleague. He was particularly proud of his service with the Royal Navy – and so he should have been.

Keith had undertaken a study on the dockyards which became known as the Speed Report. It said that the short-lifing of naval ships was a serious option for policy – that is to say, paying off ships early before they went into the dockyard for a long and very expensive refit. To keep the maximum number of hulls floating in the water, frigates and destroyers underwent a refit in the dockyards costing up to £70 million each. The carrier refits cost more than £100 million, and *Endurance* was to cost about £30 million. Yet the cost at that time of building and equipping an entirely new and more modern frigate, the Type 23, was around £90 million.

Keith's conclusion – and I have to summarise it – was that short-lifing was not possible, because it would have reduced the number of surface ships and therefore was an unacceptable 'political' proposition; not an unacceptable dockyard proposition, not an unacceptable defence proposition, but an unacceptable 'political' proposition. In the appendices to the Speed Report – Appendix J – the arguments for short-lifing were pretty overwhelming.

I was accused of not having a full and proper discussion about short-lifing with the Navy, but it was all there in their own report and had been considered by them in great depth. But it was too difficult 'politically'. It was the same with Chatham Dockyard, redolent with great tradition and wonderful architecture, but hopelessly vulnerable to tides and access and an air attack in any conflict. The Royal Navy had wanted to close it for years, but it was not 'politically' possible – they were nearly right.

I probably handled Keith badly, because I liked to be able to speculate privately with my junior ministers on what we could do with the programmes. In our ministerial discussions, which were always attended by my two excellent Parliamentary Private Secretaries, David Hunt (who became a Cabinet minister and is now in the Lords) and John Wilkinson (who is still in the Commons), we ranged over a wide number of problems. No doubt, I remarked how difficult and unsatisfactory I had found my meetings with the Naval Staff, which clearly must have alienated Keith. Fortunately or unfortunately, my exasperation was shared by Tom Trenchard, the Minister of State for Procurement, and by Philip Goodhart, the Army Minister, and Geoffrey Pattie, the Air Force Minister. They were a good team and I was particularly sorry to see Philip Goodhart go – no one ever consulted me. He was replaced by Peter Blaker, who was also a good man. Jerry Wiggin also joined the department, but he gave me some problems as his arrogant approach consistently put up the backs of the military. In retrospect it is really quite disgraceful that I was never consulted at Defence about my ministerial team. It was simply decided by the Prime Minister, Whitelaw and the whips.

When Keith made a speech in his constituency in May 1981 hinting at the dangers of the Defence Review, I was speaking somewhere in Merseyside and staying the night with Jock Bruce-Gardyne at his home. The *Sunday Times* made Keith's speech their lead story. Jock said 'That's the end of Keith.' I said, 'I hope not, as I find him helpful and pleasant.' Unfortunately the Monday papers also led with the story and the Prime Minister called me in. Whitelaw – he was a nuisance throughout my whole political career – agreed with Margaret Thatcher that he had to go. I tried to persuade them to shift Keith to another department, but they would not have it. The First Sea Lord organised for the Naval Staff, some in uniform, to line the corridor as Keith departed the building, and they piped him down the steps of the Ministry of Defence in a public gesture of support for him and of defiance to me. If I think about it, it was near to mutiny – a capital offence!

Another similar incident occurred not long afterwards. Henry Leach in his intense lobbying against what he called Nott's naval cuts – as if they were personal to me – had entertained, mainly in his flat in the Admiralty Arch, a succession of MPs and other distinguished persons who either disliked me or who were staunch and loyal members of the naval lobby. No one was more distinguished, staunch and loyal to the naval interest than Jim Callaghan, former Naval Petty Officer and Prime Minister in that order. Jim was briefed by Henry into the internal details of what was happening. It was all heavily classified – and although Jim was, of course, privy to the highest level of security, it was wholly contrary to Queen's Regulations and to the rules prevailing for military officers and, quite probably, to the Official Secrets Act.

Jim Callaghan, whilst fully supportive of Henry Leach's protests, was nevertheless somewhat embarrassed. He knew that he would not have allowed something of this sort to happen in his administration. So being the decent man he is, he telephoned me to tell me that he had been briefed by Henry Leach, against my interest, and he felt that he had a duty to let me know. My Private Office, which had listened in to Callaghan's call, must have informed Clive Whitmore, the Prime Minister's Private Secretary, because, as in the Keith Speed case, I was asked to go across to No. 10.

I arrived to find the usual team of Thatcher, Whitelaw and Clive Whitmore.

I am not sure that Robert Armstrong was not there as well. Margaret and Willie expressed a sense of outrage that Henry Leach was briefing the Labour Party and going around undermining me, his political boss. Willie said that Leach must go, it was intolerable, he was letting the Services down. Margaret agreed. I said that I didn't agree. Whilst it would have cleared the air – and I might have got Fieldhouse, a better choice – it would have interfered with a process that was going along all right. I knew by this time that I had found the way to go and I was confident that I could get it through the Cabinet and party. To get rid of Leach would be an unnecessary distraction, taking up time when I had so little of it. I also said, 'Look, Prime Minister, Henry Leach has had forty years of distinguished service and he is shortly to retire as an Admiral of the Fleet. I don't want his career to be blighted by removing him at this time.' It might have meant, of course, that he would have retired in glory as a naval martyr – and I was not to know that he was anyhow at that time consulting with his colleagues whether he should tender his resignation. They advised him against it, as it would not have been more than a one-day wonder for the press. They were right to persuade him to stay and fight his corner.

~

At the launch of the Programme Review following the issue of my request to the Military Staffs in the so-called Bermudagram, I asked them to cost out their own programmes based on the new numbers that I had given them. These revised budgetary numbers – which had been prepared for me by the Central Staff, based on 1 per cent growth in defence expenditure in the later years of the ten-year programme – produced a sense of shock and, in certain quarters, outrage. The 1 per cent growth element – i.e. excluding 3 per cent volume growth in the later years – meant that over the ten-year period we had to take up to £10 billion in total off the long-term programme, the annual budget at that time being about £12 billion a year. This in fact formed the financial basis of what was finally agreed by parliament. I gave each of the Service Chiefs one month to come back to me with their own proposals for rebuilding their budgets from the bottom up. In other words, they were to list their own programmes in their own order of priority.

Their response was disappointing. Each of them had done their best to protect their long-term programmes by salami-slicing at the margins, reducing stocks and training – in other words, generally conducting the sort of cheese-paring exercise which had been forced on them in successive earlier Treasury squeezes. For its part, the Royal Navy listed the surface ships that they were prepared to lay off, placing *Britannia* and *Endurance* near the top of their list because, of course, these were the most politically difficult for me to undertake. I am not sure that, even at this stage, the Royal Navy took me seriously.

However, Round I was useful because it clarified both the near-impossibility of finding savings in the mainly contracted programmes of the RAF and the huge disruption to the NATO alliance that would arise if we were to breach the Brussels Treaty, which had set out our military contribution to continental defence. The Royal Navy, on the other hand, offered substantial savings by going for a short-lifing policy for their surface ships – a policy which seemed to have great merit anyhow, but involved of course a very large and painful reduction in naval infrastructure and the closure of Chatham, Gibraltar and Portsmouth dockyards for the refitting of surface ships. It meant also a reduction in the frigate numbers from sixty-five to fifty – with some of the fifty in reserve.

Round II went better and, with the help of the Central Staffs, we put a draft programme together for examination by the Overseas and Defence Policy Committee of the Cabinet, chaired by the Prime Minister. Not only was the 'Nott' Review, as described by the Naval Staff, not the Nott Review at all but an amalgam of advice from very many quarters (the tri-Service military staffs, civil servants, scientists and the rest), but I also needed of course the support of Carrington, a former Defence Secretary, at the Foreign Office, and my other Cabinet colleagues, some of whom were close to the naval lobby.

Henry Leach asked to see the Prime Minister, as was his right and obligation. He saw her twice in the early summer of 1981. I leave it to him to describe the second meeting:

> On the morning of 8 June I personally saw the Prime Minister as First Sea Lord. Calling at the Defence Secretary's room before walking across to No. 10, John Nott was kind enough to suggest that I should go alone so as not to inhibit the discussion. 'Thank you, S of S,' I said, 'that is generous of you but I really must insist that you come too …'
>
> Mrs Thatcher listened patiently whilst I briefly summarised the main points of my case (which had not changed since my recent submission), then looking gravely at me she asked:
>
> 'What would you do instead?'

'Prime Minister, I would start by hiving off £2–3 billion to the Army,' I replied.

'Why on earth would you do that?' she broke in.

'In order to reprovide in this country the necessary barracks, etc., which are currently in Germany with a view to rotating front-line units to a frequency selected by the Army (say every nine months, like naval deployments), thereby saving the recurring and crippling annual bill in foreign exchange.'

For a moment the PM looked uncertain and glanced inquiringly at the Defence Secretary.

'We've studied that and it's too expensive,' said John Nott curtly.

I have explained already that the cost of achieving a withdrawal or partial withdrawal from Germany was crippling at the time – and, since sterling was floating and it was embarrassingly strong anyhow, the foreign exchange argument was completely irrelevant. The overriding objection to the Naval option was, however, the need to hold the US commitment to the land defence of Europe; they had 200,000 ground forces in Germany against our 55,000. If we had decided to rescind our Brussels Treaty commitment, pressure from Congress for the Americans to do the same would have been intense, in the face of the American contribution being more than 50 per cent of the total defence of Europe.

My paper to the Cabinet, seeking their approval for the Defence Review, began as follows:

We need to reshape our Defence programme to provide within our growing spending on Defence a force structure which is cost-effective for the future and capable of being sustained surely and adequately in the long haul. The memorandum which I attach explains the need for change, the options for its direction and the industrial employment and budgetary implications. This note summarises the key issues.

The central message is that we are at present trying to do too much with the certainty of not doing it well enough. Now is the time to face radical adjustment and to settle a stable and realistic long-term course. If we duck decisions now they will confront us more acutely and in more difficult circumstances later.

I had, in fact, put two options to the Cabinet: one was a crash reduction in the programme which would have reduced expenditure on the Defence Programme quickly and controversially; the other, a more phased reduction, was difficult but less dramatic. I recommended the second approach, pointing out that with the faster reduction I would require an extra £300 million a year for a few years to fund the cost of Trident. That killed it, at least for the Treasury.

No doubt this is the cause of an anecdote in the Lewin biography:

An official close to John Nott recalls that a special subvention was argued for; and Lord Howe, who was then Chancellor of the Exchequer, records a limerick scribbled by Lord Carrington, the Foreign Secretary, at the Cabinet table.

The spendthrift and bellicose Nott
Is involved in a nuclear plot;
He's impaled on the fork
Of his Tridential talk
And Howe has to finance the lot.

The long and detailed proposal was agreed by the Cabinet Committee and endorsed by the whole Cabinet. A White Paper (*The Way Forward,* Cmnd. 8288) was published on 25 June 1981. Later that summer it was passed by parliament with only six Conservatives voting against, mainly MPs whose constituencies were adversely affected by the closures.

I made a visit to Chatham dockyard – a sad day. The unions representing the men (some 7,000) who were to lose their jobs were restrained. I had other meetings with the unions representing the ordnance factories which also had a bad hit from the Review; altogether my changes to the programme were to lead to many thousands of redundancies, representing some 40 per cent of all the reductions in the civil service during the Thatcher Government. I somehow managed to get through these meetings without too much unpleasantness. The main grief, I regret, fell on Admiral Pillar and those below him.

When, however, I made my visit to Portsmouth dockyard it was a different story. Somehow it became known that I was on the dockyard premises talking to the unions. I noticed hundreds of menacing-looking dockyard workers converging on the glass-covered headquarters building where my meetings were taking place. Gradually the anger from the assembled men grew in intensity, with massive shouting, yelling and abuse. I asked the admiral commanding the dockyard if he had sufficient Ministry of Defence police on duty:

'No, they are all at the International Defence Equipment exhibition in Southampton.'

'How many police do you have?'

'About six.'

'Well, I think we are about to have a violent riot on our hands. You had better call in the Hampshire police as a precaution.'

'We can't do that. We never invite civilian police on to dockyard premises.'

By this time, the assembly was in a very ugly mood and another officer whispered to the admiral that the men wished to talk to the Defence Secretary. Saying that I would go out and see them if that was the decision, I added, 'But I don't think it will do any good.' However, the union officials urged me to do so – so a soapbox was erected outside the main door for me to address the multitude. As soon as I opened my mouth a hail of metal bolts and other dangerous missiles were hurled in my direction and the glass of several windows and doors of the headquarters building was shattered. Amazingly nothing struck me, and I was hustled back into the building and the doors were locked. This time the Hampshire police were called in plus two coaches, and some time later we were ushered into the coaches and led by a police car out towards the exit. However, the men had not dispersed and hurled their missiles at the coaches. Several naval and civilian officials were covered in shattered glass, but we escaped, rather surprisingly, without any casualties. None of this appeared in the press. These same men who had been so violent were, as I shortly relate, the very same chaps I talked to the following spring at the beginning of the Falklands campaign.

There was a sequel to my Defence Review which helped to trigger the end of my political career. In the paper which I had submitted to the Cabinet I included an appendix, setting out the agreed budget for defence following the Review. It showed volume growth of defence spending at 3 per cent per annum until 1985–86 and 1 per cent thereafter. However, my Treasury experience standing me in good stead, I included a line setting out the agreed expenditure in cash terms as well. I knew the Treasury would try and undermine the agreement by fiddling the cash.

I made a note of the actual numbers at the time. The Cabinet in June had agreed cash expenditure in 1982–83 of £13.78 billion, having rejected the

Chancellor's bid for a reduced number of £13.58 billion. In October, the Treasury came back again with a bid for £13.71 billion – £700 million less than the Cabinet had agreed.

So sure enough, not more than four months after I had put the Defence Review to bed in July with an agreed set of numbers, the Treasury was in its annual PESC crisis and it came to me for a substantial contribution to their shortfall – this was in October 1981. I refused to see the Chief Secretary and the Chancellor even to discuss it. I said the numbers had all been agreed a few months earlier and ratified by the Cabinet. The day before the Cabinet met to agree the public expenditure totals, Defence still had not been settled. The Prime Minister asked to see me. We went hammer and tongs at each other for nearly an hour. I refused to budge by even £1, giving my reasons. It would have been impossible to find £700 million or anything near it. To her fury, I read back to her the concluding sentence of the Cabinet minutes in July, drafted by Robert Armstrong, the Cabinet Secretary, which had specifically agreed and endorsed the columns of expenditure in both volume and cash.

As I walked back across Whitehall to my office, I began to feel that – although I had right on my side – I had behaved rather badly. I knew that Thatcher could hardly dismiss me so soon after removing Francis Pym, but I had taken advantage of the strength of my position. When I got to my office I called in Frank Cooper and said: 'Frank, I think that I may have behaved rather badly. I refused to give an inch to the Prime Minister and I know in my heart of hearts that the business of government has to go on. Why don't you go across to No. 10 and settle an amount with Robert Armstrong and I will abide by your joint decision?' The amount agreed was £200 million off the Defence Budget for the coming year.

I remembered the impossible problem that I had faced in finding the £200 million cut that I had inherited from Francis Pym; even more serious, I had conducted my whole Defence Review on the basis that we were not to salami-slice at the margin but were to look at the fundamentals. Now I could only find £200 million by cheese-paring on food, training and stocks – everything else was more or less contracted. I was not going to do that to help the Treasury, which had been consistently obstructive, negative and unhelpful during my Defence Review. They had not been in the slightest bit interested in the £10 billion or so that I cut off the long-term defence programme. Like stockbrokers looking to the end of the next fortnightly account, they were only interested in the next two years –

for which my Defence Review had offered them nothing from the government's announced and agreed plans. There was, however, one opportunity. The Defence Review had agreed that we should reduce the carrier force from three to two and I still had not sold *Invincible* for £175 million to the Australians.

So I went back to the Cabinet Committee and the Prime Minister, asking them to endorse again the sale of *Invincible*, which in general terms they had already agreed. To be faced with the specific case, however, was a different matter. They knew the grief that such a sale was causing in the Royal Navy and that it was also a deeply unpopular move in the Tory Party. With political misgivings all round, not least from me, the sale of *Invincible* was agreed to fund the Treasury's £200 million. The Treasury did not care, of course. They would have been happy for everything to be sold to square their books. Leon Brittan was by this time the Chief Secretary. But still I did not sign the contract of sale with the Australians, as somehow I hoped that something yet might turn up to help me out, at least until *Ark Royal* and *Illustrious* came into service.

As I might have expected after my fierce disagreement with Thatcher – because such it was – quite shortly the whole thing found its way into the press, not from me I hasten to say. The No. 10 machine led by Bernard Ingham, from which I had been relatively immune (at least until the big Cabinet disagreement on public expenditure that July), began to brief against me. 'John Nott is on his way out ... he is not tough enough to sustain his control over Defence ...' 'He has reneged on his previous beliefs about public expenditure now he is in a spending department,' etc., etc.

I set out the version from Hugo Young's *One of Us*, undoubtedly based on the unattributable briefings that, as a political journalist, he had been getting from No. 10:

Nott, having been sent to Defence as a loyal monetarist with instructions to bring the military budget under control, had lost his faith and was failing in his task. At the famous Cabinet meeting in July 1981, he had shockingly withdrawn support for more spending cuts. Throughout the winter, he had lobbied for his department and used the press to help him. Downing Street was not amused. Two months before the Falklands invasion, the Prime Minister's office was putting it about that Nott would soon be on the way out. He was too flashy, too febrile, definitely unsuited to the long, slow grind of taking on the

Ministry of Defence and forcing it into a managerial regime that would succeed in reconciling its commitments with its resources.

Newspaper articles began to appear. I remember a particularly vicious one in the *Daily Express*, written by one of Thatcher's favourite journalists, and he could only have been briefed by No. 10. It was underhand and unpleasant, but none of us could expect any better from this source. Nothing was said about the £10,000 million that I had cut from the long-term programme: it was all about the £200 million, right on top of the new financial year, making a nonsense of sensible planning. It is a sad commentary on the Thatcher years that almost all of her closest and most loyal supporters, Howe, Lawson, Tebbit, Biffen, each suffered from this disreputable practice whenever they had a disagreement on a point of policy. Although not a leading player in the Thatcher story, I was always a significant one – and now it was happening to me.

I had told my wife at Cambridge that I did not intend to spend more than fifteen years in politics. She still has the letter that I wrote to her. She and I never wavered in that intention throughout my time at Westminster. We had agreed at the 1979 election that it was to be my last. The fifteen years were up in 1981, and I had enjoyed nearly every moment of them. But it was time to go. I was also debilitated at the time by a nasty intestinal bug called giardia which I only discovered many months later; I was quite a sick man.

I liked Margaret Thatcher and admired her courage, but I was upset at the disloyal way in which she treated her friends and allies by allowing her coterie at No. 10 to brief against her ministers. I was so fed up by this press that in December 1981 I told her that I would not be standing at the next election and that I wanted to step down from Defence. She would not have it. She insisted that I carried on as Defence Secretary and said that I might change my mind. In the meantime, I had arranged through an old Warburg colleague, Bernard Kelly, to return to the City to join Lazard – so I had to telephone Ian Fraser, the chairman, to say that my return to the City had to be postponed. Not long afterwards, the Falklands intervened.

However, one final punch-up with the Treasury was still to take place. After the Falklands – when I had been asked to stay on for a time, in order to conduct a post-mortem on the lessons of the campaign – our finances were, rather understandably, in a parlous state unless I found new money. The officials pleaded with me that I would still go ahead with the sale of *Invincible* because, quite correctly, they believed that we could not afford three carriers in the 'high intensity' scenario of the time. Unfortunately, Malcolm Fraser, the Prime Minister of Australia, had publicly announced during the Falklands campaign that 'as a gesture of support' for Great Britain he would forgo the purchase of *Invincible*. He actually had no choice as I had never signed the contract. I decided that, for political reasons in the aftermath of the Falklands victory, I should reprieve her. I did so against my better judgement; I was not to know that ten years later I would have backed a three-carrier fleet. I did not prophesy the collapse of the Soviet Union – but nor did anyone else.

The Treasury proposed that the cost of the Falklands campaign should be found from within the existing Defence Budget – including the replacement of all the ships, ammunition and equipment lost. It was what the Treasury would describe as their 'opening bid'. The very idea was pathetic, not least because, unusually, there was a high degree of public interest in our forces at the end of the campaign. I saw no purpose in bargaining with the Treasury; their ministers were politicians like me and they must have known that they were wasting everyone's time. In all my time at Defence, they had never offered me any help, so there was not much purpose in helping them.

However, Margaret Thatcher asked me to go over to No. 10 and discuss it with her. Leon Brittan, the Chief Secretary, was in attendance. He reiterated the Treasury request. I said that he was behaving like 'a Pakistani accountant'. I like the Pakistanis, but it was politically very incorrect to use such language. It was unfair on Pakistani accountants to compare them unfavourably with the Chief Secretary to the Treasury. Margaret Thatcher said I was being 'very rude'. Also correct. Leon argued that the Treasury could not afford to provide any more money to Defence. Perhaps the stupidity of the argument was based on some resentment that the Treasury had rightly been excluded from the War Cabinet. There is no purpose in reciting all the arguments. Suffice to say that I won a further £1,000 million from the Contingency Fund to provide many enhancements to the Defence Programme, including five new Type 22 frigates, with enhanced defence capability; a replacement for the logistic landing ship RFA *Sir Galahad*; and the replacement of all lost Harrier aircraft and Sea King, Lynx and Chinook helicopters.

Together the enhancements added up to the most valuable orders for the Royal Navy for very many years – and they were well deserved. Together with the additional £500 million of expenditure on the Royal Navy conventional programme between 1979 and 1983, it actually came out in my time, as Defence Secretary, stronger, not weaker. But the misrepresentations still continue.

I end this necessarily rather detailed chapter with my valedictory appearance in the House of Commons as Defence Secretary, following the publication in December 1982 of my White Paper on the Falklands campaign. 'I regret it always when men of ability like the right hon. Gentleman leave the House in mid-life,' Jim Callaghan was kind enough to say after my speech. 'The House and democracy need the best of our talents from all parts in the country. I wish that the right hon. Gentleman were not going, despite our disagreements on policy.'

In my own speech I was at pains to counter the increasingly fashionable, post-Falklands argument that we needed to shift the emphasis of our defence policy away from its principal focus on Europe and towards a wider world role. Of course, I recognise that today, with the suspension of the Soviet threat and our virtual withdrawal from Germany and all our overseas bases, our military forces must have something to occupy their energies, some worthwhile function to perform in order to maintain their readiness and discipline. An Army located in Aldershot, and training in gorse bushes around Fleet, would grow bored and restless, ill-prepared to respond to an unforeseen emergency that threatened the security of the United Kingdom.

The Royal Navy, on the other hand, having cast around for, and failed to find, a coherent strategy in the likely scenario of a high-intensity 'short war' against the Warsaw Pact, now has a role again, in what Correlli Barnett has described as 'the neo-imperialist do-goodery' of the Blair Government. The evacuation of British civilians from far-flung corners of the world, launching rapid reaction forces in East Timor and Sierra Leone, posturing with ship deployments in foreign ports to emphasise our ability to 'punch above our weight' – all this can be a reminder of the Royal Navy's great imperial past. It enables Blair and the Foreign Office to use our forces as an instrument of prestige, their prestige, but it has nothing to do with defence.

The same can be said of the so-called European Rapid Reaction Force. It will never be rapid and it will seldom react. The Balkans conflict demonstrated the inability of the European Union to come to difficult politico-military decisions without the leadership of the United States – something the French detest. Defence capacity continues to decline in all European countries; and even if the European Union had the ability to take decisions, which it does not, it has neither the heavy lift nor the sophisticated weapon systems to intervene effectively. The European Army – however the European enthusiasts dress it up as part of NATO – is a threat to our long-term security because it is a challenge to the United States, the only nation that can defend us should the need arise.

Thus the dilemma is stark. What are our forces to be doing in a climate where there is no obvious threat to the independence of the United Kingdom? It is, after all, a relatively recent phenomenon in our history that we have a standing army in times of peace.

The threat to our security exists all right, but from the much more insidious dangers of a single European currency and a European army, both of which would emasculate our ability to act speedily and independently in our own defence. Both would fortify the deep-seated unwillingness of the British ever to identify and then react to danger before it is too late. The innate caution of the British political classes, so vividly demonstrated in the 1930s, would be multiplied if decisive action were to be subject to a committee of our European allies, and our currency were to be controlled by a group of unelected bankers in Frankfurt. Yet large sections of our political world fail to see this. Not for the first time in our history we will be thrown back on the instincts of the British people generally, rather than on the political classes who have let us down before.

Chapter Nine

FALKLANDS: THE FIRST WEEK

King Philip of Macedon said to his son, Alexander: 'You see the glory, but war is above all else horror. It is blood, sweat, excrement; it is dust and wind; it is thirst and hunger, unbearable frost and unbearable heat. Let me face all this for you, for so long as I am able. Stay here [with Aristotle, your tutor] for one more year.'

(Alexander: Child of a Dream, Valerio Manfredi)

I hate war; the thought of sending young men and women away to fight is repugnant to me. Yet on the night of Thursday, 1 April 1982, I agreed, with my immediate colleagues, that we had no option but to do so; and we sent them to the other side of the world, at huge risk, across 8,000 miles of ocean. It ended in triumph and tragedy – 255 British lost their lives and many more were wounded. Nor should we forget the Argentine dead, brought about needlessly by the fascist leaders of their country.

Those who had experienced war – Terry Lewin, William Whitelaw and Francis Pym, my colleagues in the War Cabinet – must have felt as I did. Margaret Thatcher, as a woman and a mother, must have been just as deeply affected as us men. But all of us managed, in the crisis which engulfed us, to conceal these feelings from each other. Sometimes Francis, in his determined quest for a negotiated settlement, perhaps allowed his emotions to show a little; but it was his job as Foreign Secretary to seek a diplomatic exit – an exit to a situation that had vexed successive governments ever since the Second World War.

Whitelaw, Pym and I, as members of the Cabinet Committee under Margaret Thatcher's chairmanship, had all agreed to an earlier proposal by Nicholas Ridley to attempt a negotiated settlement with Argentina, based on a long-term lease-back of the Falkland Islands, but this proposal had been sabotaged by a cross-party alliance in the House of Commons. When a gun is pointed at your head, diplomacy has a tendency to veer towards appeasement. Yet appeasing the fascist junta in Argentina, once they had invaded British territory, was not on our agenda. There were only two choices: war or surrender. As circumstances later showed, there was never an honourable negotiated settlement in between.

Throughout the Falklands conflict, Margaret Thatcher was at her best, showing great courage and determination. I had some disagreements with her when I urged restraint, and occasionally I aligned myself with Francis Pym, not entirely to Margaret's liking. But generally there was a remarkable sense of unity among us – and that was surprising, given the rather diverse personalities involved. There were only five of us as politicians: Thatcher, Whitelaw, Pym, Parkinson and myself. We were later joined by Michael Havers, the Attorney-General.

There were strong differences of view on the handling of the negotiations, which were being conducted by Francis Pym; but generally, the atmosphere was good. There was none of the hectoring or personal antipathy which had characterised our debates on domestic economic policy. Fortunately, on Harold Macmillan's advice, the Chancellor of the Exchequer was excluded from the War Cabinet, so that money was never mentioned and the institutionalised negativism of the Treasury was avoided.

The handling of the Falklands crisis was a personal triumph for Margaret Thatcher and for Terry Lewin – and both of them deserve their high place in military history.

In time of war there is no room for the post of Defence Secretary; that role must necessarily be performed by the Prime Minister of the day. I found it difficult, because I knew that I would be the first scapegoat for any military failure. Truly, I had responsibility without power. I participated in, and I hope influenced, all the key decisions in the War Cabinet – but it was a very different set of circumstances from when I had been very much in charge on my own patch in the Ministry of Defence. I tried, and I believe succeeded, in redefining my own role within the MoD, questioning but not overly influencing the decisions of the military.

At the beginning of this book I talked about my grandfather's experience of war and his insistence, as a general, that it was the job of politicians to set out the objectives and the framework of activity, but that it was for the commanders in the field to decide the 'manner' by which they put those directions into effect:

The Envoys and Ministers – will state to you from time to time the services
which they may wish the troops to accomplish; when the 'manner' of performing and carrying them into full effect must depend entirely on your
judgement … (General Nott to Lt. Col. Wymer, commanding a detachment
– Kandahar, 1840)

My experience as a soldier was limited, but I had seen how things can go
wrong, particularly if consensus overrides command. Someone must be in
charge; war cannot be waged by a committee; nor for that matter must its conduct, in today's conditions, be unduly influenced by press and television.

Napoleon had said:

Nothing is so important in war as an individual command … Long discussions and councils of war … will terminate in the adoption of the worst
course which in war is the most timid, or, if you will, the most prudent. The
only true wisdom in a General is determined courage!

Thankfully I had agreed and implemented, not many months before, a change
to the status and authority of the Chief of the Defence Staff. I had placed Admiral Lewin in charge *de jure,* and his outstanding personality guaranteed that
he was also boss *de facto* within the MoD. Lewin scrupulously consulted daily
with his principal colleagues on the Chiefs of Staff Committee – Leach,
Bramall and Beetham in particular – but ultimately his decision was paramount
before he presented it to the War Cabinet. Each day he and I had a private
meeting to ensure that we were in accord in presenting the military options to
the War Cabinet. Terry Lewin himself established the shortest chain of command directly from the War Cabinet through him to Admiral Fieldhouse, the
Commander in Chief, down to Major General Moore on the battlefield and
Rear Admiral Woodward in the Fleet.

I have also explained in a previous chapter how the shambles of Suez had
influenced me. It was not just the interminable time that it took for the British
forces to reach the Canal Zone, but the deception which the senior politicians
practised in Whitehall in order to ensure secrecy about their intentions. I know
that Whitelaw, Lewin and I, in the early stages, thought 'Suez, Suez, Suez' in
many of our waking hours. Not least, we needed the support of the Americans.

If you go to war you have to trust the system – the relevant parts of the
bureaucracy must be kept informed. This was one of the principal failures of

Suez. It means widening the circle of information and consultation far beyond what is wise; but in an emergency the key people must be made to feel part of a team, for exclusion breeds resentment. In the early days several of my parliamentary colleagues were a real threat to national morale and good order, not least because of their incestuous relationship with the parliamentary press, but with difficulty (as I shall explain later) we managed to neutralise the worst speculation and gossip in the newspapers.

I hope that this account of my experiences of life is not too immodest, but as these reflections are in the form of a memoir rather than a biography I have to say where I think I got it right.

My principal contribution to the success of the Falklands campaign lay in my determination to ensure the shortest chain of command. I have already mentioned that I had to redefine my role within the Ministry of Defence, but it was also essential to get it right within the War Cabinet. I needed to transfer my efforts more to the collective decisions of the War Cabinet, rather than deciding military issues within the MoD and recommending them to my colleagues; I left this task to Terry Lewin. At our first meeting to decide the procedures for OD(SA), hereafter called the War Cabinet, I insisted, although it did not need much urging, that the Chief of the Defence Staff should attend all our meetings. In retrospect it seems an obvious decision, but at that time it was unusual to include a military officer as a regular member of a sub-committee of the Cabinet. Moreover, Margaret Thatcher at that stage did not know Terry Lewin very well.

More importantly, Margaret had discussed with me personally how I wanted to present the military intelligence and advice to the War Cabinet. I had no hesitation in saying that I thought this function would be better deployed by the Chief of the Defence Staff rather than by me. Again, it seems obvious now, but it was not so then. Richard Hill's biography of Lewin puts the matter accurately:

> John Nott had early decided, and cleared with the Prime Minister, that the military voice in OD(SA) [the War Cabinet] should be that of the CDS and not the Defence Secretary. He himself might sometimes take on the role of devil's advocate if he thought political sentiment was getting too hawkish, but generally he would keep a low profile.

General Bramall in his book, *The Chiefs*, describes it rather differently, but he puts the position of the Defence Secretary in time of war with clarity:

John Nott played a well-judged and significant part. In war, the position of a Secretary of State for Defence, who is not also Prime Minister, can be anomalous. There has to be a direct relationship between the Prime Minister and the Chiefs. Nott cast himself as something of a devil's advocate in his discussions with the Chiefs within the Ministry of Defence, ensuring that political requirements and military planning were co-ordinated, and that realism always prevailed.

I do not know in retrospect whether I got my function right – and certainly, the 'low profile' which I chose led to criticism. The Naval Staff, always happy to talk to the press, remained unforgiving of my reductions to their naval programme, so they were quick to claim that my contribution within the Ministry of Defence was ineffective. But they could not have it both ways: either they wanted their political boss to assert himself within the chain of command, or they had to be happy that they were left alone to get on with the military planning. It was my job to keep the budgetary programmes of Defence within the resources available; it was their job to fight a war. After all, as General Nott had long before said, the military command should have 'a becoming jealousy of the independence of a commanding officer of a military detachment engaged in a responsible duty'. So I backed away in the Ministry of Defence, leaving Terry Lewin to bring our joint recommendations to the War Cabinet. He then reported our decisions to Admiral Fieldhouse, the Commander-in-Chief, who communicated them to Admiral Woodward in the Fleet and General Moore on land. This chain of command was short and simple.

I had an uncomfortable time – not as uncomfortable or as dangerous as the sailors, soldiers and airmen that we sent to war, but difficult nonetheless. I was the spokesman for our forces in the House of Commons and had to explain and answer for events over which I had very limited control. I had to agree statements that were, by necessity, based on the shortest and flimsiest information from the Fleet whilst at the same time the world media, led by the BBC, was pumping out contrary Argentinian propaganda. I had to argue against the Foreign Office, which frequently wished to postpone military activity when it conflicted with diplomatic negotiations. I had a particularly difficult time with some colleagues – alternately doubting and frenetic – in the House of Commons. Sometimes I had to disagree with a bevy of admirals on how and when we would issue statements about casualties and losses to the Fleet.

Others had equal problems, and even today, nearly twenty years after the event, I have nothing but praise and admiration for everyone in the MoD and in Northwood, the command headquarters. No-one, of course, deserves greater praise and admiration than the Chief of the Defence Staff himself. Terry Lewin, with whom I had a very close and good working relationship throughout, was an excellent man. I have read his account of the Falklands and I am sad that he is no longer with us to read mine.

When I stepped down as Defence Secretary at the start of 1983, I wrote an account of some of the key events of those times. I did not keep a diary – I was too busy – but my record of events is reasonably contemporaneous. I cannot guarantee the accuracy (including the chronological accuracy) of every memory, and of course my opinions will be disputed, but it is not my intention to fight the war yet again. Many others have done that before me. This is a book of recollections, not a work of history. The most accurate and full historical record of the Falklands is, in my view, contained in the two chapters of Margaret Thatcher's memoirs; an excellent section, which I am sure she wrote herself.

~

Throughout March 1982, the month preceding the Argentine invasion on 2 April, I had been preoccupied with the typical round of events that fill the days of a Defence Secretary. There was a state visit by the Sultan of Oman – important for Defence as we were trying to establish ourselves as a major supplier of equipment in the Gulf. There was a one-week NATO war game, in which I had to participate. I was trying to make a start on the reorganisation and privatisation of the Royal Ordnance factories, then one of the largest businesses in the country. I was trying to agree with the Army the number of armoured personnel carriers – costing nearly £1 million apiece – that we intended to buy. British industry, in the form of Sir Robert Hunt and Sir Austin Pearce of British Aerospace, were at me, rightly, to get British offset work for Trident, following the statement to Parliament on 11 March of our intention to purchase the American nuclear system. It was a busy time, but not unusually so.

On 19 March I attended an Anglo-German summit at Chequers, and it was on that same day that I was shown the Defence contingency plans to meet any emergency in the Falkland Islands. I took this paper with me down to Cornwall where I had constituency engagements for the weekend of the 20th and 21st. It was on 20 March that we heard of the Davidoff landing on South Georgia and the hoisting of the Argentine flag, together with a message from the Governor (Rex Hunt) requesting that we despatch *Endurance* to South Georgia.

I read the contingency plans over the weekend and they seemed to me to be very negative. I said that I couldn't clear the paper without a meeting with the Naval Staff, which occurred on the Monday morning just before my departure that day to the United States. After a discussion, in particular about the deployment of our submarines, I agreed the paper. As I departed, news came through that the Argentine flag had been taken down and that a party of only twelve Argentinians had been left behind. So when I arrived in Colorado Springs for the bi-annual meeting of NATO's Nuclear Planning Group, the Falkland Islands were not at the forefront of my concerns. It seems odd to say so after the event, but even up to ten days before the Argentine invasion I was preoccupied with the problems of Trident.

The added firepower or, to be precise, the greater number of warheads on Trident II was causing considerable difficulty with our European allies. It had been discussed at the Anglo-German summit at Chequers the previous week. The Germans, whilst favouring the British nuclear deterrent in principle, were nevertheless carping at its impact on the nuclear arms reduction programme. They took the view that our choice of system was excessive. I had to explain to all our European allies in NATO, without disclosing the full extent of our knowledge of Soviet developments, why we needed more sophisticated accuracy, penetration and decoy capabilities in order to maintain the credibility of our deterrent in the eyes of the Soviets. Although NATO intelligence briefings to our allies were frequent and wide-ranging, only we, the British, shared the full intelligence picture with the United States.

The main parliamentary debate on Trident was due to take place on the following Monday, 29 March – four days, as it happened, before the invasion – and I had to avoid any rash press comments by our European allies that might strengthen the opposition to it, which was already very strong in the Labour and Liberal Parties. The Germans in particular, with their Social Democratic coalition, were a constant problem to me at this time – and they remained so throughout the Falklands conflict.

I succeeded, however, in getting not only Trident on the agenda, but a statement agreed by all the Social Democratic coalition countries of NATO that Trident was necessary for the defence of Europe. To get the Germans, Danes, Dutch and Belgians with their coalition governments to be unanimous about anything positive was something of a triumph. I also managed to agree a valuable degree of offset work for British industry on both the American and British Trident systems, with the ever-helpful and friendly Caspar Weinberger, the US Defence Secretary.

There were many defence journalists in Colorado Springs. The BBC had a team of around fifty people, though ITN did a rather better job with six. I was asked about the situation in South Georgia but the questioning was relaxed. I was in touch with Jerry Wiggin, the Parliamentary Under-Secretary, back in London about the deployment of RFA *Fort Austin* to replenish HMS *Endurance* and the proposed doubling of the Royal Marine contingent on the Falklands. Even so, there was little sense of the impending crisis.

I returned from Colorado Springs direct to Cornwall, the RAF VC10 dropping me off at RAF St Mawgan, near Newquay, on the Friday morning. After a short snooze I attended my constituency surgeries in Penzance, saw a pile of correspondence and attended the St Ives Conservative Association annual dinner in the evening.

It was not until Saturday morning, 27 March, that I opened my red boxes for the weekend work; as soon as I did so, I could see that the South Georgia situation was worse than I had expected. It had been discussed at the Cabinet meeting on Thursday in my absence. I had not been sent the intelligence reports, which arrived later on Saturday. These indicated that Argentine warships had been despatched to intercept *Endurance* on her passage to South Georgia. But even without them, there was sufficient information to give grounds for concern. On Sunday I telephoned the Navy Duty Officer at the MoD and asked to see the First Sea Lord first thing on Monday morning.

I met Henry Leach and the Naval Staff as soon as I arrived in London. I wanted them to put some frigates on standby and to discuss again the deployment of a nuclear submarine. A number of our nuclear submarines were operationally deployed in the far north and others were not suitably equipped for a passage to the Falklands. However, he went away and returned later in the morning to say that *Spartan* might be available, but that it would take two or three days to equip her with the necessary weapons, provision her for a very long mission and fit her out with the right torpedoes.

Quite by coincidence the Prime Minister's Private Secretary, Clive Whitmore, had telephoned mine, David Omand, to say that Margaret Thatcher and Peter Carrington had come to the same conclusion on a journey that they were making to Brussels – and their concern gave added urgency to the despatch. We also agreed that whatever the detriment to other operational activities, a second submarine should be put on standby. Equally important, we agreed that RFA *Fort Austin* should not only be provisioned for *Endurance*, but she should carry the maximum amount of stores in case we decided to send frigates subsequently. I sent a telegram to Brussels to tell the Prime Minister what was happening. In the afternoon we had the Trident debate in Parliament, which we won by 297 votes to 149.

After the debate, I returned to Admiralty House, where I was living. I did not sleep well. Next morning, Tuesday 30th, I returned to the office and asked the Naval Staff to prepare the second submarine. I then asked to see the Chief of the Air Staff, because I wanted to be sure that we could not land reinforcements of the Parachute Regiment with Hercules aircraft. He confirmed that as we could not risk a military aircraft being diverted to a South American country in the event of problems, this could not work. Even with refuelling the Hercules it would have been at the limit of its range – and therefore only able to carry a very small team. It had to be ruled out as an option.

In the meantime, I was not consulted or involved in the diplomatic negotiations over the Argentine landings, which were being conducted by the Foreign Office. If I had been asked, I would have agreed that any overt military reaction by us at this stage would have been very foolish, as it would have precipitated the very action by the Argentines which we were trying to avoid. 'We believe it would not have been appropriate to prepare a large task force ... before there was clear evidence of an invasion,' was how the Franks Committee later put it. With the benefit of hindsight, I should, of course, when I saw the Chief of the Naval Staff the week before my departure to the United States and we discussed the situation in South Atlantic, have pressed the question of an early submarine deployment. I knew, however, that at that particular juncture no suitably equipped submarines were available. In any event, such a submarine could hardly have reached the South Atlantic in time, as it took around fourteen days to get there.

But the more interesting 'what if?' question is this. What would we have done if a nuclear submarine had been on station and we had disclosed its presence? Would it have deterred an Argentine invasion? Knowing the subsequent problems that we had with the rules of engagement, I find it a little hard to believe that, at that moment, we would have given it orders to sink approaching

Argentine merchant ships in the area. Moreover, even if we had done so, it could hardly have prevented the landing of sufficient forces to overpower our Royal Marine contingent on the Islands.

In the debate on the Franks Report on 25 January 1983, David Owen claimed that deployment of a nuclear submarine in 1982 would have averted the crisis. Later he said that for this reason 'the Falklands was an avoidable war'. It led to a public disagreement with Lord Lewin who had, by that time, retired. All war, thankfully, is avoidable; but the Falklands war was never avoidable by the earlier deployment of a nuclear submarine.

The Franks Committee made an exhaustive independent study of the internal papers and the circumstances which preceded the invasion on Friday, 2 April, so I will not repeat them here. Its conclusion vindicated the government. Nevertheless, criticism persisted that the invasion had been encouraged by my announcement in June 1981 that HMS *Endurance* was to be withdrawn from service.

The cost of running *Endurance* was about £3 million a year – not an intolerable amount of money, but that was not the issue. As I have already explained, I had taken a decision, which had been endorsed by the Cabinet, to cease mid-life modernisation of surface ships, using the savings to bring forward more building of the new Type 23 frigates. I was closing Chatham, Gibraltar and part of Portsmouth dockyards. HMS *Endurance* had been listed for disposal ever since the Labour Defence Review in 1974. She had been reprieved repeatedly; but she was getting very old, had no defence capability of any real consequence, as events subsequently showed, and she was overdue for a refit costing up to £30 million – and this at a time when I was stopping this very practice. We were, moreover, desperately stretched for funds.

More important, the Royal Navy had themselves listed *Endurance* near the top of their list for disposal at the outset of my Defence Review. In pure defence terms they were right, as although she was a symbol of our continuing interest in the Antarctic dependencies and the Falklands, she had little deterrent value whatsoever. Having cut the Royal Navy's frigate force from sixty-four to fifty, with all the controversy that this had caused, I did not feel justified in taking on the Naval Staff once again over an ageing and expensive ship, albeit one that had symbolic importance in the South Atlantic. In my final minute to Lord Carrington, dated 3 February 1982, I had observed, 'I think there would be considerable depth of feeling in the Royal Navy if further inroads had to be made on the Naval Programme to make room for *Endurance* which, quite frankly, is a low priority in defence terms.'

Again with the wisdom of hindsight, I regret that I so stubbornly refused Carrington's pleas for a reprieve, but at the time I had no suspicion of any kind of a threat to the Falkland Islands. I had agreed that we should jointly approach the Treasury to see if she could be retained on a non-defence vote or out of the contingency fund; but the Treasury would never have found the money. Nor was *Endurance* the only 'symbol' of Britain's rather relaxed approach to the South Atlantic. The Labour government had showed no great resolve when the Argentines landed on Southern Thule in 1976; the Treasury had rejected Lord Shackleton's recommendation made that year to strengthen defences in the Islands, by lengthening the runway; and an earlier government had refused to extend, without conditions, British citizenship to the inhabitants of the Falkland Islands.

Possibly the weakening of our stance went as far back as the Defence Review in 1966, when decisions were taken to withdraw the Commander in Chief South Atlantic and the frigate on station in the area, and in 1974 to terminate the Simonstown agreements and our naval base in South Africa. If I can be accused of some guilt for the announcement of the withdrawal of *Endurance*, I share it with a very large number of my ministerial predecessors of both major political parties right from 1966.

In any event, having agreed to the despatch of two submarines to the South Atlantic – and having convinced myself that it was impossible to reinforce the Islands in short time – I decided to carry on with my programme.

On Tuesday I was due to leave London early in the morning to visit Marconi at Neston on Merseyside. I had postponed this trip on several occasions, but it was important as Marconi was responsible for building the Stingray torpedo and was about to gain the contract for the heavyweight torpedo, both contracts running into billions of pounds. I also wanted to do a Territorial Army visit following my Reserve Forces statement in Parliament, so I stayed the night with Lord Derby, the President of the Territorial Army Association.

That took me to the fateful Wednesday 31st, when the crisis finally broke. However, as I was up in the north anyhow I had arranged to visit British Aerospace at Wharton. I have explained in the previous chapter that there was grave concern in the industry because it was running out of work. Unless I took a decision to start work on the so-called advanced combat aircraft, which became the

European Fighter, the whole of Wharton was going to disintegrate. I met the management and the unions, but I was not ready to make a decision.

I then flew back to Northolt in an HS125 and went straight to the House of Commons to vote. I had to see General Allen, the head of the United States Air Force, with Sir Michael Beetham; but my thoughts were on the Falklands, and I called a meeting in my room in the House of Commons at around 6.00 p.m. to be updated on the situation.

In the meantime there had been a meeting of the Defence Operations Executive, a creature of the Chiefs of Staff Committee; and it is clear in retrospect that, following the decision to deploy submarines to the South Atlantic and despatch RFA *Fort Austin* from Gibraltar, the Royal Navy began, on their own initiative, to run with the ball. Initially there had been some resistance to a diversion of effort and thought away from an important NATO exercise to meet a rather minor political incident in the South Atlantic, but the mood changed on the Monday and Tuesday. Although I had suggested it at the beginning of the week, I was unaware that Admiral Fieldhouse (who was to become the Commander in Chief of the Falklands Task Force, based at Northwood) had considered with the Naval Staff the option of despatching a contingency surface force should the problem escalate. Fortunately, a large part of the surface fleet was on the NATO exercise called Spring Train, off Gibraltar, so that a significant part of our naval force was already at sea. It may explain the confidence which Henry Leach displayed at the meeting with the Prime Minister late on Wednesday evening.

Unfortunately, although it was possibly too late to be relevant, Richard Luce, the Foreign Office minister, had made a statement in the House on Tuesday about the situation in the South Atlantic and had been given rather a rough ride. Later, at a private Conservative Party meeting upstairs, the Falkland Islands lobby had attacked him for the lack of any action by the government. In reply he must have hinted that the government had taken some action. I am sure that he did not specify, but a number of Tory MPs rushed downstairs to speculate with the parliamentary press among others that the government had despatched a submarine. Next day this speculation was all over the press, and the despatch of *Endurance* to South Georgia to take off the Davidoff scrap dealers clearly provoked the Argentine junta. The presence of *Endurance* was already causing more trouble than it was worth. Possibly the junta had already taken a private decision to trigger the invasion, but Wednesday's British press about the despatch of a nuclear submarine, together with the riots in Buenos Aires the day before, put pressure on them to act.

Having seen off the head of the US Air Force, at my request a briefing team from the intelligence staff, led by Roger Jackling from the Ministry of Defence, assembled in my room in the House of Commons. Although the Falklands problem was beginning to escalate, I had no conception as late as six o'clock that Wednesday evening that a major crisis was about to hit us. They then produced a series of intercepted signals and other intelligence which left little doubt that an invasion was planned for the morning of Friday 2 April. We knew four things: that an Argentine submarine had been deployed to the area around Port Stanley (we were subsequently to learn that its task was to reconnoitre the beaches); that the Argentine fleet, which had been on exercises, had broken up into smaller units and seemed to be reassembling for an invasion; that an army commander had been embarked separately on a merchant ship and seemed likely to be the commander of an amphibious force; and finally, that the fleet had been ordered to destroy all its documents.

I said to my Private Secretary, David Omand, that we must see the Prime Minister immediately. He telephoned No. 10. I saw Ian Gow, Margaret Thatcher's Parliamentary Private Secretary, and slowly we assembled in her room. I believe that this informal meeting consisted of Clive Whitmore and Peter Blaker, Humphrey Atkins and Richard Luce, the two Foreign Office ministers, and Ian Gow. Margaret Thatcher herself suggested that Sir Antony Acland, the new Permanent Secretary at the Foreign Office, should join us, and I asked for Sir Frank Cooper to come over from Defence. Our initial conversation was somewhat unstructured, but mainly concerned itself with how we could react diplomatically. A message was prepared for Margaret Thatcher to send to President Reagan asking whether he was aware of the Signals intelligence that we had just received. David Omand was sent to ensure that our Intelligence material had equally been received by our US counterparts. At this early stage it had not. A message was prepared to send to our Ambassador in the United States, Sir Nicholas Henderson, and to the Governor of the Falkland Islands.

At this juncture, a secretary took me aside and said that Henry Leach was outside the Prime Minister's room and had asked to see me. After I had suggested to Margaret Thatcher that he should join us, Henry did so in full naval uniform. The sight of a man in uniform always pleases the ladies and Margaret, very much an impressionable lady, was always impressed by men in uniform.

She asked for Henry's views. With great assurance, he said that it was possible to prepare a large task force. This would include *Hermes* and *Invincible*, together with the greater part of our destroyer and frigate forces, which were exercising off Gibraltar. He declared that the task force could be ready to sail early the following week, so long as he had authority to prepare it, with instructions to sail to follow later. This assertion greatly boosted the confidence of Margaret Thatcher; it was met by some scepticism among the rest of us.

Eventually the meeting broke up late at night and I was left alone with Margaret. I thought that Henry had performed very well – and I have great praise for his supreme self-confidence and assertiveness. He had appeared, quite by chance, at a critical moment. I have already, describing my long series of disagreements with him, said that Henry was a sailor in the best Nelsonian tradition. 'Sail at the enemy!' and do not hesitate about the consequences.

However, unlike his immediate superior Admiral Lewin, who was away in New Zealand, Henry was not exactly 'cerebral man'. Such an epithet might have been applied to Edwin Bramall, the Chief of the General Staff, and perhaps, but rather less so, to Sir Michael Beetham, the acting Chief of the Defence Staff. I was pleased with Henry's performance, but I was not going to take his assurances just like that. The latest Defence briefing, such as it was, had indicated considerable uncertainty about our ability to recapture the Falkland Islands – and on Wednesday night I had my own doubts, not least about the logistics of fighting a war 8,000 miles away without air cover from land-based aircraft. I had confidence in what I had seen of the Royal Navy's Harriers, but no one had briefed me on the capabilities of the Argentine Air Force.

The first chapter of this book is about the extraordinary logistic operation which saw the Indian Army, 50,000 strong with 30,000 camels, cross the plains of India and move into the mountains of Afghanistan, where it suffered one of the greatest disasters in British military history. I have also explained at somewhat tedious length the impact which the disaster of Suez had upon me whilst I was at Cambridge.

If I had had confidence in Henry Leach's judgement, no doubt my hesitation might have been partially dispelled. But I did not have such confidence – there had been a full year of misunderstanding between us. So I expressed my qualms to Margaret Thatcher about the viability of such an operation. Reasonably enough, she has often reminded me of them. In particular, I recall the following exchange between us. She said, 'I suppose you realise, John, that this is going to be the worst week of our lives.' I responded, 'Well, that may be so, but I imagine that each successive week will be worse than the last.' It was not a helpful exchange at that particular juncture. Nevertheless, we gave Henry Leach authority to make preparations for a task force.

The following morning, Thursday 1st, I went to the MoD at 8.15 for a meeting with a group of senior civilian and military personnel under the chairmanship of Michael Beetham. We discussed the whole situation, ahead of a Cabinet meeting which was due at 9.30. I was told that the Defence Operations Executive would meet later to advance planning on the military options and I suggested that Beetham and Leach should make themselves available for a meeting of OD after Cabinet was concluded.

At Cabinet there was a brief discussion of the Falklands. The Prime Minister described the situation as being very grave; but neither at that meeting nor at the subsequent meeting of OD, which concerned itself with our diplomatic proposals, did we reveal the intelligence information that had been received the night before. As was customary, signals intelligence of this kind (only revealed some nine months later in the Franks Report) was treated on a 'need to know' basis.

After the OD meeting concluded, I believe that we met the Prime Minister as a small group consisting of Beetham, Leach and Whitelaw, who had not been present the previous night. I have no record of the meeting, but I believe it took place.

When I returned to the MoD I was given a full Minute from the acting Chief of Defence Staff, which had been prepared whilst I had been at Cabinet, laying out all the military options including the deployment of a full Task Force. Set out clearly, it indicated that a task force was a viable proposal and had a good chance of success, although the risks were to be studied further in the next few days. This gave me much greater confidence than I had felt the night before, as I knew that all three Services had been involved in putting this advice together. There was a further proposal – to deploy communications equipment and some men to Ascension Island, in order to join up with the RFA *Fort Austin* which was already on its way to the South Atlantic. Later in the day I was to have a further meeting to discuss the deployment of a team of SAS and SBS to join up with *Fort Austin* and the second nuclear submarine respectively. By the early evening I was much more fully briefed than on Wednesday night and my confidence was increasing. I also asked whether the Royal Marines on the Falklands could destroy the airfield, but I was told that they had already been dispersed around the island to await a possible invasion. I did, however, feel extremely foolish when I was told that there was anyhow insufficient explosives on the island to do the job.

At two o'clock I had to be on the steps of the MoD to welcome Mr Hernou, the French Defence Secretary. In the circumstances, I was hoping that I could make it a reasonably short meeting. No such hope.

Mr Hernou looked like a rather tubby French provincial mayor, which no doubt he may have been. I do not recall whether he spoke any English. I think not, and my French is inadequate, so everything had to be translated. Mr Hernou, a good socialist, was nonetheless a great enthusiast for the French nuclear deterrent. He was benevolent and exceptionally voluble. He regarded this meeting as of great importance because he was very anxious to get closer to us on nuclear issues. I had been briefed that there were several areas where we could co-operate together; but there was very great reluctance to allow the French to get anywhere near our technology, which of course was of American origin. I wanted to discuss how we could do more together on the conventional side, but Mr Hernou was not to be diverted and he talked with immense enthusiasm, almost obsessively so, for over an hour in French about what he was doing to improve France's nuclear capability. The more he talked the more uncertain I became about the effectiveness of the French nuclear deterrent – and the more relieved I was about our Trident decision. Unfortunately whilst Mr Hernou's monologue continued, I could not help drifting off into thoughts about the Falklands. My guest was a charming man and he, Mitterrand and the French government were, as I shall explain, very helpful to us during the coming weeks; but I was relieved when I managed to say goodbye to him at five o'clock in the afternoon.

Margaret Thatcher, meanwhile, had called another meeting at No. 10 in the evening, but she did not want it to start until Peter Carrington had arrived back from a trip to Israel. Accordingly, it was ten o'clock by the time she, Whitelaw, Carrington and myself got together.

In many ways this was a smaller and more useful meeting than the night before. Peter looked exhausted – he had had a difficult time with the Israelis in Jerusalem and was under quite some strain. After a lengthy discussion, it was decided that he should speak to Alexander Haig, the US Secretary of State. I think it was on this occasion, rather late at night, that Haig told him that following a talk between Thatcher and Reagan earlier in the day, the

Argentine President, General Galtieri, had refused to take Reagan's call. Further intelligence came in late the same evening that sections of the Argentine forces had been ordered to rendezvous at 0600 hours the next day at a particular point off the Falkland Islands. Peter Carrington, new to the crisis, did not hesitate to say that we had no option but to put the Fleet to sea.

At this point we decided to ask Henry Leach to join us. Unfortunately he had been asked to be on standby and had been sitting for an hour or more in an anteroom at No. 10. He confirmed that the ships on exercise could be reprovisioned in Gibraltar and told to sail back to the UK, but turned south thereafter; such a deployment would not remain covert, because anyhow we needed *Hermes* and *Invincible* and other ships to sail from the UK. He said that if he had the authority to put the Fleet on alert, much of it could sail within three or four days. We were tremendously impressed. The speed with which the task force put to sea was critical and no-one deserves greater credit than Henry Leach himself. It was a triumph of determination and executive will. Later in the campaign, he and the Naval Staff in Whitehall tended to pass several of their personnel and much of their authority to Admiral Fieldhouse in Northwood as the operational command; but of course, they continued to play an important role in Whitehall. At about one o'clock in the morning Henry Leach left No. 10 in order to place the Fleet on alert; and we agreed, subject only to a Cabinet meeting the next day, to set it for sail at the beginning of the following week.

In his memoirs, John Major asserts that 'if the Cabinet had not sent the task force Margaret Thatcher would not have survived as Prime Minister'. He adds that 'she took a great risk, requiring huge nerve, but the alternative was certain catastrophe'. Actually, I do not agree with that judgement. I would not have survived, but I think that Margaret Thatcher would have done so. But that is another 'What if' of history. Who can know?

~

Friday 2 April was a day of some confusion. The Cabinet met in the morning but there was not a great deal to report; it parted in some gloom. A statement was organised for 11.30 a.m., but we had no communication from the Falklands. There was a high-frequency system, interrupted by very bad weather; a Cable & Wireless telex, which had presumably been taken over; and a satellite link with *Endurance* which was on its way to South Georgia. Humphrey Atkins was not able to confirm that an invasion had taken place, but he did say that the Governor had been in touch with the Foreign Office some hours earlier, which was incorrect. Humphrey felt bad that he had given inaccurate information to the House – but it was not his fault. I never saw why he needed to resign with Peter Carrington. It was only around lunchtime that we heard via a British Antarctic Survey vessel that the Falklands had indeed been occupied.

We met in the Prime Minister's room, after Humphrey Atkins' statement, to decide what to do. Suggestions were made for a statement in the afternoon, because by this time the BBC and other stations were relaying from Buenos Aires that the Falklands had been taken. However, we had no corroborative information at all. We were all against another statement in the afternoon, but really bought off the protests by proposing an emergency debate on Saturday morning. It proved to be an unwise move. It would have been better to have waited until the following Monday.

One of the most constant aggravations was the inability of Parliament and the press to understand the nature of our communication problems. Huge amounts of technical effort were put into maintaining signals contact, even in a nuclear conflict; but whatever provision for redundancy you construct into your communications, they can go wrong. There was always the feeling among wide sections of the press that people engaged in conflict had nothing better to do than send messages back home for them.

Friday represented also the first spat between the Ministry of Defence and No. 10 about how many journalists should accompany the Fleet. Understandably the Navy fought against taking anyone, on the good grounds that the limited satellite facilities were needed for operations. I insisted that they should embark a number of journalists (six, as I recall) initially, each to cover a range of media outlets. The editors made their protests to Bernard Ingham, the No. 10 Press Secretary, who sounded off loudly at such a paltry number. Frank Cooper, who was in charge of the negotiations with No. 10, and I increased the number to up to fourteen, to be chosen by the Newspaper Publishers' Association. The NPA then nominated a team which excluded *The Times*, the *Sun*, the *Guardian* and other newspapers, so we had to add them. I had a disagreement with the Navy, but called rank and insisted that the key television channels and newspapers were included.

Bernard Ingham was a constant nuisance throughout the Falklands campaign – jumping up and down and causing no end of difficulty, criticising the Ministry of Defence on trivial issues. But Frank and I were determined to keep the press under the tightest Ministry of Defence control and, as far as possible, away from No. 10, with its obsession for background briefing and for spin. Margaret Thatcher in her memoirs has the temerity to claim that 'too much talk was giving the Argentinians warning of what we intended, though the fault did not always lie with the media themselves but also with the media management of the MoD'. In fact, we had a constant problem trying to prevent Ingham in No. 10 from adding his largely uninformed opinion to the No. 10 spin.

Even just one photograph took up an inordinate amount of satellite time, to the detriment of operations, and explains why I was often having to make statements to the House of Commons based on a single terse signal. It was good military practice, but it made the job of keeping everyone on side really very difficult. The fault lay, of course, in the ships' limited communications systems, as they had never been prepared for a press contingent embarked at sea. Of course it was necessary all along to embark the press, but it did cause severe problems in handling the media at home.

Frank Cooper chose a Ministry of Defence official, Ian Macdonald, to be press spokesman. He spoke slowly and methodically, uttering each word as if he was savouring a delicious plum. He did it very well and no-one ever questioned his integrity. It was painfully obvious to the whole world that Ian could only speak the truth. It was a huge contrast to all the lies coming out of Buenos Aires, but sometimes the Argentine statements were more lurid and therefore to the liking of the members of the British press. However, generally the press was very helpful. Only the BBC was quite appalling – seeing its role as requiring dispassionate even-handedness between their own country and its enemies.

About halfway through the campaign there was a well of growing criticism of Ian Macdonald's style. The Americans, in particular, were astonished at this strange Englishman, and PR smoothies worldwide, including Ingham at No. 10, demanded a change to a more professional style. Frank Cooper, in one of his better moves, said that he thought the way around the problem was to send Ian up to Glasgow for a weekend with his mum. In his place we put on parade a number of polished young officers to do the job. Sure enough, as soon as Ian was gone there was a surge of demand for us to reinstate him. Ian Macdonald was borne back to the world's screens in triumph. There he remained to the end.

At 7.30 on Friday evening the Cabinet met again and gave its backing to the despatch of the task force. Only John Biffen expressed some doubts, but without in any way opposing the move outright. I thought it was courageous of him to speak up in this way – no-one else did so. Considerable discussion took place as to how we could get a resolution condemning the invasion in the United Nations, condemnation from our so-called friends in the European Community, and a freezing of Argentine assets.

Sir Anthony Parsons, our man at the UN, with Sir Antony Acland and Sir Michael Palliser, the present and former Permanent Secretaries of the Foreign Office, together with the legal adviser, Ian Sinclair, were at many of our meetings. Parsons played a key role by obtaining Resolution 502 through the Security Council, demanding the withdrawal of Argentina. This was an absolutely crucial success and had required lobbying around the world to gather sufficient support; somehow Parsons managed to get an abstention from the Russians. Without Resolution 502, which gave us the moral authority for our actions, I doubt if we could have held international opinion over the next few months. We would have been in deep trouble, as well as making our task in Parliament infinitely more difficult.

Here I must interpose a comment about the Foreign Office. Throughout this book I have been critical of their attitudes and approach. Yet face to face in critical meetings about how to handle the long drawn-out negotiations with Haig, the Peruvians and the United Nations, Parsons, Acland, Palliser and, in particular, Sinclair, their admirable legal adviser, were helpful, pragmatic and constructive. Why is it that one can respect and enjoy the company of so many outstanding individuals when one holds their institution in such deep contempt?

Margaret Thatcher, recalling the events of Friday the 2nd, poses this dilemma very well:

> I received advice from the Foreign Office which summed up the flexibility of principle characteristic of that department. I was presented with the dangers of a backlash against the British expatriates in Argentina, problems about getting support in the UN Security Council, the lack of reliance we could place on the European Community or the United States, the risk of the Soviets becoming involved, the disadvantage of being looked at as a colonial power.

It might have been the duty of the Foreign Office to warn of all these obstacles, which were very clear to all of us, but it is the never-ending feebleness of the institution and its demeaning role as a spokesman for foreign interests that rankles so deeply with Tories like myself. All of this was to break out in a ruthless attack by Tory MPs on Peter Carrington the next day.

I retired to Admiralty House on Friday night, after further meetings in the Ministry of Defence, bearing a draft of my speech for the emergency debate on Saturday. I glanced at it and, not unusually, realised that I had to bin it and write it myself. However, I was too tired to do so; I went to bed and got up at four o'clock to prepare it for myself.

The Saturday emergency debate (the first since the Suez crisis) has gone down as a famous event in Parliamentary history. The House was full, worried and concerned; but there was an underlying ugly mood – a developing desire to find scapegoats for the national humiliation that had occurred. The Prime Minister opened the debate, wisely in a low key, and expressed the government's anger at what had happened. She announced the preparation of the task force and this somewhat mollified, albeit temporarily, the more hawkish members of the Tory Party.

Michael Foot, the Leader of the Opposition, could be relied upon in any crisis to make an emotive and impressive speech. With the passing of Iain Macleod, he was the last outstanding orator in the House of Commons. His principal attack was against the fascists in Argentina, but quite correctly he posed the question of how such an event could have been allowed to happen. How could there have been such a failure of British intelligence and diplomacy? So far, so good.

There were then speeches from Enoch Powell, who attacked the Royal Marines for surrendering, and Julian Amery, who fiercely attacked the Foreign Office. The most unpleasant contributions came from a predictable direction, namely from the Tory benches. Edward du Cann and Patrick Cormack both made contemptible speeches, dressing up naked self-advertisement in patriotic clothes.

As I was about to wind up the debate, the Whips asked for more time for backbench speeches. As a result, my prepared and reasonably balanced observations, intended to last half an hour, had to be compressed into a shortened timescale of fifteen minutes – always a problem, because the House feels that its concerns have not been answered. Rule No. 1: be very wary of any advice coming from the Whips. However, the speech went quite well initially. I said that if, after the South Georgia incident two weeks before, we had sent a task force of sufficient size to the South Atlantic, it would not have arrived in time to perform its task. I added that 'certainly in deterrence terms, had it been successful [i.e. in strengthening our negotiating hand], that large task force would have had to remain indefinitely in Falkland waters, in detriment to its other tasks'. However, 'as my right hon. Friend the Prime Minister said in opening this debate, we were throughout seeking a peaceful solution through the United Nations and by other means'.

At this point things began to go wrong, because I tried to answer the criticisms of Jim Callaghan and David Owen. I was correct in what I said but it did not help:

> The other option would have been the deployment of a small force insufficient to resist the Argentine Navy, as was done [by the Labour government] in 1977. May I comment first on this particular proposal, because there seems to be a difference of view between the then Prime Minister [Callaghan] and the then Foreign Secretary [Owen] about the events in 1977. The right hon. Member for Cardiff South-East [Callaghan] said that this force in 1977 became known and that a diplomatic solution followed, whereas the right hon. Member for Plymouth, Devonport [Owen] said yesterday on the radio that it was done in total secrecy – (Interruption) – but he added that it gave him confidence in his negotiations, whatever that might mean – (Interruption).

At this point, one interruption followed another and Michael Foot joined in, noisily supported from the Labour benches. The description given by Alan Clark in his diary well captures the gathering drama:

> Poor old Notters was a disaster ... The *coup de grâce* was delivered by David Owen, who had spoken earlier. He forced Nott to give way and he told him that if he could not appreciate the need to back negotiations with force he did not deserve to remain one minute as Secretary of State.

I mentioned at the beginning of this book that politics is a performing art and that a politician is only as good as his last performance. This was a good example of that abiding truth.

I only had a few minutes left before the debate was curtailed at two o'clock. I now made the most serious error of my debating career – I attacked the Labour Party. It was foolish in the circumstances. I said:

The military problems are formidable, but they are certainly not insoluble because of the professionalism, the preparedness and the quality of our defences, which for our nation's size are unique in the free world. I do not believe the claim that the new Labour Party, with its well-known and well-advertised anti-defence bias and lack of commitment to defence spending, would have done any better ...

There was uproar and calls for my resignation. The debate ended with the House in a very ugly mood. The full speech is reproduced in the appendix.

Again, I resort to Margaret Thatcher's memoirs:

I faced a crisis in the Government. John Nott, who was under great strain, had delivered an uncharacteristically poor performance in his winding-up speech. He had been very harshly treated in the debate. He was held responsible by many of our backbenchers for what had happened because of the Defence Review which he had pioneered. This was unfair. The budget for conventional naval forces (that is excluding the Trident programme) was £500 million higher – and also higher as a share of the Defence Budget – than when we took office ... But there was no doubt that the Party's blood was up: nor was it just John Nott they were after.

It was understandable that I should be the scapegoat for the whole affair. The Foreign Secretary was in the House of Lords; I was the spokesman for the government. The anger of the House was bound to fall on my shoulders – and I was expecting it. I had seen the House of Commons turn into a mob before. Or in Alan Clark's apposite words, 'Like the pack that they are they always smell the blood of a wounded animal and turn on it.'

Immediately, with hugely long faces all around, with a general feeling that I had made a complete cock-up in the debate, we moved back into the Prime Minister's room behind the Speaker's chair. I am an excitable person by nature, though normally I get excitable about little and unimportant things. But in a major crisis of this kind, for reasons that I do not quite understand, I go extremely calm. When we arrived in the Prime Minister's room, I was indeed the calmest person there. Willie Whitelaw, not unusually, was in a frightful flap.

At that moment Michael Jopling, the Chief Whip, arrived and said that the party was in a state of chaos, that many people were saying that they wished to resign the whip, that the government had been humiliated; the lobbies, he added, were seething with press and discontented Conservative Members; and he declared that he could see no other choice but to call an immediate meeting of the party, which he suggested that Carrington and I should address. Peter had had an easy ride in the House of Lords and I don't think he realised how bad it was. He shrugged his shoulders and said, 'Oh dear, well yes, we'd better go up and talk to the party.'

I quote from my near-contemporary record:

So he and I went upstairs to the Party meeting and Peter made a short speech which was met by an element of cat-calling, derision and jeers from the assembled Members. I suppose there must have been about 150 to 200 Tory Members there – it was a very full meeting. I then made an intervention which was received marginally better than Peter's, because I made it clear that we intended to sail the Fleet and, if necessary, we intended to use it. It was easier to play the hawk in a private meeting of the Party than it had been in the House of Commons, where I had to justify and explain the government's policy up to then. Whereas in the Party meeting upstairs I was able to sound the note of a forthcoming war, which, in a way, responded to the mood of the Party, Carrington was there for the first time in front of the Party and he was on the defensive. It was his policy on the Falklands which was under attack, and all the resentments of the Party now came to the surface about what had happened in Rhodesia and the election of Mugabe and a long, long history – going back over ten, fifteen years, going back to the Heath Government when Carrington as Minister of Defence, I remember it very well, had been under attack for his policy in Northern Ireland. Several of the more elderly backbenchers felt that Carrington was a consensus man, and the whole fury against the Foreign Office came out more against him than against me. Mind you, there were many Members there who were determined that I should go. I had, I would say, ten or so bitter enemies in the Tory Party as a result of my Defence Review and there were sufficient numbers of people in the Party who were gunning for me. Although the Defence Review was all finished and behind us, the memories of it were fairly recent. The Party meeting, which went on for two and a half hours, developed more into an attack on the Foreign Office than on me, and I emerged from it slightly less under total siege than I had emerged three hours earlier from the debate in the House.

Alan Clark's version is as follows:

After the debate we all trailed up to Committee Room 10. Carrington and Nott were both present. Thirty-three Members asked questions and, with the exception of three heavy-weight duds (Patten, Kershaw and van Straubenzee), every single person was critical. I asked a long, sneering question about the failure of our intelligence. I made a point of addressing it to Peter Carrington whom, with my very long memory, I had not forgiven for snubbing me at a meeting on Afghanistan in December 1980, in the Grand Committee Room. As my irony developed, people in the Committee Room started sniggering, but poor Notters was still so rattled and blubbery that he leant across and answered it, while Carrington sat staring at me in haughty silence.

As Peter Carrington and I left the meeting on our way back downstairs to tell the Prime Minister how it had gone – we could not give her much encouragement – he said to me, 'You know, I really think I must go. I don't think that I can possibly stay. The Party regard it as being all my fault, there is no way that I can sustain my position and I shall tell the Prime Minister that I intend to go.' To which I replied, 'Peter, I think that you must stay. You can't leave at this particular moment. We've got to see the next few days through and it would be a catastrophe if you left now.'

It seemed to me then – and still does now – that it was the party meeting that did him in, not the newspapers that called for his resignation. The sadness was that Peter Carrington, being in the Lords, did not know the characters in that party meeting – whereas I could say to myself, 'A' is an idiot, 'B' always talks nonsense, 'C' is a pompous twit, you only need to be bothered about 'D' and 'E' who carry some respect among their colleagues. Peter possibly saw them all as having equal relevance.

Having reported back to Margaret Thatcher – and leaving Peter Carrington with her (I never saw him again as a ministerial colleague) – I escaped back to the Ministry of Defence. I was conscious that I had responsibility for a task force which was due to sail in two days' time. Whilst the political war had been raging in the House of Commons, the Chiefs of Staff had been planning for the real war in the South Atlantic. By this time the MoD had got itself into top gear and confidence was building everywhere.

One of the earliest problems lay in the status of Ascension. Although the island was British we had entered into an agreement with the State Department, placing the airfield totally under American control. The use of the airfield was an absolute precondition to our getting the full complement of provisions, equipment, ships and men to the South Atlantic. It was by no means certain at this stage that the State Department would not be obstructive. When the Fleet sailed on the Monday, it was in the knowledge that a host of additional equipment would have to be shipped by air to join the task force at Ascension. The island also, along with Dakar in Senegal on the west coast of Africa, became the essential air bridge for flying extra RAF Harriers to the Fleet. Dakar was important because refuelling there enabled the Hercules supply aircraft to carry heavier loads on their way to Ascension.

It was at this very early stage that the immensely close military relationship between the Ministry of Defence and the Pentagon proved its value. The Royal Navy and the US Navy were extremely close. The intelligence agencies of the two countries virtually worked as one, while the recent negotiations on Trident and co-operation in NATO meetings had brought the two ministerial teams together. Weinberger was splendid from the outset. Ignoring the jealousies and rivalries in Washington, he ordered his staff to give maximum and urgent support to the British. We needed additional fuel supplies in Ascension, which the Americans supplied with their tankers. Certain valuable weapons systems, in particular the Sidewinder air-to-air missile, supplemented and upgraded the capability of the Harriers, and a host of other incremental stores were all forthcoming without cost ever being mentioned.

Looking back on it, this all seems rather academic and unremarkable; but anyone who has dealt with Washington will understand the incoherence of the United States' government system. The Washington agencies work independently of each other and often in contradiction, so you could never expect too much. The State Department at this time was dominated by the Latinos who saw President Reagan's Latin American policy going down the drain. Mrs Kirkpatrick, the US Ambassador to the UN, dined with the Argentinians on the evening that they invaded British territory.

For all Margaret Thatcher's friendship with Ronald Reagan, he remained a West Coast American looking south to Latin America and west to the Pacific. Sometimes I wondered if Reagan knew where Europe was – although he was certainly conscious of the Russian 'Evil Empire'. It took weeks of determined diplomacy by Sir Nicholas Henderson, our Ambassador in Washington, before the White House was prepared to declare itself wholeheartedly on the side of the British. Moreover, it did so, I suspect, only because Congress and American public opinion had come down heavily on our side. By doing so, it destroyed the support of the South American dictators for Reagan's anti-communist crusade in Central America. It would have been impossible in those crucial early days to muster support from the US Administration; where it was forthcoming, wholly independently of the State Department and the White House, was from Weinberger and the Pentagon.

Many influential Americans, furious at Britain's later unwillingness to support the US invasion of Grenada, have claimed that we could not have recovered the Falklands without American support. Certainly the use of Ascension – a British island – was essential. In Weinberger's memoirs, *Fighting for Peace*, he says: 'Some said later that the British could not have succeeded if we had not helped. This is not so – I believe the decisive factor was Mrs Thatcher's firm and immediate decision to retake the Islands, despite the impressive military and other advice [in the Pentagon] to the contrary.'

I too believe that we could have succeeded without US logistic and equipment back-up – though certainly the whole operation would have been infinitely more extended and hazardous. We would not have succeeded if the Americans had positively turned against us, as they had at Suez. But for those, like me, who oppose our political integration into Europe, do not imagine that the United States is in some way 'an alternative' to Europe. It is not.

On Sunday morning, the 4th, I attended my first meeting of the Chiefs of Staff Committee. Terry Lewin was still away in New Zealand and there was great hesitation about where I should sit. The Secretary of State did not attend these meetings normally; his forum was the Defence Council. I was offered, out of courtesy I imagine, Mountbatten's chair – Mountbatten being the first Chief of the Defence Staff. I insisted that Michael Beetham chair the meeting, so this awful high-backed chair – Mountbatten's chair – was shifted to his right and I was forced to sit in it. Two days after the invasion there was a host of decisions outstanding. We had, for instance, to decide whether to charter or requisition civilian ships. We chose the latter course, requiring an Order in Council, and action was put in hand to acquire the *Canberra*. We had to agree contingency plans, which in the event were not needed, to evacuate the thousands of British nationals living in Argentina.

We also had to establish procedures for considering the rules of engagement – the basis which set out the limits of action by the military. Each day this question became one of the most difficult decisions for the War Cabinet.

What authority were we to give the forces if civilian aircraft and merchant ships were used to spy on the Fleet? How was the task force commander to react to Russian vessels, submarines and fishing boats, equipped with listening and reconnaissance devices? What was to be done about South American scheduled aircraft overflying the task force and passing back information to the Argentine Navy? The rules of engagement, setting out the degree of response, defensive or aggressive, towards the Argentine Navy, were rather more straightforward; not least in the case of the aircraft carrier whose aircraft could easily be within striking distance of our ships. We had no hesitation in recognising the danger to the Fleet posed by the *Belgrano*.

The rules of engagement for our submarines posed rather different problems. As the submarines moved fast and submerged underwater, they only emerged infrequently to send and receive burst signals from satellite; so with two submarines fast approaching the Falklands, forethought was needed about what orders they should have when they encountered Argentine naval shipping or merchant vessels supplying the invasion force. It was this discussion which led to the recommendation for a maritime exclusion zone, which I announced in Parliament the following Wednesday.

One of the most vexing questions, extraordinary as it seems, was whether we could say that we were at war. Evidently not; we were strongly advised by the excellent Foreign Office lawyers not to declare war but to act entirely under Article 51 of the United Nations Charter, which gave the right to countries to act in their own self-defence. This legal distinction caused no end of puzzlement in the Ministry of Defence – and when asked the question in the Commons, I said, 'No, we are not at war,' which caused some mirth.

On Admiral Lewin's return the Chiefs of Staff meetings settled down into a regular routine throughout the conflict. After the first meeting on the Sunday, I expressed a wish that I should not attend the full meeting, which really agreed the military plans that later came forward for consideration by the War Cabinet. Terry Lewin saw me after each meeting to brief me on the outcome and then went on to a gathering of senior officials who, in turn, briefed their ministers in advance of the meetings of the War Cabinet.

On most days, however, I did join the meeting for the first few items on the agenda. Each day General Glover, the Deputy Chief of Defence Staff Intelligence, gave a briefing on the deployment and state of the Argentine forces; then we heard where the Soviet forces were operating and the extent to which they were gathering intelligence, either by means of satellite or from their ships in the area. We had several scares about covert Argentinian plans to attack Gibraltar dockyard with special forces. And in the early days, before our nuclear submarines arrived on station, we were informed of the situation of the Argentine Navy, which was all at sea between the Falkland Islands and South Georgia. After the *Belgrano* incident the Argentine Navy, which was not insubstantial, largely stayed in port – but up to then it posed a very major threat to our forces.

We had landed reconnaissance teams on the Falkland Islands long before the task force arrived – and some of the most effective, Spanish-speaking sections from the SAS, dug into holes in the ground near the Argentine trenches, reported back to their HQ in Hereford on a daily basis the state of morale of the Argentinian forces around Port Stanley. We learnt where the regular forces were positioned and where the poor Argentine conscripts were located. The conscripts were being brutalised by their officers, were short of food and clothing, and generally suffered from very low morale. 'In war', said Napoleon, 'the moral is to the physical as three to one.' And so it proved. On occasions General Glover gave us a run-down of the Argentinian menu for the previous day and what the soldiers in the trenches were saying about their food – or lack of it!

There was then a briefing about the disposition of our forces, where the long, strung-out task force was located, and other information about the need for stores and weapons. The problem of what to do with *Endurance* kept on coming up. In the days preceding the invasion of South Georgia she had been ordered from one place to another, first in order to avoid provocation and then to escape the attentions of Argentine submarines. Once the conflict happened she had little relevance in a military sense; but she remained an important political symbol, and so the captain of *Endurance* was given orders to avoid all Argentinian shipping and hide himself in the ice south of South Georgia.

Another item on the agenda of the Chiefs of Staff was the press. I normally stayed for the discussion about how much we could release to the press and in what form. Frank Cooper, as Permanent Secretary, was in charge of the 'D' Notice system and discussed with the editors the way in which we might voluntarily control the flow of information from the task force. We knew that we were going to encounter severe communication problems; and censorship of press copy sent back from the Fleet. The communications overload was much more severe than we had anticipated, possibly because we embarked too many media representatives in the first place.

We received a report from the Americans, I think at the first meeting, about the likely reaction of other South American countries to the invasion. With the single exception of Chile, they declared their support for Argentina. If we had been able to use a South American airfield, even for a diversion in an emergency, it would have made the whole operation easier. The importance of Chile, with its long-standing rivalry and fear of Argentina, was therefore very great. We wanted to use their airfields for stationing our Nimrods, the maritime patrol aircraft, so that they could hunt down the Argentinian submarines, which were a real threat to the Fleet. They would also have been valuable to monitor the movement of the task force. For reasons of NATO priority, we had no satellite coverage at all of the South Atlantic and, even later in the campaign, we had considerable difficulty persuading the Americans to divert satellite coverage from NATO tasks to ours. I don't think we ever expected that the Chileans would allow us to station combat or support aircraft on their soil, though as they wanted to buy some maritime patrol aircraft from us, we tried to do a deal. We were never successful, but in several respects the Chilean link proved very valuable to us later.

~

I return to the account which I dictated not long after the Falklands War was concluded, picking up the story on the morning of Sunday, 4 April:

> I did not stay to the end of the Chiefs of Staff meeting because I had made arrangements to appear on *Weekend World* – one of the influential current affairs programmes at that time. After my disaster the previous day, Brian Walden had personally asked if I would be prepared to go on his programme and, after some heart-searching, I agreed to do so. It was, I think, a very valuable occasion for me and I am still very grateful to Brian Walden for giving me the opportunity. I do feel that, as we were friends, it was not just topical news; he also had some sympathy for the way in which I had been treated in the House and wanted to give me a chance to have my say. I went on the programme and took a very hawkish stance. I said we would not be sending the Fleet to sea unless we were prepared to use it. As soon as I had left the television studio I was deluged with a great volume of telephone calls from my Parliamentary colleagues, congratulating me on my performance and saying that it had greatly raised everybody's morale and confidence. Rather cynically I recall

that at least two of the people who congratulated me were the very same people who'd been rushing around like madmen the day before demanding my immediate resignation. That is the nature of politics. The Prime Minister also passed a personal message to me at lunchtime – saying that she had watched the programme, how well it had gone and how delighted she was that the thing was beginning to turn back. That *Weekend World* programme, which had a very large audience that Sunday morning, began to restore confidence in the Conservative Party, which had totally collapsed as a result of the invasion and the Saturday debate.

I then hurried from the studio to the City heliport and took a helicopter straight down to Portsmouth to visit the Fleet. Over the weekend, apart from the hectic efforts of the Royal Navy and all the dockyard workers, effectively the whole of the Army in southern England had been mobilised to move the war reserves to the Fleet. The Territorial Army, in particular, played a key role in transporting equipment and stores to Devonport and Plymouth. Without the Territorial Army we would have been hard put to it to get the Fleet away on time. My visit was, in a way, very difficult but, at the same time, an emotional occasion. My visit was well-publicised and led the national news. I was met by the Port Admiral when I arrived off the helicopter – the same man who had handled my earlier visit to Portsmouth when we had been besieged by rioting dockyard workers who had heaved these enormous steel bolts at me and smashed the windows of the Headquarters building.

As I was about to go on board *Hermes*, I saw a group of the same dockyard workers standing on the dockside and I went up to speak to them. During the course of the next two hours I met several groups of dockyard workers and I had a word with each of them. I think it was one of the most poignant memories that I have of the whole Falklands affair, because these were the very same men whom I was putting out of work. Several of them had received their redundancy notices a few days before; but in spite of that they'd all rallied around over that weekend, working day and night, and had done a splendid job. I must have been a real nightmare to them, but they nevertheless spoke to me with courtesy – not with any enthusiasm, but there was no rudeness, there was no attempt to be abusive. They made their feelings very clear about the dockyard measures, but at the same time they behaved with great dignity and restraint.

I cannot read this record of events even today without a great sense of sadness – and the feeling of what a wonderful country we live in and the greatness, yes the greatness, of our fellow countrymen and women.

My account continues:

I went on board *Hermes* where there was an enormous amount of activity going on. It was tremendously impressive. The Harriers were flying in from Yeovilton and landing on the deck. I took the opportunity, which was a rather unique one for me, of meeting more of my naval constituents on *Hermes* than I had ever met in one place before in my sixteen years in Parliament, because a very large number of men came from RNAS Culdrose, which is in my constituency in West Cornwall; they had flown on to *Hermes* with their Sea King helicopters the day before.

I went around the ship and, to my intense astonishment I must admit, in spite of repeated questioning of the chief petty officers, those responsible for the radar, the weapons systems, the stores, I could not get a single chief petty officer to say that he was short of any spares or of any of the supplies which he considered to be necessary for the deployment. Having in the earlier months discussed with the Admiralty Board the problem of where we were to make our reductions in supplies and in stocks, I was surprised but very impressed by the fact that there was no major shortage in the key stocks and spares which were necessary for this deployment. It says an enormous amount for the Royal Navy that, living the life they do, constantly ready to put to sea, their logistics were brilliant. I had my disagreements with the Royal Navy on their strategy but I have to admire their readiness, which showed itself so clearly on that Sunday.

I went down to the engine room of *Hermes* to find that her boilers had been completely defective three days before and a team had worked all day and all night to get them repaired. By the time I got there on the Sunday they were confident that they'd done a sufficiently adequate job for her to be able to go to sea the next day.

It was an enormously encouraging visit and the astonishing part of it all, looking back on it now, is that although I had been in the centre of a major row, a very emotional row, about the future of the Royal Navy over the preceding six to nine months, and although there must have been a number of officers on board who felt that I was responsible for having taken totally wrong decisions about their future, nevertheless none of this came out at all during my visit.

There was an intense feeling of unity between all of the people on board and I sensed the reaction that they did not see me as a visiting politician, but acknowledged that I was there as the Minister of Defence; that the nation had a crisis and that we just had to all work together to put on a good show. And that feeling did pervade itself through all the Services, and between the Navy and myself throughout the Falklands conflict. It shows how much this country does come together in times of crisis and in a quite astonishing way.

I left *Hermes* and took a helicopter straight back to Windsor. We had some difficulty in finding the rendezvous in Windsor and we flew round and round the town but eventually we found the place to land. The colonel commanding the Blues met me on the barrack-square and drove me up to the Castle, where I was met by Robin Fellowes, the Queen's Deputy Private Secretary, and a number of other Palace staff whom I knew. John Biffen, Francis Pym and I attended a Privy Council meeting where the requisitioning arrangements for civilian ships were agreed as an Order in Council. After the short Privy Council meeting, the Queen offered us a glass of sherry, a most unusual act of generosity, and we had a little chat, dwelling somewhat on polo ponies and their Argentine grooms!

Monday was another day of drama. I was in my office with Frank Cooper and David Omand preparing a number of organisational matters when Jerry Wiggin telephoned me from Brize Norton. He had been with Richard Luce to meet the returning Royal Marines from the Falklands, who had flown back from Uruguay by an RAF VC10. Jerry Wiggin told me that Peter Carrington was about to resign and that he, Richard Luce and Humphrey Atkins had decided to resign with him. Was I aware of it? I knew that everybody was trying to persuade Peter otherwise, but no-one had told me that he had been in to see the Prime Minister earlier in the morning and insisted on tendering his resignation.

Imagine my consternation when I received this call – not having heard anything at all from No. 10 – when I, with him, was regarded as the principal culprit for the whole affair. It seemed to place me in a totally impossible position. Although I had not been responsible for policy over the Falklands, I was depicted as having been so, equally with Peter Carrington. For him to resign and insist upon it, and for me not to tender my resignation, would make him the 'honourable man' and me the 'dishonourable' one who wanted to cling to office. I was astonished that no-one had told me. I could not understand how the polished Whitehall system could work in this way. I had also heard a few minutes earlier that the Chief Whip had advised that if Peter Carrington were to resign, I should not be told in advance. No doubt he did this with the best of good intentions, thinking that if both of us went it might have been the end of the government. It was no doubt a passing remark and was not in any way intended to let me down, but it was reported to me nonetheless and I was very angry.

I said to Frank Cooper that I must resign immediately. Frank said he didn't think that was necessary, but I insisted. I told my Private Secretary to ring the Prime Minister immediately. David Omand spoke to Clive Whitmore and said I wanted to talk immediately to the PM. She came on the line. I said, 'Prime Minister, I have just heard indirectly that Peter Carrington is about to resign. I cannot understand why I have not been told. Indeed, I am appalled. My own resignation is already on its way.' Indeed, having heard the story, I had sat down and written out my letter of resignation, going over the drafting with Frank Cooper and David Omand in Frank's room. The letter had been despatched and I told her so. She said, 'John, you cannot resign. I will not allow it. There is no possible circumstance under which this is your responsibility. I insist that you do not send your letter over. Tear it up and the matter must end there.' I said, 'Prime Minister, I understand your position but I am afraid I cannot do so. You have my resignation. If you wish to refuse it, then you must say so publicly. I cannot be placed in the position where Peter Carrington is said to be the "honourable man" and I am the "dishonourable" one. I do not want to stay in office. As you know, privately I have told you, I no longer intend to fight the next election and, in my view, I should go with Peter in view of the public outcry.' 'I will not accept it,' she said. I replied, 'Well, I have sent it over.' And that was that.

When the call was over, I thought about it less emotionally and I asked my Private Secretary to speak to Clive Whitmore again. I said to Whitmore that the only way in which I could be persuaded to remain was if my letter was published, so that the whole world knew I had tendered my resignation with Peter Carrington. If the PM wished to refuse it, then she should publish her rejection of my offer, so that the whole world could see the full position. Clive Whitmore said she was calling in Willie Whitelaw to consult him immediately. Within ten minutes I had a call back from Ian Gow to say that there had been a great misunderstanding. There was no question of hiding Peter Carrington's resignation from me. No. 10 had just not had time to tell me, but certainly the PM would publish my letter of resignation and her reply. And he read out her reply to me. It could not have been more generous. As I did not feel responsible for what had occurred, I did not feel the necessity to press my resignation as Peter had done.

Peter Carrington's resignation was on the one o'clock news. Passing mention was made of my resignation and of the refusal of the PM. The news came as a bombshell to the Party. Many of those people who had called for his resignation had joined in the hunt at the Party meeting on Saturday and now deeply regretted what they had done.

For all the fact that he was criticised for being a real Foreign Office man, and had often been accused of appeasement, for instance on Rhodesia, there was not a soul in the Party, except for a few of his enemies, who did not recognise that, although he was a diplomat through and through with all that that implied, he had marked up many achievements for the country. I have to confess that I did not agree with his politics or with his policies, particularly those on the EC, as I had often felt him not to be strong enough, not to be emphatic enough; but I could not deny that he had added greatly to the prestige of the government. Most people felt likewise and were deeply ashamed at the witch-hunt the previous Saturday. From a personal point of view, I too regretted Peter's departure, but to some extent I could not help reflecting that it made my position easier. It would clear the air. Blood had been shed. Peter had gone. A victim had been offered up for sacrifice and the funeral pyre had been lit.

Almost every decision in the MoD needs political authority. Many of the actions we took came near to flouting the letter of the law, but in the chaos of the past few days the Whitehall system had been hit below the solar plexus. A great tangled mass of co-ordinating committees, Cabinet sub-committees, the great panoply of bureaucratic checking and double-checking had been completely flattened. The horrendous way in which Whitehall ensures that it retains control through an excess of co-ordination means that nothing happens with any kind of urgency. The whole system had been caught with its trousers down. It was partly due to the fact that Whitehall was virtually in suspense, shell-shocked and useless, that no obstacles arose in getting the Fleet to sea. The shackles of bureaucracy just fell off. I felt a blessed sense of relief that all the committees, which were always there to prevent anything being done, were not there to frustrate us.

On Monday, as well as Peter Carrington's resignation, the news was full of the sailing of the Fleet. I prayed that they would come home safely. I had been accused of wishing to ruin the Royal Navy. The charge was totally untrue. Changes that I had proposed were for the best for the Royal Navy. They were not just my whim. They were also the best advice that I had available from the Defence Staffs and the Intelligence Staffs. Several of my Party were quite unable to understand that money must always be a constraint on the Defence programme. We were greatly over-programmed and we had to claw it back.

As the Fleet sailed, like everybody else I had tears in my eyes. It was a great achievement. The Royal Navy had done a magnificent job. The RAF too had played their part and the Army, as I have said, helped to get everything to the dockside on time.

There is one other event that I remember that day, and it will remain in my memory for a long time. It was the *Panorama* interview given by Peter Carrington that evening. I had been asked the previous Saturday if I would do *Panorama* on Monday night. Knowing that they were an unpleasant bunch, knowing that whatever one said they would twist it, knowing that the BBC was anti-patriotic, was out of control, using opinions rather than facts, I decided that I would not go on *Panorama*. Beside the quality of ITV and, in particular, ITN, the BBC is a disgrace.

The interview with Peter Carrington was a classic of its kind. It was handled by a man called Robert Kee, who was rude, combative, totally inaccurate and badly prepared. Peter Carrington batted the questions well, but his exasperation at the futility and asinine nature of the questions came through. It was, I think, a classic interview because it showed the low depths to which the BBC descended throughout the Falklands campaign.

Tuesday was a less hectic day within the Ministry of Defence and I was able to spend some time in the House of Commons, concluding with a meeting with my awkward squad – the Conservative backbench Defence Committee. They were a strange bunch under the chairmanship of Anthony Buck, who had once been a Parliamentary Under-Secretary for the Navy and I was never allowed to forget it. Tony was rather a sad figure and I fear that he liked the bottle. Other members included Victor Goodhew, Winston Churchill, Julian

Critchley and Alan Clark. I had a very difficult time holding them together over the Defence Review; but I had taken the trouble to invite all the Tory backbenchers to my room to brief them on Trident, and my relations with the backbenchers generally were rather better than with the Defence Committee zealots. Although I maintained a friendly, if somewhat tense, relationship with the officers, they were always a potential source of trouble.

Fortunately I was well served by two excellent men: the person responsible for Defence in the Whips' Office, Bob Boscawen, and my Parliamentary Private Secretary, John Wilkinson. Bob is a Cornishman, the brother of Cornwall's then Lord Lieutenant, Lord Falmouth, and he had been the Conservative candidate for Falmouth & Camborne when I was first selected for St Ives. We worked together quite closely; I won my seat and he unfortunately could not shift the Labour man from his. Throughout my Defence Review and the Falklands, Bob did a wonderful job calming the more frenetic members of the Party; he had been a brave soldier during the war, which helped, and he was greatly respected by his colleagues. John Wilkinson, a younger man, had doubts about my reductions to the Naval Programme, but he too reported back to me when trouble was brewing. Both of them attended all our ministerial meetings in the MoD, so they were well-informed of what was happening. They were loyal, constructive and ready to criticise where appropriate.

To understand the flavour of these feverish days, I cannot do better than recommend a reading of Alan Clark's second published set of diaries, *Into Politics*. I knew Alan well and enjoyed his company, but we were never close. A great part of his diaries describes his determination to replace Buck as chairman of the Defence Committee. Why this mattered to him so much is beyond my comprehension, because I do not believe that the Committee had any influence except, perhaps, that the chairmanship was seen in some quarters as a rung on the ladder to promotion. But I do not even believe that.

What I find valuable about the diaries is the way they illustrate the dangers of the parliamentary lobby, members of which spend their whole life cohabiting 'off the record' with disaffected MPs. Every piece of tittle-tattle finds its way as gospel into the newspapers – so it was damaging to read that the Harriers were no match for the Argentinian Mirages (untrue), that very few Harriers would reach the Falklands due to attrition on the way (luckily untrue), that it was suicide to attempt an opposed amphibious landing without air superiority (luckily untrue), that the Army's boots were no good (true). There was an endless stream of damaging gossip from the Defence buffs and Bob Boscawen, John Wilkinson, my ministerial team and I had to spend an inordinate amount of time correcting it.

Typical examples from Alan Clark's diaries include:

Hermes was suffering from mechanical trouble and her propellers were seizing …

Michael Mates dwelt at length on the prospects of very heavy casualties and how we ought to warn the public, etc …

Callaghan … said it was the most frightful situation and fraught with danger, that it was important to find a way out, short of a full-scale amphibious assault with all the casualties that might accompany it …

It was not just in the corridors of the House of Commons that this kind of speculation was rife – and certainly some of it had a degree of truth – but a few MPs and even some ministers were indiscreet at dinner parties in foreign embassies. I was kept informed of the conversations which took place around the dinner tables of foreign ambassadors in London, which must have given considerable joy to President Galtieri.

The armchair generals – the retired senior officers of the three Services constantly on television to give their expert opinion – did no harm but became something of a bore. I learnt that you cease to be an expert in anything the day that you step down from Whitehall or the military. The very day you leave you are a goner, and you had better know it.

John Major's memoirs record how one day he 'overheard a washroom conversation in which two Cabinet ministers denounced the expedition as "ludicrous" and as "a folly" due to the lack of air cover for the fleet'. This 'gave me a glimpse of the tension that existed at the heart of the government'. I know who they were – and neither spoke up when the matter came before the Cabinet. On another occasion I happened to drop into the Chief Whip's office to find two Cabinet colleagues denouncing Thatcher and the whole government response.

Finally, I leave Tuesday with this extract from Alan Clark:

People who should know better are striding up and down the Smoking Room corridor telling anyone whom they can apprehend that the *Invincible* is sailing without her radar operative; that many of her weapons systems have already been removed, that the Sea Harrier cannot land on deck in a rough sea, that many of the ships in the task force have defective power trains, etc., etc.

It is monstrous that senior Tories should be behaving in this way. It is only on occasions such as this that the implacable hatred in which certain established figures hold the Prime Minister can be detected. They oppose government policy whatever it is ... They are within an ace they think of bringing her government down. If by some miracle the expedition succeeds they know, and dread, that she will be established for ever as a national hero.

So regardless of the country's interests they are determined that the expedition will not succeed. The greater the humiliation of its failure, the more certain will be the downfall of The Lady's Government, the greater the likelihood of a lash-up coalition ... One angle from which [it] can be attacked is via the so-called 'expert' opinion, which is that we just do not have the equipment to launch and sustain an expedition of this magnitude.

Just imagine how this kind of thing must have encouraged the Argentine junta in those early days. No wonder that they were not prepared to make any concessions in the diplomatic negotiations.

Chapter Ten

FALKLANDS: LANDING AND VICTORY

Nothing except a battle lost can be half so melancholy as a battle won.
(Wellington's dispatch from the field of Waterloo)

The first meeting of the South Atlantic sub-committee of the Overseas and Defence Policy Committee of the Cabinet OD(SA), usually known as the War Cabinet, took place on Wednesday, 7 April. I had discussed its composition with Margaret Thatcher at the same time that I recommended the full membership and participation of Terry Lewin. I was nervous about its political balance. Suspecting that Francis Pym, as the newly appointed Foreign Secretary, would be likely to take a very cautious line, and knowing that Pym and Whitelaw were politically close and were former members of the Chief Whips' club, I proposed the selection of a fifth political member. I am not a hawk by nature, far from it; but as Defence Secretary, with the responsibility of giving every possible support to the military, I was concerned that Margaret and I would find ourselves opposed by a combination of Pym and Whitelaw. She and I discussed who the fifth member might be and agreed on Cecil Parkinson. As the Chairman of the Conservative Party, and as a keen and adept performer on the media, he seemed a good choice. Cecil, who had been my deputy at the Department of Trade, proved to be a valuable addition when it came to putting forward the government's case on television. In retrospect I need not have worried about political balance because Whitelaw – who always supported Margaret Thatcher anyhow, whatever the merits of the issue – became with Margaret herself the most hawkish political voice in the War Cabinet. And Michael Havers, who attended nearly all our meetings in his capacity as the government legal adviser, proved to be more of a pragmatic former Fleet Air Arm officer than a typical, pernickety, nitpicking wordsmith of a lawyer. We also had no Chancellor of the Exchequer, but that had been decided earlier.

Francis Pym therefore found his determined efforts to achieve a diplomatic solution somewhat frustrated by the balance of sentiment in the War Cabinet. But it was important to understand his position and help him with it. Margaret Thatcher was not good at conciliation with her colleagues. She preferred the bludgeon to the rapier.

She and Francis approached the negotiations for a diplomatic settlement from opposite directions, and there was a frequent clash of wills. Both took an entirely honourable position but they were in fundamental conflict. Francis seemed to want to avoid an ugly and dangerous battle at all costs; I think he was genuinely upset at putting all these young soldiers and sailors – at very great risk – into an opposed amphibious landing without air superiority. He had seen war himself. Moreover, on his several visits to Washington he must have been increasingly influenced by Haig and other US military opinion to the effect that this whole exercise was beyond our capability.

Nicholas Henderson's excellent published diaries make this clear:

> … the facts disclosed the scepticism of the US Navy at the outset about the prospects for the success of the British Task Force. Britain was ill-equipped to fight a war in the South Atlantic. They lacked air surveillance; their satellite communications were inadequate. They were short of an effective air-to-air missile for the Harriers. They had no base in the South Atlantic.

Later, he quotes Weinberger admitting that 'we all knew of the enormous military odds against Britain'. Weinberger's own memoirs say:

> Our military leaders advised that lack of shipping made Mrs Thatcher's position and plans impossible to carry out. Also they noted that the UK's lack of air transport, the length of time the Argentinians would have to prepare defences against the British and all the normal difficulties inherent in making an opposed landing, not to mention the difficulties of doing that after an 8,000 mile trip with no real intermediate bases – all of those factors led our military leaders to conclude that the UK action could not succeed.

As a former Defence Secretary, Francis Pym may – and I emphasise may – have been horrified at the likely financial cost of garrisoning the Falklands against a subsequent military threat from Argentina. He knew, as I knew, that we were insufficiently resourced to meet the threat to NATO, let alone future threats 8,000 miles away in the South Atlantic. Francis wanted to do a deal and was flexible in his approach to achieving this objective.

Margaret Thatcher had, I believe, made up her mind from the outset that the only way we could regain our national honour and prestige was by inflicting a military defeat on Argentina. She was sufficiently pragmatic to understand that if the negotiations could bring about a total withdrawal of the Argentinians and the restoration of some kind of British administration, then her Cabinet would accept it. A myth grew up about Margaret Thatcher that in some way her word was law. It was never the case in my day; she was very well aware that she had to keep her Cabinet, her parliamentary supporters and the party in the country with her. The painful and endless negotiations for a diplomatic settlement produced the only significant personal clashes of the war. The only positive thing that can be said of them in retrospect is that they filled a horrible vacuum, whilst the task force made its long, long voyage towards Antarctica – as far laterally as Hawaii.

The first clash between the military imperatives and the requirements of diplomacy came on Wednesday 7th, only five days after the invasion. *Spartan,* our first nuclear submarine, was approaching the Falklands, and we needed to decide on the appropriate rules of engagement for its captain. The Chiefs of Staff, by now headed by the returned Terry Lewin, had recommended the imposition of a 200-mile maritime exclusion zone; the principal purpose being to stop further Argentinian supplies reaching the troops embarked on the Falkland Islands. I had to get this through the War Cabinet and announced as soon as possible. In the end I agreed to announce it at a debate in the House of Commons on the Wednesday, the first major debate since the debacle on the previous Saturday. I wanted not only to give this support to the military, but also to show to the world after the sailing of the task force that we really meant business.

From the beginning of the week the position of the Americans was becoming clear: they stopped arms sales to Argentina, but were unwilling to take more effective economic measures. Nicholas Henderson, our Ambassador, reported back that the Americans were not prepared to 'tilt' too heavily against Argentina; to do so, they said, would deprive them of their influence in Buenos Aires. They did not want Galtieri to fall – whereas we saw him as an outright fascist dictator and aggressor. Galtieri was for the Americans a central pillar of resistance to communism in South and Central America, and all of Reagan's and the State Department's efforts were concentrated on the crisis in El Salvador. The United States did not wish to choose between Britain, their principal NATO ally in

Europe, and their interests in Latin America. Apart from Weinberger and the Pentagon, the Americans were very, very far from being on our side.

Al Haig was due to commence his mediation – although we resented his use of such a term – on Wednesday, but because of the debate it was postponed until the Thursday. The War Cabinet met for the first time that Wednesday morning and again in the evening. My 1983 record describes the drama that occurred at that evening meeting, for me one of the most important of the war:

> It took place informally at seven o'clock in Margaret Thatcher's room in the House of Commons. It had been decided that we should meet to confirm the declaration of the maritime exclusion zone. We had discussed this in detail that morning and it had been agreed that, subject to any second thoughts, the declaration of the exclusion zone should be included in my own winding-up speech [due to be made later that evening]. It had been a struggle to get it agreed but I had done so at a meeting of the War Cabinet that morning, subject to final decision in the evening. I heard, as I was sitting on the front bench – nervous, of course, at my approaching speech – that the Foreign Office was now absolutely determined, and passionately so, to avoid the declaration of the MEZ that evening. Their reason was that Haig was coming to London and that it would be a slap in the face to ask him here as a negotiator and an intermediary and then, just before he arrived, to declare the zone, an act which was hostile to the Argentinians. I was absolutely horrified. The whole thing was on course and the Royal Navy needed it. It was the central part of my speech. It was a climb-down at a critical moment when our resolve needed to be shown to the whole world. It was typical of the Foreign Office. Margaret Thatcher was on the bench beside me listening to the debate. I whispered to her that I was deeply upset at this change of plan.
>
> It was clear to me as we sat down in her room that Margaret, who had just appointed Francis Pym as Foreign Secretary, was not going to come out against him. She did not agree, but she felt having just appointed him that she had to back him up. I think she must have realised that this made my position very awkward indeed, but at the same time I knew that she was not going to back me up. Francis opened the discussion by saying that he thought there was no question, now that Haig was coming, of going ahead with this declaration. It would make Haig's mission impossible and he could not agree with it; he realised what a foolish decision we'd made that morning. I said that I

could not disagree more strongly. In fact, although I never said so, I felt that I could hardly stay as Defence Secretary if the decision went against me. I knew that Willie would be likely to back up Francis, as was Margaret. Cecil Parkinson was my only hope. I said that I fundamentally disagreed. If Haig came to London and we had not already started on military measures, we would be in balk thereafter. How were we ever going to take a necessary military measure if, every time he came, we were concerned about upsetting him? I said that it was absolutely vital that we now showed our determination to the Argentinians; this would improve the peace process, the negotiating process, it would help Haig. We could not declare it after he arrived, and it was urgently necessary now that our submarines were approaching the Falklands to get on and show that we meant business.

Margaret did not come down on my side. She wondered whether we could not declare it the next day. I said that was impossible. It was the last day before Parliament went into recess. Why, if there was a speech by me in one hour's time, would we not have declared it but waited till the next day to make a statement? The following day was Good Friday. We could not make the statement on Good Friday. If we waited till Saturday, it would seem very odd that when we had had a major debate on the subject, we had deferred a decision until Saturday. And, anyhow, by Saturday Haig would be in Buenos Aires and we could not send him back there to negotiate a settlement and than announce a maritime exclusion zone when he was there. Willie Whitelaw came in, concerned not so much about the substance of the matter but about parliamentary opinion. I could see a Chief Whip's mind grinding through. The parliamentary situation was very difficult, he said. This was the time to announce it, and yet he saw how difficult this would be for Francis. He was worried that if we did not announce it now, it would look as if we had been frightened out of doing so. Cecil Parkinson then came in. He too said he thought it was very difficult. We were reaching a stalemate in a decision. I knew that I had to plough on. I once again protested that the submarines were there; the Fleet had put to sea; the public and international recognition of our resolve following the passing of Resolution 502 was absolutely crucial; the Party would not stand for any weakness; this was the last occasion on which we could do so before Parliament left for the Easter Recess. Haig would place us in balk. We had no choice. The argument went on and on and on – but gradually, slowly, I pulled it round my way.

We then discussed whether we had to tell Haig in advance. I said I did not mind informing him, but it must be information and no more. About an hour and a half had passed when, somewhat to my surprise, Francis, who saw that the argument was going against him, suddenly said well, he would accept it. It was one of the most relieving moments of the crisis. We agreed to inform Haig, and the statement, which had already been prepared by the Foreign Office lawyers, was re-incorporated in my speech.

I made the statement right at the beginning of what I had to say. It completely transformed the atmosphere of the House and met with universal agreement from the Labour Party, Callaghan and the rest, and brought great cheers from our side. I believe it was one of the most important decisions that we took throughout the crisis. We indicated to the world that we meant business. Haig, when he arrived the next morning, knew that we meant business. The Argentinians now realised that we were not fooling around, and at least it made possible my political recovery from the disastrous speech I'd made the previous Saturday. I had not had time to prepare my wind-up, but David Omand and others had put together a rather boring, flat and dull speech for me. As it turned out, the House was in a much better mood. It allowed me to speak. I was unprovocative. For the first time since I had done the Defence Review the House actually listened to what I had to say about the Royal Navy. I was able to explain that we were spending more, not less, on the conventional Navy. As I sat down the House was appreciative. Margaret and Willie and Francis beside me were genuinely relieved. It had been a difficult occasion. Afterwards Miloska and I went round to Margaret's room for a drink, and the mood was very different from the previous Saturday's. I could now carry on with my work.

I have dwelt on that single occasion at some length because it illustrates the problem of managing the intricate relationship between military and diplomatic requirements. If we had not given priority to the military on this first occasion when the clash of interests arose, I doubt whether the resolve to support the task force against all the diplomatic, international and parliamentary pressures could have been sustained. Thereafter, I don't think there was another occasion where such a problem went against the military imperatives. It had been a close-run thing, but it set the right precedent for thereafter. The maritime exclusion zone itself took effect from the early hours of Easter Monday morning, 12 April.

The Haig-led negotiations were interminable – and it would be tedious to go over again all the twists and turns that encountered us. If Washington had been in the hands of the East Coast WASPS (White Anglo-Saxon Protestants) instead of the West Coast Americans, with their overriding concern for the Americas, it might have been different. The State Department, the White House security staff, led by Judge Clark, and Reagan himself were never wholly committed to our case, although they came out publicly in our support on 30 April. Even thereafter the Americans gave every assistance to the Peruvians, the United Nations and every other mediator – Brazilian, Mexican and the rest – to bring about a negotiated settlement, on terms which would have been seen as a surrender by political, press and public opinion in the United Kingdom. In the closing stages, when we had already lost many ships and men and were already safely back on the Falkland Islands, the Americans leant heavily on us, backed up by telephone calls from Reagan to Thatcher, to find some way of saving Galtieri's face. 'Magnanimity before victory' became their watchword. Fortunately the military, apart from Terry Lewin, were kept largely ignorant of the hesitations of the wider Cabinet and the considerable international pressures on us to call it a day, not least from Germany, Ireland, Italy and Spain. Only Mitterrand and the French remained staunch allies to the end. Bravely Margaret Thatcher held firm – and it needed a massive exercise of will to resist these pressures, but she did so.

When Haig and his party returned from Buenos Aires after their initial talk with us, there was a classic demonstration of how Whitehall's undoubted skills can be unhelpful. After various talks on the morning of 12 April, we all gathered in the Cabinet Room to discuss the draft proposals that he had brought back with him. Unfortunately Robert Armstrong, who performed a valuable role as the Secretary of the War Cabinet, had included several senior civil service colleagues in the meeting. The meeting was far too big.

Haig talked and talked, speaking up for his proposals with some vigour and skill. Margaret Thatcher, Whitelaw and I resisted him. The civil servants (Robert Wade-Gery, a Foreign Office man, among them) started passing amendments up and down the table. We reached the point where they were trying to broker a drafting compromise between us and Haig – typical Foreign Office practice but thoroughly unhelpful. At one stage, with the assistance of these Whitehall draughtsmen, we had nearly reached a stage where we were being asked to withdraw 4,000 miles to Ascension whilst the Argentinians were withdrawing 400 miles to their mainland. I protested and it was taken out. Eventually, after some eleven hours of discussions, we had reached a sort of compromise: the Argentinians would withdraw to the mainland; we would position a naval force the same distance from the Falklands; and there would be a joint United States-Argentine-British administration acting in conjunction with the Falkland Islanders, who would agree for one or two of the Argentine resident population to join the Executive and Legislative Councils. It was a nonsense, but we were under great pressure to agree something positive with the Americans.

Haig departed, saying that the Argentinians would never accept the final draft but that he would put it to them. When he arrived back in Buenos Aires he was met by organised riots in favour of the occupation, and his discussions with the junta, which was deeply divided, were chaotic. As soon as one point was agreed there were protests from senior officers of the Services and the position was rescinded. So it went on.

The final drama of the Haig negotiations occurred almost a fortnight later, on Saturday, 24 April. By this time, Haig was getting nowhere very fast between the intransigent Argentine junta and the determined Margaret Thatcher.

Francis Pym returned from one of his visits to Washington with an amended set of American proposals. There is no need to give the details – the text is available in several other memoirs of the time. But by the time the War Cabinet was called to consider them that evening, Francis was advocating acceptance with some vigour. I quote from Margaret Thatcher's accurate record:

> Francis Pym's document [brought back from his latest negotiations in Washington] ruled out the possibility of a return to the situation enjoyed by the Islanders before the invasion. We would have gone against our commitment to the principle that the Islanders' wishes were paramount … Did Francis realise how much he had signed away?
>
> Francis put a paper to the War Cabinet recommending acceptance of these terms … I asked Willie Whitelaw to come upstairs to my study. I told him that I could not accept these terms.

At the meeting itself, there was a long discussion which led to something of an impasse. The Foreign Office representatives were in favour of acceptance, but the rest of us were not. Margaret again:

It was John Nott who found the procedural way forward. He proposed that we should make no comment on the draft but ask Mr Haig to put it to the Argentinians first. If they accepted it we should undoubtedly be in difficulties: but we could then put the matter to Parliament in the light of their acceptance. If the Argentinians rejected it – and we thought that they would, because it is almost impossible for any military junta to withdraw – we could then urge the Americans to come down firmly on our side, as Al Haig had indicated they would as long as we did not break off the negotiations. This is what was decided.

And so a great crisis passed. I could not have stayed as Prime Minister had the War Cabinet accepted Francis Pym's proposals. I would have resigned.

I am always surprised when support for me comes from unexpected quarters, and I am especially pleased with the nice comment which Terry Lewin made about me that is quoted near the start of this book. But to receive praise from a senior Foreign Office mandarin, albeit one for whom I had considerable respect, came as a real bonus. In his account of this critical episode, Nicholas Henderson describes my 'brainwave' as 'a finesse of which Talleyrand would have been proud'! The Argentinians did not respond in favour of the American proposals, and in consequence the United States announced their support for the United Kingdom on 30 April – nearly one month after an armed aggression on the territory of their closest NATO ally.

Before I finally leave the subject of the negotiations and return to the more important subject of the war, it is worth mentioning the meeting which took place at Chequers on 17 May.

By this time the peace negotiations had passed to the United Nations. Our support remained quite fragile among our allies, and we were concerned that the whole subject might return to the Security Council. International opinion had not been assisted by our sinking of the *Belgrano* with her large loss of life. Tony Parsons and Nicholas Henderson were asked to return here from the United States and join the meeting, which was also attended by Francis Pym, Tony Acland and Michael Palliser. A clutch of five men from the Foreign Office.

I have to say that Margaret Thatcher was pretty aggressive at this meeting. As Nicholas Henderson reported very accurately, Margaret accused them 'of being wet, ready to sell out, unsupportive of British interests, etc., etc.' And: 'Did the Foreign Office have no principles? She said that while we [i.e. the Foreign

Office] were content to be dishonest and consult with dishonest people, she was honest.' At one stage I thought that this was all getting a bit much and I intervened in some exasperation. She then rounded on me and accused me of being rude to her! It is true, I had been. 'Those who live by the sword, die by the sword.' I am afraid these polite, civilised, intelligent mandarins as good civil servants were hardly able to retaliate, so it rightly fell to me.

In his entertaining account of this extended meeting, Henderson then goes on:

> Right at the end of the meeting Nott protested about the American attitude. Did they realise the bitterness in the UK about them?
>
> I asked him in what way the Americans had fallen short of expectations since they had declared their support for us on 30 April. Surely they had met all our demands for intelligence and equipment? With less than enthusiasm the PM referred to Reagan's recent telephone call to her urging us not to undertake military operations against the mainland. She exclaimed once again against 'ingratitude' ...
>
> Nott came up to me after the meeting was over to say that perhaps he had given the wrong impression. It was simply a feeling he had that some of the speeches were bad (which is true) and that there were people, e.g. Jeanne Kirkpatrick, who were against us (also true).

The call from Reagan about avoiding military operations on the mainland reminds me of my last disagreement with Margaret Thatcher, and in this case I was also opposed by Terry Lewin.

Towards the end of the conflict, when the outcome was not in much doubt, one of our nuclear submarines found the Argentine aircraft carrier lurking within Argentinian territorial waters. We had agreed rules of engagement which allowed our submarines to sink the aircraft carrier fairly early in the conflict, as she posed a very real threat, with her A4 aircraft, to the safety of our ships. I had fully endorsed this necessary action, but we never found her right up until this late moment – and the rules of engagement did not permit an attack within Argentinian territorial waters. The Navy sought a change in the rules, although the shallow water would have posed a hazard to our submarine. Margaret Thatcher was keen to agree the change, on the basis that the aircraft carrier would present a continuing threat to our ships and to the Falklands even after we had recaptured them. I opposed the change, arguing against her and Terry Lewin on the grounds that action in South American territorial waters could bring in other countries on the Argentinian side, just as we were about to achieve a victory. We did not agree the change. Another 'What if?' of history.

~

It was while the task force was still sailing south that I heard that my mother had died in the night after several years of serious disability following a stroke. I wish she had lived to see the conclusion of the Falklands, though I have no way of knowing whether she understood it all; I imagine she did because she sat in front of the television day by day, but she could not communicate. Her funeral was in Northam Church, North Devon, where she had been baptised, confirmed and married. Frank Cooper had kindly arranged for an RAF HS135 to be put at my disposal. On Wednesday, 21 April I woke up my daughter, who was living with me in Admiralty House, and we were in the air from Northolt by eight o'clock.

We flew down to Chivenor, near Barnstaple in North Devon, and as we came in the beautiful Taw/Torridge estuary lay before us. Drawn up on the apron were a large number of Hawk Jet trainers, a most impressive sight. Chivenor is where we train our RAF pilots for their advanced jet and weapons training. I was met by the captain of the station, who walked with me over to the buildings nearby where I chatted to quite a large group of ground crew – young men in their early twenties and even younger than that. They all seemed very cheerful and were highly curious about my arrival and what I would have to say. I told them that the RAF was putting up a splendid job, particularly on the air bridge to Ascension. The Royal Navy was getting more of the publicity, but behind the scenes a tremendous amount of valuable work had already been undertaken. I thought it wise to let them know, although the information was very restricted, that we had placed air-flight refuelling on the Vulcans and Victors, and I said that the Victors had been performing a valuable role on reconnaissance in the South Atlantic. When I said that the Royal Navy was getting more publicity, one of them said there was nothing new in that and there was laughter and agreement all round.

Saša and I then drove in an RAF car to my father's home. My father had decided that we would not all parade into the church, so it was nice to find our places. Northam Church was quite full and, although my mother had been disabled and had really been unable to speak for many years, there was a good congregation, very much of families who had grown up with her in the past – many people, now in their seventies and eighties, who had shared their childhood with her in Northam and the surrounding area.

It was a sad occasion and several of us were in tears, but it was a lovely sunny day; and as my mother's coffin was lowered into the grave, we looked out from Northam churchyard across Bideford Bay and the estuary of the River Torridge with ships coming in and out across the bar – a sight I had seen so many times when I was young. She will lie there in peace with one of the most beautiful views in all of this country stretched below.

We returned to my father's home for lunch, and I had only just completed it when Wendy, my social secretary, was on the line. Francis Pym was making a statement in the Commons that afternoon and if I left immediately I could be back there in time. I gathered up my three children. William, the youngest, was due back at Eton that evening so I had to take him with me. Saša also was starting at Chelsea Art College the next day and Julian was due to return to Oxford. My wife and I had a quick discussion as to whether all the children should travel with me on the same aeroplane and, in the end, we agreed to take the risk.

We were back in London fifty minutes after leaving Chivenor and my second Private Secretary, Nick Evans, met me with the latest papers, including notes of the War Cabinet meeting which had taken place that morning in my absence. Terry Lewin's notes gave me a good feel for what had been discussed and I was, therefore, able to join Francis Pym in the House with the knowledge of what had taken place in the previous few hours.

Francis made a good statement, but the impression left on me that afternoon was an unhappy one. The House of Commons seemed to me a million miles from understanding the gap that remained between the Argentinians and ourselves. By emphasising our desire for a peaceful settlement with almost every other word, Francis, I fear, gave the impression we could see one in sight – it was only a question of one final heave and we would be home and dry. This feeling of optimism had translated itself into the House, particularly on our side, and Healey, of course, went on about the United Nations. He cannot really believe that the United Nations will provide anything other than a catastrophic defeat for us, but he goes on saying it; presumably it's the only way of holding his own Party together. I came away from that session in the House feeling depressed.

We then had to take a decision whether we should recapture South Georgia. Terry Lewin and I had discussed it several times. The Naval Staff and Northwood were anxious not to be distracted by a diversion into South Georgia and, looked at from a strictly military point of view, they were right. But Lewin had a well-known dictum that 'there is no such thing as a purely military operation, all operations are politico-military', and he was right. As a member of the War Cabinet he could see that, as politicians, we were under enormous pressure in the House of Commons and internationally to get the campaign finished; but he and I knew that the amphibious force was going to take longer to arrive in the Falklands than anyone anticipated. So we agreed that we had to go for this diversion to fill the vacuum. It was pure politics.

That evening we had another meeting. From my memory, there was the PM, Francis Pym and me and a few of our officials. It was a discussion about Francis' journey next day to the United States but, in particular, we had a major disagreement surrounding our decision to carry on with the attack on South Georgia. This had been a difficult decision earlier in the day because the mood of Parliament and, indeed, the country, had been that no shot should be fired in anger whilst the negotiating process was still going on.

Such a position would have placed us in an intolerable situation because there was no reason to believe that the Argentinians were seriously intending to negotiate. We could not detach the *Antrim* group [a naval detachment] to South Georgia and then leave it hanging around there without our orders. In every way it seemed essential to confirm our earlier decision that the reoccupation of South Georgia should proceed. Francis resisted but by this time we'd been joined by Willie Whitelaw. He supported the decision to continue with the South Georgia operation, which involved landing a team of SAS and the Special Boat Squadron on the island in order to attempt at least a partially bloodless reoccupation. The FO put up some resistance, but in the end the decision was taken: we went ahead.

Just as we were breaking up, Michael Palliser said that he thought it was necessary to inform Nicholas Henderson of what we were doing. I disagreed with this rather strongly. It did not seem to me a matter for the British Ambassador in Washington. The PM clearly agreed with me, but Tony Acland, Michael Palliser and Francis Pym all pressed the point and, in the end, we seemed unable to resist it. It was agreed, therefore, to send a message to

Nicholas Henderson telling him that the South Georgia occupation had already begun and pointing out that Francis Pym would be in Washington negotiating, possibly when the news began to break.

Later that evening we had a message back from Nicholas saying that he quite understood our decision, but he felt that it would be very wrong for us not to inform Alexander Haig. He did not intend to put it other than as firm information to Haig – a decision had been taken, it was going ahead, but we wanted him to know. This was the position when we broke up that evening. It was a tense meeting but a friendly one and we resolved the difference satisfactorily.

I had dinner in the House with a group of colleagues. I remember John Stokes and two others were sitting at my table. I said how depressed I had been with the mood of the House of Commons, its belief that a settlement was near and its seeming unwillingness to face the consequences of what was likely to happen. They did not agree with me. They agreed that there was a difference of view in the Party but, on the whole, there was an acceptance that if force became necessary it would have to follow. I voted at ten o'clock and got back to Admiralty House feeling very tired. It was, after all, the day of my mother's funeral and I had just got to sleep around about 11.30 when the telephone rang. My Private Secretary asked to come round and see me, he had some messages.

The first message indicated that the SAS had already landed on South Georgia some ten miles from one of the Argentinian bases. This was a factual statement and said nothing more. But the other message was a long rambling telex from Nicholas Henderson about his talk with Haig. Haig expressed his shock that we would go ahead and re-occupy South Georgia at the present time. The peace process was still going on – it would certainly damage him in the eyes of the Argentinians. He was deeply concerned about how he would be seen, and it would certainly be thought that he had connived, if not agreed, to this military action. He said that he had no course but to inform the Argentinians of our forthcoming military action. Nicholas Henderson replied that this was quite impossible – this would be giving up our military secret and could damage lives. Haig continued to protest but in the end agreed that he would not tell the Argentinians. Was it not possible, he asked, for him to tell the Argentinians that American intelligence had discovered that we had a group of ships in the area, and that the Argentinians could be warned in this way? Henderson again protested that this would be intolerable and so their meeting broke up; but it also became apparent that Costa Mendes [the Argentine Foreign Minister] had tried to telephone Haig that evening on an urgent matter, and I believe that other members of the State Department informed the Argentinians of what we were about. It is a frightening thing that our greatest ally is not wholly on our side. I only hoped that if information had been passed by the Americans to the Argentinians about our impending assault that this did not lead to loss of life.

The week before it had been agreed that we [the War Cabinet] should have a military briefing. It was difficult fixing the time and it was necessary that it should be done before Francis Pym departed. I had had a difference of view with Terry Lewin about how the briefing should be presented to my colleagues. Normally I would have had a dress rehearsal with the Chiefs, but in the end I left them to it and they prepared it in my absence, so that the next morning they could present a set of military options.

The briefing took place in the Ministry of Defence at about nine o'clock. There were about fifteen officials present and the Chiefs of Staff. It was very well done. We went over the list of military options. The difficulty with it was – and I should certainly have warned against packing so much into such a short time – that there was such a mass of information, the decisions were so difficult and so far-reaching, that the PM protested that she could not carry on the discussion at that time.

This is how Margaret Thatcher herself describes the meeting:

It was clear that we had a period of some two to three weeks in May during which we might land without terrible casualties. And then there were decisions to be made about how much more equipment, aircraft and troops to send, how to deal with the resulting prisoners of war, what to do about South Georgia and when. There was to be no respite at all. And these decisions must be made quickly. I looked from the Chiefs of Staff to my colleagues. It was a lot for them to take in. With the exception of John Nott, who of course was already briefed on the difficulties, they seemed somewhat taken aback. By this stage the press had learnt that we were at the MoD and I asked that everyone look confident as we left.

We went into a smaller group with just Margaret, Willie, Francis and myself. There were really three decisions that needed to be taken that day. First of all, we had to decide whether to deploy the Vulcans to Ascension. They'd already been fitted with air-flight refuelling, and from Ascension it would be possible for them to bomb the runway at Port Stanley. However, that morning we had received information that the American Air Force station commander, who up to then had been extremely helpful, would deny us aviation fuel for the Vulcans and that we were not to bring them there. This was an intolerable and disgraceful episode, indicating that the State Department had got in touch with Ascension to block the Vulcans going there. This can only have come from Haig himself. I said to Francis that the Americans had no right to take such measures, they were our allies, and the first thing he should do on arriving in Washington that morning (he was going on Concorde) was to protest loudly that the Americans, under the agreement, had to make the air-field available to us in an emergency.

The second issue was whether we should sail the advanced amphibious group from Ascension on Saturday and Sunday. I had been against doing this because I did not want the amphibious group to set sail and, having set sail, for it to turn back as a result of the negotiations. I was therefore in favour of hold-ing it for a few days until Francis had returned to London. In the end it was decided not to sail on the Saturday. I recommended that we had a meeting at Chequers at which we could spend four or five hours knocking the whole thing around and so, just before Francis's departure, it was agreed that this should happen.

Richard Hill's biography of Lewin covers this disagreement as follows:

> There was one occasion when he was overruled. John Nott intervened to delay by two days the sailing of the force south from Ascension when it appeared that there might be some chance of Haig's latest initiative (one more spin of the 'Haig Shuttle') succeeding. This, he knew, would irritate all the naval authorities because they were working to a desperately narrow window of opportunity … But he reasoned that if the task force sailed south and it then turned round because there had been a settlement, it would look as though it had turned tail in defeat.

The most important thing of all, however, was to get Francis back from Wash-ington in time. If Francis was to remain there negotiating for ever without get-ting anywhere then we were in a hopeless state. The negotiating process over-lapped and conflicted with the necessary military measures. The amphibious group could not remain for ever on Ascension without our credibility being at stake. So I pleaded with Francis – you must be back by Sunday. We had to get a clear decision as to whether it was really worthwhile Haig going back to Buenos Aires or not, because the military timetable and the diplomatic negotiations were beginning to get in conflict with one another. The meeting broke up, Francis went off to catch Concorde to Washington and, after a short pause, Cabinet began.

Whereas at Cabinet on the previous Tuesday there had been a full briefing by Francis on the diplomatic situation, on this occasion I gave a very full briefing to the whole Cabinet on where the Argentinian forces were; where our troops were deployed. I announced for the first time that Special Forces were already embarked on South Georgia and I listed some of the military options. I think this came as a shock to the Cabinet but, on the whole, it went down well. I had preceded my remarks by pointing out the difficulties of the diplomatic process. I read out another cable, which had come from Nico Henderson the previous night, indicating that there were fifty or so people to negotiate with in Buenos Aires, but that they were always changing their view and that Galtieri was drunk.

The Cabinet was quite contrary to Tuesday, where it had been drifting off in high-flown views about international law, with Geoffrey Howe mumbling on as usual and Leon Brittan trying to display his legal pyrotechnics. Tuesday's Cabinet had been depressing but Thursday helped to concentrate people's minds and Willie, as usual, came in as an enormous help. The only dissenting voices were Jim Prior and Peter Walker. Jim Prior was clearly upset about the whole thing. The previous night I had been on my way home to bed and had drifted in to pick up a piece of paper out of the Chief Whip's office from Michael Jopling, I found Willie there. He'd been out to dinner and was in his normal after-dinner state. He, Jopling and Jim Prior were all together. I joined them. Willie and I tried to persuade Jim that we just had to go forward with military preparations, we could not hold them up. Jim, in fact, was OK at Cabinet but he was obviously deeply concerned that we were going to fire a shot and the whole peace process was going to break down. Peter Walker too expressed his great concern about the South Georgia operation. He, like Jim Prior, was concerned that we should be actually embarking on an operation in South Georgia at the same time as we were negotiating in Washington. Neither of them seemed to see that, on the whole, we'd got as far as we had already purely because we had kept up our military pressure. I pointed out that exactly the same arguments had been used against the declaration of the exclusion zone at that very critical meeting on the night of the Wednesday debate. The Cabinet agreed the way forward with only some dissent from these two colleagues. Perfectly reasonably, they were more cautious than the others.

I had told Margaret that I'd had three weeks without any rest at all and that I intended to fly back home to Cornwall for a day or so. All I wanted to do was to go home to see my wife and our farm! She said she was happy with that, so I went back to the office to sign off some papers with the idea of picking up my bags and flying down to Cornwall. At that moment I was paged and I went to the telephone. I was needed urgently in the Ministry. I went back there. My Private Secretary, David Omand, clearly had had a terrible shock and Terry Lewin came in to see me – they had bad news. In fact, it could not have been worse. We'd had a telephone message from Northwood which indicated that two Wessex helicopters had had a white-out in a Force 11 blizzard and had crashed in South Georgia, probably in the mountains, with their crews aboard. Evidently the SAS, as we subsequently found out, had been caught in a terrible blizzard and the men were beginning to get frostbite and needed lifting off. Clearly the captain had decided the danger of leaving them there was too great, and so in these appalling conditions he despatched two Wessex helicopters. They evidently managed to pick up the crew, but coming off they were hit by this white-out and the helicopters crashed. We knew no more about it.

I said that I thought we should not await a further signal but should immediately inform the PM. Terry Lewin and I went across to No. 10. They had been warned that we had unhappy news. When we got there, Margaret was sitting in the Cabinet Room with her two Private Secretaries and Robert Armstrong. I said I feared that we had some unhappy news to tell her and Terry Lewin then told her what had happened. It was a great shock to all of us. However, just as we were going in to see her, we heard slightly better news, namely that four of the SAS and one aircrew had been picked up by another helicopter. This did at least give us hope. When we got back to the Ministry the news was even better. It seemed that the helicopter had found the other SAS and their crew and, although the helicopters were broken down and smashed up against the mountain, maybe everybody was all right. We then waited to see the latest news. I decided not to hang back and I went to Northolt. I telephoned

David Omand from there and he said he had no more news. Evidently ten of them were still on the mountain.

When I arrived at St Mawgan I asked to use the secure line. I got on it to David and we were able to talk. The men were still on South Georgia, but they'd got a helicopter to them and there seemed to be no casualties. In the evening I found out that they had managed to lift them off and abandoned the helicopters on the mountain. When they returned to the ship it was found that they had bad frostbite and were in a poor condition; but nevertheless, that same day members of the Special Boat Squadron had been landed further down the coast, so it was too soon to say that the operation had been aborted. Subsequently I heard that, although we were minus two helicopters which we hoped to pick up later, the force commander had decided not to abandon the assault. The relief was great – it would have been an appalling situation had our very first operation resulted in loss of life as a result of the crash of a helicopter. One could imagine the sense of dismay at home that some accident of this nature had occurred before we had made contact with the Argentinians.

'Still, it worked out not too badly,' I wrote next morning sitting in the sun in my garden at Trewinnard. 'We have no helicopters and I am worried about how we can get ashore but, basically, the position is infinitely better than it was a few hours ago.' On a more personal note, I added that 'the cattle look fit' and that 'already after three hours at home and one short night I feel better and ready to go again'.

It was around this time that we heard of one of the most tragic accidents of the whole campaign. A helicopter transporting a whole team of the SAS crashed into the sea, and all were lost. It was devastating to lose so many of our most valuable, brave and effective soldiers in such an accident.

After this short break, I returned to London to await the news from South Georgia. It was recaptured without loss of life. Quite late on Sunday evening, the 25th, I went across to No. 10 with a draft statement, as I felt that this first victory should be announced by Margaret, but she was insistent that the task should fall to me. We went out into Downing Street and I read out the agreed statement. I remember the occasion for two reasons.

I had returned from Cornwall on my RAF plane wearing an appalling spiv's suit, which had been made for me by the only tailor in my constituency. It never occurred to me that it would see the light of day; but as soon as I had completed my statement, the large number of assorted hacks and newshounds, accompanied by a huge congregation of cameramen, started shouting questions at me. 'What happens next, Mr Nott? Are we going to declare war on Argentina, Mrs Thatcher?'To which Margaret replied in a high-pitched voice, 'Just rejoice at that news and congratulate our forces and the marines ... Rejoice.' Somehow it was highly embarrassing, although she was only trying to get the wretched media to acknowledge our success. We retreated hastily into No. 10.

Second only to my interview – or non-interview – with Robin Day, this incident known as 'Rejoice, Rejoice' was to dog me on the television for the next twenty years. Every time I see it, I cringe at that awful suit and the millions of people around the world who have now been able to judge the quality of Cornish tailoring.

~

In the early stages of the campaign, it had been very much a naval operation, which was sensible. The Chiefs of Staff of the Army and the Air Force were intimately involved through the Defence Operations Executive, but the contributions of the Army and the Air Force, apart from their gallant efforts in helping to get the Fleet to sea and operating the air bridge to Ascension, were limited. The RAF, in particular, was anxious to get involved and sought my political view as to whether a bombing raid on the runway at Port Stanley would be acceptable. I was wholeheartedly in favour. With amazing despatch the RAF equipped all the Hercules, the Victors and the last remaining Vulcan bomber with air-flight refuelling. In retrospect it is amazing what was achieved in a few weeks; it would have taken years of dithering bureaucracy to get anything similar decided and accomplished in times of peace. Another example was to equip the helicopters on the carriers with Searchwater radar, which had been used for years successfully for anti-submarine warfare on Nimrod maritime patrol aircraft; but no one had pressed forward to adapt the same radar for the airborne early warning of approaching aircraft.

The Vulcan practised bombing runs in the Highlands of Scotland and, just three weeks after the Argentine invasion, it set out to bomb the runway at Port Stanley and needed seven tanker aircraft to get it there and back. The impact of the raid was more psychological than real – only one bomb actually hit the runway – but it was an early indication that we meant business. More important was the equipping of the RAF Harriers with air-flight refuelling and, in an utterly remarkable feat of skill and endurance, the RAF pilots flew them down to join the carriers – stopping off only at Dakar and Ascension on the way. I met some of the young RAF pilots before they left, and it was remarkable to see their confidence and courage.

In so many ways Mitterrand and the French were our greatest allies. In earlier years we had equipped the Argentine Navy with our former destroyers, while the French had supplied them with the Mirage and Super-Etendard aircraft. The ships, especially the *Belgrano*, and the aircraft were equipped with modern Exocet missiles. As soon as the conflict began, Hernou, acting on the instructions of Mitterrand, got in touch with me to make available to us a Super-Etendard and Mirage aircraft, so that our Harrier pilots could train against them before setting off to the South Atlantic. The French supplied us with detailed technical information on the Exocet, showing us how to tamper with the missiles.

A remarkable worldwide operation then ensued to prevent further Exocets being bought by Argentina. I authorised our agents to pose as bona fide purchasers of equipment on the international market, ensuring that we outbid the Argentinians, and other agents identified Exocet missiles in various markets and covertly rendered them inoperable, based on information provided by the French. It was a remarkably successful operation. In spite of strenuous efforts by several countries, particularly the Israelis and the South Africans, to help Argentina, we succeeded in intercepting and preventing the supply of further equipment to the Argentinians who were desperately seeking resupply.

I had spoken to Henry Leach at the beginning of the campaign to ask him why he was so determined that the Royal Navy could do the job with so few men. He assured me that this was an amphibious operation suited to the Royal Navy's experience and that the Royal Marine Commando, supplemented by battalions of the Parachute Regiment, was sufficient to meet the objectives of the task force.

I did not believe him, although I understood that he wished to make it the Royal Navy's show. It was not my job to interfere. I consulted Dwin Bramall and senior civil servants, and their attitude was that plans would change and that the Navy itself would decide in favour of a back-up force. As I expected, General Bramall came to see me a week or two later to say that the Chiefs of Staff had decided to embark another brigade and wished to requisition the *QE2* to take it there. There ensued an amusing conversation:

Nott: Who are you intending to send, Dwin?

Bramall: We will send the 5th Brigade at Aldershot, but as it has lost two parachute battalions which are already part of the Commando Brigade's landing force, I will supplement it by two Guards battalions.

Nott: Where are the Guards battalions now?

Bramall: I am taking the Scots Guards and the Welsh Guards off ceremonial duties in London.

Nott: But how can you do that? They will be hopelessly unfit. Haven't you got other infantry battalions available which are already fit and well trained?

Bramall: I am sending them this weekend to the Welsh mountains for a period of concentrated battlefield training – they will be fine at the end of it.

Nott: Oh! Which is the third battalion making up the Brigade strength?

Bramall: The 7th Gurkhas who are already part of 5th Brigade.

Nott: Dwin, you can't send the Gurkhas. We are having frightful trouble holding things together in the United Nations and it is more than likely that the Indians will kick up a frightful fuss. It is just too risky politically to send the Gurkhas in my view.

Bramall: The 7th Gurkhas are part of 5th Brigade, the designated strategic reserve, and if we recoil from sending them now there will always be some reason for not sending the Gurkhas on future operations.

Nott: I agree that point and, as an ex-Gurkha, I would, of course, be mortified if we spoilt their chances.

Bramall: Look, Secretary of State, I am the Colonel of your Regiment [the 2nd Gurkhas], and I am telling you that they must go and I am requiring your support to fight our corner with the Foreign Office.

Nott: If you are instructing me in your capacity as Colonel of the 2nd Gurkhas, then of course, Dwin, I have no option but to obey!

So the matter was settled without more ado. My devil's advocacy had been heard and rightly rejected out of hand. Dwin Bramall was correct to call rank and, as the Colonel of my Regiment, I obeyed his instructions. It was nice for me to feel like a junior officer once again.

This anecdote reminds me of my mood in the middle of the crisis whilst the task force was still proceeding south. Immediately after the conclusion of the war, Dwin Bramall wrote me a delightful letter, which I quote towards the end of this chapter. In my reply, dated 20 June 1982, I expressed my feelings:

> Of all the letters that I have received yours was the most generous and welcome. This is partly because you were just close enough to the centre of the stage [i.e. the War Cabinet] to understand what was happening, but also because you will have understood some of the personality problems and tensions which will always play a key role in such great events. Having had a good 'start' (not a good speech!) and having helped in the government's initial recovery, I confess that I found the 'middle' weeks very difficult. This was partly because the diplomatic phase saw the PM at her most belligerent and inflexible – and partly because there was so little information coming from the Navy with which to conduct the political and PR campaign. In spite of distance – and the overriding need for commanders to be free of interference – there will always be other (equally) important battles being waged consecutively with the soldiers'/sailors' battle on the ground. I think we need a Staff College session on this subject. Once your magnificent soldiers were ashore – and we had the simple task of winning the war – everything became easier again.

On 30 April the 200-mile maritime exclusion zone, which had first been announced by me in the House of Commons on the 7th, was extended into a total exclusion zone. This made it clear that any ship or aircraft was liable to be attacked if it was carrying supplies or reinforcements for the Argentine forces. There was an additional clause, which was subsequently to become an item of contention, that these measures were 'without prejudice to the right of the UK to take whatever additional measures may be needed in its exercise of the right of self-defence, under Article 51 of the UN Charter'. A week earlier, on the 23rd, a message had been sent to the Argentine government and published internationally. It stated:

> That in this connection (with Article 51) Her Majesty's Government now wishes to make clear that any approach on the part of Argentine warships, including submarines, naval auxiliaries or military aircraft which could amount

to a threat to interfere with the mission of British forces in the South Atlantic, will encounter the appropriate response.

This was the very least that we could do – and it is often forgotten that the only reason why *we* had not suffered serious loss of life to the Royal Marines in the initial assault by Argentinian forces was that following our receipt of the intercepted Argentine signal to invade, we had instructed the Royal Marines to abandon their barracks at Moody Brook and disperse themselves around the Island.

When preparations were made by the Argentine forces on 2 May to make a strike with their carrier-based aircraft against the task force, we were aware that a pincer movement was also being organised for the *General Belgrano* and her escorting destroyers to exploit the air strike on the Fleet. We had already given Admiral Woodward rules of engagement, enabling him to attack the Argentine carrier *Veinticinco de Mayo* wherever he found her, inside or outside any exclusion zones; the extension of this right to attack the *Belgrano*, given the clear warnings given, was really not more than a formality. The two nuclear submarines given the task of shadowing the *Veinticinco de Mayo* seemed to have lost her temporarily, but *Conqueror*, the third submarine, was following the *Belgrano*. Terry Lewin asked me whether there would be any political problems in extending the rules of engagement to cover an attack on the *Belgrano*, knowing the grave danger she posed with her Exocet and other armaments to our ships. I agreed that we should attempt to neutralise her.

As it happened, we were due to meet at Chequers on Sunday, 2 May to discuss a range of matters, and Terry Lewin, Margaret Thatcher and I agreed there that we had no option but to agree to an attack on the *Belgrano*. It was one of the easiest decisions of the whole war and was subsequently endorsed by the War Cabinet at its meeting later in the morning.

Next day I received a terse, one-line signal from the Fleet just before I was due to make a statement to the House of Commons. I hardly had time to compose my statement, so I knocked the final version together in the car. My final statement was not seen – and vetted – by officials, as there was no time for this to happen. I remain astonished to this day, although knowing the House of Commons I should not have been, that anyone should consider the momentary compass bearing of the *Belgrano's* passage to be of any consequence whatever. Any ship can turn about in an instant. She was sunk in international waters in strict conformity with the warnings that we had given

– and for us to have taken any other decision, given her threat to the Fleet, would have been a serious dereliction of duty on our part.

I was shocked when I heard of the terrible loss of life that followed, and I regret it deeply, but I fear this was the consequence of a war that we did not initiate. I do not know why the Argentine destroyers did not stay in the area to pick up the survivors – I believe that our ships would have done so. I have no doubt that, although this incident turned international opinion against us, particularly in neutralist-minded Germany and in Argentina's cousin countries Spain and Italy, it did in fact save many British lives. If we had been forced to contend with an aggressive Argentine navy, as well as the courageous Argentine pilots, things might have been different. As it happened, Admiral Anaya, the most aggressive member of the Argentine junta and more than anyone responsible for the conflict in the first place, decided to keep the Argentine surface fleet in port following the sinking of the *Belgrano*. By neutralising the whole of the Argentine navy, our decision proved to be correct and fully justified.

Two days after the sinking of the Belgrano, on 4 May, the Argentines attacked HMS *Sheffield* with an Exocet missile. It was the first British naval tragedy of the war. The ship sunk, with some forty casualties, and it was my job to announce this loss to the House of Commons – an unhappy task. The sinking of the *Sheffield* at last brought home to the British public that we really were at war. Because I knew of the hazardous nature of the whole enterprise, I may have been anticipating a disaster more than most.

As the task force moved south, plans were being made at Northwood in consultation with Admiral Woodward about the timing and place of the amphibious landing. I quote from my account soon afterwards of the relevant discussions in Whitehall:

It was on Tuesday, 18 May that one of the most important meetings of the war took place. An informal gathering with the members of the War Cabinet was called, partly at my prompting, to give the Chiefs of Staff collectively an opportunity of setting out to the PM and her colleagues the risks attached to the landing at San Carlos, following the briefing which I had received at Northwood about the place of the landing on 14 May.

I had been anxious throughout the conflict to get the Chiefs of Staff collectively together as often as was reasonably possible without interfering with the day-to-day decision-making process, so that my political colleagues were fully aware of all the problems and risks attached to the decisions that they were taking. We all knew that the actual amphibious landing was the most critical and difficult of all the operations, so the day before the meeting with the War Cabinet we had a rehearsal in my room in the MoD at a long three-hour lunch.

At the meeting, as might have been expected, the Chiefs of Staff could not restrain their enthusiasm for making political comments. Henry Leach implied that our national honour was at stake. Dwin Bramall said the same. Terry Lewin, as usual, kept more or less to the military implications and Michael Beetham concentrated on the air side. The meeting went very well indeed.

Terry Lewin spoke first. He said that it was the unanimous view of the Chiefs of Staff that a long blockade was not feasible. This was supported later by Henry Leach, who said that the rate of attrition from accidents to aircraft, ships and men, if the whole operation were to be extended further, would probably lead to greater loss of life and greater loss of equipment than if we went forward and conducted the landing at the earliest possible time.

In a way the most striking of all the four presentations by each of the individual Chiefs was that by the Chief of the Air Staff, Sir Michael Beetham. He made the point very graphically that we had not succeeded, as we had hoped, in neutralising the Argentinian Air Force. This point was also confirmed by Bramall, who said that it was an established principle of modern war that a hazardous amphibious landing should not normally take place without air superiority. Both of them agreed that this had not yet been achieved. The Argentinians, said Michael Beetham, had already succeeded in locating our ships; they had clearly solved the problem of how to find out where they were; and, as the task force approached in one group to perform the amphibious landing, they would be even more exposed than up to now and, of course, would bring themselves within easy range of Argentinian land-based aircraft. He pointed out that the Argentinians still had a substantial force of Skyhawks, Mirage and Super-Etendard and that the threat was significant. Some aircraft would be likely to get through our defensive shield. He thought that ships might well be lost, and it was very important in his judgement that the approaching task force should come in at night and limit their exposure-time to the absolute minimum essential. Beetham took the view, as did all the other Chiefs, that the risks were substantial, that a blockade made no sense because of attrition in the appalling weather and conditions of the South Atlantic, that delay was possible but only at the expense of even greater risks; given all the worries that we undoubtedly possessed, he thought we had no political or military option but to move forward as soon as possible to establish a bridgehead and then go ahead to reconquer the Islands.

We also discussed at that meeting the threat that existed from the Argentine forces on the land; the lesser threat was from the naval forces, but we believed they had been more or less successfully neutralised since the sinking of the *Belgrano*. There had also been considerable discussion internally in the MoD and at my earlier briefing on 14 May about the danger which still existed from the Argentinian submarines. But the whole tenor of the meeting with the members of the War Cabinet was concern about the dangers from Argentinian aircraft, and there was no doubt that we went into this amphibious landing at San Carlos with our eyes wide-open, knowing very well that we were likely to lose ships and men. My own private view at this stage was that we were likely to lose up to five or six ships; and it was vitally important that we spread the troops around as many ships as possible, so that if we lost a ship with all its crew and all its equipment and all its men, at least we would limit the number of casualties and deaths to the absolute minimum. The meeting agreed that we should go ahead with the landing as proposed, leaving the actual timing to the force commanders on the spot.

We were also aware of the pressure that was bound to mount internationally as soon as our troops were ashore. We, as politicians, expressed our collective view to the Chiefs of Staff that the length of time between establishing a landing and total repossession of the Islands was a matter of concern to all of us. We thought that international pressures were bound to mount and mount and, therefore, speed was of the essence to this whole operation.

In discussion in the MoD afterwards it was felt that the air threat was probably higher than the Cabinet realised, and there was a general view, which I supported, that colleagues should be told and should realise that we were about to embark on a highly hazardous operation and we needed all the luck that we could get. It was, however, decided because of the vital security aspect of the whole affair not to inform Cabinet colleagues about the date of the landing, although of course all of them were conscious of the fact that this had to be within the foreseeable future.

We did have luck on our side – and with the heroism and skill of the Royal

Navy and the Royal Marines, the initial landing took place in darkness on 21 May without a single life lost. The place of landing, San Carlos Water, had been the subject of some concern as the Army, in particular, was worried at its distance (some sixty miles) from the main defensive positions of the Argentines around Port Stanley. There was considerable worry that, if the Argentines counter-attacked our forces, we could get bogged down half-way across the island in winter weather, with international opinion building up against us. This danger was enhanced when the *Atlantic Conveyor,* carrying a huge amount of stores and the crucial troop-carrying Chinook helicopters, was sunk. But the choice of San Carlos proved correct: it had space, some protection from submarine activity, depth of water, accessibility for ships and landing craft and, crucially, a hilly terrain which made it difficult for sea-skimming Exocet attack and low-level bombing. We did lose HMS *Ardent* and *Antelope* in the Sound, and *Coventry* outside it; had not so many of the Argentine bombs failed to explode, our casualties and ship losses could have been much worse. Many ships were hit, but the fuse setting on the bombs was not in conformity with the low-level attacks forced on the Argentine pilots by the hilly terrain and air-defence missiles on ships and shore.

After the conflict was over, I flew down to the Falklands in a Hercules, with the aid of several air-flight refuellings, and I had the privilege of inaugurating the cemetery overlooking San Carlos Water. Whenever I travelled around the world on duty, as Chairman of the Commonwealth War Graves Commission, I visited our war cemeteries and they were always sad and contemplative occasions. But the immediacy of the Falklands conflict – and a beautiful, clear sunny day shining on the beautiful San Carlos Water – made this one of the most moving occasions of my life.

The loss of the *Coventry* created a very unfortunate but not untypical dilemma in the Ministry of Defence. The timing for the announcement of casualties always generated problems, because often we knew that a particular ship had been hit but, understandably in the confusion surrounding such an incident, it was some time before we were aware of casualties. We had an overriding obligation to inform the next of kin before a public announcement, but the Argentinian media with their propaganda broadcasts often forced our hand prematurely.

The day of the *Coventry* disaster (25 May) was one of the worst at sea. It was also the day that we lost the *Atlantic Conveyor,* the Exocet attack by the Argentine Air Force failed to target a carrier, but hit this large and vital converted roll-on roll-off ship instead. Fortunately her Harriers had been flown off just in time before she sunk, with loss of life, including her Captain North.

That evening I was due to make a broadcast on ITN just after the 10 o'clock news, so we gathered in Terry Lewin's room at 9.30 to decide what I should say. There were three admirals – Lewin, Leach and Fieldhouse – and one politician, me. I wanted to announce that *Coventry* had been hit, but the admirals did not want to give specific information away to the Argentinians at that stage. They had a justified operational point. I argued that, in spite of their operational view, it was unwise to talk about the loss of an unnamed ship. However, in the end, I had to defer to their judgement.

I was much criticised for my announcement – as the telephone exchanges were jammed all night by calls from families of the entire task force worried about their sons and daughters. My judgement was often wrong, so I could hardly criticise others for taking a different view, and anyway it was my function to take the media flak whether the blame was mine or not.

Another occasion of a similar kind took place soon afterwards in connection with the attack on Goose Green, when we lost Lieutenant Colonel Jones, VC, and a number of his gallant men of the 2nd Battalion, the Parachute Regiment. Colonel Julian Thompson, a Royal Marine who had been in charge of the amphibious landing and had handled it brilliantly, was understandably concerned to consolidate and build his bridgehead at San Carlos. But in London we were in severe trouble both with domestic and international opinion, and it was urgently necessary for our troops to establish early contact with the Argentine forces – it was just as possible for us to lose the war in London as it was to do so on the battlefield of the Falklands. It was a classic case of the military priorities on the ground conflicting with the wider political requirements thousands of miles away. As politicians, we were determined not to interfere with military decisions. Fortunately, Lewin and Fieldhouse understood the dilemma, and Julian Thompson was pressured by them to break out of the bridgehead, perhaps before he would have chosen to do so.

Although it was obvious to the world that British forces were about to move forward, we were shocked in the MoD to read in the newspapers that our troops were about to attack Goose Green. It was a classic case of why we had tried to keep the No. 10 briefing machine as much in the dark as possible. The obsession with unattributable background briefing – what today goes by the name of spin – remains the curse of politics.

Following the ghastly tragedy to the Welsh Guards when *Sir Galahad* was attacked at Bluff Cove, the Argentines believed that our casualties were even worse than those we had sustained. We got in touch with the next of kin but did not release the full casualty list, as the final assault on Port Stanley was about to begin with an attack on Mount Longdon, Two Sisters and Wireless Ridge.

On Saturday, 12 June, HMS *Glamorgan* was hit by a missile. The signal from the Fleet simply said, 'HMS *Glamorgan* struck by suspected Exocet missile. Large fire in vicinity of hangar and in gas turbine and gear room. Power still available. Ship making 10 knots to the south.' There were no details of casualties. It was the morning of trooping the colour on Horseguards Parade, so it was not an auspicious start to the day. Meanwhile, back in the Falklands, John Witherow of *The Times* reported:

> As the sun climbed into the sky next day the Welsh Guards attempted to get what sleep they could in the open. Colonel Reckitt, lying in his sleeping bag, said that at the moment the Guards should have been at the Queen's Birthday Parade in Horseguards. 'We are celebrating the Queen's Birthday by lying here in the cold. We tuned into the World Service and heard them marching down the Mall.'

I joined Margaret Thatcher on the stand with my young son, William, to watch the parade, and afterwards we adjourned to No. 10 for lunch. Margaret had asked Rex Hunt and his wife, but really made it an occasion to entertain the children of her staff in the large dining room upstairs. I remember David Wolfson and his wife and their children, together with several other youngsters. I asked Margaret who had prepared the lunch. 'Oh, I did,' she said, 'Mary and I stayed up late last night to put a meal together.' I recall it so well because here was the Prime Minister in the middle of a war, provided with no staff whatsoever, and yet she had found time personally to prepare a meal late at night for the children. Her image as a ruthless, uncaring harridan was misplaced; no-one took more care of her staff and she was always scrupulous in showing her concern for the health and well-being of her friends. It was strange how she could be so cruel and unreasonable to her ministers, but so kind and thoughtful to her immediate circle. Margaret had a warm and generous heart – and yet she presided over an unhappy Cabinet, continuously undermined by gossip and malicious unattributable briefing.

By the end of lunch, Margaret and I had heard that after fierce battles Two

Sisters, Mount Longdon and Mount Harriet had been secured. Again, I leave it to John Witherow, who filed this pooled despatch (appearing in the press on 15 June), to describe these battles:

> Red tracer bullets lit the night sky and hillsides were engulfed in explosions and sheets of flame as British forces on the Falkland Islands launched their offensive on Port Stanley early on Saturday morning.
>
> The attack was made on three fronts at key strategic points, defending access to the capital, and by daylight all the positions had been secured, pushing British troops to within five miles of Port Stanley. The first raid was made by 3 Paratroop battalion on Mount Longdon to the north.
>
> They approached Argentine positions stealthily soon after midnight GMT, observing radio silence. As soon as the first clash took place field artillery opened fire, blasting enemy trenches and dugouts.
>
> To the south Royal Marines of 42 Commando seized Mount Harriet after a five-hour battle and then 45 Commando attacked and captured the mist-enshrouded Two Sisters.

It had been the intention to push straight on that night to strike at the well-defended positions on Mount Tumbledown and Mount William; but the troops were tired and more time was needed to bring up ammunition, so it was decided to wait.

In London we knew that everything now rested with our soldiers and sailors. So we all kept strictly to our self-imposed rule not to pester Northwood for news about operations in progress.

On my trip to the Falklands, just after the war, I tramped around the battlefield and spent some time on Tumbledown, which had been taken at night by the Scots Guards in one of the fiercest battles; they were one of the battalions previously on public duties in London. Tumbledown was defended by some of the best Argentine regular troops and on the ground it looked well-nigh impregnable. Nevertheless, with great bravery and skill, the guards managed to get in amongst the trenches at night and fought a hand-to-hand battle with the defending troops. I met some of the wounded guardsmen in Woolwich Military Hospital on my return.

Next door to Mount Tumbledown was Mount William, which saw the final episode of the war just before white flags began to fly over Port Stanley on 14 June. The 7th Gurkhas, to their immense frustration, had been held back by

General Moore until this final moment. When the Argentine troops saw the Gurkhas approaching, kukris drawn, they abandoned their positions and fled down the hill into the town.

The war was over.

~

My feelings at this moment of victory were surprising. I just felt an intense sense of relief that it was over. Although I recognised the tremendous achievement of our forces and their leaders – and the courage and determination shown by Margaret Thatcher – personally I felt no sense of triumph. I wanted to sneak away and hide. I knew what the Duke of Wellington had meant when he said that 'nothing except a battle lost can be half so melancholy as a battle won'. Just over a thousand had died on both sides and it all seemed so unnecessary.

Casting around to find something that I might have written at the time which could express my private thoughts, I have come across the copy of a private, handwritten letter that I wrote to Peter Carrington on 28 May, in the middle of the crisis:

> I feel very bad about my failure to drop you a line about the tragedy of your resignation. Over the past few (hectic) weeks I have several times sat down to do so, but a series of interruptions has driven it out of my mind …
>
> I shall always remember that Thursday evening when you returned exhausted from Israel but where you showed immense determination to get the Fleet to sea.
>
> I suppose you must long to be part of it all still – I wish that I could exchange my place for yours. The crisis brings me no pleasure at all. I am hating every minute of it! But we are all trapped by events as is so often the case in politics …

Yes, I felt a sense of sadness about the waste of it all. Of course I am proud that I played a small part in our victory, but I would rather have been elsewhere. Fame is the spur but fame is an empty chalice. Each generation has to discover that for itself: I had drained the chalice dry.

Nonetheless, it was nice to receive the normal ration of congratulatory letters. I only mention one, not because he was the Chief of the General Staff but because he was the colonel of my old regiment – much more important to me than a letter from a general. Part of it read:

My dear Secretary of State,

... If I may say so (and it doesn't sound patronising) I think you have done splendidly in every possible way. You have always ensured that political decisions were ready to match the military needs; you have performed brilliantly on television (*Panorama* last night was another triumph) and never shirked being on the front line when bad news was around; and you have skilfully and admirably prepared Parliamentary and public opinion for all the steps and shocks which were needed to complete this difficult and dangerous operation; and you stood up to the PM when necessary which is never easy!

Yours ever, Dwin

Victory on the battlefield had been won, but there were a hundred problems still to solve: how to handle the 11,000 Argentinian prisoners; how to accommodate large numbers of our soldiers and airmen in the coming Falklands winter and how to get the majority of them home; how to defend the Falkland Islands in the future when we still faced a major threat to NATO; how to go through a tedious argument with the Treasury about replacing all the ships and equipment that we had lost.

And then there were the victory parades and dinners, the self-congratulatory speeches about our will to resist aggression, and the strengthening of the deterrent posture of the alliance. All true. Great Britain emerged from the Falklands a more self-confident nation. It had taken a quarter of a century to recover our pride after the shambles of Suez. But I did not enjoy the celebrations.

I least of all enjoyed the stupidity of the bishops of the Church of England when arranging the thanksgiving service at St Paul's at the end of July. No-one was more in favour of reconciliation with Argentina than I; we could all say prayers privately, if we wished, for the dead and maimed of both sides; but this was a service for the veterans of the war and, in particular, for the families of the British dead. It almost seemed as if our disagreements on the form of worship were more about the Church of England's own war against Margaret Thatcher and her policies than about comforting the families of our dead. Archbishop Runcie had been a brave soldier, but he got drawn into a purposeless argument about the appropriateness of the hymns and prayers. Enough said – the modern Anglican Church is beyond my comprehension. It should be laid to rest alongside the BBC.

As soon as I could decently do so, I went back to Margaret Thatcher in late

August and reminded her of my intention to retire from politics. She said she was very surprised, after the Falklands victory, that I did not want to change my mind. My immediate colleagues in the Ministry of Defence were equally surprised when I told them that I had informed her as far back as the previous December of my intention to retire from politics. I was keen to step down straight away, because I thought that my successor should have a reasonable period to acclimatise himself before the general election – and I knew that as the deployment of US Cruise missiles in Europe was imminent, nuclear policy would be a major source of controversy during the campaign.

My preference was for joint control of these weapons. 'John Nott before he left his post as Defence Secretary had been attracted by the dual-key option,' Margaret Thatcher correctly notes in her memoirs. 'But neither Michael Heseltine, his successor, nor I shared his view.' It was another reason to make the change in time. Our policy had to be decided. However, Margaret insisted that I stay on to conduct a review of the lessons arising from the Falklands campaign, which we published (as Cmnd. 8758) a few weeks before I eventually stepped down from the MoD four months later at the end of December.

Perhaps foolishly, I insisted that we should clear the air straight away and get an announcement made of my intentions – not least because I wanted my Conservative Association in St Ives to have time to select my successor.

So on 1 September, a few weeks before the Conservative Party conference in October and the interview with Robin Day, I made the following statement:

> When I entered the House of Commons in 1966, I did so with the intention of spending around fifteen years in Parliament. Towards the end of last year, I told the Prime Minister that I wished to leave politics at the next General election and return to business.

The Prime Minister's announcement said:

> I told him of my deep regret at his decision, which will be a great loss to Parliament, to his constituents and to me personally ... I understand and respect the reasons which have prompted him to make public his decision now. He will continue as Secretary of State for Defence as a most valuable and trusted member of the Cabinet.

Unlike her ritual expression of regret each time she sacked a colleague, I like to believe in the generosity of her remarks, which were largely undeserved.

It was a mistake. 'The King is dead, long live the King.' I should have insisted on going immediately. The press took great joy, egged on by the Royal Navy, in describing me as a 'lame duck' minister, and there were even suggestions that I wanted to hang on for myself. I had, of course, no authority any more, but I did as I was asked.

On 1 January 1983, when I stepped down and handed over to Michael Heseltine, Margaret Thatcher allowed me to remain in Admiralty House until the general election in June. It was there that I decided to follow up my new career, whilst I was at fifty young enough to take a full-time job. I therefore contacted Ian Fraser once again, with a view to going to Lazard whilst I looked around for a job in industry. But it was not to be – I stayed on in Lazard and became its chairman.

But I also sat down and dictated my recollections of the Falklands, which have formed the basis of these chapters. When I left parliament – and I had been a rather keen Commons man – I had no feelings of nostalgia. I never look backwards; it is always on to the next challenge. I missed not having somewhere to go for a drink before dinner; getting home at six o'clock each evening was quite unsettling; this had never happened in my life before. But the pleasure, the sheer bliss of not having that endless round of constituency weekend engagements was heaven.

In the interregnum between leaving Defence and retiring at the general election in June, I did, however, write to Margaret Thatcher. The letter was dated 23 January 1983:

My dear Margaret,

I shall not be speaking in the Franks Debate but I wanted to send you this personal letter of support and encouragement.

The Report itself puts our case better than we could ever have dared to hope and I can add nothing to it. Leaving aside the predictable disappointment of the Opposition and the media, the Country generally is sick, I believe, of the whole affair. It is neither in a mood for recrimination or self-justification. We won – and that is good enough for the overwhelming proportion of the British people.

In my letter of resignation I said a number of things publicly about your Leadership, but public letters cannot say what I really feel about our friendship over fifteen years in Government and Opposition.

Our friendship has been sustained for me through years of happy co-operation and occasional fierce disagreement (tinged with moments of positive dislike on both sides, I suspect) by your wonderful personality.

It is inexcusable to say so nowadays, but I actually admire you as a Woman! I think your instinctive approach to so many issues, so very unmasculine, is the secret of your success in the male-dominated world of politics.

Today there is no way that a consensus approach to the Nation's problems can overcome them. Until you gained the Leadership we were a Whips' Party. I am glad that we are now a gut-instinct Party.

Well, I am glad to be gone and, truthfully, the Government is better off without me. I lost my spark after the Defence Review, during those awful PESC [public expenditure] negotiations in 1981. Perhaps unreasonably, I came to harbour a resentment that the Lords of the Treasury could not see the immensity and long-term nature of the problems I was trying to tackle in the MoD and, in Geoffrey's case, the overriding importance and the nature of the Defence dilemma. I always wanted to go at the end of this Parliament, but, feeling as I did, it was important to go quickly because it began to show. I am so glad to be out of it all and enthusiastic about the next challenge.

Given the immensity of your task and the support that you need to sustain your courage and conviction, it would be invidious of me to offer any caution, but I cannot restrain myself from one remark which you will not like. The Government will succeed or fail in the next six to seven years because the British people approve of it collectively. The personal loyalty and dedication of your Political Press Advisers in No. 10 I do not question, but the Lobby and the Corridors of Parliament are a dangerous place. I think it is utterly divisive and destructive to good Government if the Parliamentary Lobby-system is used to sustain the PM, or No. 10's view of life, against the Cabinet generally, or individual colleagues. You would never countenance such a thing I know, but it should not happen.

I do not mean to end on a sour, patronising or critical note because that, I hope, is not the tenor of my final letter. I wish you God speed. You are doing a marvellous job in an almost impossible environment. Fortunately we are blessed by an outstanding Civil Service, for whom I have nothing but praise and admiration, albeit they need pushing and shoving now and again.

I wish you and Denis every personal happiness and success as the task continues.

Love,

John

She did not reply.

I have often wondered since whether it could have ever happened thus if the Prime Minister had been a man. In her relationships with a male-dominated Cabinet – and one that had traditional attitudes to the place of women in society – she often behaved in ways that would have been unacceptable for any man. Above all, she had a woman's courage. A different kind of courage from a man's.

Whilst I was researching for my next chapter on Lazard, I came across a remark of André Meyer, the French senior partner of Lazard Frères, New York, and probably the most famous financier of his generation. He was asked why he spent so much time with famous women – Katharine Graham, Jackie Kennedy, Jane Englehard. He replied, 'I have to see men for business reasons. But I don't like men. They have no courage. All my friends are now women. They have more courage.'

It was true of Margaret Thatcher. She had more courage and more obstinacy than a man. She really did believe that men were 'wet', and particularly the species called 'gentlemen'. Of all the men that I knew in my time in politics, I cannot think of any who would not have sought an honourable settlement. I am sure that Margaret never meant to do so, but she went along with the diplomatic game – because to 'win' she had to do so. In my letter I said that her approach was instinctive, 'so very unmasculine'. She was confronted with a crisis for her government and she shut her mind to the risks of conducting such an adventure 8,000 miles away. Of course, it is always easier to be in charge; to be leader if you have it in you, rather than to be the staff officers who make it happen. But, in the last resort, it was a woman's war – and the woman in her won.

Chapter Eleven

LAZARD: THE CITY REVOLUTION COMPLETED

You want loyalty – hire a cocker spaniel.

(trader at Salomons)

When I first joined the City in 1959, Lazard, Morgan Grenfell, Hambros and Schroders were at the top of the pile – and Warburg was still climbing the greasy pole. The battle for British Aluminium in 1958–59 changed everything in the City – the arrivistes Warburg quite quickly overtook the establishment firms by being more determined, clever and ruthless than their sleepier British counterparts. By the 1970s Lazard Brothers had lost its prime position as Warburg grew into the leading investment bank in the City of London.

The American branch of Lazard, Lazard Frères in New York, had been dominated by a remarkable man called André Meyer, whose views on women I have mentioned; he had risen from a modest background, beginning as a button boy on the Paris Bourse. He became the best-known financier in Wall Street, and he created a powerhouse which was the undoubted US leader in the business of mergers and acquisitions – or financial engineering as we called it.

'The most creative financial genius of our time in the investment banking world,' was how David Rockefeller, chairman of Chase, described Meyer. Giovanni Agnelli of Fiat came to rely on him totally and said: 'André was always the main architect, the last judge, and the last word.' World Bank President Robert McNamara described Meyer as 'a giant, absolutely unique'.

I start my Lazard story with André Meyer, not because I met him several times when I was Siegmund Warburg's personal assistant, and later as the chairman of one part (Lazard Brothers, London) of the Lazard family empire which he ignored; but because he exemplified so much that is distasteful in the world of finance. The naked acquisitiveness and greed of Wall Street is poisonous to

European sensitivities – as indeed it is to so much of American industry. Meyer's behaviour is so true of the famous characters of Wall Street, described in brilliant books like *Liar's Poker, Financier* and *Barbarians at the Gate*. Bruce Wasserstein, the new chief executive of Lazard, is in the Meyer mould; a consummate deal-maker, restless, rumpled, greedy – but a star all the same.

As a junior executive in Warburg I was aware of Lazard even before my visit to New York with Siegmund Warburg. Warburg used to rile about Lord Kindersley, the chairman of Lazard, whom he considered to be a very stupid man. There were five peers on the board of Lazard in the 1950s and they had their tentacles into all the leading British industrial firms. Warburg also sensed, I suspect, that Kindersley was anti-Semitic, almost certainly the case. Sitting in a room between Siegmund Warburg and Henry Grunfeld, I was used to Warburg crashing across my room and into the open door of Grunfeld, where he would complain endlessly about the 'useless' Kindersley. He had more time for Lord Hampden of Lazard, but Kindersley represented everything that he despised in the English character and in the culture of the City.

André Meyer had much the same attitude to the English as Warburg developed in his later years, and he held Kindersley and Lazard Brothers in London in equally low esteem. This is not hearsay on my part, because on my trip with Warburg to Wall Street in 1964 I was present at private meetings, in the Carlyle Hotel, between Warburg and Meyer. Before discussing any business, the conversation always went like this:

Warburg: André, you are the most brilliant man in Wall Street.

Meyer: Siegmund, you are without question the most brilliant man in London.

They used to sit around for an endless period of time congratulating each other on their brilliance, indulging in the most absurd mutual flattery.

Although Lazard was the creation of three French brothers (Alexandre, Simon and Lazare, from Lorraine), it was in fact founded in New Orleans. It started trading, as Cary Reich in *Financier* relates, as a dry-goods business in 1848. Within a year the firm was wiped out by a fire which destroyed a large part of New Orleans and the brothers moved to San Francisco. Gold had just been discovered nearby and a mass of prospectors descended on the Lazard business, needing everything from 'gold pans to overalls'. They sent for a

French cousin called Alexandre Weill to become their bookkeeper. It did not take very long before the three entrepreneurs started dealing in gold itself and in foreign exchange. By 1852 they had opened a Paris operation called Lazard Frères et Cie.

The son of Alexandre Weill, David David-Weill ran the Paris firm along with André Lazard, the last of the Lazards. It was David David-Weill who in 1926 recruited the twenty-seven-year-old trader, André Meyer, to the Paris firm with the promise of a partnership in a year if things went well. They did.

By the 1930s André Meyer and Pierre David-Weill, David's son, dominated the Paris firm. When the Germans marched into Poland in September 1939, André Meyer packed his bags. As a leading Jewish banker working for a well-known Jewish bank, he had been to the fore in an organisation started by his friend Baron Robert de Rothschild that sought to help Jewish refugees from Nazi Germany. In 1941 Lazard Frères was placed under 'Aryan' direction by the Vichy government. As with Charles de Gaulle, he was stripped of his citizenship and all his property in France was confiscated. The man who signed the decree was an 'old friend'. It reminded him of the limits of trust and friendship. He left for New York. Similar experiences had already led to the departure from Germany and Austria of Warburg, Grunfeld, Korner and Thalmann, the four Jewish refugees in Warburg. These experiences marked them all and tailored their attitude to risk and the fragility of relationships.

I dwell on the background of Lazard because it helps to understand what I inherited when, quite by an accident of timing, I became the top man in London. Michel David-Weill, who was the son of Pierre and had done his training in New York under André Meyer, had by this time become the senior partner and controlling shareholder of Paris and New York. André Meyer had died and Michel David-Weill's approach to life and banking was a strange mixture of his aristocratic forebears and his rather ruthless mentor, André Meyer. In personal terms, his most important inheritance was the presence of Felix Rohatyn in New York, who had been the right-hand man of Meyer, and two Frenchmen, Jean Guyot and Antoine Bernheim in Paris.

Michel inherited great wealth from his father – a major art collection, a 'private palace' in Paris on the Left Bank, a French country house, a house on Cap d'Antibes, a country house on Long Island and a large apartment overlooking Central Park. There were other properties, all fully staffed, but I never counted them. Jean-Claude Haas, a partner in Lazard Frères, Paris and the administrator of

Pierre David-Weill's estate, said (according to Cary Reich) that he counted eighty-four full-time gardeners without any of the indoor staff. Michel had also inherited his father's charm and courtesy, modesty and amiability.

Of the two men, Siegmund Warburg and Michel David-Weill, the latter virtually unknown in England, I much preferred Michel. Siegmund had in his behaviour many of André Meyer's characteristics – 'manifestations of affection and emotional outbursts, unbridled flattery to achieve his ends, tantrums, self-pity', as well as 'the shouting and the slamming' of the autocratic founder. But both men were interesting, immensely able and skilful. I am privileged to have met one of them, André Meyer, and worked with the other, Siegmund Warburg.

Because Lazard Brothers in London had passed out of the control of the David-Weill family after the First World War, into the hands of Pearsons, relationships between London and the other two houses were traditionally strained – and made worse by André Meyer. He had no control over London, it frustrated him. It bore the Lazard name and yet Kindersley and co. had the cheek to adopt a somewhat haughty, Anglo-Saxon disdain towards the wheeler-dealers in New York.

Although Meyer was on the board of Lazard Brothers in London, he never attended any of its meetings. He forbade any contact between the people at Lazard Frères and the London firm. It is possible that Lord Poole – a former chairman of the Conservative Party who had succeeded Kindersley as chairman of Lazard in 1965 – might have brought the three houses slightly closer together over time simply by deferring to Meyer, but it was not to be. Poor Oliver Poole was devastated by a stroke in 1974 which left him incapacitated. Lord Cowdray, chairman of Pearsons and the controlling shareholder of London, put the charming Daniel Meinertzhagen in charge of London. Consequently, Lazard Brothers went to sleep and remained in a somewhat dormant state, albeit with one of the best client lists in London, until Ian Fraser took over in 1980. Ian has recalled how 'two or three times' he tried to explain the London business to Meyer – 'but he just got bored'.

I had a problem when I became chairman of Lazard Brothers. I had great support from Michel David-Weill, but there was always a sense in London that we were the poor relation of the three Lazard houses: not because we were unsuccessful, but because Michel had absorbed something of André Meyer's negative and pessimistic attitude to the City of London and to the English. I think the problem was that when he came he found it an alien and strange environment. In New York, Michel was a 'Great Man' because he was very rich; and in Paris he was feted everywhere as a cultural and commercial hero. But in London he was unknown, and London had no heroes, no stars – it was not the way we did things. Michel felt lost.

I had many conversations with Michel. 'What you need in London is some "stars"' – acknowledged 'rainmakers' that attract business and make things happen – he used to say. I said: 'There are no stars in London – it is the reputation of the firm that matters.' He demurred.

About a year after my arrival at Lazard in 1983, Rupert Murdoch started an assault on Pearsons, with the objective of gaining control of the *Financial Times*, the most prominent of its subsidiary companies. Michel David-Weill saw his chance, and after long negotiations with Lord Blakenham (a nephew of Lord Cowdray, a son of Macmillan's Conservative Party chairman, and the chairman of Pearsons) a deal was done. Michel offered to buy 10 per cent of Pearsons' equity, which together with the Pearson family holdings made the company virtually impregnable, in exchange for a controlling interest in Lazard Brothers. Pearsons also received a larger stake in the New York and Paris houses.

By this time, although I had no inkling that I was Ian Fraser's choice to succeed him as chairman, I was on the Managing Directors' Committee of Lazard, effectively the bank's board. I was already earning four times the income of a Cabinet minister. This committee numbered about eight of the top executive directors of Lazard.

Michael Blakenham called the Managing Directors' Committee together one day at Pearsons to explain the agreement that he, Michel David-Weill and Ian Fraser had constructed. All my colleagues nodded in agreement; but being an outspoken politician, with no particular ambition to succeed Fraser, I expressed my doubts about the proposal, although it was much too late to influence the outcome. I said I was unhappy that Lazard Brothers could pass into the control of 'an absentee landlord'. It was a perfectly appropriate comment, because for all Michel's ability and judgement, all of which I valued greatly, that is exactly what he was. A frown appeared across the face of the relatively inexpressive Michael Blakenham, while Jean-Claude, the delightful French henchman of the absentee landlord, went rather pale. Rightly, the deal went through without more ado.

I was completely mistaken in my doubts. I had not been in Lazard long enough to understand why it had remained rather dormant under the chairmanship of Daniel Meinertzhagen; although it retained a remarkable client list, the best in the City, its position had slipped in favour of competitors like Warburg, Morgan Grenfell, Schroders and Kleinworts – now, ironically, all owned by foreign interests. It was partly the attitude of the older generation in the bank. As Ian Fraser had found (after leaving the Takeover Panel in 1972 to go to Lazard), the principal block to giving a sharper edge to the firm were the so-called 'Four Colonels', namely Mark Norman, Kit Dawnay and Denny Marris as well as Meinertzhagen himself. Oliver Poole had billed them in advance as 'unhungry', and it did not take long for Fraser to agree:

> Charming though the Four Colonels were, they were all useless for our purposes. Norman's chairmanships included Gallahers and Dawnay's Wiggins Teape. On the rare occasions when they were in their offices at 11 Old Broad Street, they seemed to spend their time dictating letters to their (Lazard) secretaries about their outside companies or the management of their country estates. Meinertzhagen was memorably lazy and it was quite usual to find him sitting at his desk after lunch, asleep with a copy of *The Times* over his face. Marris went on endless travels to Persia, bought beautiful carpets and talked, talked, talked …

Fraser also quotes Meinertzhagen's attitude to getting new corporate clients: 'They know where we are and if they want our services, they will come to our door.'

There was, however, another, more fundamental reason for Lazard Brothers' sluggishness: the inhibiting and conservative ownership of Pearsons. The Pearson family had made a great fortune, and their motivation was the safeguarding of that fortune – not its multiplication by taking risks in the field of financial services. I still see Michael Blakenham, and I like him very much; but his mandate, although not openly expressed as such, was to protect the Pearson inheritance, not to allow Lazard or other subsidiaries to hazard it. Michael Blakenham came every Friday to our weekly meeting and his contributions were always useful. Yet, in the last resort, Pearsons was a drag on Lazard. Ian Fraser saw, as I did not, that there was a greater future for Lazard Brothers if it broke its connection with Pearsons and threw in its lot with the other two Lazard houses and with a man, Michel, who had investment banking in his blood.

When I became chairman in 1985 on Ian Fraser's retirement, I sat down with my immediate corporate finance colleagues, David Verey, Marcus Agius and Michael Baughan, to draw up a list of the best and most successful corporate financiers in the City – the 'stars' of the business, if you like. We had four individuals on the list – John Nelson of Kleinworts, Nicholas Jones of Schroders, Roger Seelig of Morgan Grenfell and Michael Pescod of Slaughter and May. Without, I fear, any hesitation about stealing good men from other competitors, I arranged for each of them to be approached by their Lazard contemporaries with a request that they came along informally and talked to me. We recruited Nelson and Jones, nearly Seelig (before the Guinness dramas), and the only refusal was Pescod of Slaughters, who wanted to remain with the law. We created a team of outstanding corporate financiers that included a number of exceptional younger insiders, John Dear among them. I could never have achieved this without a new and very generous remuneration structure provided by Ian Fraser and Michel David-Weill. It has, moreover, provided me with a comfortable old age.

There was one other, even more fundamental decision taken shortly before I became chairman. In the context of the impending 'big bang', which saw the London securities industry for the first time being opened up to outside ownership, Lazard – like all the other banks, merchant and clearing – had to take a view whether it wished to acquire a stockbroking and/or jobbing firm. Ian Fraser arranged for the forty or so London directors (including myself) to gather at Leeds Castle in Kent for two and a half days of brainstorming.

As a result a unanimous decision was taken not to enter the securities industry but the key voice belonged to Ian. Both in his time and my time, the chairman and chief executive of Lazard was an autocrat, albeit an autocrat willing to have everything discussed. I'm sure that Ian, in taking this strong line, was much influenced, as I was, by his years at Warburg back in the 1950s and 1960s. Siegmund Warburg, as I have already explained, had the deepest contempt for stockbrokers and indeed for stock markets generally; he relentlessly inculcated the principles of *haute banque,* which did not embrace getting into brokerage and market making, as opposed to sticking to corporate finance, banking, and other similar activities; and, moreover, he had such a gloomy streak to his character – always believing that another slump was just around the corner – that the thought of plunging into such a cyclical activity in markets would have appalled him.

Even so, the matter was constantly to the fore in the mid-1980s, because we were acting for a number of financial institutions who were contemplating moving down the 'big bang' route. Several of the major broking and jobbing firms approached us to see if we were prepared to be a candidate for them to join us – not surprisingly, given that in those days we were seen in the City as a much friendlier, more reasonable place to team up with than, say, Warburg. Indeed, at that time Lazard might have been almost the top choice of Rowe & Pitman, Akroyd & Smithers and Wedd Durlacher, because we had a marvellous client base and, being a bit sleepy, would 'culturally' have joined very easily with those firms.

But as I say, our fundamental attitude did not shift, and by the time of the 'big bang' itself on Monday, 27 October 1986 we were the only merchant bank that had decided to stay entirely aloof from the securities business. 'Profit rather than size is still the target' was the headline for the *FT*'s interview with me published that day. This was a historic moment, as our rivals entered uncharted waters, and I quote from part of Barry Riley's article:

> For the past year or so, since becoming Lazard's chairman, John Nott has continued to steer the merchant bank along the independent path mapped out by his predecessor.
>
> In particular, Lazard has refused to engage in the kind of expensive purchases of Stock Exchange firms that have been implemented by rival merchant banks such as Warburgs, Kleinwort Benson or Hill Samuel.
>
> One reason is that Lazard wishes to remain relatively small and flexible. 'We don't really want to grow to more than 500 people or so in number,' Sir John explains. 'We felt that, in our traditional corporate finance advisory business, we could retain the advantages of a private banking house, and the personal relationships which are so vital for that, more easily if our numbers and overheads were kept restricted.'
>
> Lazard also decided that buying a British stockbroking firm would have been irrelevant to the need for distribution of securities in the international markets, 'which are going to be more important as the years go by than the domestic market'.
>
> Sir John adds: 'Thirdly, we felt that the prices being paid for the good will of these firms were excessive, not least the payment for good will with feet. Since these very large sums have been paid for these firms, many of the best people have left and moved on.'

I was careful not to claim that the strategy of other merchant banks, in seeking to combine corporate finance and distribution, was misguided – but little that has happened in the last fifteen years has made me feel that we got the decision wrong as far as Lazard itself was concerned.

~

The City of London to which I returned in the 1980s was a very different place from the one I had left in 1966. It had, for one thing, become much more meritocratic, more like Warburg in the early days, with the new blood being symbolised by the traders in their colourful jackets – the proverbial barrow boys from Essex. The financial rewards in the City suddenly shot up – to previously unheard-of levels – and for the first time it became a place where high-fliers from the top universities wanted to enter, in preference to, say, the Foreign Office.

In my time it was not unusual for us to have 800 applications from the top universities, and we could only take two or three a year. This led to a clash between my junior directors and myself. Understandably, they had to narrow down the applicants mainly on the basis of their academic achievement – whilst I wanted youngsters with commercial acumen, energy and character, barrow boys, if you like. These qualities are not inseparable from a first at Oxford, but they are rarely found together.

The principal attraction of the merchant banks for the intelligent young in the 1980s lay in what they saw as the drama, excitement and romance of the City. It had captured me at Cambridge when I read of the shenanigans surrounding the battle for the control of British Aluminium. The fact that bright young men could secure advancement and a high income far faster than in British industry was, I think, a lesser factor. I did not keep a diary of all our high-profile battles, so it is difficult, in retrospect, to recreate the atmosphere of those events – the late nights, the panning of big reputations, careers ruined and made. The leading corporate financiers were indeed seen as the SAS of the City.

The key factor was that the stakes were very high, not just for the predator and the victim but also for the merchant bank advisers, whose reputation and fees were closely related to success. There was always a temptation to cut corners and to be seen to be tougher than your competitors. Industrialists looking for advice, when their own reputation and success were at issue, naturally turned to the merchant bank with the most ruthless and clever reputation; they were much less concerned at the outrageous fees that often ran into millions of pounds. Morgan Grenfell played the game with skill under Magan and Seelig, but when Morgans overplayed its hand it led to the near-collapse of the bank in the Guinness scandal.

To the outsider in the 1980s, the City was depicted in the press as a cockpit of scandal and greed, albeit it was a child at the game beside the goings-on in Wall Street. Power struggles for position, huge salaries and personal indulgence, lunches at the Savoy Grill, a week at Ascot, shooting parties, chauffeurs, butlers and the rest, much of it at the expense of shareholders, were the stories of the time. It had little truth, and with 'big bang' happening they were hectic times and it became a struggle for the survival of the fittest – a new City phenomenon.

In spite of Westminster's envy of the City, it was the only truly dynamic part of the economy. And the City establishment, which was changing into a meritocracy, had contempt for the politicians, while they in turn regarded the City as an unregulated jungle unanswerable to them and independent of them. This led to the Financial Services Act, a damaging and ill thought-out measure to protect investors, strangling every financial firm with needless bureaucracy when the same objective could have been achieved by a compulsory insurance levy. It would never have got through me at Trade.

I remember reading in the press that when Nigel Lawson, the Chancellor, tried to persuade a reluctant Margaret Thatcher to put a 'cap' on the amount of a salary that could be transferred untaxed into a pension scheme, he cited John Nott's income as a case in point. According to press reports, Margaret then agreed to the reform with alacrity! This is a good example, if it's true, of the envy of the politicians for the money-makers in the City.

As the Americans expanded their presence in the mid-1980s in order to try to take advantage of the coming 'big bang', the City as a way of life began to change in spite of what Westminster thought about it. The much longer working hours, the advent of the American breakfast, the shorter lunches – these things changed the very rhythm of the City's time-honoured way of life. Still more fundamentally, the City traditions of loyalty, of working for one or at the most two firms through a lifetime, of an implicit bond between employer and employee that did not reduce everything to cash were comprehensively shot to pieces by the American influence. The head gilts trader quoted in *Liar's Poker* put it perfectly: 'You want loyalty – hire a cocker spaniel.' I used to compare the traders that I interviewed with the masons who built the cathedrals of Europe; their loyalty was to their trade and to their immediate fellows, not to the benefactors who employed them.

Inevitably I wondered what Siegmund Warburg (who had died in 1982) would have made of this new, harsher world. He would surely have welcomed the ambition, the intensity, the ruthless breaking-down of complacent, entrenched City assumptions, practices and coteries. It was no surprise that in his last few years he became a great admirer of Margaret Thatcher, who was trying to do much the same in the country at large. The Americanisation of the City has proceeded apace since I left in 1990, and we seem to be breeding a race of highly intelligent, highly focused young bankers and brokers who work phenomenally long hours and do their jobs very proficiently, but hardly have the time or the energy to see what is going on outside their frenetic world. Nor do they have time to spend with their families. The pursuit of their inflated expectations has turned them into slaves, and their wealth is not to be envied. A friend told me recently that Morgan Stanley in New York conducted an internal study and found that 80 per cent of their young men wound up in the divorce courts. It is hard to know who to pity, them or their wives. I am so glad that my two sons never entered today's City.

When I went to Lazard in 1983 it was far from my ambition to succeed Ian Fraser as chairman and chief executive – indeed, as I have mentioned already, I was much more interested in using Lazard as a springboard for an outside industrial post. Others may have perceived the matter differently, but that is the case. Ian was due to retire in August 1985, and naturally during 1984 the question of a successor became actively mooted. The strong preference at the London house was for someone British to succeed him; but for various reasons, neither of the two obvious internal possibilities, both of whom had spent their entire lives in the City, were deemed suitable. Ian gives the impression in his memoirs that that had been in his mind right from the time he recruited me from politics – and before long he was recommending me to Michel David-Weill as the popular internal choice. Michel, however, was reluctant – and understandably so, in that I had recently opposed him taking control of Lazard London and he did not think I would bring London closer to the Lazard family.

Accordingly, he got a head-hunter to line up a series of all the obvious candidates from other merchant banks. Unfortunately for him, none made a favourable impression – probably a reflection less on them than on the way in which the whole culture of London was alien to Michel. Still, he was wise enough to recognise that in those days a British bank, heavily dependent on British clients, needed a British chairman; and eventually, after the whole process had dragged on and on, he bowed to pressure (mainly from Ian Fraser, but also Michael Blakenham) that he had no choice but to turn to this rather English former politician.

Although regretting the fact that I did not take up a position in industry, I look back on my seven years at Lazard with satisfaction. The firm had something of a regimental feeling, which I enjoyed, while at the same time trying to stimulate a sharper, more competitive atmosphere in the context of a rapidly changing business environment. We ran a truly independent operation, co-operating with our American and French cousins but never subservient to them. Overall, it was an extremely pleasant team at Lazard (full of nice intelligent people, but entirely lacking the bitchiness which I remembered from my days in Warburg) and the prevailing mood was positive, particularly so in the final two or three years as we climbed to the top of the league tables.

Once it became clear that I was taking over from Ian Fraser, I set about recruiting a top corporate finance team, as I have mentioned. But I was well aware that it always takes time for business to come. The problem therefore was how to get the profits up while we waited. Accordingly, having consulted Michel, I decided that the only thing was to broaden out the base of the bank. However, in one respect I narrowed it by closing down our international division. This employed some forty or so talented people, led by an excellent man called David Gemmill. There were two reasons: first, I wanted to keep the bank small and, second, whilst they worked extremely hard, the profits never exceeded the costs. It was sad when the top team left to join Standard Chartered.

Two aspects of this broadening of the base proved successful. First, we recruited a small team from Cazenove's and became the only bank operating as a broker in the stock-lending business. This was against the background of a hugely increased number of market-makers in the gilt-edged, bond and equity markets, which inevitably led to a large multiplication in the volume of trading business as a whole. Secondly, I recruited, with Michel's help, a man who had started trading for Morgan Stanley in London in the 1970s – an interesting character called Gil Scharf. He and I got on very well and we developed a sort of wary respect for one another. He got together a team of three or four traders, including a couple from Morgan Guaranty, and we set them up in the floor below me at 21 Moorfields. Gil and his very clever team set to work trading in the debt market – in any part of it where they could make money. This included Japanese warrants, which at that time was one of the most profitable areas, and also the fixed-interest eurobond market. What they did was mainly arbitraging, not risking much capital, and each evening they closed their positions within their limits unless I had given specific permission to exceed them for a specified period. Gil's team made good money for Lazard (fluctuating, but generally in the order of £10m a year). Gil used to come into my room most days to tell me of the deals he was doing and, like all traders, he sometimes wanted to extend his position beyond the limits. Whilst I trusted Gil, I knew from an apprenticeship under Henry Grunfeld that you must never feel safe with traders. Very often he wanted to carry the position over for a few days. Often I refused, with the upshot being that Gil banged his fist on the table and declared, 'I'm going!' These were the sort of shouting matches that happened every hour of the day in New York among the traders, but I found them rather tiresome. I also set up an oil trading team, but it was unsuccessful and I closed it down a year later with accumulated losses of £1 million.

In addition, I chaired the Banking Committee, where I made myself very unpopular with the Banking Department by more or less refusing to let them lend money to anybody. This department was run by a good chap called John Harvey Bathurst, who'd been in Lazard for many years, and they wanted to lend overnight money to the Japanese banks, at that time very much the flavour of the month. Our exchange of views went something like this:

Why do you want to lend to the Japanese banks?

Well, because we can get an extra sixty-fourth overnight.

I don't think any of the Japanese banks is solvent. I don't want to lend to the Japanese banks. There's only one bank in the world I really want to put my overnight money in and that's Morgan Guaranty.

The general principle that we followed was to stay incredibly liquid. We placed 90 per cent of our money – around £3 billion – in very short-term deposits with major banks. I took the view that we needed the banking business really as a stand-by to finance the underwriting of securities. Michel didn't much like banking – Lazard had no banking business in Paris and New York – but agreed that we should keep going the banking business in London.

My natural obstinacy, and ability to say 'No', was to the fore during an amusing episode in October 1987. The occasion was the government's largest privatisation issue to date – £7,250m of British Petroleum shares. Rothschilds led the underwriting group, and Michael Richardson rang me to confirm that Lazard was willing to take its share of the prime underwriting. 'I've just been speaking to Margaret and Nigel,' he announced in his typically rather unctuous way. 'They really want every bank in the City to participate in the underwriting. I'm sure you'll join in.' But when I pressed him about what the underwriting commission would be, it turned out that the Treasury had got involved in the matter and decided, in their ignorance, that underwriting was just money for jam for the banks and that they would cut the commission right back. It transpired that we were being asked to underwrite £100m for the less than princely remuneration of £18,000. It simply did not seem worth the risk, and I told Richardson so. 'But everybody else in the City is taking the BP underwriting,' he protested. 'A bank like Lazard, which has often acted for BP, can't refuse to underwrite. It's not the practice of the City.' In a sense he was right – in the old City, if you started turning down underwriting, then it wasn't long before you weren't offered it. But this carving of the commission by the Treasury was so outrageous that I was determined to stick to my guns.

I told my colleagues of my intention, which led to a certain amount of humming and hawing, and I also rang Michel to tell him. He was concerned, because for him the prestige of Lazard and its name was important. Then came the inevitable phone call from the governor of the Bank of England, Robin Leigh-Pemberton:

> I understand that Lazards is not going to take the BP underwriting and I'm very surprised. How can a name like Lazards not take the underwriting?

> Governor, we've decided we won't take it because the fees aren't sufficient, and this is a risk business and unless we're paid for our risk we won't take it.

The following week the world's stock markets crashed (Black Monday followed by Black Tuesday); BP's share price went down in two days from 350p to 286p, way below the underwriting price of 330p; and even though a 'floor' arrangement was eventually made by the government, we would have lost up to £25m if we'd taken it. If your annual income is wholly dependent on a share of the profits, it concentrates the mind wonderfully. Lazard was just about the only bank in the City that did not take a big hit as a result of this episode, while Lazard Paris was taken to the cleaners – at which, I have to admit, I smiled inwardly. The leading Canadian investment bank went bust.

Corporate finance was at the very heart of what Lazard was about, and during these years we were closely involved as advisers in three much-publicised episodes: Westland, Guinness, and Plessey/GEC. There was also Jimmy Goldsmith's and Jacob Rothschild's bid for BAT, which we successfully defended, but there is not space to tell of it here.

Neither is this the place for a detailed account of the tortuous, feverish Westland affair, which reached a climax in January 1986 with the resignations of Michael Heseltine and Leon Brittan from Margaret Thatcher's Cabinet. Thatcher and Heseltine, among others, have written full accounts. It was interesting for me as I had recently rejoined civilian life after politics, and this was a clash between politics and the City, between political power and City independence. Essentially the affair turned on whether Westland, a troubled helicopter manufacturer, was going to be rescued by an American or a European takeover. In the first camp was Sikorsky, a subsidiary of the giant US-based United Technologies; in the other was a European consortium, including British Aerospace and GEC. Incredible as it now seems, this insignificant question came within an ace of splitting the Tory Party and causing Margaret Thatcher's downfall.

Throughout the Westland imbroglio I had three main concerns. The first, naturally, was that we would do our very best to enable our client – Westland – to get the solution it wanted. Quite quickly it became clear that this was the American solution – partly because the management at Westland tended to see the whole European option as being politically motivated by Heseltine and the MoD. My second concern was to keep the politicians as much as possible off the back of the company and, in particular, its chairman, John Cuckney. 'Take absolutely no notice of Whitelaw,' I remember saying to him at one point. 'He's always in a panic. Forget the House of Commons and politics.' My third, more personal concern was to keep as low a profile as possible. With my immediate successor at Defence, Michael Heseltine, pushing the European solution with all the considerable force and rhetorical ingenuity that he could muster, I had no wish for this to be depicted in the press as a Nott versus Heseltine punch-up, as it could so easily have been. Apart from anything else, it would have been very damaging to Lazard's reputation if that had happened. So on the whole, I tried to keep my distance, for example by only attending the Westland meetings that took place in Lazard but avoiding going to those in Cuckney's office at Thomas Cook (where he was also chairman) or indeed those in the company's London offices, where the press was always lurking.

All three aims were largely fulfilled, though any success we had in the second aim owed much to the tough-minded, broad-backed character of John Cuckney himself. Although he could not help being dragged into meeting after meeting at the DTI and the MoD, he had, after all, spent ten years in MI5, knew something about Whitehall, and took the whole situation extremely coolly. We were also fortunate that Cuckney had taken on Gordon Reece as his PR adviser. Gordon had helped Margaret Thatcher in her early days as leader, knew her well, and was generally a source of strength.

There were many twists and turns in the battle for control of Westland – a battle that at times had echoes of the long-ago Aluminium War – and Westland itself was fortunate that its brokers were Rowe & Pitman, whose senior partner, Peter Wilmot-Sitwell, did an outstanding job. To this day, Michael Heseltine, a good friend of mine, finds it a mystery as to how exactly Sikorsky won the bid. Despite Stock Exchange and other investigations into mystery millionaires buying sizeable blocks of Westland shares, mainly through Swiss banks, the ultimate identity of these buyers was never revealed. In his memoirs Michael, in a chapter headed "A Very Good Resignation", goes into the greatest detail of how he believes that Sikorsky won the day. He clearly feels that the City conducted a series of manoeuvres to deny the victory to the European consortium. My recollections do not coincide with Michael's but nothing is to be gained from re-engaging in a contest which almost everyone but Michael has forgotten long ago. Certainly it will go down in political history as a massive drama about a relatively trivial event. I have often wondered what attitude I might have taken to the whole affair had I still had his job. I find it inconceivable that I would have sought to intervene in a decision which was ultimately one for Westland. But then I am not an enthusiastic 'European' and that is possibly where we differ.

It was just as the Westland affair was reaching the boil that Guinness and Argyll began their controversial takeover battle for Distillers – a battle eventually resolved in favour of Guinness in April 1986. As it happens, Lazard might easily have acted for Argyll, the other suitor for Distillers. It had looked at one stage as if we were going to, thanks to discussions that Peter Grant (my deputy chairman) and Ian MacGregor (whom I'd made a non-executive director not long after his triumph over Scargill) had had with Argyll's Jimmy Gulliver. All three were Scotsmen and they had cooked it up together, I think in Glasgow. Gulliver, though, also had a close connection with Samuel Montagu and Charterhouse, and it became apparent that his plan was to use three advisers,

Private Eye, 9 April 1982

'We are doing everything to seek a negotiated solution' (Garland, *Daily Telegraph*, 26 June 1981)

'Nott's Navy Cuts' (Garland, Daily Telegraph, 27 April 1982)

'Ah, John! The good news is we've got a job for you in the city – the bad news is it's in Palermo!'

(Jak, *Evening Standard*, 7 October 1982)

playing them off one against another to get his way, although we were to take the lead. Anyway, three advisers never work – too many cooks etc. 'This is a frightful mess', David Verey had said to me, 'and the relationship between three advisers will become impossible.' Accordingly, I decided we would step down as advisers to Argyll – to the considerable disappointment of Peter Grant and Ian MacGregor. Soon afterwards the takeover battle between Guinness and Argyll for Distillers began, but we were not involved.

The story now moves on to July 1986. Guinness's chief executive, Ernest Saunders, had made a promise during the takeover battle that in due course Sir Thomas Risk of the Bank of Scotland, one of the great upright Scottish establishment figures, would become chairman of Guinness – in other words, as a sop to Scottish sensibilities as a result of the takeover of Distillers. Now, however, Saunders wanted to become chairman himself as well as chief executive, and this was leading to major rumblings in the City – including a semi-public dressing down for Saunders from the Governor, and Guinness's joint brokers Wood Mackenzie resigning. Morgan Grenfell, Guinness's merchant bank, by contrast announced that it was standing foursquare behind its man; but in fact, there were by this time distinct rumblings between Saunders and Morgan Grenfell. I'm not quite sure what the underlying problem was; perhaps he sensed that Morgans was beginning to get into trouble, on account of its generally over-aggressive tactics during takeover battles.

Anyway, for one reason and another, Saunders decided he needed additional financial advisers, and he turned to us. Initially we were appointed as adviser to the chairman of Guinness, Lord Iveagh, who had been with me at Trinity; it was something of a fiction. The link was made by Gordon Reece, whom after the Westland affair I'd appointed as an adviser to us. Gordon loved going to parties – in fact, he was one of those impossible people who whenever you saw him said, 'Let's open a bottle of champagne' – and there was nobody in Lazard, in spite of my urging, who was prepared to go to all those business parties. I remember Robert Maxwell reprimanding me: 'Do you realise, John, that none of your younger directors knows my two sons and they are the future of my business?' I repeated the reprimand to my colleagues but they just smiled sweetly. This was perhaps a mark of the firm's civilised outlook, but it did not help with new contacts. And it was at a party that Gordon met Ernest Saunders, who was casting around for additional financial advisers. On the actual principles of the case, I took the robust view that there was nothing in the Companies Act or anywhere else that meant that there was a binding undertaking to Risk in the event that the Guinness board met and decided that they didn't want him. I'm not sure that my predecessor Ian Fraser, a Scot himself, would have taken such a cavalier view of the small print, but anyhow I did.

The battle became how to support Saunders and Guinness in ensuring that Risk was not appointed, at a time when the Scottish Office had worked No. 10, and in particular the DTI, into an absolute fury. Michael Howard, a junior minister at the DTI (Paul Channon, the Secretary of State, standing aside as a member of the Guinness family), was even threatening Guinness with a Board of Trade enquiry unless Risk was appointed chairman. It was a disgraceful abuse of the DTI's legal powers – and I should know, as a former Trade Secretary. So I decided I had to go along and see Michael (who has always been a good friend of mine), taking with me two very clever lawyers: Robert Alexander, then one of the leading QCs and subsequently chairman of NatWest; and Thomas Ward, Saunders' clever and cunning right-hand man. We told Michael, who was being pressed by the Scottish Office, that he had absolutely no right to threaten us with a Board of Trade enquiry and that it was a matter solely for the Guinness board to decide. Eventually, both sides sought a compromise and, at the suggestion of Ward, agreed that there would be no Board of Trade enquiry so long as we appointed some outside non-executive directors to ensure that Saunders, when he became chairman, behaved himself. It was agreed also that Lazard – in effect, me – would be responsible for finding them.

Finding these non-executives caused me considerable difficulty, not least because it had been further agreed that there should be a strong Scottish element to them to placate Distillers and Scottish sensibilities. The Bank of England was pathetic, suggesting a succession of geriatric City establishment figures. One whom I plumped for, and eventually got through, was Ian MacLaurin of Tesco, whom I thought was a Scot but in fact wasn't. Eventually, after being submitted to the DTI and the Bank of England, the names of the non-execs were announced in mid-August. 'The new board proposed by Guinness yesterday will satisfy those in the City who wish to kiss and make up,' the *FT*'s 'Lex' commented. Saunders, meanwhile, had never stopped grumbling about having these outside directors (who also included Sir David Plastow, chief executive of Vickers, and Sir Norman Macfarlane, chairman of Macfarlane Group) imposed on him. Marcus Agius, the key man on our side, remembers to this day how on one occasion I exploded: 'Ernest, you remind me of Mrs Thatcher. The trouble with you is that you are never satisfied with victory – you always want unconditional surrender.' Marcus was convinced that this was going to lead to the end of a beautiful relationship, but in fact Ernest was highly flattered to be compared with Mrs Thatcher. Anyway, this clutch of new non-executive directors did the trick, and in September Guinness's institutional shareholders voted overwhelmingly to ditch Sir Thomas Risk and to back Saunders as chairman.

During this time I got to know Ernest pretty well and found him a not unattractive character. The problem was that he had a different perception of what most people would call the truth; he used to say things which one knew were completely inaccurate, and which he knew that one knew this, but it didn't faze him a bit. He was, though, becoming increasingly paranoid. His office at Guinness was on the second floor on the corner of Portman Square, directly opposite the Churchill Hotel, and he was convinced that the security services had a camera in the hotel and were monitoring what was going on in his office. He was so sure of it that he used to pull the curtains, and we would have to sit round the corner so that we couldn't be seen.

I find it impossible to say whether he knew that the roof was about to fall in on his career and indeed his life. I am doubtful whether anyone guessed the extent to which 'Guinness' was about to blow up as one of the great historic City scandals. It was shortly before it did so that I met Margaret Thatcher at a party, where she took me aside, indicating the concern felt in the Tory government about the goings on in the City.

John, is it the case, as I am told, that the sort of manoeuvrings conducted by Morgan Grenfell, and the use of fee commissions as a means of compensating banks for share support, is normal in the City? I am told that Morgan Grenfell has not done anything that was not becoming commonplace in the City.

Prime Minister, I'm afraid I have to tell you that, although this sort of thing is often discussed, I believe that Morgan Grenfell has pushed out the limits of what is done. It is certainly not City practice to use fees as a means of compensating individuals and banks for buying shares in a takeover situation.

In late November, Saunders summoned me to Portman Square and, with Ward and two other colleagues alongside him, informed me that the disgraced American arbitrageur Ivan Boesky was about to reveal the secret financial arrangements that he had entered into with Guinness during the battle for Distillers. 'I think this is going to cause immense trouble', I replied, 'and I really think that was a grave mistake.' A day or two later it was announced that the DTI was beginning an investigation into an alleged share-support operation during the closing weeks of the takeover battle. Ernest at once got hold of Marcus Agius and pressed him hard to say something publicly in support. This did not, to put it mildly, strike me as a good idea, especially if we wanted to hold on to Guinness as clients. 'Marcus,' I instructed him, 'say absolutely nothing. We keep our mouths shut and events will take their own course. We're stuck in the middle between Saunders and the non-executive directors who are gunning for him. If we go and say anything in favour of Saunders, the non-executive directors will sack us. So we'll say nothing.' In short, it was not a time for unnecessary heroics.

Events did indeed unfold over the next few weeks. Shortly after Christmas it emerged that Patrick Spens of Henry Ansbacher had given details to DTI inspectors about the informal indemnification arrangements that had been made between Seelig and himself during the closing stages. Seelig's resignation from Morgan Grenfell was announced on the 30th. Early in the new year we received a copy of a letter written by Guinness's finance director, Olivier Roux, setting out all that had gone on. It was clear to me that there was no alternative but for Saunders to stand down immediately. The day before a Guinness board meeting was due to take place, Marcus Agius and I went to see him in Portman Square. 'Ernest', I said, 'you have no choice, you must step down.' He wavered and looked for excuses, all the time insisting on his innocence. He was very upset with us, because we weren't taking his side. Some time after we left, before the board meeting, Ernest tendered his resignation.

What followed was little less than a political witch hunt. A series of arrests was made, and eventually, in August 1990, Saunders was one of four people found guilty of conspiracy, theft and false accounting. Three, including Saunders, received prison sentences. As I have said, the Thatcher government in the late 1980s had been determined to allay public concern about malpractice in the City but it raised a more fundamental issue of some constitutional importance. I have always opposed the incestuous relationship that exists between the law officers and the government. I have always taken the view, for instance, that the Lord Chancellor should not be a member of the government and that the Attorney General's relationship with the Director of Public Prosecutions should be redefined. At the time, I was particularly cross about the way in which the evidence that helped to convict Saunders and the others was obtained by the DTI under duress. Ironically, it was I who in 1979 had reframed the rules for these Board of Trade enquiries – but their purpose was to establish the facts and thus enable the Director of Public Prosecutions to reach a decision on whether to prosecute. It was contrary to fair justice for DTI investigations to become a court of law, in a situation where those alleged to have created an offence had no right of silence. In the Guinness case, the DTI should never have given transcripts to the Crown Prosecution Service for use in a criminal investigation. I am delighted that the European Court of Human Rights, to which Saunders and other defendants have appealed in the last few years, came to the same conclusion.

Anyway, was Saunders really guilty? Certainly he behaved foolishly; certainly he didn't always tell the truth, and certainly he allowed manoeuvrings to go on which he shouldn't have allowed. Against that, not only was he badly advised by Morgan Grenfell, but it is arguable that the other side in the battle, Argyll, was bending the rules just as much as the Guinness camp. Yes, he committed a series of misdemeanours, but the way in which he was given a five-year prison sentence was quite excessive. For my taste, it smacked far too much of a show trial. The DTI should be ashamed of its behaviour, and the trial judge got it wrong. But justice is fickle, and it is wise in life to keep the maximum distance from both the law and lawyers. This affair still rumbles through the courts, but I suspect that the House of Lords will find some excuse to overturn the European Court; retrospection, probably. You can expect the judges to support each other. I doubt if justice will prevail against 'political correctness'. The judges are often more political than politicians.

~

'The City was last night preparing to sound the death-knell of Plessey,' was how the *FT* in November 1988 announced the start of what was to be the third of these episodes, as GEC (in alliance with Siemens) launched a £1.7 billion bid for Plessey. The key figure at Plessey was John Clark, who was the founder's son and had been chairman and chief executive since 1970. The *FT* also set the scene for what turned out to be a memorable few weeks:

Pugnacious and often accused of Byzantine manoeuvrings in Plessey's boardroom politics, Sir John has had a stormy relationship with the financial markets.

Briefly, he enjoyed support after Plessey defeated the last bid from GEC in 1986. Since then, Plessey has once again fallen from favour, seen in the City as having failed to deliver on its promises ...

Sir John will not surrender his independence easily to his old antagonist. On the record of the last bid, the in-fighting may well get as nasty as the shoot-out at the OK Corral.

Clark's 'old antagonist' was of course Arnold Weinstock, who had been running GEC even longer, since 1963. Naturally, Plessey rejected GEC's bid (emphatically), but this time round the general City expectation was that Weinstock would nail his target.

Lazard had been Plessey's adviser only since Bobby Henderson's retirement from Kleinworts in 1983. Clark did not like his successors, and we got the billet instead. I had met John Clark many times as a purchaser of Plessey products at the MoD, so there was already a sort of relationship, but the real social spadework was done on our behalf by Gordon Reece. John Clark himself was something of an acquired taste. I would go to see him at Plessey's offices on the Embankment, and every time I walked in, he used to bawl out, 'James, James,' or whatever the name of the butler was, and the butler used to come stalking into the room with a silver tray, and amidst a lot of backslapping Clark would say, 'Have a glass of champagne, John, have a glass of champagne,' and this to me was always the worst start to any meeting. Moreover, despite all the champagne swilling round, it was not a happy atmosphere at Plessey. The chief executive was James Blyth, whom I knew very well because I had recruited him as chief salesman at the MoD, before he was recruited by John Clark. At Plessey he grew to detest Clark, whom he thought was hopeless and interfered with everything. I am not sure that James Blyth was right. John Clark had a certain street-fighter's credibility and he certainly knew the industry.

All in all, I was very pessimistic about Plessey's chances – especially once it became clear that the MoD (whose Chief of Defence Procurement, Peter Levene, was close to Weinstock) was, against apparent economic logic and simple monopoly considerations, in favour of a merger between these two electronics businesses. As I pondered during the closing weeks of 1988 what we should do, I realised that my poor relationship with Arnold Weinstock could lead to unpleasantness. It did.

Back in my days at the MoD he had been a bidder for the Navy's torpedo contract, potentially a huge contract for GEC, and I had had to decide between it and an American bid. Arnold had come into my room and started lecturing me about Trident. It was a waste of money, a foolish decision, etc., etc. I thought that he was patronising and objectionable. I said, 'Arnold, I am not interested in your views on Trident. We are here to discuss your torpedo bid.' In the end, I accepted GEC's bid for the torpedo contract. Then, when I got to Lazard, our international division was very busy acting for GEC around the world, but it seemed to me that he never came forward and paid the fees without further argument. Eventually, I informed him that we weren't prepared to act for him any more. Arnold did not expect to be told that by a merchant bank.

I was aware that my experiences were far from unique, not to mention the City's general lack of enthusiasm for GEC's cautious piling up of a cash mountain, so I came to the conclusion that there was a small chance that we might be able to launch a counter-bid, using the so-called 'Pacman' defence. Apparently the term comes from the video game in which a creature turns round and eats another which has been pursuing it. It was not, I must concede, a strategy for which there was much enthusiasm at Lazard; but it seemed the only possible means of turning the tables on GEC, which was in a much more powerful position than Plessey. Anyhow my colleagues and I thought it was worth the gamble – and initially it was warmly supported by the board of Plessey.

So, with the bit between our teeth, we bought a tiny company (Metsun) off the shelf, set it up with an equity capital of £2, and began to put together a consortium to bid for GEC on Plessey's behalf. I had no difficulty persuading John Cuckney (no great fan of Weinstock) to lead the consortium, while Barclays – which at this time, under John Quinton and Andrew Buxton, was very much in the business of funding big takeover bids – was happy to take a lead role in assembling the necessary finance, which amounted to a £3.5 billion package to be secured against the assets of the victim. Kenneth Keith, chairman of Standard Telephones and legendary for his piratical instincts, was also quite keen on having a crack at Arnold Weinstock, not least because the combined telecommunications business of Plessey/GEC would have been of great interest to Northern Telecom of Canada, the owner of Standard Telephones. In addition, there was the possibility of General Electric of America getting involved on our side as a buyer of the GEC name and some of its assets.

Unfortunately, just before the first weekend of 1989, there was a leak to GEC, possibly more than one. It also leaked to the press. As a result, we were compelled on a Saturday morning to make an immediate press announcement about the possibility of a Metsun bid for GEC, several days before we were quite ready to do so. At breakfast I rang up Jim Prior, who was then the chairman of GEC, to tell him what was about to happen. Jim replied, 'I'm just going off shooting. Why do you have to ruin my shooting on a Saturday morning? Why can't you do this on Monday?' Press reaction about a bid for GEC by a £2 off-the-shelf shell company was pretty sceptical, epitomised by Lex's observation on the Monday morning that 'the cynical response to the proposed bid for GEC is to ask whether it exists outside the imagination of the corporate financier'. There is no doubt that the premature nature of the announcement was most unfortunate, in that it meant that necessarily difficult negotiations were henceforth conducted in the full glare of publicity.

Other things soon started to go wrong. At Standard Telephones, Kenneth Keith's chief executive, Arthur Walsh, suddenly reappeared after several months sickness, to find that his chairman was negotiating to bid for his old employer, GEC. Unfortunately, Walsh had been chief executive for many years at Marconi, had worked very closely with Weinstock for a long time, and they clearly had a bond together. The upshot was well expressed in a headline on 11 January: 'GEC bid is less likely after STC has doubts'. The following day STC had definitely dropped out, and I tried in vain to bring in AT&T to fill their place. Nor was General Electric any more reliable as an ally. By this time Jack Welch, the most famous American businessman of our era, had arrived in London and he and I had several meetings. I found him an attractive character – very much an Irish American and none too fond of the Brits. It probably did not help me that he was being represented by Michael Richardson of Rothschilds, whom Welch complained about at every meeting with me. In due course Welch decided he would be better off to cut a deal with Weinstock. This he duly did, leading to the headline on the 14th: 'General Electric and GEC to join forces in Europe'. This meant it was all over bar the shouting, and within a week it was known to the world that the counter-bid against GEC had collapsed. Such had been the high-profile nature of the episode – with at one point television cameras circling round Lazard's premises in the City – that inevitably there was a certain amount of egg on our faces.

~

Although we were a happy ship in London – and although with the rising profits and reputation of the bank our morale and *esprit de corps* were high – my relationship with the New York team was unsatisfactory. Michel David-Weill may have been senior partner there, but the key business-getter was Felix Rohatyn. When André Meyer died, Felix had been his obvious successor; but he was uninterested in running the bank, and Michel David-Weill, as the leading shareholder, assumed his rightful position as senior partner. Meyer himself had observed of Rohatyn, after it became clear even before Meyer's death that he did not want the succession, that he was 'a very able man in making deals', but was 'no good in dealing with garbage' – and, Meyer added, 'a good banker must, above all, be good at dealing with garbage'. We will have to see whether the latest recruit to Lazard, Bruce Wasserstein, is good at 'dealing with garbage'!

Lazard Frères had its headquarters in the Rockefeller Center and it was famous for the shabbiness of its offices. Unlike the big American investment banks which pretended an extreme English-style olde worlde décor – much favoured by the interior decorating community – Lazard had no decoration of any kind at all. On entering the bank you were confronted with a very old sofa. Michel used to say that Lazard spent no money on its offices – that is not what clients came to see – but instead kept their extravagance for their own homes. It was a sentiment that attracted me. The chichi offices of the big US investment bankers are normally rather revolting and are decorated in an upmarket 'brothel' style – an appropriate decor.

In my time it was an eccentric atmosphere in New York. Michel and Felix, the two key men, conversed in French; but what struck a visiting Englishman in the 1980s was the astonishing greed of Wall Street. Money had truly corrupted its denizens. Whereas in London I spent fifteen minutes or so each year telling my senior colleagues what share of the profits they would receive in the coming year, and no-one ever grumbled even though sometimes they must have been disappointed, Michel, performing a similar function in New York, used to spend hours and hours with each partner, many of whom complained bitterly that they were misunderstood and badly done by. Money was everything to them. It established their position in life, the respect that they felt for themselves, and their attitude towards the pecking order in the firm and on Wall Street generally. They would be astonished if anyone suggested that they had been utterly corrupted by money, but that was the way it was; they were slaves to the prestige of where they worked and the peer pressure to be rich. Unfortunately that money culture has now found its way to the City of London, which is no longer a nice place at all.

The essential difference between Englishmen and Americans, or at least between English and American bankers, is this. Most Englishmen have a hinterland, a family background, a sense of holding some position in the world, even if they are poor. The Americans have no hinterland; they burn their family tree when they arrive as immigrants at Ellis Island. It is the first step in their ritual of assimilation as Americans. The English know who they are, the Americans do not. An American's position in society, and how he sees himself, is entirely dictated by how much he earns. 'Joe Stacey, jnr, works for Goldman Sachs and takes home $20 million a year.' Joe Stacey has a position in American society, and its financial and social pecking order. His identity is his job and how much he earns. He is like a battery hen – he is encapsulated by his place of work and by how many eggs he lays.

As I was always looking for new activities in London to supplement our corporate finance fees and so on, I went to New York on several occasions to sit at the desk of the traders. There I had the misfortune to spend two days sitting beside the most foul-mouthed woman it has ever been my misfortune to meet. Her language was disgusting, but she seemed proud of it – and Damon Mezzacappa, the head of trading in New York, seemed to encourage this kind of behaviour with his own vituperative language. It was not a pleasant place. Moreover, although I much preferred Michel's regime to that of Siegmund Warburg, he never walked around his firm; he simply did not know the junior members of the team, whilst Siegmund knew everyone and would never have tolerated bad language or arrogance in his bank.

Paris was altogether a more civilised place. The Paris partners lived very well and it was a gentlemen's bank – something which, Michel apart, could not have been said of the culture of New York. Because it had just survived as a private partnership when Mitterrand had nationalised all the Paris banks above a certain size, including Rothschilds, it had a near monopoly of advice to the French corporate sector. I liked the French, in particular Jean Guyot and Jean-Claude Haas; they were utterly civilised. It was difficult for me and rather shaming that I did not speak French – disgraceful really – but I was an English war child and never had the chance to go abroad at the critical time.

I had two specific disagreements with New York. First, Ian Fraser had recruited two very strange, eccentric but remarkable young men called Hock and Pope; they traded in Third World debt – and made very large sums of money. Michel, who was always being pressed for higher partnership payments by his New York team, insisted that we divided their profits equally between the three houses on the excuse that it was an international business. I protested, as all the capital, responsibility and trading took place in London. I gave in; but it rankled. How we divided the fees of the three Houses was always a source of contention, given that our incomes were dependent on the result, but I always found Michel helpful and reasonable except on this one occasion.

Second, I had difficulty over a character called Robert Agostonelli. He was a charming and intelligent hustler. Michel was always keen to have his man in London to safeguard the interests of New York, acting as a useful bridge for two-way business between the houses – and reporting back to him on what was going on in London. I was often concerned that Michel, based in New York, was captive to the greed and ambitions of his New York team. I was keen on Robert joining us, as he had been with Goldman Sachs in London and knew something of the City's customs. But, as he was operating from our London base, I was conscious of my regulatory responsibilities, even though I did not employ him. Robert made it his business to visit our UK clients, but I insisted that he should do so in partnership with the relevant London director. On several occasions I discovered that he was using the Lazard Brothers client base to drum up business for New York, without keeping us informed. There was always an underlying tension between the 'transaction' culture of New York and the 'relationship' culture in London. Finally, after several discussions with Robert on how we could best work together, he broke the rules that I had established – and I told him that he must go. I informed Michel that I had dismissed his employee, and this was supported by my colleagues. Michel was upset. It was an unfortunate incident, but happily my good relationship with Michel was only temporarily suspended.

I stepped down from the bank about six months later, in 1990, as I had found the weekend commuting to Cornwall an increasing burden. In parliament, by the time Thursday evening came I got restless; I was dying to return on the sleeper to Cornwall to see my wife and our farm. At Lazard it was even worse; I sneaked down the back stairs after lunch on Friday but as chief executive of the bank, I had to return on Sunday afternoon. It ruined my weekends, and my freedom. I also felt that five years of running a merchant bank, in booming times, was long enough for anyone. On my recommendation, Michel David-Weill and Michael Blakenham chose David Verey as my successor; Marcus Agius, the present chairman of Lazard in London, was a close runner-up.

Lazard has lost the almost unique position that the three houses occupied in the 1980s. It no longer comes near the top of the league tables in either New York, Paris or London. Financial advice has become dominated by the likes of Goldman Sachs, Morgan Stanley and Merrill Lynch – and the creatures of the big money banks, such as Warburg, Morgan Grenfell and Kleinwort, owned respectively by UBS, Deutsche and Dresdner. But this will change. Money is a corrupting influence on advice. One-stop financial shopping is the current fashion, but it will not last. The internet bubble has already revealed the lack of quality control being exercised by the big investment banks, and it is only a question of time before a mighty scandal demonstrates the inherent flimsiness of their so-called 'Chinese walls'. There will be an irresistible demand to separate again the integrity of advice from distribution and investment analysis. Moreover, so substantial are the overheads of the big investment banks, and so spoilt and greedy are their key 'rainmakers', that rather than deny these people their inflated expectations, they will over-trade to sustain bonuses and profits. Trading, trading, trading – that way lies disaster, mark my words.

Until last year it was quite hard to see where Lazard was going. Its position in the galaxy had been slipping for some time, especially in New York. I believed that if Lazard had kept its cost base and employee numbers low, relying on brains and inventiveness rather than capital, leading business would eventually flow back its way as problems began to multiply for the big investment banks. But a collective loss of self-confidence seems to have set in; again, I blame New York. Its dilemma became the hinge that held it all together – that hinge was not the 'big money' of the bulge bracket banks but one man, Michel David-Weill, and at the age of sixty-nine, people were aware he could not go on for ever.

In an attempt to avoid squabbling over fees all the Houses were joined together so that the partners drew their income from a single profit pool. Then the US partners were unprepared to accept that their reduced contribution merited a lower share of the take – they saw their friends in Goldmans, Morgan Stanley and Merrill Lynch grow richer whilst they got poorer. Things began to wobble. So, somewhat in desperation I suspect, Michel David-Weill turned again to Bruce Wasserstein, whom he had tried to recruit before. I remember a previous incident quite well. Bruce may have been an elderly star of silent films – or, to be fair, of the black and white films of Wall Street in the 1980s, but he was still a star – a Wall Street diva. Frank Sinatra, after all, went on for ever. Whether Bruce 'bid em up' Wasserstein will prove to be a manager – 'a good garbage handler' to use Andre Meyer's phrase – only time will tell. He is unlikely to be such a brilliant manager as Michel David-Weill, who held together all those tiresome, greedy New York partners for more than twenty years; but maybe a consummate deal-maker can do the trick. What would be a tragedy for choice in markets is if a pure advisory business like Lazard winds up as just another Wasserstein Perella in the maw of another vast great German banking empire.

Today the City makes a huge contribution to the British economy, vastly greater in relative terms than when I joined Warburg in 1959. Its overseas earnings – around £22 billion a year – play a vital part in the UK's balance of payments, largely offsetting the long-standing deficit in the trade of physical goods, most of it with Europe. By a combination of history, luck and an eye for the main chance, London has become the world's leading offshore banking centre. Its growth in the past forty years or so – since the coming of the euromarkets in the 1960s – stems partly from its professional infrastructure, the English language and its favourable time zone; but also from a peculiarly un-English culture, which was very much the post-war creation of Jewish immigrants like Siegmund Warburg and Henry Grunfeld. Finally, it is the invasion of foreign banks and institutions that has sealed its international pre-eminence – and here credit, in short supply in this book, must go to the flexibility and opportunism of the Bank of England and its Whitehall master, HM Treasury. A visitor to Frankfurt or Paris – the aspiring competitors of London – is struck by the conservatism and *dirigiste* approach of the authorities in both these centres. Beside the liveliness of London, with its openness and transparency, Frankfurt seems half-dead, corporatist, bureaucratic and stolid, like the German character.

Not everyone, even in the square mile itself, seems to understand that the City prospers independently of sterling and its economic hinterland. British banks are not seen as dominating the City in the way that the big German banks so obviously dominate Frankfurt. London as a financial centre is quite unlike New York or Tokyo, or Frankfurt or Paris; it is more akin to Hong Kong and Singapore. In fact, London has the most international character of any financial centre in the world – and, as long as it retains that character, it will continue to prosper as remarkably as it has so far.

But there is a dark cloud looming on the horizon: the euro. The City has thrived on the basis of a business-friendly tax and regulatory regime, but British membership of the European single currency would undoubtedly increase the number of Brussels-initiated regulations – of which the recent row about an EU-wide withholding tax presaged a useful lesson. London is viewed by the international financial community – stretching far beyond Europe – as being even-handed, with no signs of favouritism. As an independent entrepôt between the dollar and euro blocs, it can continue to dominate trading in the euro without sacrificing its much more important role as a dollar money centre, which it has largely been since the 1960s.

In short, we are at a cross-roads. A decision on how much further we proceed with European integration will in turn determine the future of the City of London, the greatest economic success story of the post-war years.

Chapter Twelve

RETURN TO THE PLOUGH

Last night I dreamt I went to Manderley again.

(Daphne du Maurier, *Rebecca*)

I left the City in 1990 without regrets. I had been with Warburg and Lazard for a total of fourteen years – not much less than the time that I had spent in politics. Warburg had been a valuable apprenticeship for business and had taught me the tools of the banking trade: Lazard had proved an interesting and profitable end to my business career – or that is what I intended. A dozen or so years after Robin Oakley had written of me that 'he shoots, fishes and farms without a hint of tweed or the merest whiff of retriever coming through as part of his Westminster persona', I wanted to spend more time on the farm in Cornwall and to devote myself to what are known as country pursuits.

I thought that if I went 'pluralist' it would help to finance my leisure activities, which included fishing, shooting, boating and golf – all of which I did badly, but that did not limit the pleasure that I obtained from them. So I agreed to join the boards of several public companies, to all of which I made a most limited contribution; being a non-executive director of a public company is a job of the utmost worthlessness.

I did, however, enjoy being chairman of Etam, a rather downmarket women's clothing chain. It had recently fought off a bid from a South African group and I presume my City experience was thought appropriate. I have always been interested in the fashion industry, but the real pleasure that I obtained from this particular job was visiting all the shops in the High Street. I had encountered my fellow countrymen for the first time some forty years earlier in the barracks at Aldershot; now I was to meet my fellow countrywomen who managed and ran the Etam shops. Without exception they were charming, courteous and competent, and attractive to boot. I thought that this thirty-year-old generation of young working mums was tremendously impressive. They were truly descendants of that remarkable European species, the British memsahib. I remember John Smith, one-time MP for the Cities of London and Westminster, saying of his then secretary that she could 'govern the Punjab standing on her head'. The Etam managers had the same determination and competence. This was recession time, and I was shocked to find that up to half our women managers were the family breadwinner with the husbands out of work.

All this kept me half-employed, and I was able to spend a little more time in Cornwall; but not for long. One of our clients at Lazard had been a large food conglomerate called Hillsdown Holdings – a high-volume, low-margin commodity business. My colleague John Nelson had been a good friend of its chairman, Harry Solomon. I had met Harry a number of times at Lazard and shared the universal liking for his friendliness and charm. When I announced my retirement from Lazard, he and Gordon Reece tried to persuade me to take the chairmanship of Hillsdown. I told Harry that I did not want to take on any new business responsibilities or directorships. The moment passed. About eighteen months later, however, Harry became disillusioned with City criticism of Hillsdown's performance – combined, I suspect, with frustration at the thuggish behaviour of the supermarkets towards their suppliers, of which Hillsdown was one of the largest. A conspiracy developed between Harry Solomon and Miloska to get me back to work. Eventually I was persuaded to succeed Harry as full-time executive chairman.

On 17 December 1992 the *Financial Times* announced that 'Sir John Nott's arrival in the hot seat at Hillsdown, the most lowly rated company in the food sector, raises the inevitable question of whether former Defence Secretaries make good butchers'. I may have been a good butcher but I never succeeded in dishing up a satisfactory meal for shareholders.

It was no small task. Hillsdown had been one of the high-fliers of the 1980s. When it went public in 1985, the offer was nine times oversubscribed. Using its fashionably high share price, it had bought a series of failing companies that no-one else wanted in the food and related industries. It had also entered the property development, furniture, venture capital and house-building industries. Just before I became chairman it had put together the largest food company in Canada, formed out of Canada Packers, the long-standing but failing Canadian meat-packing business, and Maple Leaf Mills. Taking all these companies together, Hillsdown boasted a turnover in 1993 of some £4 billion with 43,000 employees around the world. Harry Solomon's co-founder, David Thompson, had sold out for some £350 million, leaving Harry to pick up the pieces. The market was awash with Hillsdown shares.

I took the job for two reasons; and it was to become the only real failure of my career, although I enjoyed my time at Hillsdown much more than my two stints in the City.

First, as it was the largest agricultural business in the country, it marked for me a return to the plough, albeit in a suit. We had around 20 per cent of the UK poultry and egg market, as well as a very large pork and bacon business called Harris. With Heinz we were the largest canners of vegetables and beans in Europe. We owned Pinneys, the seafood business, and had a big share of the salad business in Germany and France. We bought up to 10 per cent of the UK's feed wheat crop in order to feed our chicken and pigs. We had about 15 per cent of the UK's potato market. I had wanted to get back into agriculture, and here it was in a big way. Second, I must have developed the arrogance of all investment bankers, about which Siegmund Warburg had warned me many years earlier. I believed that, with Harry's advice in the background, I could sort Hillsdown out. It was also a real challenge.

Actually, we had only one problem in Hillsdown – our customers! That sounds trite and foolish. What else is business about but the satisfaction of customers? But Hillsdown, in the food business, only had around five or so significant customers: Sainsbury's, Tesco, Safeway, Asda and Marks & Spencer. Together they represented a complex monopoly, using their overwhelming buying power to squeeze their suppliers, most of them in the farming industry.

As a leading food analyst told me recently, 'the domestic UK food producers – those producing food for supermarket brands – have gone down the plughole; they were squeezed to death when the supermarkets went to war with the discounters, cutting food producers' margins into shreds'. The Stock Market was no longer willing to finance the UK food industry – only the international brands managed to survive in their original form. Not just Hillsdown disappeared but United Biscuits, Rank Hovis, Hazlewoods, Unigate, Northern Foods, Perkins and Albert Fisher have all been broken up – or have gone to private equity. The UK milk industry, the mainstay of generations of farmers, is rapidly diminishing, inevitably giving way to foreign imports.

Hillsdown, with its wide spread of food products, had some protection against the practices of its supermarket customers; but it was under constant siege from the threat of sudden de-listing unless discounts were offered, the return of unsold products, and blackmail to contribute financially to the cost of 'promotions', to the better positioning of products in stores, to artwork and packaging, and even to the building of new stores. The farmers in West Cornwall were expected to pay the travelling, hotel and entertainment expenses of the supermarket buyers who come to seek out new sources of supply. At its most ruthless stood Sainsbury's. On several occasions I visited its headquarters to see the Purchasing Director. The atmosphere in Sainsbury's headquarters was poisonous: apparently miserable staff and an arrogance towards suppliers, consistent with the bullying approach of a third-rate corporal in a bad regiment – or a rude officer in the Metropolitan Police. Later, Sainsbury's began to change its culture for the better under the more civilised approach of David Sainsbury – now a Lord of New Labour – but it remained a classic case of the overmighty subject.

In my last year as chairman of Hillsdown (I stepped down in 2000), we were, among other things, the largest supplier of poultry and eggs to the supermarkets, and yet our profits in the poultry division fell from £30 million to a loss of £1 million. There were, of course, a number of international factors which accounted for this dramatic change – commodity markets are subject to large swings – but none of Hillsdown's customers made any great effort to show loyalty to their traditional UK suppliers. They simply purchased abroad from places like Brazil and Thailand where the welfare and health of the animals, and safety practices and cost, fell far below British regulations and standards.

The supermarkets, without exception, conduct an utterly disingenuous marketing campaign to convince the housewife, naturally gullible in this particular area, that 'organic' food is safer and more wholesome than traditionally produced food. The whole campaign has been a device to widen food margins further at the expense of the housewife. Those farmers who have converted to organic production, urged on by the supermarkets, will inevitably be driven out of business when the buyers start to squeeze their margins as supplies from overseas and domestic sources come nearer to meeting this artificially stimulated home demand. Hillsdown was the country's largest supplier of 'free range' eggs, for which the housewife was prepared to pay a much higher price, yet they are certainly a less healthy product than the cheaper traditional cage and barn eggs. Again, it is a pure marketing gimmick. The housewife has visions of free chickens pecking their way around a farmyard, whereas the truth is that ten thousand birds have to be pushed outdoors each day, where they are supposed to roam in so many acres per thousand birds. In fact, the birds hang around the entrance of their sheds, picking up worms and disease, until they can return more happily to a controlled environment indoors. The housewife should ask, 'What is the definition of a "free range" egg?'

How is it possible that the ruthless practices of the supermarkets have been allowed to continue in such a way? As I suggested in the chapter on my childhood, it is because governments, since the first Thatcher Government, have abrogated their responsibility to hold the balance between consumers and producers. They have surrendered to the consumer interest – or what is now termed the focus group voter. The customer is God. Superficially, of course, the supermarkets compete with each other on price; but such is their buying power that they can simply follow each other's pricing practices and structures, in a complex conspiracy against their suppliers. As the number of domestic suppliers declines (milk is an example), the supermarkets are forced more and more – contrary to their denials – to purchase food from abroad where the health and welfare regulations are less harsh and, therefore, the costs of production lower.

Does it matter? The government of which I was a part in the early 1980s allowed the run down of the traditional shipbuilding, coal, steel and car industries of this country, causing much dislocation and misery among the workers in these sectors. Why should the farmers be treated differently? Fortunately, most of the industrial areas affected by the dramatic changes in the structure of British industry have risen from the ashes – and the people of these areas are generally employed in more modern and healthy working environments, to the benefit of their families and of the country. The impact of the closure of a factory can be traumatic, but it is normally short-term and can be addressed. But land is something else. It is permanent, unlike a factory. The French recognise this. We are an urban society, and we do not.

In the West Country and elsewhere, the livestock farmers are under a state of siege. BSE and foot and mouth are decimating the structure – and equally important, the morale – of farming families who have preserved, cared for, and loved the countryside for untold generations. The price of beef and sheep meat has not fallen in the supermarkets. Oh, no! The profits of the big supermarkets have risen consistently to more than £1 billion a year; but according to a recent study by Deloitte and Touche, in the five years up to autumn 2000, 'the net farm income' of a 200-hectare (450-acre) family farm has fallen from £80,000 to just £8,000.

City buyers, and the big cereal barons, have held up the price of land (the

200-hectare farm mentioned above is still worth up to £1m); but when the recession comes, the price of land must fall – and the security of the banks, who hold land against loans to the farmers, will be imperilled. The banks, as always, will panic and there could be an accelerating spiral of dispossession and falling land prices. The government, caught up in this crisis when it comes – which is only of their own making in their unwillingness to tackle the difficult problem of the over-mighty supermarkets – will then try to preserve the structure and beauty of the British countryside by turning the land into a rural theme park. Fewer cows, fewer sheep, more horses, more gymkhanas, but no hunting. There is a total incomprehension in Whitehall and Westminster that the landscape enjoyed by the millions of members of the Ramblers' Association, the National Trust and the Royal Society for the Protection of Birds has not only been man-made by farmers and landowners but kept in trim by the millions of animals now being slaughtered for foot and mouth. All the publicity coming out of government is about transforming the cost of agricultural support away from headage payments (e.g. for each cow and sheep) into conservation.

It is a nonsense. The only way to preserve the viable and beautiful landscape for the benefit of our urban population is to find some mechanism to transfer the piratically acquired wealth (as a result of their monopoly power) of the retailers back into the hands of the farmers and the producers. As has happened since the beginning of time, they will protect and build the beauty of the countryside in which they spend their daily lives. Once government gets into the conservation business – nationalises it with subsidies – the land will go the way of all public-sector undertakings from the NHS to London Underground. Government will destroy what it claims to support.

~

This brings me to the real world of farming itself and, in particular, to our farm in Cornwall. My great-great-great-grandfather William, with whom this book began, abandoned the family farm for military service with the East India Company in 1798. He was the third son of a farmer and innkeeper and had to seek fame and fortune elsewhere. Six generations later, the most satisfying thing that I have done with my life is to return to the land.

Why do Englishmen have this strange compulsion to own a country estate? We leave it to others to multiply their millions and enhance the wealth of the country; many successful Englishmen just want to return to nature as soon as a moderate fortune enables them to do so. A friend of mine said the other day that only two things in life really interested him, 'Cash and women'. I can understand the necessity of the former and the desirability of the latter, but I do not share this lust for wealth creation. I think that I know the reason why.

There are a limited number of true natural pleasures in life and they are mostly connected with the soil – or at least with nature. It is a sort of primitive territorial imperative. There is no greater satisfaction in life than being able to walk over one's own land, see crops and young trees grow, and watch as the soil is turned by the plough.

I have no idea whether my grandsons, William and Thomas, will feel as passionate about the countryside as I do. No longer is it possible to earn a living in the world of mixed farming – it is factory farming or poverty – but there is still a niche for the part-time farmer who earns some of his living elsewhere but sustains his spirit close to nature. I am proud to be a part-time peasant descended from my yeoman ancestors.

Our Cornish home, Trewinnard, built around 1700 and redolent of Daphne du Maurier's Cornwall, lies some twenty miles or so from Land's End; the land grows some of the earliest crops in Europe, warmed by the Gulf Stream which surrounds us. It means that our acreage is worth more than elsewhere because we can double-crop the land, growing vegetables in winter and cereals in the summer. Possibly the maintenance of the house and grounds, the seven cottages and the land itself will prove too great a financial burden on my descendants and it will all be sold. But even if that were to happen, I will have added more to this world by sustaining a rather beautiful and historic Cornish manor house than by anything I could have achieved in politics. Others will have their life immeasurably enhanced by the trees that I have planted and by the beauty of Trewinnard, even if it is not my descendants. In the modern world every incentive exists to take more out than you put in – in farming it has to be the other way around.

I found this fantastic place quite by chance. One weekend in 1967 I was alone in our cottage above the fishing port of Newlyn and chanced to glance at the property section of the *Sunday Times*. I saw an advertisement for a house and grounds within my parliamentary constituency, but it was tucked away between the north and south coasts – and had escaped my canvassing of the area. The property agent, Michael Newman, happened to be treasurer of my local Conservative Association, so I telephoned him at home on Sunday evening to say that I was catching the sleeper back to London in three hours' time, but was there any chance of popping in to see the property on my way to the station? When we arrived in the cobbled courtyard outside the ancient stable block – and then entered the panelled hall – I knew instantly that I had to buy it. I told the owners, well-known local farmers, the Pascoes, that I would pay their asking price, subject only to Miloska seeing it the following morning. I telephoned her in London and said that she had one hour to catch the sleeper at Paddington and that Michael Newman would meet her at Penzance station. By ten o'clock on Monday morning my offer was accepted. The house, stable block and fifteen acres of land cost me £18,000.

Fortunately, instinct told me that the surrounding agricultural land might also come on the market in due course, as the Pascoes were going through difficult times. This was hardly surprising, because although Tom Pascoe had made an excellent living growing winter cabbages for the British population during the war – and he was a good farmer – the burden of keeping up the house and grounds on a farmer's income was something of a strain. I sought and was granted a right of first refusal on the land and farm buildings should the Pascoes ever want to sell. Sure enough, a year or so later I was able to buy the farm for what was then a top price of nearly £300 an acre. I had no spare capital but my credit was good. I borrowed the entire sum. I remember driving past the bankruptcy courts in London to see my solicitors and I had a horrible premonition that I had overreached myself.

As indeed I had. The farm cost £40,000 – a paltry sum for grade I and II land today – but I did not have it. The fact that we survived through severe financial setbacks was entirely due to Miloska. Whilst I played politics in London, she was saddled with the responsibility of the farm mid-week. She is a phenomenal worker who, as she has related, was raised during the war on a small farm in the hills of northern Slovenia. So although we had to learn everything from scratch, she had an instinct for the land – and even to this day has an astonishing knowledge of subsistence farming and survival. To sustain the bank account we grew everything – snowdrops, primroses, violets, pinks and anemones – and she sat up half the night bunching flowers in the garage.

When we bought the farm, I had no money for working capital or equipment, so I entered into an agreement with a local landowner called Charles Le Grice to rent him the land for growing daffodils. It brought in a significant income and, as we watched the flower business going on around us, we decided after four or five years that we could do it for ourselves. We bought a ton of bulbs from Charles Le Grice and started with six rows of flowers. Bulbs double in weight every two years, multiplying quickly; by the time we gave up daffodil growing some twenty-five years later, we had nearly seventy-five acres of daffodils with thirty different varieties and quite a thriving business. Miloska ran it, with charm and discipline. We had up to sixty flower pickers, all needing supervision, with each picker having to be paid on piece rates – as well as selling up to 300 boxes daily. In preparing this book, Miloska and I found ourselves reminiscing about our experiences on the land, and I pass the story to her.

Miloska's Story (3): The Daffodil Business

I have to start with the flower pickers. Some of my professional pickers were able to earn over £100 a day, quite a lot of money in the 1970s. They were very fast, they were like machines. They would arrive around seven o'clock in the morning and would stay late; often they would be 50 to 60 years old and they would go from farm to farm. These were amazing women, very hardworking locals, and I used to get really fond of them. I got to know them very well and, when I gave up farming, I really missed them.

I could write a whole book about my flower pickers. So many incidents happened in my fields. I used to drive our Massey Ferguson 35 tractor into the field to collect the flowers and, as you know, a tractor is quite high up so you can see over the hedge. One day we had a very attractive girl who was around 30 to 35 years old, and as I drove into the field I thought that's very funny, what is happening over the hedge? She was making love to another flower picker. I was so embarrassed, I didn't know whether to go back to the farm, but anyhow I kept very quiet about it. I didn't tell anybody, but as they came very sheepishly back to the field trying to straighten up their clothing, everybody else was laughing. I thought that nobody knew, but in fact this woman tried out any new picker who came on the farm. 'She's just trying them all out,' they said, and all the pickers used to really laugh.

At the weekends John would arrive. I had to work with the flower pickers at the weekend too, because on Monday morning there was usually quite a good market. Three to four hundred boxes of flowers would go off on Saturday and Sunday, that is around 300,000 stems, we tried to get as many flowers away as we could. Unfortunately my dear husband John, he loved the young females, and he would come on the field and there were all these young females around, and he would flirt with them in the fields. Now I didn't mind that, but I would have preferred that he flirted when I had my quota, but you see he didn't understand that. I used to get more and more irritable, and he used to think that I got irritable because he was flirting with the girls. I didn't. I was very irritable because I had to get the amount of flowers away over the weekend.

It's true. My military training had taught me to keep up the morale of the team! I enjoyed chatting up the flower pickers, young and old. I admit that some of the younger girls were very attractive, but the thing about them all was that they were great characters. There was a lot of ribaldry and teasing. I did not dare take up too much of their time, because they were all on piece rates and they didn't want to lose out by wasting their time being chatted up by an old bugger like myself, even if he was their landlord. Often the weather was appalling; Cornwall is not like the Caribbean in February and March, but somehow the flower pickers remained cheerful. Picking flowers is back-breaking work and the speed of each of them varied enormously – some earned over £100 a day, as Miloska says; others took home £15. Normally the slow pickers dropped out, it was not worth the hassle. Miloska used to take them out in the field first thing and show them the technique. That was partly the secret of how to make good money. It was a moveable feast, they came and went, and although we could not engage anyone for more than a day at a time, that was the Inland Revenue rule, we had a good core of loyal and reliable pickers, from the local area. Miloska built up a very good reputation in markets, and I was not welcome in her flower-packing shed in the mornings because so much time was taken up flirting with the salesmen in the markets. To accuse me of flirting with the flower pickers when Miloska's flirtatious telephone calls to Sheffield, Glasgow or Cardiff might add a penny to a bunch of ten is a bit ripe. I felt quite excluded from my own farm! But at least I was allowed to load the boxes into the van and take them to the transport depot or the railway. By ruthless grading, good packing and banter with the salesmen in markets, Miloska always got two or three pence more for a bunch than many other local growers – and two pence was a lot of money at the end of the season.

The flower business was profitable and it became the principal activity on the farm for many years. But it became a real burden in the end. It took up nearly three months in the spring, and then the bulbs needed to be sprayed every week to keep the leaves healthy. In July we had to lift up to half the acreage, grade the bulbs, sell off the surplus and replant the rest – that took up much of August and September, with another team to employ. The huge amount of work made little economic sense because I could earn as much from one or two non-executive directorships as we could make in five months' work on the daffodils. It also became too much for Miloska.

The trigger for our decision to cease the business was, however, the appalling hassle of dealing with anything to do with government. We were quite inured to raids by the Social Security. Every so often they were spotted arriving over the hedge by a flower picker, and the whole field scarpered in an instant. We lost all the flowers that day. The idea was to catch flower pickers who were on social security. Our sympathies were with the pickers, because most of them wanted to work; but there was so much delay and bureaucracy signing on and off, and the weather was so uncertain, that there was no real incentive for them to seek work at all. This would not have been the case if government had introduced a 'negative income tax system' of a kind that I described in an earlier chapter.

I have to say that agriculture is beset by more needless form-filling and regulation than any other area of economic activity. Were it not for farmers' love of the land, no-one in their senses would engage in agriculture. Over the years I have filled up annually at least five censuses. Most of them ask exactly the same question as the one before; everything goes on the computer, no-one ever sees the result. It is the civil service passion for information gathering. The livestock farmer has the worst time of all – the degree of bureaucracy and regulation is unbelievable. Now the supermarkets are up to the same tricks, burdening the farmer with needless rules, just to protect themselves against press and consumer complaints – they call it traceability. Just as we gave up daffodils they were introducing 'bulb passports' to accompany the sale of bulbs. Sometimes I think that only a total breakdown of law and order – complete anarchy – can ever get this country back to economic foundations where everything is governed by one simple rule: *'caveat emptor'*, or buyer beware, where the responsibility is yours. The problem with parliamentary democracy is that every government feels compelled by pressure from the media to protect the British people from themselves.

Back to Miloska – my small businessman tirades are a bore but they are no less valid for that.

Miloska's Story (4): The Hereford Herd

Harvest and hay-making times were a busy period of the year. My neighbour farmers used to be very amused because I would turn the hay and one of them, Gordon Geoffrey, leant over the hedge and shouted at me, so I stopped the tractor and went to see what he wanted, and he said, 'Do you wear a bra?' I was really quite embarrassed and I said, 'Why do you ask that?' 'Well, I have to tell you, my dear, if you don't wear a bra your bosom will go up and down, up and down, and it's going to be very painful.' I had a lot of good male friends who were terribly helpful to me, local farmers and non-farmers. They would sit with me and plant cabbages on the cabbage planter. We were really a horticultural business at that time. You sit in a row of four, and it is such a stupid job because all you do is to take your plant and stick it into the ground as this machine goes forward, so you chat and chat, often about the silly sexual exploits of the local characters. One day they were talking about some farmer who was terribly promiscuous, and the man who was sitting next to me on the planter was saying 'You know what. You know this chap when they tried to put the lid on his coffin they couldn't,' and I pretended I didn't understand why. He said, 'Even in his death, he couldn't keep it down.'

When we were making hay I had a lot of good friends who volunteered to help me. I had a dentist friend who came every season, Don Hobson, then there were Dell and Gareth, tenants in our cottages. They were lovely friends and still are today. I have to be very grateful for a lot of help. The other person who was so helpful to me was Gordon Geoffrey – him with the advice about wearing a bra – because when I didn't get the straw in he would come to me and say, 'Dear woman, you can't leave that straw out there. Come on, I'm sending over my workmen to get the straw in,' and he would. When John had the Special Branch detectives with him, they enjoyed working in the fields, it was better than sitting around doing nothing. I have been extremely lucky with my friends, particularly Nevile Noye; he knew a lot about flowers. Nevile is another farmer who is a good horticulturist and he really looked after me. Another man who looked after our bulb tank – all the bulbs had to be sterilised in hot water and chemicals every other year to counteract eel worm – was Alan Scrimshaw. When we couldn't get the temperature thermostats to work properly, he used to travel thirty miles from the Lizard Peninsula to help put them right.

As only part of the land was used for bulbs and vegetables, which we had to circulate around the fields, we decided to buy some cattle. We chose pedigree Herefords with the idea of providing young bulls to the local dairy farmers. They were based on the Merryhill herd in Herefordshire, which had won the Burke Trophy at the Royal Show for its females; so we bought a bull called Merryhill Upstart and four cows. So while we were doing the daffodils we also started with a few Herefords.

I was looking after these four cows which were in calf, and it was interesting because I had never in my life farmed. I grew up during the war on a little farm in Slovenia, and it's very interesting because the instinct of those five years as a child on the farm were still there, and of course the people, my family, always had land although they didn't work on the land. So it wasn't something completely new to me to live out on the farm. We built up our herd to nearly a hundred head, and that was quite hard work because I found myself very often completely alone with calving. In the early years there was a problem with a calf and I had to tie calving ropes on this calf's legs. I put myself on my tummy and I pulled the calf out like that, and the calf was alive, and I think that is the first time when I felt this amazing exultation about being able to calve any animal safely. And that is something that nobody will ever understand unless they have done it. I always think of *Anna Karenina* when Levin came from St Petersburg very disappointed about love, and when he went back to his estate the servant came out with a cloak and said, 'Daisy's had a calf.' Levin forgot completely about his love affair in St Petersburg, society in Petersburg, because this was his prize cow and she had a calf and it was safe. I must have read *Anna Karenina* in different languages at least three or four times, but I did not really understand it until I started to farm.

With the Herefords we just about broke even, but the problem with Trewinnard was that the land was too rich for Herefords and the bulls lost their size and they got rather fat, so we were all the time losing the scale of the bull calves. But we did sell thirty or forty bulls for putting on the Friesian dairy cows – my progeny are well established in West Cornwall!

Neither of us was an expert on farming. We were learning the hard way. When John came back on Friday off the sleeper quite exhausted to work on his red boxes, it was not unusual for us to be woken up at around five o'clock in the morning by a neighbour saying, 'Your bull calves are running up the river,' or 'Your bull calves are in our garden,' or 'Your bull calves have been seen in the village.' So we used to rush out in our pyjamas and run for miles up the river to try to find these damned cattle to get them back to our farm, yelling at them, of course to no avail. I think we must have been quite a joke to our neighbours at the weekends, seeing the MP and his wife running around in their pyjamas.

There were some incidents that were quite terrifying. Because our grass was very luscious we had a great problem with magnesium deficiency, which is called staggers, in spite of the fact that we pumped magnesium into the cows in the spring. One year we lost three valuable pedigree cows and the vet could not come in time, so John and I had to learn how to stab the cow to let out the gases from its stomach. The vet showed me the area, but of course it is the most difficult thing to do because the cow's skin is so hard. There was me stabbing and stabbing, and unless I succeeded the cow was going to die. Anyhow eventually I managed to stab correctly and all these terrible gases came out. It's really quite revolting. Then the cow got up and fell down, and then got up again and fell down, because they suffer shock. I really thought I would lose the cow, but in fact it survived. I have never had an experience of doing something like that. It took another ten years off my life.

Yes, we had a lot of fun and games with the Herefords. Frankly, it was an unsuccessful experiment. But I cannot tell you the joy and contentment that I gained at the weekend when I returned from the hectic, introverted world of Westminster and saw those beautiful animals in the field. A pedigree suckler herd of Herefords with cows and calves at foot is a wonderful sight – only, I think, beaten by a herd of Ayrshire cows for sheer beauty.

Only one incident is worth recalling. We had an excellent vet called John Hardern, who is still my shooting partner in Cornwall. We were undertaking the annual TB test on the cattle, as required by the rules and regulations. Our Herefords were not handled daily like dairy cattle, and the young bulls were quite difficult to manage – rather like my young grandsons. We had passed several young bulls through the cattle crush and they were loose in the farmyard. Unfortunately, the stock bull, Merryhill Upstart, normally a calm animal, somehow escaped out of the crush and started a massive fight with his male offspring. Unbeknown to me, a German businessman, who was renting one of the holiday cottages, had parked the great love of his life, his spanking new Mercedes, in the corner of the farmyard. Merryhill Upstart crashed into the

Mercedes, and he then sat on it. This beautiful piece of German machinery crumpled under his weight. Our German tenant broke into floods of tears. We paid out, but I felt that Merryhill Upstart was only obtaining reparation for my wartime upbringing. One year we lost four pedigree cows from milk fever and staggers, and it was so upsetting seeing those lovely animals die on us that we decided we'd had enough. We disposed of the Herefords, but we still needed animals on the farm to keep it fertile, so we decided to buy some sheep. Back to Miloska.

Miloska's Story (5): The Sheep

We went to an auction and initially bought some Devon Longwool ewes – this was before we changed to Dorsets. Now, what a game you have when you're not an experienced farmer. I was lambing during the week and John helped me at the weekend. The Devon Longwool are big sheep, and when the ewe is in lambing difficulty she gets frightened and you can't help her if she runs away, with the lamb's head hanging out. If it's a breech birth, you have a great problem. I had to call the local vet. The vet, the ewe and I were all dragged round the shed trying to catch these big animals. The vet would always say to me, 'Oh, you take the lamb because you have much smaller hands.' So I became quite expert at lambing over time and we did not have to call the vet too often. I used to sleep in the lambing shed at peak times and John used to come from the Cabinet to help with the lambing at weekends. Between us we used to produce up to five hundred spring lambs and we lambed them all ourselves. I loved the lambing but it was very tiring. We normally left the lambing shed at midnight and got up early at six o'clock to deal with any problems. During the week I was often visited at night in the lambing shed by the local police, who used to drive up to the farm to see if everything was OK.

Because grass grows for most of the year in our area, we changed over to Dorset ewes so that we were able to lamb in November and December and fatten the lambs on the spring grass without using any feeding stuffs, except perhaps a little home-grown barley for the ewes. Our lambs all went for the luxury market in France, and in the 1980s we were getting something like £65 per lamb – today you would be hard pressed to get £40. Then the European Community got involved with sheep for the first time and introduced the European Sheepmeat Regime – this brought in an export clawback and our profits were diverted to subsidise the uneconomic hill farmers. So that killed a perfectly economic business.

The sheep were lovely – they had such a beautiful character and they were excellent mothers. We brought them indoors to lamb. We could not lamb out of doors because the foxes used to take the newly born lambs. As lambing time drew near the foxes came into the fields and quietly passed between the ewes and befriended them. Then they took the lambs as soon as they were born. I have not much sympathy for foxes. They are cruel and vicious animals which are put down much more humanely by hunting than by shooting. Shooting is a hit-and-miss affair which leaves too many wounded foxes.

Sheep are the biggest enemy of sexual attraction, because if you have sheep, you smell of sheep – a mixture of lanolin and urine – all day long. You are perpetually covered in dung. I have never come across a man before who could go into a field and find the only pat there, only one, and step into it. If it's there, John will step in it. Whenever during the weekend John came back either from the cow shed or from the fields, he was always covered in cow muck or ewe manure. I would farm the whole week and I wouldn't bring into the house so much manure as John. I have never understood in twenty-five years of farming whether he looked for the cow pat or the cow pats looked for him. He had to change from top to bottom in order to be able to sit down. He couldn't go and sit down in his trousers because he smelled of sheep manure and was covered in it.

What you must understand is that John is not a farmer. He is a great lover of the country. He is a lover of fishing, shooting, trees; he is interested in his greenhouse. He had this hectic life in London: politics kept the adrenaline running. But there is no peace in politics. I personally think it's the worst sort of life, but he's enjoyed it and it's never dull. But he could do it because he came home at the weekend and it was a complete contrast. He had children at home in the summer. He had his wife down there, and he had his home that he loved. He loved the farm and the animals. Actually he was regenerating his energies in Cornwall.

Yes, I like being covered in manure, but time wore on. Some years we made a good profit on the daffodils. Occasionally we had a windfall when a frost up-country, as we call it, enabled us to send away winter cabbages at high prices. But

West Cornwall is gamblers' country because so much of horticulture there depends on the weather. Everyone made a killing on spring greens, broccoli and early potatoes when frosts in the main horticultural areas, like Lincolnshire, meant that markets were short of vegetables and prices rose accordingly. We never made a profit on the cattle, but they kept the farm fertile; and before the European Community got involved we built up an excellent business in the export of spring lambs to France. There are many traditional rules in farming. I introduced a new one. Never have anything to do with a farm product that is part of the Common Agricultural Policy. Regulation, subsidy and the consequent overproduction will kill it, as night follows day. And never have too much to do with the National Farmers Union, which will always be in the pocket of government. And government – all government – is bad news for farming.

We still have the farm, about 200 acres, but neither Miloska nor I have the energy to be livestock farmers any more. We miss the animals very much – they were part of the family. Perhaps we are fortunate, because it means that we have avoided the dramas of foot and mouth and BSE, and their accompanying sadness and bureaucracy. Now I just grow cereals with the help and encouragement of my contracting farmer neighbour – the admirable Billy Collins – and I have had no choice but to break my own rule. I get up to £100 an acre subsidy from the Common Agricultural Policy, although the metric maniacs express it all in hectares these days. When asked what we do on the farm, I say that we draw social security from the European Union – even so, most years the farm still loses money however hard I try to make a profit. But I get so much pleasure from the land that I could never give it up. Nowadays, we only have one excellent Yorkshireman, Tony Farnaby, to look after the farm whilst we are away.

~

As I was pondering this final chapter, I came across a scribbled note, in pencil, that I had written in Malaya nearly fifty years ago. It was the yearning of an expatriate young Army officer for home, for England. It is clear that I was never cut out to be an Army officer, even less a merchant banker, certainly not a farmer. Politics, on the other hand, was about my country; it gave me roots, not as it should have been in Devon, but in Cornwall. My instinct, my ambition for the countryside shines through in these, my 'jungle reflections', written so long ago:

It was a warm close evening and dusk was falling. I had been on patrol all day in the Malayan jungle and now, having had my curry bhat, I was lying on my bed of leaves thinking of the day that had passed. It had been like any other really, exhausting, hot and tiring, and as I went along I thought of the peace and quiet of the camp at night. This was the ninth day of our patrol and this evening was much like the other eight. I suppose I was satisfied – anyhow I was physically tired and it was a pleasure to lie back and think.

I thought of the men with me, the Gurkhas, tough and loveable. I thought of the valley that we had crossed and what a lovely ambush position it would have made. I thought of the wild boar we could have shot but dared not do so for fear of giving our position away. I thought of Corporal Bhimbahadur who had helped me over that fallen tree when he himself was exhausted too. Of the monkey who screamed at us, of the lovely waterfall that we had crossed; and then, the same as every night, I thought of home.

I might have been asleep but I think I was drowsing; anyhow I was no longer in Malaya, I was in Devonshire again, and wandering over the green fields to the trout stream beyond. There was no-one near, I was by myself and only with my own thoughts:

Thou art free, my Country

And 'tis joy enough and pride

For one hour's perfect bliss to tread the grass of

England once again.

And then climbing the stile I saw it once again, my old friend that had not been disturbed, had never had to leave its native land, the River Tamar. It is where I had spent one whole week before I left to go abroad [at the Arundell Arms near Lifton]. It was also quiet and lovely, and there lying under the bank was a small trout. I got out my rod and pulled out my fly boxes from the bulging pockets of my tweed jacket. This jacket of mine was another love and it always reminded me of home. It was much older than me and had be-longed to my grandfather; it was terribly stained and dirty and full of holes. For twenty-three years it had been condemned by my mother, but it was part of me and could never be thrown away.

And then I was up to my thighs in the river and the water swelled around my waders and I watched my fly floating back towards me. There was a jerk on the line and letting the small trout struggle for a moment, I pulled him in and after holding him in the water, he swam away.

I had not heard her coming. The rush of the water on the pebbles, the hum of the flies on the water and the soft breeze rustling the trees. Yet there she was, watching me from the bank. She was short and slim with a country girl's figure and high colouring with soft brown hair that blew across her face. Her rough tweed skirt and high-necked sweater added to a picture which seemed quite natural. I knew her too. I had always known her.

I waded out of the clear, fast-running river and took her hand, and we wandered together down the side of the river past the deep pools that were the home of Salar the Salmon, over the muddy path that the cattle used on their way to the water, and up to the little stone bridge that carried the lane over the stream. We never said a word but every now and then I would turn and look into her eyes and there, reflected in them, I saw the secret of the English countryside; they were soft and understanding, they were quiet and misty like the morning haze over my river.

Then through the trees, I saw our cottage. I knew that I had been there before, but it seemed new to me tonight for she was leading me there. It was small and tumbling down with an old thatched roof, but the paint was new and the brass on the door was bright and shiny. Lying on the doorstep were two spaniels and, as we approached, they came rushing towards us full of welcome and love and, as I leant down and stroked their silky coats, I smelled the clean breath of the fields where they wandered.

Pure nostalgia, of course. Written a long time ago in a foreign country. The river, the trout, the country clothes, the cottage and the spaniels – maybe that is all I ever wanted out of life. And amazingly it has all come to pass.

~

I remember, when I was a small boy in Devon during the war, passing Beam, the first weir pool on the River Torridge, and thinking that one day I might have the opportunity of fishing there. My grandfather used to take me higher up the River Torridge to fish for trout; and when King's Mead, my evacuated preparatory school, was still in Bideford, Douglas Shilcock, the headmaster, had the lease of Rosemoor, also on the River Torridge. He used to take us out for weekends and show us how to cast a salmon fly – he got very angry if he found a boy with a knot in his cast. 'No fisherman would ever cast a fly without checking his cast,' he would say. We used to go hunting for pearls in the freshwater mussels which were then prolific on the riverbed. And he showed us how a poacher would creep up on a salmon lying up against the river bank and slip his hand under the fish's belly before whisking it out of the river. The River Torridge was the place that I learned to fish. I have fished in all the great rivers of Scotland (Tay, Spey and Tweed), for Pacific salmon off Vancouver, for Atlantic salmon in New Brunswick, in New Zealand, in Iceland. I have a rod on the River Test; but nothing compares with my own river, the River Lynher on the borders of Devon and Cornwall. It flows into the estuary at Plymouth, alongside the Tavy and the Tamar. It is there that I draw towards the end of my story, with the creation of a small sporting estate.

Alec Douglas-Home, in his wonderful, evocative little book *Border Reflections*, captures the life of the young sportsman so very well:

> Whether the young man shoots or fishes or both, he will move among the birds and the beasts and the mountains and the valleys, and he will learn about nature's ways. He will know the excitement of anticipation, and the luxury of reminiscence, and I hope he will conclude, as I have done, that when shooting and fishing no day can ever be dull.

So what is so exciting for me about the River Lynher? 'In 1868,' noted Augustus Grimble, the author of *The Salmon Rivers of England and Wales*, 'the Lynher was reported as entirely destroyed owing to the discharge of mineral refuse at the rate of 100 tons a week. This was formerly the best river in Cornwall.' One hundred years later I joined a few friends who were trying to buy some two miles or so of fishing rights on this same river. By then the mines on Bodmin Moor and in the Tamar Valley, which had produced tin, copper, wolfram, lead arsenic and silver, were abandoned. The ancient adits and tunnels still drained into the river; and even now, when the water is low, copper-coloured water trickles from some streams into the river. But the Lynher is a spate river which has its source on Bodmin Moor. All that was needed to bring life back to the river was rain, and there is no shortage of rain in southwest England. Nature is a great healer and salmon and sea trout are resilient. When a small group of us came across the opportunity of purchasing the best stretch on the whole river, the migratory fish had returned.

The Lynher's history as a polluted river saved it. Consulting engineers, looking for a new reservoir for Plymouth, proposed two sites on the river. One of them would have flooded the valley at the lower end of our beat and cut off the salmon and sea trout from their spawning grounds. A defence committee of some 20,000 people was formed to save the river for the future. We fought the authorities off by saying that the arsenic residues in the river could poison the whole city of Plymouth. Many Devonians might have welcomed that, but the project was abandoned.

Then a few years later a nasty fungal disease called UDN (ulcerative dermal necrosis) struck the West Country rivers. Just as now, the destruction of the salmon was predicted. I remember sitting next to Alec Douglas-Home at a dinner of our club in Westminster – The Farmers' Club, the oldest dining club in Parliament. Alec was our chairman. I said the salmon was threatened by UDN; he did not believe it. The game books for Tweed, going back 150 years, had shown that UDN came and went in cycles, but the rivers always recovered. Happily, he was right. Although we saw some traces of UDN in our river, it appears that the copper residues draining from the old mines on Bodmin Moor acted as an effective fungicide. The River Exe rod catch before UDN ran at over 2,000 salmon each season. In 1975 the Exe catch was down to 109 fish and we caught 177 fish on the River Lynher.

Five of us bought 4,000 yards of freehold fishing rights in perpetuity, with extensive covenants to protect the fishing and the rights of way, for about £1,500. It worked out around 36 pence a yard, at the same time as a stretch of the River Exe was purchased for nearly £9 per yard. My investment of £300 not only purchased the fishing in perpetuity but, as I shall explain, it also brought us over 500 acres of the most splendid shooting rights, also in perpetuity. Although this small sporting estate will never be sold and will be passed down through our respective families, it has been the best investment that I have ever made – and brought me unequalled pleasure.

We bought the fishing, and subsequently obtained the shooting, rights in the river valley from a famous West Country family – the Foots. I knew Michael Foot quite well in politics, and he told me of his upbringing and his joy on his long walks in the Lynher Valley. The Foots' family home was at Pencrebar just outside Callington, overlooking the river.

Michael's father, Isaac, was the son of a builder and carpenter. He became a successful Plymouth solicitor, a well-known Methodist preacher, a Privy Councillor, Liberal MP for Bodmin, and was famous for his left-wing principles. He also fought my seat of St Ives at a by-election in 1937. He had been President of the National Commercial Temperance League and the Liberal

Party. But his greatest achievement was to breed four remarkable sons. Perhaps Michael was the most famous, but Hugh Foot was Britain's envoy at the UN and became Lord Caradon; Dingle Foot became Solicitor General; and John Foot was given a Liberal life peerage and became the senior partner of Foot & Bowden, solicitors in Plymouth. It was with John Foot that we dealt when he was winding up Isaac Foot's estate, which incidentally included a famous private library of 80,000 volumes that was bought by the University of California.

Isaac Foot may have been a militant left-wing apostle, but he was not wanting in commercial acumen. He bought several farms on each side of the Lynher Valley which were later sold, but he never parted with the fishing and shooting rights on his estate, which he protected with extensive covenants. It was strange because Isaac and his sons, so far as I know, had no sporting inclinations; but he must have thought that sporting rights would increase in value over the future years. Anyhow, John Foot put them up for sale as part of the settlement of his father's estate and we bought them.

The salmon fishing has declined, as has every other salmon river, mainly because we have lost our spring run of fish; but the river is healthy and is still teeming with fish in the late autumn – and nowadays the season ends on 15 October, just as the run of autumn salmon seems to be at its peak. The spring run of salmon will return quite naturally, and I quote again from the Home family – this time from David, Alec's son:

> There is no doubt that runs on Tweed do change from autumn to spring and back again approximately every forty-five years, give or take five years … Records confirm that these changes have taken place for the last 150 years, but no-one has any idea why they do. An enormous amount of rubbish has been written about it, mostly by people who call themselves scientists, all of which can be disproved. I actually think it is quite comforting that we don't know why and the salmon can still keep us guessing …

In the early days of our purchase, in the late 1960s and 1970s, I would say that the average catch on our beat, which was seldom fished, was around twenty to thirty salmon and a hundred sea trout. Today, after years of struggle, it looks as if the nets in the estuary at Plymouth have largely been bought out, and there has been a major run of big sea trout in the past two years. Our record sea trout is 12lbs; they are good strong fish, and the sea trout is the cream of West Country fishing.

I think the two greatest activities that any sportsman can experience are sea trout fishing with a fly at night and the flighting of teal at dusk. A river at night, although quite eerie, is a wondrous thing: the buzz of flies on the river, the occasional bark of a fox, the splash of a sea trout as it jumps out of the water to retrieve a dragonfly. Similarly there is something equally exciting about waiting beside a shallow pool for the teal to flight into their pond. They circle around you in the dusk and then descend vertically into the water with a splash.

The Lynher Valley is a real sanctuary for a wide variety of wildlife. The ancient woodlands on the old Foot estate, which we bought to protect our shooting rights and have replanted with a range of oak, beech and chestnut, are the home of a herd of fallow deer and roe which are growing in number, somewhat to the hazard of our trees. Mink and cormorants, equal pests that destroy wildlife and fish, are sadly present. But we have seen an otter and her cubs. Otters live mainly on the eels that prey on the eggs and fry of trout and migratory fish. Kingfishers are common and there are always buzzards in the sky.

On 19 May 1967 I fished the Lynher for the first time. It proved a dramatic if unlucky beginning to my relationship with the river. I hooked two salmon and lost both of them. The first was a monster, it could have been anything up to 20lbs; it set off to the sea, stripped off all my line, and I could not hold it. We christened the pool the Sand Pool. I also lost a fish of around 12lbs in Big Pool – it wrapped itself around a sunken tree and was gone. Two days later, after three hours of rain, I caught my first Lynher salmon of 8lbs in Junction Pool. On 2 June I had another fish of 7½lbs in rising water. When the river cleared the next day, the whole stretch was full of sea trout, but I had to return to Westminster.

One of the more satisfying episodes was on 12 October 1991. It was the first outside day on our shoot, when we wander around the edges of the woods with our dogs to chase the birds back into the main coverts. If they offer a sporting shot we have a go at them. I decided to go for a Cornish MacNab so I arrived early and met the guns with a beautiful fresh run salmon of 6lbs. I should have brought my rifle and tried for a deer the same day. The satisfying part of this incident was that I had recently returned from Islamouth on the River Tay, possibly its most famous beat, and the week had cost me £2,500. The only salmon was caught by my daughter from a boat. Who says that we have to fish on the world's most famous beats?

Michael Charleston, one of the five of us, which now include my son William, has been responsible for the river and the shoot. He has done a wonderful job in creating our little sporting estate. He spent most of his career as a *Daily Express* journalist in the West Country. Michael is one of nature's gentlemen; indeed I think he is rather a great man, high in the tradition of West Country sporting gentlemen. Taking time off the hectic round of a local journalist one day, he connected with three salmon and five sea trout, including a six pounder. Michael spends most of his time, in retirement, working with Orri Vigfusson, the remarkable Icelander who has led a successful crusade against the netting of Atlantic salmon. If he can persuade the Irish government to control commercial salmon fishing off the coast of Ireland, it might restore West Country salmon fishing to its former glory.

The development of our shoot in the Lynher Valley does not inspire quite the same enthusiasm for me. Before we put down reared pheasants, slightly against my inclinations, we had a very natural and exciting wild bird shoot, especially for woodcock. Indeed we call our little sporting estate the Woodcock Club. Twice a year I used to take a group of farmers from the Treloweth shoot, the next-door farm to mine near Penzance, to the Lynher Valley. We had plenty of dogs and the principal members of the shoot, Michael Eddy, my next-door neighbour, John Hardern, my local vet, and Michael Giles, another farmer, used to fight their way through the young, tangled forestry to put up the odd wild pheasant and woodcock. This was rough shooting as it was meant to be. On average we used to shoot four or five pheasants, fifteen or so woodcock, some pigeon and the occasional mallard. That is great sport. I have some contempt for the recent development of the businessmen's commercial shoot of 400-plus high pheasants – a rather pointless slaughter.

Nowadays we put down about 1,500 reared pheasants in two pens and consistently shoot up to forty-five per cent of them in the season. We try to limit each day's bag to 80 birds so that the sport stretches out from November through to the end of January. The real triumph of our little sporting shoot is, however, the low-cost approach. Roger Bunkum, the local farmer's son over whose land we shoot, looks after the birds in return for a free gun. We have no gamekeeper. And on shooting days the volunteers of the Dartmoor Gundog Club do the beating with their splendid trained dogs. For the last twenty years they have steadily rejected offers to go to a larger, more fashionable shoot. They are very much part of the Woodcock Club and everyone is equal – and equally important. It is what sport should be about; it is sad that commercial necessity has destroyed so much in the English sporting tradition, but without the shooting income from foreign visitors and business leisure so many traditional estates would be unviable today.

The Woodcock Club has been one of the highlights of my life, and I look forward to my grandsons gaining equal pleasure from it.

~

Trewinnard Farm, unlike the Woodcock estate, is poor shooting ground. It is flat farming country. There are no hills. Accordingly, soon after I bought the house and farm I set about planting one mile of shelter belts around the top fields of the farm, which is quite exposed to the southwesterly gales that sweep in from the Atlantic. My farming neighbours must have felt that I was some kind of nutcase to take up valuable and expensive arable land to plant trees. In those days all the farms around me in the Parish of St Erth employed at least five or six people, as the early land was ideal for winter vegetables. The produce went into the markets and made the neighbouring farms, including Trewinnard, quite prosperous. Gradually economic pressures increased and the farm workers were dismissed; the final blow being the arrival of the supermarkets with their centralised distribution and the import of huge quantities of foreign vegetables. The supermarkets, more than any other factor, have been responsible for the destruction of rural England, its prosperity, culture and way of life. Today a cauliflower will travel a hundred miles or more from west Cornwall to a centralised depot, and then back again, in a huge lorry on the overcrowded A30, to a supermarket in the district of its origin.

Anyhow my shelter belts, somewhat inimical to good farming, have been the creator of an oasis of wildlife at Trewinnard. This has come about via the humble rabbit – truly a real farming pest – but it has had its impact. The rabbits – now vast in numbers, and quite out of control until myxomatosis depletes their numbers in the high summer – have brought in buzzards and foxes up the food chain; whilst the rabbits' droppings and other predations have increased the insect life down the food chain, which in turn has increased the numbers of songbirds. The only songbirds which seem to have visibly declined are the thrush and sparrow. The other puzzle is, although we have plenty of swifts and swallows in the summer (especially along the river and beside our three-acre lake), the house martins, which used to nest in all the farm buildings, also have declined. I expect it is more to do with nesting conditions in Russia and Scandinavia than anything we have done to discourage them. The fly life must be there, because on a warm summer evening sitting in the garden we can shine a torch into the sky and it is full of bats circling around us. There are plenty of owls as well. Last year I took my tractor and my rifle into one of the fields at night to shoot foxes. I opened the roof of the tractor, stood on the seat and used my artificial screecher to imitate the sound of a wounded rabbit. Sure enough, I could see several pairs of bright-eyed foxes approaching to investigate; but suddenly out of nowhere an owl swooped on me, almost brushing against my face. It was quite a frightening experience to be the victim of a night-time predator.

But one bird seems as healthy and numerous as ever – the woodcock. In the valley, adjoining our lake, there is a ten-acre area of natural wetland, covered in trees. Each year we shoot it twice and the woodcock return year by year; you can almost guarantee that you will find woodcock in the same place – that is within a few yards – each year. They arrive from northern Scandinavia and Russia on the first full moon in November and disappear completely by the end of January. They form the basis of Trewinnard's wild shoot. Nowadays I put down a few redleg partridges and pheasants. We walk up the hedgerows, putting a few guns forward. It is great sport. Our average bag is around 25 pheasants, 5 woodcock, 3 mallard, 2 teal, 3 snipe, 1 rabbit, 4 pigeon, 4 redlegs. The farm is full of partridge, but they are so crafty that I doubt at the season's end whether we can account for 60 or 70 of them. The foxes, buzzards and owls get a larger share as, unlike pheasants, partridges do not roost and they are vulnerable on the ground at night.

The greatest shooting day, in all my experience, is not the 167 wild boar shot in Austria on 19–20 November 1999, or the 830 pheasants and 57 duck shot by a party of which I was a guest on Tony Lambton's shoot in Durham on 31 October 1998, but the following bag at Trewinnard recorded in my game book for 3 January 1997. It is very remarkable but true: 1 pheasant, 1 grey partridge, 1 redleg partridge, 1 teal, 1 mallard, 1 woodcock, 1 snipe, 1 pigeon, 1 rabbit. A mixed bag of nine.

~

'A Mixed Bag of Nine' might have been an apt title for this book, had Robin Day not intervened. At the outset I warned that it would be a 'hotchpotch' of recollections – and so it has proved.

Publishers do not like 'a Life' – unless it is the story of a celebrity or the biography of some historical figure, however obscure. They have a point. Taking this book as an example, as soon as the reader's interest is grabbed by an incident, say the Falklands, he is snatched away to the City. He reads about the Gurkhas and the jungle only to find himself unwillingly transported to academia in Cambridge. If it were long-gone history, then it might hold the attention; but a story of our times – seventy years seen through the life of a living person – is of more interest to a historian one hundred years hence than to someone now struggling with his own life and career.

Political memoirs, in particular, are generally considered something of a bore. With only a few exceptions, no-one reads them. In my passage through life I noted that politicians generally develop an aura of self-importance out of all proportion to their worth. One can only say in their defence that they are infinitely less arrogant, pompous and self-satisfied than their City counterparts. The incestuous world of Westminster, easy to report by lazy journalists, is all-consuming for its participants. But few people outside that closed world care about it very much at all. One of the great strengths of our democracy is that hardly anyone thinks that politics matters. In other countries, more corrupt than ours, politics matters very much.

It is quite a culture shock to move from the hothouse world of Westminster into the real world outside. Politics does matter. We are about to make a constitutional decision on our place in Europe which will determine our people's future for many generations to come. But although there is an instinctive feeling that 'Europe' is important, and it remains a heated topic of political debate, people much prefer to concentrate on the village bypass, the future of their cottage hospital, and their local school. My last mission in life will be to help persuade them not to concede the independence of this country which their forefathers fought so hard to retain.

When I started on my recollections, I had a clear objective. It was to provide a record, hopefully an interesting one, for my descendants. Memoirs, like a family tree, should be on every family bookshelf. Certainly the biography of my ancestor, General Nott, has brought me pleasure. I don't believe it matters whether the subject of a memoir is widely known or not. Often the most humble and obscure contribute more to society than the best-known politician. The simple life of a housewife living in suburbia, undertaking good works through the Women's Institute, will be of consuming interest to historians in AD 3002 – probably more so than the antics of the Home Secretary of the day. To repeat my favourite quotation from Shakespeare:

And what have kings that privates have not too
Save ceremony …?

I suppose that all of us have some influence over the lives we lead, although chance and fortune play a greater role. I had the ambition to place myself in the centre of affairs, in politics, where opportunities might come my way. On the whole, when those opportunities were offered, I took them. Others might have let them pass; either because they lacked ambition, or were perfectly content with what they had already. In my case, 'Fame' was the spur (Milton this time), but I found out long before most of my political contemporaries that it was an empty chalice. I got out, they chose to stay. What is a throne? A bit of wood covered with velvet.

If I had had the stamina and application to stick with one profession – politics, business or the Army – I might have been more 'successful', whatever that treacherous word may mean. But I would not have had such a satisfying life. Perhaps it was my low boredom threshold, oft remarked upon, that propelled me from one experience to another. I think that I might have been happier had fortune and ambition not intervened in the life of William Nott, and I had found myself as a farmer in Herefordshire or Wales. But of one thing I am quite certain. I will have contributed more to life by planting trees, by nurturing the land at Trewinnard, and by preserving for future generations my home in Cornwall, than anything I did, or might have done, in politics, business or the Army. What could anyone ask for more of life than that? So I rest, content.

SPEECH TO THE HOUSE OF COMMONS, 3 APRIL 1982

1.45 pm

The Secretary of State for Defence (Mr. John Nott): I wish to join the right hon. Member for Deptford (Mr. Silkin) in saying that today all our thoughts are with the British people of the Falkland Islands. I know that the whole House agrees with him on that.

Two main criticisms of the Government have emerged in the debate, certainly in my area of responsibility. There. will be another debate on the subject very soon, so I cannot answer every point made by my hon. Friends. The first main criticism is that in some way the changes that we have made to our Naval programme and our other defence arrangements have diminished our capability to respond to such a crisis. The second criticism is that the specific events that developed 14 days ago in South Georgia have caught us unprepared militarily.

The pledge of the right hon. Member for Deptford yesterday that we could count on the support of the official Opposition was welcome. Of course, there is much criticism of the Government on both sides of the House, but I hope that we can unite behind our Armed Forces and that they will have the full backing of the House in the difficult circumstances that we face. It is clear that the whole House accepts that the guarantee of political integrity granted to the Falkland Islands by successive Governments has been breached by an act of flagrant territorial agression in the face of a determined diplomatic effort to solve the problem peacefully – without any sabre-rattling by the British Government. Our attempt to achieve a peaceful resolution of a long-standing dispute stretching back for many years under Governments of both parties might have been expected to appeal to the Leader of the Opposition. He welcomed our peaceful attempts to resolve the dispute. We shall all remember that, speaking for the whole House, he said that we would not wish to see foul brutal agression succeed anywhere in the world. My right hon. Friend the Member for Taunton (Mr. du Cann) and the whole House applauded him for that remark, which we shall remember.

I wish to dispose of the question raised by the right hon. Member for Down, South (Mr. Powell) about the conduct of the Royal Marines at Port Stanley. He referred to what I said at a press conference yesterday. I was asked:

"Will the Royal Marines be told to surrender?"

I took that to mean, naturally, that they would be told to surrender without a fight. I replied:

"Of course not. No British soldier would be ordered to surrender."

By that, I meant without a fight. What else would anyone have answered at such a press conference?

The other major criticism that has been echoed on both sides of the House is that we should have reacted earlier with the despatch, either covertly or overtly, of some surface ships. There are two questions on that issue. First, should we have despatched earlier than we did a Naval task force? [HON. MEMBERS: "Yes."] Secondly, should we have deployed covertly some frigates, as the right hon. Member for Cardiff, South-East (Mr. Callaghan) did in 1977? With the wisdom of hindsight, the despatch of a large surface task force sufficient to deter or destroy the Argentine navy might have given pause to the Argentines. [Interruption.] Perhaps the House will allow me to argue the point through. As the incident at South Georgia began just 14 days ago, such a task force would not have reached the Falkland Islands in order to perform its task. It is impossible, as the right hon. Gentleman said, to know what psychological impact such a force might have had on Argentine intentions, but certainly in deterrence terms, had it been successful, that large task force would have had to remain perhaps indefinitely in Falkland waters in detriment to its other tasks. But, as my right hon. Friend the Prime Minister said in opening this debate, we were throughout seeking a peaceful solution through the United Nations and by other means.

Viscount Cranborne (Dorset, South) *rose –*

Mr. Nott: I have only a few minutes in which to answer this debate. The

Prime Minister said in opening this debate that we were throughout seeking a peaceful solution to this dispute, and such an act, at a moment when we might have been going to the United Nations, would have seemed highly provocative and would probably – *[Interruption.]*

Mr. Eldon Griffiths (Bury St. Edmunds) *rose* –

Mr. Nott: The other option –

Mr. Griffiths *rose* –

Mr. Speaker: Order. It is clear that the Minister will not give way. He is now prepared to give way.

Mr. Griffiths: I have this precise question to put to my right hon. Friend, and I speak as one of his supporters. Understanding full well, as I do, the psychological difficulties of a large surface fleet, why did he not put the hunter-killer submarines on station two weeks ago?

Mr. Nott: If my hon. Friend will allow me to continue with what I was saying. The other option would have been the deployment of a small force insufficient to resist the Argentine Navy, as was done in 1977. May I comment first on this particular proposal, because there seems to be a difference of view between the then Prime Minister and the then Foreign Secretary about the events in 1977. The right hon. Member for Cardiff, South-East said that this force in 1977 became known and that a diplomatic solution followed, whereas the right hon. Member for Plymouth, Devonport (Dr. Owen) said yesterday on the radio that it was done in total secrecy – *[Interruption]* – but he added that it gave him confidence in his negotiations, whatever that might mean. *[Interruption.]*

Mr. Speaker: Order.

Mr. Nott: Presumably to deter, the presence of the force must have been known. If so, to have sent it, then it would have had precisely the same objections to a peaceful solution. *[Interruption.]* If this were a covert deployment, which I believe that it was, it could not have deterred if its presence was not known; and even if the size of the force had been revealed, it could have provided nothing more than a tripwire of exactly the same kind provided by HMS "Endurance" and provided by the Royal Marine garrison on Port Stanley.

Mr. Foot: The right hon. Gentleman is trying to say that there was some difference of opinion, but it was clearly stated by my right hon. Friend when the fact became known without fuss and publicity, and it had a success. That is the difference. What happened in 1977 was a success. This is a terrible failure.

Mr. Nott: I do not think that one is able to draw that conclusion.

Dr. Owen: If the right hon. Gentleman as Secretary of State for Defence has not understood the value to a Foreign Secretary of being able to negotiate in a position of some military influence and strength, he should not be Secretary of State for Defence.

Mr. Nott: Of course I understand that. However, as the Leader of the Opposition said, there can be no evidence that the position of the frigates in the South Atlantic at that time brought about the settlement of that dispute.

Several hon. Members have spoken of the problems that we now face. I do not seek to hide from Parliament the formidable difficulties with a crisis 8,000 miles away. However, the United Kingdom has the ability to mount a major naval task force and to sustain it for a period at that distance. The charge that the Royal Navy cannot do this is flagrantly and patently untrue. We have that capability, as will certainly be evident, and it amounts to a formidable force which no other nation in the world possesses with the exception of the Soviet Union and the United States.

If we were unprepared, how is it that from next Monday, at only a few days' notice, the Royal Navy will put to sea in wartime order and with wartime stocks and weapons? That force will include the carriers HMS "Invincible" and HMS "Hermes", the assault ship HMS "Fearless" and a number of destroyers and frigates armed with anti-surface and anti-air missiles, together with afloat support. A strong force of Royal Marine commandos and a large number of Sea Harriers and anti-submarine and troop-carrying helicopters will also be embarked.

I suggest that no other country in the world could react so fast and the preparations have been in progress for several weeks. We were not unprepared. I must make it clear to my right hon. Friend the Member for Brighton, Pavilion (Mr. Amery) that the carrier, HMS "Illustrious" is now undergoing sea trials. She will be joining the carrier HMS "Ark Royal" and we shall retain an out-of-area capability during the 1980s and 1990s to deal with this sort of problem – *[Interruption.]*

Mr. Speaker: Order. The Minister should be allowed to be heard.

Mr. Nott: I conclude by saying – [HON. MEMBERS: "Resign".] – that the Government do not pretend that the situation is anything but extremely grave. The resolution of this problem will undoubtedly be all the more difficult since the occupation. We intend to solve the problem and we shall try to solve it continuingly by diplomatic means, but if that fails, and it will probably do so, we shall have no choice but to press forward with our plans, retaining secrecy where necessary and flexibility to act as circumstances demand.

The military problems are formidable, but they am certainly not insoluble because of the professionalism, the preparedness and the quality of our defences, which for our nation's size are unique in the free world. I do not believe the claim that the new Labour Party, with its well-known and well-advertised anti-defence bias and lack of commitment to defence spending, would have done any better. The Government will accept criticism – [HON. MEMBERS: "Resign".] But I believe –

Hon. Members: Go.

Mr. Speaker: Order. There is less than a minute left for the Secretary of State.

Mr. Nott: I believe that the Government will have the support of the opposition parties in what we now intend to do. We can at least – and I should like to say this – give to the Armed Forces the unanimous backing of this House in the difficult task that they are being asked to undertake.

It being Two o'clock, MR. SPEAKER *adjourned the House without Question put, pursuant to the Order this day.*

Adjourned accordingly till Monday next, pursuant to the Resolution of the House of Friday 2 April.

Acknowledgements

I am especially indebted to four people. David Kynaston read the drafts of all my chapters, suggested many improvements and reduced the length of some of my more prolix passages. Shortly after leaving politics, I had a series of discussions with Jon Connell, then defence correspondent of the *Sunday Times*, about my time as Defence Secretary, and the transcriptions of those conversations, which were prepared by Bobby Brasier, have proved invaluable. Finally, I am grateful to my long-serving and loyal personal assistant, Debbie Emerson.

Many books have been helpful during the preparation of these memoirs. They include: Sir Robin Day, *... But with Respect*; Karl Meyer and Shareen Brysac, *Tournament of Shadows*; J.H. Stocqueler, *Memoirs and Correspondence of Major-General Sir William Nott, GCB;* Patrick Macrory, *Signal Catastrophe*; Naomi Shepherd, *Ploughing Sand*; Peter Chambers and Amy Landreth, *Called Up*; Peter Carrington, *Reflect on Things Past*; Tony Benn, *Years of Hope*; Ian Fraser, *The High Road to England*; Peter Stormonth Darling, *City Cinderella*; Edward Heath, *The Course of My Life*; Stuart Ball and Anthony Seldon, *The Heath Government*; Nicholas Henderson, *Mandarin*; John Ranelagh, *Thatcher's People*; Cecil Parkinson, *Right at the Centre*; Margaret Thatcher, *The Downing Street Years*; Hugo Young, *One of Us*; Sir Henry Leach, *Endure No Makeshifts*; Sir William Jackson and Lord Bramall, *The Chiefs*; Richard Hill, *Lewin of Greenwich*; Alan Clark, *Diaries: Into Politics*; Caspar Weinberger, *Fighting for Peace*; Cary Reich, *Financier*; Lord Home, *Border Reflections*.

I am also very grateful to a host of people for providing me with helpful comments and information. They include: Marcus Agius; Douglas Allen; Alan Budd; Frank Cooper; John Chapple; Michael Charleston; Nicholas Jones; John Nelson; Peter Spira; Michael Willis.

John Nott
January 2002

INDEX